ISSUES IN SECONDARY EDUCATION

ISSUES IN SECONDARY EDUCATION

The Seventy-fifth Yearbook of the National Society for the Study of Education

PART II

By
THE YEARBOOK COMMITTEE
and
ASSOCIATED CONTRIBUTORS

Edited by
WILLIAM VAN TIL

Editor for the Society
KENNETH J. REHAGE

19 | NSSE | 76

Distributed by THE UNIVERSITY OF CHICAGO PRESS • CHICAGO, ILLINOIS

The National Society for the Study of Education

The purposes of the Society are to carry on investigations of educational problems and to publish the results of these investigations as a means of promoting informed discussion of important educational issues.

The two volumes of the seventy-fifth yearbook (Part I: *The Psychology of Teaching Methods* and Part II: *Issues in Secondary Education* continue the well-established tradition, now in its seventy-sixth year, of serious effort to provide scholarly and readable materials for those interested in the thoughtful study of educational matters. The yearbook series is planned to include at least one volume each year of general interest to all educators, while the second volume tends to be somewhat more specialized.

A complete list of the Society's past publications, including the yearbooks and the recently inaugurated series of paperbacks on Contemporary Educational Issues, will be found in the back pages of this volume.

It is the responsibility of the Board of Directors of the Society to select the subjects to be treated in the yearbooks, to appoint committees whose personnel are expected to insure consideration of all significant points of view, to provide for necessary expenses in connection with the preparation of the yearbooks, to publish and distribute the committees' reports, and to arrange for their discussion at the annual meeting. The editor for the Society is responsible for preparing the submitted manuscripts for publication in accordance with the principles and regulations approved by the Board of Directors.

Neither the Board of Directors, nor the Society's editor, nor the Society is responsible for the conclusions reached or the opinions expressed by the Society's yearbook committees.

All persons sharing an interest in the Society's purposes are invited to join. Regular members receive both volumes of the current yearbook. Those taking out the "comprehensive" membership receive the yearbook volumes and the volumes in the current series of paperbacks. Inquiries regarding membership may be addressed to the Secretary, NSSE, 5835 Kimbark Avenue, Chicago, Illinois 60637.

Library of Congress Catalog Number: 76-2220

Published 1976 by
THE NATIONAL SOCIETY FOR THE STUDY OF EDUCATION

5835 Kimbark Avenue, Chicago, Illinois 60637

First Printing, 9,000 Copies

Printed in the United States of America

iv

Officers of the Society

1975-76
(Term of office expires March 1 of the year indicated.)

JEANNE CHALL
(1977)
Harvard University, Cambridge, Massachusetts

LUVERN L. CUNNINGHAM
(1976)
The Ohio State University, Columbus, Ohio

JACOB W. GETZELS
(1978)
University of Chicago, Chicago, Illinois

JOHN I. GOODLAD
(1976)
University of California, Los Angeles, California

A. HARRY PASSOW
(1978)
Teachers College, Columbia University, New York, New York

KENNETH J. REHAGE
(Ex-officio)
University of Chicago, Chicago, Illinois

RALPH W. TYLER
(1977)
Director Emeritus, Center for Advanced Study in the Behavioral Sciences
Stanford, California

Secretary-Treasurer

KENNETH J. REHAGE
5835 Kimbark Avenue, Chicago, Illinois 60637

The Society's Committee on Issues in Secondary Education

WILLIAM VAN TIL

(Chairman)
Coffman Distinguished Professor of Education
Indiana State University
Terre Haute, Indiana

VIRGIL A. CLIFT

Professor of Education
New York University
New York, New York

HAROLD G. SHANE

University Professor of Education
Indiana University
Bloomington, Indiana

J. LLOYD TRUMP

Director, Model Schools Project and Associate Secretary Emeritus,
National Association of Secondary School Principals
Reston, Virginia

GORDON F. VARS

Professor of Secondary Education
Kent State University
Kent, Ohio

Associated Contributors

ROBERT D. BARR

Associate Professor of Education
School of Education
Indiana University
Bloomington, Indiana

ROBERT H. BECK

Professor of History and Philosophy of Education
College of Education, University of Minnesota
Minneapolis, Minnesota

ARTHUR W. COMBS

Professor of Education
Department of Foundations in Education
University of Florida
Gainesville, Florida

vii

RONALD C. DOLL

Professor of Curriculum and Instruction
Richmond College, City University of New York
Staten Island, New York, New York

ARTHUR W. FOSHAY

Professor Emeritus of Education
Teachers College, Columbia University
New York, New York

WILLIS W. HARMAN

Director, Center for the Study of Social Policy
Stanford Research Institute
Menlo Park, California

RONALD T. HYMAN

Professor of Education
Graduate School of Education
Rutgers University
New Brunswick, New Jersey

LAWRENCE E. METCALF

Professor of Education
University of Illinois
Urbana, Illinois

VERNON H. SMITH

Professor of Education
School of Education
Indiana University
Bloomington, Indiana

Editor's Preface

In 1972 the Board of Directors of the National Society for the Study of Education sought the advice of several educators with respect to the nature of a possible yearbook on secondary education in the United States. A large majority of the respondents urged that such a yearbook should focus on central issues. An advisory group, consisting of Arno A. Bellack, Louise M. Berman, Catherine McKenzie, Harold G. Shane, J. Lloyd Trump, William Van Til, and Gordon F. Vars, was then convened to give further consideration to the nature of an issue-oriented yearbook.

At its meeting in September of 1973 the Board acted favorably on a proposal for the yearbook and appointed a yearbook committee consisting of the following persons: Arno A. Bellack, Virgil A. Clift, Harold G. Shane, J. Lloyd Trump, William Van Til (chairman), and Gordon F. Vars. The committee met with Robert J. Havighurst and Kenneth J. Rehage and agreed upon the central issues to be treated in the volume, the related issues and topics to be considered, the immediate cutting points and concerns, the basic structure of the yearbook, and the names of individuals to be invited to write on selected issues. Because of other commitments, Professor Bellack withdrew from the committee in 1974.

Following an introductory chapter by William Van Til, the yearbook turns to a history of issues in secondary education in a chapter prepared by Robert H. Beck. Chapters devoted to each of nine central issues follow. The authors of these chapters are Arthur W. Combs, Lawrence E. Metcalf, Willis W. Harman, Arthur W. Foshay, Vernon H. Smith and Robert D. Barr, William Van Til, J. Lloyd Trump and Gordon F. Vars, Ronald T. Hyman, and Ronald C. Doll. The yearbook concludes with speculation on the future of secondary education in a chapter by Virgil A. Clift and Harold G. Shane.

The Committee is especially grateful to Herman G. Richey, formerly Secretary-Treasurer and Editor for the Society, who prepared the index for the volume.

WILLIAM VAN TIL
Terre Haute, Indiana
December, 1975

Table of Contents

xi

CHAPTER I

The Crucial Issues in Secondary Education Today

WILLIAM VAN TIL

In the United States, public secondary education is being vigorously examined today. The criticism has been sharp during the past decade. Some critics have concluded that there is no hope whatever for public secondary education as currently conceived, organized, and practiced. Others have called for reform through new educational partnerships between the school and community.

Current Criticism
DESCHOOLERS

Among the critics are the "deschoolers" who tell us that what is needed is the abolition of the social institution of secondary education. They call for the dismantling of "the present school machinery." Writing in the *Saturday Review*, Paul Goodman said:

> Since the growing-up of the young into society to be useful to themselves and others, and to do God's work, is one of the three or four most important functions of any society, no doubt we ought to spend even more on the education of the young than we do; but I would not give a penny to the present administrators, and I would largely dismantle the present school machinery . . .[1]

Goodman also wrote:

> In the adolescent and college years, the present mania is to keep students at their lessons for another four to ten years as the only way of their growing up

1. Paul Goodman, "Freedom and Learning: The Need for Choice," *Saturday Review* 51 (May 18, 1968): 75.

in the world. The correct policy would be to open as many diverse paths as possible, with plenty of opportunity to backtrack and change. . . Most of the money now spent for high schools and colleges should be devoted to the support of apprenticeships; travel; subsidized browsing in libraries and self-directed study and research; programs such as VISTA, the Peace Corps, Students for a Democratic Society, or the Student Nonviolent Coordinating Committee; rural reconstruction; and work camps for projects in conservation and urban renewal.[2]

Goodman elaborated on his viewpoint in *Compulsory Mis-education* and *Growing Up Absurd*.[3]

Theordore Roszak, in an address to the annual conference of the Association for Supervision and Curriculum Development in 1970 in San Francisco, condemned "the culture of industrial society" and "compulsion," then advised his listeners simply to "let go" of the students:

Let them go. Help them to escape, those that need to escape. Find them cracks in the system's great walls and guide them through, cover their tracks, provide the alibis, mislead the posse, . . . the anxious parents, the truant officers, the supervisors and superintendents and officious superegos of the social order.[4]

Ivan Illich, currently the best-known of the deschoolers, proposed in *Deschooling Society* a substitute for schools at all levels through the creation of "opportunity webs" or "networks" such as:

Reference Services to Educational Objects—which facilitate access to things or processes used for formal learning. Some of these things can be reserved for this purpose, stored in libraries, rental agencies, laboratories, and showrooms like museums and theaters; others can be in daily use in factories, airports, or on farms, but made available to students as apprentices or on off-hours.

Skill Exchanges—which permit persons to list their skills, the conditions under which they are willing to serve as models for others who want to learn these skills, and the addresses at which they can be reached.

2. Ibid., p. 74.

3. Paul Goodman, *Compulsory Miseducation* (New York: Vintage Books, 1966); idem, *Growing Up Absurd: Problems of Youth in Organized Society* (New York: Random House, 1960).

4. Theodore Roszak, "Educating Contra Naturam," in *A Man for Tomorrow's World*, Twenty-fifth Annual Conference of the Association for Supervision and Curriculum Development (Washington, D.C.: Distributed by the Association for Supervision and Curriculum Development, National Education Association, 1970), p. 27.

Peer-Matching—a communications network which permits persons to describe the learning activity in which they wish to engage, in the hope of finding a partner for the inquiry.

Reference Services to Educators-at-Large—who can be listed in a directory giving the addresses and self-descriptions of professionals, paraprofessionals, and free-lancers, along with conditions of access to their services. Such educators, as we will see, could be chosen by polling or consulting their former clients.[5]

THE COMPASSIONATE CRITICS

The deschoolers are not alone in their scathing repudiations of public education. The smell of death permeates the titles of several books by the "compassionate critics" who find American public elementary and secondary schools sadly wanting. To the compassionate critics, education in America kills the minds, hearts, and spirits of defenseless children and youth. Some of their book titles are indicative of the tone of their criticism: *Death at an Early Age: The Destruction of the Hearts and Minds of Negro Children in the Boston Public Schools,* by Jonathan Kozol; *Our Children Are Dying,* by Nat Hentoff; *How to Survive in Your Native Land,* by James Herndon; *The Naked Children,* by Daniel Fader.[6]

Schools are prisons, said John Holt in "The Little Red Prison;" they are places where students are taught to fail, he said in *How Children Fail.* Educators pay no heed to crises in the lives of the young, is a message of George Dennison's *The Lives of Children.* We need to help our troubled children, indicates Esther Rothman in *The Angel Inside Went Sour.* We dangle illusory carrots of the future before our junior high school youth and things are never *The Way It Spozed To Be,* said James Herndon. The best thing to do when confronted with a course of study is to ignore it, advises Herbert Kohl in *36 Children.* In a time of *The Underachieving School,* we need *Education as a Subversive Activity.*[7]

5. Ivan Illich, *Deschooling Society* (New York: Harper & Row, 1970), pp. 76, 78-79.

6. Jonathan Kozol, *Death at an Early Age: The Destruction of the Hearts and Minds of Negro Children in the Boston Public Schools* (Boston: Houghton Mifflin, 1967); Nat Hentoff, *Our Children Are Dying* (New York: Viking Press, 1966); James Herndon, *How To Survive in Your Native Land* (New York: Simon & Schuster, 1971); Daniel Fader, *The Naked Children* (New York: Macmillan Co., 1971).

7. John Holt, "The Little Red Prison," *Harper's Magazine* 244 (June 1972): 80-2; idem, *How Children Fail* (New York: Pitman Publishing Corp., 1964); George Den-

To many of the compassionate critics, the only way out is through the establishment of nonpublic schools. For instance, Jonathan Kozol advocates a "passionate, angry, realistic education" in free schools.[8] Allen Graubard wrote in the *Harvard Educational Review* that nonpublic alternative schools have "increased dramatically" and that a "movement" has emerged.[9]

Unlike many earlier critics of American education, the deschoolers, the compassionate critics, and the supporters of nonpublic alternative schools have not been talking simply to themselves. Nor are they simply addressing themselves to the American educators. The large majority of their books are "trade" books, addressed to the American public, not "professional" books directed to educators; the large majority of their articles appear in magazines read by a highly influential segment of the general public, not in magazines edited for educators. So they are heard by a growing proportion of the American people.

THE REFORM REPORTS

In the 1970s social scientists and educators are also being heard as they document the failures of American public education through reports which propose reforms and remedies. For instance, Charles E. Silberman wrote the widely read report of the Carnegie Study, which criticized the schools he and his staff had observed. Of contemporary public schools he wrote:

> Most of all, however, I am indignant at the failures of the public schools themselves. "The most deadly of all possible sins," Erik Erikson suggests, "is the mutilation of a child's spirit." It is not possible to spend any prolonged period visiting public school classrooms without being appalled by the mutilation visible everywhere—mutilation of spontaneity, of joy in learning, of pleasure in creating, of sense of self. The public schools—those "killers of the dream," to appropriate a phrase of Lillian Smith's—are the kind of institution

---

nison. *The Lives of Children* (New York: David McKay Co., 1971); James Herndon, *The Way It Spozed To Be* (New York: Simon & Schuster, 1968); Esther P. Rothman, *The Angel Inside Went Sour* (New York: David McKay Co., Inc., 1971); Herbert Kohl, *36 Children* (New York: New American Library, 1967); John Holt, *The Underachieving School* (New York: Pitman Publishing Corp., 1969); Charles Weingartner and Neil Postman, *Education as as Subversive Activity* (New York: Delacorte Press, 1969).

8. Jonathan Kozol, "Free Schools Fail Because They Don't Teach," *Psychology Today* 5 (April 1972): 114.

9. Allen Graubard, "The Free School Movement," *Harvard Educational Review* 42 (August 1972): 355.

one cannot really dislike until one gets to know them well. Because adults take the schools so much for granted, they fail to appreciate what grim, joyless places most American schools are, how oppressive and petty are the rules by which they are governed, how intellectually sterile and esthetically barren the atmosphere, what an appalling lack of civility obtains on the part of teachers and principals, what contempt they unconsciously display for children as children.[10]

Consider, too, Christopher Jencks's endeavors. Jencks developed a voucher proposal to give individual families a sum of money for education which they could spend as they saw fit, whether for public, private, or parochial education. Some educators responded that the "tickets to school," as the press described them, were a threat to universal tax-supported public education and to separation of church and state.

Two years after his voucher proposal, Christopher Jencks with his associates published *Inequality: A Reassessment of the Effect of Family and Schooling in America* in which he documented (but not to the satisfaction of his critics) the failure of compensatory education. In *Inequality*, Jencks contended:

None of the evidence we have reviewed suggests that school reform can be expected to bring about significant social changes outside the schools. More specifically, the evidence suggests that equalizing educational opportunity would do very little to make adults more equal . . . Furthermore, the experience of the past 25 years suggests that even fairly substantial reductions in the range of educational attainments do not appreciably reduce economic inequality among adults. . . . The evidence suggests . . . that educational compensation is usually of marginal value to the recipients.[11]

Jencks argued that young people are influenced more by home and family than by schools. He summarized: "Our research suggests . . . that the character of a school's output depends largely on a single input, namely the characteristics of the entering children. Everything else— the school budget, its policies, the characteristics of the teach- ers—is either secondary or completely irrelevant."[12] He concluded

10. Charles E. Silberman, *Crisis in the Classroom* (New York: Random House, 1970), p. 10.

11. Christopher Jencks et al., *Inequality: A Reassessment of the Effect of Family and Schooling in America* (New York: Basic Books, Inc., 1972), p. 225.

12. Ibid., p. 256.

that, if Americans want economic equality, they will get it through changing economic institutions, not through the institution of the schools. Establishing political control over economic institutions, said Jencks, is usually called socialism.

Furious controversy over Jencks's contentions developed among social scientists, educators, and research specialists. But, ironically, the most apparent outcome of Jencks's *Inequality* was not a drive to change economic institutions toward socialism but was instead constant citation of the book by fiscal conservatives espousing reduction of spend--ing on schools. They asked, "If education is such a failure, why should the people support it through taxation?"

An influential study is *Youth: Transition to Adulthood*, a 1973 report of the Panel on Youth of the President's Science Advisory Committee. The chairman, James S. Coleman, an outstanding scholar in the social sciences, is the author of *The Adolescent Society*, where he argues that peer groups have become central to the adolescent experience and are undermining youth's commitment to academic success.[13] He is the senior author of *Equality of Educational Opportunity*, a massive survey indicating that family background makes a much more significant contribution to a child's educational performance than do schools.[14]

Youth: Transition to Adulthood contends that the bureaucratic cognitive-oriented secondary school does not, will not, and should not fulfill some important objectives in the transition into adulthood. "Schools are the principal formal institutions of society intended to bring youth into adulthood. But schools' structures are designed wholly for self-development, particularly the acquisition of cognitive skills and knowledge." The report indicated:

> In short, when non-cognitive activities are created for youth as ways of developing personal qualities important to a satisfactory adult life, the incorporation of them within schools places an enormous strain that is often resolved by a reversion to student role for youth and to teacher role for adults. The prospects of success for such activities appear far greater when carried on outside the school.
> Examining both sides, we feel that the benefits of incorporating non-cognitive activites into school are far fewer than those from organizing them outside schools. The principal benefit of the former path appears to be organizational "neatness" and insurance that all youth will be "covered" by such

13. James S. Coleman, *The Adolescent Society* (New York: Free Press, 1961).

14. James S. Coleman, *Equality of Educational Opportunity* (Washington, D.C.: U.S. Government Printing Office, 1966).

activity. But the costs are the distortion of such activity to fit the organizational characteristics of a school, a distortion that strikes at the very heart of the activity.[15]

The report is especially antagonistic to the concept of a comprehensive high school:

This proposal [for school diversity and student choice] goes directly against the trends in American education toward comprehensive schools. The specialized schools of the past were eliminated in one community after another (even largely so in New York City, where they were most fully differentiated). Comprehensive schools seemed to have advantages of mixing students, allowing easy transfer from one curriculum to another, and, in general, providing a democratic equality of opportunity and treatment. But these supposed advantages have been negated in many locales. Comprehensive schools drawing from black lower class neighborhoods or white upper middle class areas are very different. By specializing overtly in student body, they specialize covertly in curriculum. The comprehensive school becomes a narrow school, vainly trying to be like the others, but passively specializing around neighborhood input.[16]

The report proposes some changes in secondary school structure to expand the role of students to include, for instance, tutoring the young; to encourage differentiated alternative schools concentrating on specialized areas of activity; and to reduce the size of schools and to substructure large schools. But beyond such changes in schooling, proposed as among possible pilot studies toward change, the report looks to environments other than the secondary school to help youth make the transition to adulthood. The report especially looks to work environments.

What is needed beyond the institution of schooling, the report contends, are such developments as an alternation of school and work; the adding of educational functions to work organizations; youth communities directed toward community service or social action and possible production of goods or services; and youth organizations producing goods or services to be purchased by the government. To foster opportunities to work, the report calls for reduction of "legal constraints," such as child labor laws; the establishment of a dual

15. James S. Coleman (Chairman), *Youth: Transition to Adulthood*, Report of the Panel on Youth of the President's Science Advisory Committee (Washington, D.C.: U.S. Government Printing Office, 1973), p. 143.

16. Ibid., p. 153.

minimum wage law, lower for youth than for adult workers; and opportunities for public service through expansion of youth programs such as the Peace Corps, Job Corps, VISTA, Teacher Corps.

To reduce pressures to attend college, the report proposed that vouchers, "perhaps equivalent in value to the average cost of education through four years of college, would be given to the young at age 16, to be used at their discretion for schooling and other skill acquisition at any subsequent time of their life."[17]

Essentially what the report said is that the institution of secondary education segregates youth from adults, fosters age segregation among the young, groups the young by chronological age and ability rather than physical and social maturation, and fosters self-development while deferring productive activity. Rather than including non-cognitive activities in school, the report favored organizing the non-cognitive activities outside of school because of the necessary "organizational characteristics of the school." In sum, Coleman and the panel called for less schooling for many youths and for more work and public service experiences under the aegis of other social institutions than secondary education.

In addition to social scientists, professional educators themselves raise serious questions about the adequacy of the institution of secondary education. For instance, the National Commission on the Reform of Secondary Education stressed reform through the title of its report, *The Reform of Secondary Education*.

Like the recent Coleman report, the Commission was particularly critical of the traditional, standard, or conventional high school. It proposed multiple alternatives to the comprehensive high school which James B. Conant so strongly advocated in his influential *The American High School Today*[18] and in his speeches to conferences of educators and laymen throughout the late 1950s and early 1960s:

Many adolescents are poorly accommodated in today's conventional high schools. . . At least a million adolescents a year drop out of school. . . An equally pressing secondary school problem is the large group of students who have become disenchanted with the way things are but remain in school restlessly and reluctantly. Not all of this group are academically troubled.

17. Ibid., pp. 169-70.

18. James B. Conant, *The American High School Today* (New York: McGraw-Hill, 1959).

They are a mixed bag, sampling all levels of ability and social class background. The cost to society is high . . . The Commission recognizes the historic and significant role the comprehensive high school has played in American education. However, it believes that the near-monopoly of second-ary education by that institution, with its relatively standardized formats and restricted options, must now give way to a more diversified system of alter-native schools and programs.[19]

The National Commission on the Reform of Secondary Education specifically rejected the views of the deschoolers:

The effort to "deschool" society started with Paul Goodman's book *Growing Up Absurd: Problems of Youth in Organized Society* (1956). While it is now obvious that Goodman and Edgar Z. Friedenberg were prophetic in their criticisms of the effectiveness of the comprehensive high school, the Commis-sion sees no virtue in the efforts of their disciples to eliminate schools. "De-schooling" may be a useful exercise in scholarly discourse, but it cannot be taken seriously. The issue is not whether high schools are useful, but what role they should assume. The Commission recognizes that the primary environ-ment of the child is the home, and that the schools cannot make up for all the deficiencies of the home. This does not mean they can do nothing. . . . The Commission does not advocate abandonment of the traditional high school. It does urge, however, that recognition be given to a wide variety of available alternatives.[20]

However, accompanying the proposal for reform were suggestions that would reduce enrollment in secondary schools. Most widely remarked upon are recommendation 28 on Compulsory Attendance and recommendation 29 on Free K-14 Public Education.

Recommendation No. 28: Compulsory Attendance

If the high school is not to be a custodial institution, the state must not force adolescents to attend. Earlier maturity—physical, sexual, and intellectual—requires an option of earlier departure from the restraints of for-mal schooling.

The formal school-leaving age should be dropped to age fourteen. Other programs should accommodate those who wish to leave school, and employ-ment laws should be rewritten to assure on-the-job training in full-time service and work.

19. B. Frank Brown (Chairman), National Commission on the Reform of Second-ary Education, *The Reform of Secondary Education: A Report to the Public and the Profes-sion* (New York: McGraw-Hill, 1973), pp. 98-99. This quotation and subsequent quotations from the report are used with permission of the McGraw-Hill Book Com-pany.

20. Ibid., pp. 10-11.

Recommendation No. 29: Free K-14 Public Education

The Congress of the United States in conjunction with state legislatures should enact legislation that will entitle each citizen to fourteen years of tuition-free education beyond kindergarten, only eight of which would be compulsory. The remaining six years should be available for use by anyone at any stage of his life.[21]

Expanding further on the proposal that school attendance would be required only for the first eight years until the student reached age fourteen, thus making attendance at senior high school completely voluntary and attendance at junior high school voluntary for the large majority of ninth graders, the Commission said:

To the rights the courts have already secured for American students, the Commission would like to add another: the right not to be in formal school beyond the age of fourteen. Compulsory attendance laws are the dead hand on the high schools. The liberation of youth and the many freedoms which the courts have given to students within the last decade make it impossible for the school to continue as a custodial institution and also to perform effectively as a teaching institution. The harm done to the school by the student who does not want to be there is measured not only by the incidence of vandalism and assault but also by a subtle and continuous degradation of the tone of the education enterprise.[22]

Returning to its reform emphasis, the Commission said, "The nation does not need laws that force adolescents to go to school. It needs schools and school-related programs that make adolescents wish to come."[23] Hedging by calling for prior extensive changes in employment practices, and anticipating criticism of discrimination against low income children, the Commission added:

The Commission was deeply troubled about some of the implications of its recommendation of an end to compulsory attendance beyond the age of fourteen. Even the present situation is preferable to complete abandonment of what is likely to be the unluckiest segment of the adolescent population. The reduction of compulsory attendance laws to age fourteen must follow, not precede, the change in laws which will provide school-leaving youth real alternatives for employment or an alternative mode of education. This recommendation should in no way be considered a convenient way to "push out"

21. Ibid., p. 21.

22. Ibid., p. 133.

23. Ibid., p. 135.

unwanted youth, especially those from disadvantaged urban areas and minority families.[24]

The Commission has ventured some prophecies:

According to population projections from the Census Bureau, secondary
schools will experience a drop of more than two million in student enrollment
between 1973 and 1984. . . Even steeper declines in the enrollment of the
comprehensive high school may result from the reforms this Commission
proposes. With the burgeoning of alternative paths to the diploma, as little as
40 percent of the student population may be graduated from conventional
comprehensive high schools. Increasing numbers of students can be expected
to use bypass mechanisms or to select from a wide variety of alternatives. The
extent to which these bypass mechanisms and alternatives will employ the
services of those who are now teachers cannot be predicted at this time.[25]

Thus, the report of the Commission combines an emphasis on
reform through options and alternatives to the comprehensive school
with proposals that would sharply reduce the size and enrollment of
secondary schools.

THE LONG HISTORY PRECEDING CURRENT CRITICISMS

The continuing debate on the purposes of public secondary education goes back to the first publicly supported American high school,
which opened in Boston in 1821. One hundred and seventy-six boys
enrolled, but two years later seventy-six had dropped out. The School
Committee was alarmed because teachers had departed from the
original plan that was not only "calculated to bring the powers of the
mind into operation" but also intended "to qualify a youth to fill
usefully and respectably many of those stations, both public and
private in which he may be placed," and "to give a child an education
that shall fit him for active life, and shall serve as a foundation for
eminence in his profession, whether merchantile or mechanical."[26] In
1823 the School Committee recommended that the most useful and
most practical subjects should be offered in the first year.[27] To rein-

24. Ibid., pp. 135-36.

25. Ibid., pp. 5-6.

26. *Proceedings of the School Committee of the City of Boston*, June 17, 1820, pp. 2-7.

27. W. Richard Stephens and William Van Til, *Education in American Life* (Boston:
Houghton Mifflin Co., 1972), p. 67.

force its view, the Committee recommended that the name of the high school be changed from "English Classical School" to "English High School."

Among the contenders in the debate on the purposes of the secondary school have been the academic-oriented, the progressive-oriented, the vocational-oriented, and the compensatory-oriented. Professors of liberal arts and of education, businessmen and blacks, and many others with views on desirable education, have vigorously criticized the public high school during its more than a century and a half of existence. Proponents of these varied views are still outspoken today and are often heard in the mounting criticism of secondary education. But the recently added elements in the discussion are the contemporary attempts, reviewed over the past few pages, to replace all or a substantial part of secondary education through public schools by the deschoolers' opportunity webs, by the compassionate critics' private alternative schools, and by the expanded work and public service experience recommended by such commissions and committees as those described previously.[28]

Clearly, the social institution of secondary education is the target of vigorous critics today. The criticisms range from outright rejection of all education through public high schools to reform proposals which anticipate a marked reduction in the number of young people under the aegis of contemporary secondary schools.

The Crucial Issues in Secondary Education

In such a setting, it is appropriate that the crucial issues of secondary education today be examined by educators. Such is the responsibility of this Yearbook. The reader will find that the Yearbook Committee and the contributors to this volume are highly aware of the controversies that swirl about secondary education, are conscious of

28. Other recent commission and committee reports emphasizing work and public service experience are: National Association of Secondary School Principals, National Committee on Secondary Education, *American Youth in the Mid-Seventies* (Reston, Va.: National Association of Secondary School Principals, 1972); Ruth Weinstock, *The Greening of the High School* (New York: Educational Facilities Laboratory, 1973); John Henry Martin, "Chairman's Digest," Panel on High Schools and Adolescent Education, Office of Education, mimeographed (Washington, D.C.: U. S. Department of Health, Education, and Welfare, April 1974); National Commission on Resources for Youth, *New Roles for Youth: In the School and the Community* (New York: Citation Press, 1974).

the importance of the issues raised by current critics and reports, and are themselves highly critical of many current conceptions, forms of organization, and practices in public secondary education. Yet the Yearbook Committee and the authors are united in believing that an improved secondary education program that utilizes schools and fosters their relationship to communities can make a significant contribution to American youth and to American and world society.

The crucial issues in American secondary education today that were agreed upon by the Yearbook Committee are:

1. How can secondary education best foster the fullest development of the individual's potentialities and experiences as a fully functioning, self-actualizing person?
2. How can secondary education best help youth to develop and apply humane values so that the democratic dream might be achieved and experienced by Americans and other citizens of the world?
3. How can secondary education best equip youth with the vision, knowledge, and competencies needed to cope with the social realities that threaten survival and vitiate the quality of life for mankind in this nation and on this planet in the present and emerging future?
4. How can secondary education best utilize the winnowed and relevant experiences of mankind through drawing upon studies and knowledge in the education of contemporary youth?
5. How can secondary education best draw upon present and prospective school facilities and buildings and the life and institutions of communities and thus maximally use the total environment and setting for learning experiences by youth?
6. How can secondary education best develop a content that simultaneously takes into account social realities, humane values, the needs of individual learners, and bodies of knowledge derived from disciplinary and inter-disciplinary studies?
7. How can secondary education best create, test, and use enriching and effective ways of organization for the better education of youth?
8. How can secondary education best mobilize and use instructional resources and processes for learning experiences for youth?
9. How can secondary education best draw upon all affected groups, whether teachers, administrators, students, official bodies, interest groups, or individual citizens, in administering, supervising, and improving the educational enterprise?

The remainder of this chapter is an introduction to the nine crucial issues selected by the Yearbook Committee.

THE INDIVIDUAL

How can secondary education best foster the fullest development of the individual's potentialities and experiences as a fully functioning, self-actualizing person?

One of the oldest and most enduring insights in education is the recognition that the entire person must be educated. As long ago as the Golden Age, the Greeks recognized this insight when they insisted on education for a sound mind in a sound body. As recently as today, humanistically-oriented educators are calling for the inclusion of affective education in the program of high schools rather than almost exclusive emphasis on the cognitive.

The young person comes as a whole to secondary school. He or she brings along a body, emotions, aesthetic sensibilities, and social experiences joined with that aspect of human beings called "the mind." One in no sense derogates the importance of the use of intelligence by recognizing that human beings are complex bundles of physical, emotional, aesthetic, social, and intellectual characteristics. As a matter of fact, reflective thought is best fostered when the other aspects of human personality develop harmoniously. However little we really know of the mind, we do know that its functioning is inextricably interrelated with body, emotions, aesthetic sensibilities, and social experiences.

Yet secondary education often proceeds as if only the mind came to school. Despite the insights of scholarship in psychology, physiology, aesthetics, philosophy, and sociology, the old dualistic conception of mind as a separate entity to be cultivated prevails in practice despite refutation in theory. Yet the absurdity of the false assumption is now widely apparent in American society, even in the comic strip in which cartoonist Charles Schultz repeatedly portrays Charlie Brown's little sister as devastated by an inability to answer inane scholastic questions that are mumbled at her incoherently by an unseen teacher.

Another truism in education is that all people are individuals. Necessarily it is the individual who does the learning. And individuals differ. Consequently, a range of individual differences must be recognized and provided for by educators.

It is the responsibility of secondary education to educate the whole person, recognizing that this person is an individual. In our view, it is the responsibility of secondary education to foster healthy self-concepts in fully functioning, self-actualized persons. The evidence of failure to do so is all about us in contemporary American society. Manifestations include failing family structures, alienation, drug abuse, spectatoritis, and thwarted potentialities. No one claims that secondary education is solely to blame for these social ills or that secondary education alone can cure them. But surely the secondary schools could help by fostering more effective human beings.

A crucial issue in secondary education is whether an expanded concept of schooling, not limited solely to the cognitive, can be implemented through the secondary schools. As we have seen in preceding pages, some have concluded that secondary schools cannot do the job, and they have turned to social institutions other than schools for education beyond cognition. But others believe that through humanizing the secondary schools we can educate the whole person, treat people as individuals, and help to develop self-actualizing human beings. They believe it possible for secondary schools to help students become independent and autonomous as well as socially oriented.

This first critical issue for contemporary secondary education is examined in chapter 3, "Fostering Maximum Development of the Individual," by Arthur W. Combs.

VALUES

How can secondary education best help youth to develop and apply humane values so that the democratic dream might be achieved and experienced by Americans and other citizens of the world?

That a crisis in values exists in America today was chillingly demonstrated by Watergate. The word stands for a shocking series of events without precedent in American history. Never before had a president and his men so cynically and even casually broken laws, accepted illegal contributions, lied, covered up, fired investigators, and abused power. The corruption of the Grant and Harding administrations pales beside the abuses of the Nixon administration dueing the 1970s.

Watergate was an American nightmare. Before it was over, the President of the United States, faced with the unanimous recommendation of impeachment by a bipartisan House Judiciary Committee, had resigned. His chosen Vice-President had resigned earlier after pleading *nolo contendere* to a non-Watergate-related felony. Two of his

Attorneys General, the highest law enforcement officers of the land, had been found guilty of law-breaking. A third, who supported investigation of Watergate crimes, had been fired for not dismissing a government prosecutor. The president's closest aides, his legal counselor, some of his campaign fund-raisers and a miscellany of White House staff members had been tried by the courts and many had been sent to jail.

Today's high school students have grown up in an atmosphere poisoned by Watergate. They have learned from the actions of men in the highest reaches of American government and business that the ends justify the means, however doubtful the ends might be and however evil the means. They have heard White House staff members testify that they believed they should unquestioningly obey orders if it would help the election of the leader. They have seen equal justice under law flaunted. They have heard a sponsor of burglaries claim that former President Nixon's only defect was that he was not ruthless enough. They have observed malefactors grow prosperous through lectures and books about their crimes.

Let us hope that they have also learned from Watergate that the American system of government endures, that it works, however painfully and slowly.

In a time of disillusion and cynicism following the Watergate horrors, what an awesome task confronts American secondary education in educating students in respect to values! The task is complicated by other lessons in values young Americans have had from the undeclared war in Vietnam, the Mai Lai massacre and the bombing in neutral Indochinese lands; from both the destructiveness of the student revolutionaries and the violence of repression at Kent State and Jackson State; from the black riots of past long hot summers and the disorders related to busing during the present none-too-cool autumns; from a missile crisis growing out of Soviet Russian expansionism; from covert activities at home as well as abroad by the American Central Intelligence Agency; and from the assassinations of two Kennedys and two Kings and attempts to assassinate President Ford.

The problem of teaching humane values to achieve the democratic dream is compounded in that students learn not only from the broad social scene. They learn too at home, in school, and in their communities as well. For example, they learn what they live in their own neighborhoods. Unfortunately, in some neighborhoods they learn their values as they encounter drug addiction, police corruption, naked race hatred, the pursuit of the "quick buck," and other social evils.

So value education must deal with the real dilemmas of young people. Their dilemmas have personal referents. Yet the settings of their perplexities range widely and include school, home, community, national, and global settings. To be effective, value education must deal with personal dilemmas in ever-broadening social settings. Such value education will be effective only if based on the best we know of how moral development proceeds. The means chosen are of crucial importance. For, as we have painfully relearned in the Watergate years, the means used have a way of shaping the ends sought.

This second critical issue is examined in chapter 4, "Developing and Applying Humane Values," by Lawrence E. Metcalf.

SOCIAL REALITIES

How can secondary education best equip youth with the vision, knowledge, and competencies needed to cope with the social realities that threaten survival and vitiate the quality of life for mankind in this nation and on this planet in the present and emerging future?

Human beings have always encountered social realities—the social forces, trends, and problems that characterize the society in which they live. But has there ever been a time in human history when the surrounding social realities so threatened mankind's very survival?

Powerful nations are equipped for overkill and, in a world where nuclear secrets cannot be kept, ever more nations become knowledgeable in this area. For thirty years, a sword of Damocles has been dangling over the planet. Nuclear war could wreck the "spaceship Earth," devastating the land and decimating the people.

Even regional wars fought with nonnuclear weapons, like the undeclared war Americans fought in the quagmire of Vietnam half a world away from the United States, demonstrate the capacity of war to harm the quality of life within a nation. In America, conscripted youth felt the impact first. But who in the United States escaped the shock waves of unrest, dissent, inflation, recession, and reaction to evacuation?

The problems of pollution and population are twin time bombs. Though the more prosperous developed nations have begun to check their population growth, the birth rates in the underdeveloped nations soar. Any situation in which the rich get richer while the poor get children is potentially explosive. Within some of the underdeveloped nations, conflicting religious, nationalistic, and Marxist ideologies unite only in opposition to population controls. Yet famine stalks through many Asian and African nations.

Meanwhile, the developed nations, subject to only minimal international controls, steadily contribute to despoiling the land, air, and waters through the pollution that comes with the territory as technology grows. The higher (supposedly) the civilization, the more the air is fouled, the earth gouged, and the seas poisoned.

When the environmental drive encounters energy expectations in the United States, environmental controls often get the worst of it. The hope of raising the living standards in the underdeveloped countries through increased energy consumption fades rapidly.

Racism persists. In South Africa, racism takes the official form of apartheid. In the United States it proceeds unofficially through the white flight to the suburbs, the residential fortresses within cities, imposed segregation, and minority self-segregation. Violent opposition to desegregation moves from the South to the North. Little Rock in the fall of 1957 was matched by Boston in the fall of 1974 and 1975 as hate thronged outside the school.

Inequalities in income distribution are extreme, both in the world and in the American nation. In the United States, economic rewards for whites outstrip rewards for blacks; meanwhile the income gap between the black middle class and the black masses widens. Wars against poverty waged by liberal administrations are lost, then scrapped. Educators are told that research shows that inequality of opportunity cannot be removed through schooling; the budget-cutters joyfully capitalize on this finding. Coping with double digit inflation involves the actuality of recession and risk of depression, a choice between the devil and the deep blue sea.

Yet despite such grim social realities as those cited, there is a brighter side of the social realities coin. People of good will do struggle to reduce armaments, to achieve international understanding, and to develop United Nations activities. Though the sword of Damocles hangs, it has not fallen. Scientific knowledge about birth control expands and population growth becomes more manageable in the

Western nations. The environmentalists persist and some ecological precautions are taken and maintained. People grow more aware of the necessity of measures to conserve energy. A solid body of law supporting desegregation has been achieved in the United States; life is better for some minority group members than in earlier days. Despite inflation, Americans are better off on the whole as to buying power than were their grandparents or their parents. Inequality of opportunity is confronted by women's movements that reject subordination and take substantial steps toward full equality of the sexes.

Without minimizing social achievements, educators must help youth face the persistent problems. For such problems have been compounded into social dilemmas that lower the quality of life for some human beings and potentially threaten all of mankind.

This third critical issue is examined in chapter 5, "Coping with Social Realities That Threaten Survival" by Willis W. Harman, who speculates on a coming transformation in human history.

DRAWING UPON MAN'S EXPERIENCES

How can secondary education best utilize the winnowed and relevant experiences of mankind through drawing upon studies and knowledge in the education of contemporary youth?

One development in mankind's knowledge has immensely complicated the task of secondary education in the United States—the explosion of knowledge and the need for selection of meaningful knowledge. Leonardo da Vinci is reputed to have been the last man to know all that there was to be known in his time. Today, no single person, however Renaissance a man, can possibly master all of the world's knowledge. For knowledge has steadily multiplied, and in the twentieth century the multiplication expanded into an explosion of knowledge.

In American society, in which the conventional view of education has been an elementary education for the achievement of literacy and a secondary education for the transmission of the cultural and social heritage, with a college education for an elite minority of people destined for leadership posts, the explosion of knowledge placed a formidable burden upon the secondary school level. Within each of the major prestigious academic stems of the secondary school curriculum—language arts, social sciences, physical and biological sciences, mathematics, and world languages—more and more knowledge accumulated. Nor were the minor stems of the curriculum—the various arts, business-vocational education, and physical education—without their contributions to the multiplication of knowledge. Each broad field and each separate discipline within a broad field were represented by proponents, both within and without school systems, who urged the investment of more time in the field of the discipline for which they spoke. But the assumption was too often made that facts and techniques were more important than knowledge of processes and sources. Consequently reflective thought sometimes disappeared in the sea of facts and practical skills.

With the explosion of knowledge came expanded storage and retrieval facilities. A person simply could not carry around "in his head" the new knowledge. So microfilm supplemented books; centers for learning resources supplemented libraries; computers, like busy spiders, stored information; listening laboratories, first for language instruction then for other fields, supplemented the talking teacher. Although not always recognized by educators, the task of secondary education became less the cramming of knowledge into students and more the helping of learners to tap resources as and when needed in the quest for meaning.

The explosion of knowledge and the expansion of storage and retrieval facilities were accompanied by growing recognition by educators of the need for winnowing man's experiences to select the most meaningful and relevant. Rather than presenting a smorgasbord of unrelated facts, some secondary school educators became concerned about teaching concepts and relationships that employ selected facts and information. Rather than absurd pretensions to "covering the ground," some secondary educators recognized the need to foster inquiry and to help students learn the ways of inquiry used by scholars in varied disciplines. Since mankind's experiences and the accumulated knowledge related to human problems cut across neat disciplinary lines, the need for teaching concepts, relationships, and ways of inquiry with respect to interdisciplinary content—such as outer space, race relations, international relations, community life—also became apparent.

This fourth critical issue is examined in chapter 6, "Utilizing Man's Experiences: The Quest for Meaning," by Arthur W. Foshay.

ENVIRONMENT AND SETTING

How can secondary education best draw upon present and prospective school facilities and buildings and the life and institutions of communities and thus maximally use the total environment and setting for learning experiences by youth?

One of the early assumptions of secondary educators, along with educators at other levels, was that education must take place in a schoolhouse. This assumption worked only when education was conceived as limited to the teaching of the "three R's" and the transmission of book knowledge from a few disciplines. The assumption could not be operative in a time when needed knowledge and experiences could not be encompassed within a few books.

Secondary education adapted by changing the schoolhouse. Into a setting of desk-filled rooms geared to listening and writing came new modifications in the school environment such as libraries and playgrounds, science laboratories, shops for industrial arts, music rooms, home economic suites, gymnasiums, rooms equipped for business education, fine arts studios and laboratories, and the like.

It was a gallant response and graphic testimony to the necessity for expanding secondary education beyond the conception inherited from the little red schoolhouse. But it was not sufficient to enable the secondary school to cope with the expansion of potentially educational experiences. Outside the schoolhouse, however comprehensive, lay the community in a setting of the nation and the world. The schoolhouse could be only part of the educational environment of the young person; both the potentiality and the actuality of educational experiences through the surrounding environments were immense.

Secondary education attempted to cope through bringing into the classroom newspapers, then radio, then television. But schools, whether expanded physically or through embracing the media, could only constitute part of the total environment in which youth lived. The twentieth century in America saw the rise of protagonists of the community school. Unsatisfied with trips into the community or with observation alone, those favoring a "community school" made the case for participation by children and youth in the improvement of community living. They asked that youth be given the opportunity to serve the community and to learn the ways of democracy through social action.

The vocational education movement, which emerged in the late nineteenth century and accelerated in the early twentieth century, also quickly recognized that the schoolhouse, however equipped, could not duplicate the work setting. Soon opportunities for work experience were created, typified by distributive education and similar school-sponsored work experience.

Today experimentation in relating to the surrounding community includes schools without walls, such as the well-known Philadelphia experiment, frequently emulated in other metropolitan areas. In such programs, students "go to school" in museums, art galleries, and in various workshops, factories, and offices where man makes his living. Experimentation includes public service by youth as they accompany adults in carrying out their responsibilities. Alternation of attendance at school and work on jobs under the supervision of school personnel often takes place. In such programs, often described as "action-learning," the student works within the community with the guidance, support, and education that the trained professional can provide.

The comprehensive high school for all American youth is the characteristic model of the contemporary secondary schoolhouse. Yet even this well-established pattern of the schoolhouse is being challenged today. In an era when diversity and pluralism are valued, some educators believe that comprehensive high schools have become overly large and overly standardized. They call for experimentation with options to comprehensive high schools in order to provide stress on aspects of education in addition to the cognitive. They suspect that affective education, preparation for careers, and social responsibility may be better developed through alternatives to the comprehensive high school.

Encouraged by the compassionate critics, alternative private schools developed in the late 1960s. In the 1970s, alternative public schools have emerged as a supplement to comprehensive public high schools. The new wave of proposals for high school reforms of the mid-1970s, typified by those described earlier in this chapter, have further encouraged the development of an alternative public school movement. The proponents of a return to the "basics" recently have capitalized on the development of alternative public schools; they foster and support conservative versions of such schools. Thus, varied types of alternative public schools coexist in the mid-1970s. Some are community oriented while some stress the personal needs of learners. Some are educationally conservative, such as "fundamental" or "back to basics" schools, while some are radical in orientation. By providing options, they open up choices for students. They reflect the pluralism that has persisted throughout the history of secondary education in America. They raise an allied question—how much unity is desirable in American secondary education?

This fifth critical issue is examined in chapter 7, "Where Should Learning Take Place?" in which Vernon H. Smith discusses alternative schools and Robert D. Barr deals with action-learning.

CONTENT

How can secondary education best develop a content that simultaneously takes into account social realities, humane values, the needs of individual learners, and bodies of knowledge derived from disciplinary and interdisciplinary studies?

The past sixty years in American secondary education have been characterized by a quest for a desirable content for junior and senior high schools. A major initial twentieth century challenge to traditional education came through the 1918 report of the Commission on the Reorganization of Secondary Education which set forth "Seven Cardinal Principles."[29] Rather than simply prescribe the specific amounts of content of the various subject matter fields, the report of the Commission set forth a purpose-related conception of content for secondary education. The seven "Cardinal Principles" endorsed were: health; command of fundamental processes; worthy home membership; vocation; civic education; worthy use of leisure; and ethical character.

In the 1920s, the child and youth-centered school developed as one outgrowth of the Progressive Education movement that had begun in America in the latter part of the nineteenth century. In the 1930s, when the country was faced with critical domestic and international problems, secondary education became increasingly socially oriented as proponents of societal reconstruction were heard. In the 1940s, with the nation absorbed in the war against the fascist powers, secondary education emphasized values and the U.S. Office of Education fostered

29. Commission on the Reorganization of Secondary Education, *The Cardinal Principles of Secondary Education*, Bulletin no. 35 (Washington, D.C.: U. S. Bureau of Education, 1918).

an emphasis on "zeal for democracy." In the late 1950s and early 1960s, after the Russians sent Sputnik into space, selected academic disciplines deemed necessary for national survival were reconstructed and a process of education emphasizing relationships, concepts, and inquiry was advocated. In the mid-1960s, with the rediscovery of poverty in America, emphasis shifted to compensatory education on behalf of the disadvantaged. In the late 1960s and early 1970s, the compassionate critics of education stressed the importance of a secondary education adapted to the needs of youth and vigorously criticized the traditional education that still persisted in American high schools. In the mid-1970s, both proponents of a return to the "basics" and advocates of expanded work and public service also were heard.

American secondary education obviously has experienced great difficulty in bearing more than one concept in mind simultaneously. Emphases as to content have come, gone, then returned. Pendulums have swung and cycles have recurred. Schools of thought on what secondary education should teach have contended with rival schools of thought. Answers have sometimes been overly simplified and excessively partisan.

Yet with each swing of the cycle and each recurrence of a valid emphasis, it has become increasingly clear that secondary education must draw upon several curricular sources rather than rely on one. Although social problems change with the time, the secondary school curriculum must always take into account the existence of social realities that play a major role as social trends, forces, and dilemmas affect American youth. Although the perplexities of Americans as to values take varied forms, American secondary education must help young people to clarify their ideas and to arrive at and live by humane values. Although the personal-social perplexities of youth may vary with the generations, the curriculum of American secondary schools must be related to the needs, wants, and drives of young people if its content is to be meaningful. Although knowledge may explode and the importance of varied disciplines and of interdisciplinary problems may be reappraised, American secondary education has the task of selecting from man's experiences those insights and data which are relevant to a knowledge base in today's world.

A crucial task in American curriculum making is to interrelate necessary sources in creating a balanced curriculum. This task is examined in chapter 8, "What Should Be Taught and Learned Through Secondary Education?" by William Van Til.

ORGANIZATION

How can secondary education best create, test, and use enriching and effective ways of organization for the better education of youth?

The conventional wisdom as to academic instruction in secondary schools included several assumptions which influenced staff organization, student groupings, and curriculum organization. The typical room was to be a rectangle filled with desks facing the desk of the teacher and a blackboard. The walls were to be decorated with an occasional picture and/or a bulletin board. The lone teacher standing or sitting at his desk was to instruct the students. Mostly, he was to present lectures or to raise questions as he shuttled between blackboard and desk. The student's role was to recite (in later years this often gave way to discussion), to report, to listen or watch, or to read and write silently. In the next room down the corridor, in a design which resembled the egg carton or the ice cube tray, another teacher would be presiding over a similar setting. Each room was to be populated by young people of approximately the same age. Each class was to be dedicated to pursuit of learning in a single and separate subject.

This stereotyped secondary school classroom is deeply embedded in American culture and familiar to the experience of most of today's American adults. It is probably sadly similar to many rooms in the high school which is closest to the reader at this very moment. Often, a visitor can determine the subject of instruction only by the particular mountings on a bulletin board, textbooks on the desk, or chalk marks on the blackboard. But major departures from the conventional wisdom became necessary for fields such as the sciences, physical education, fine arts, industrial arts, and business education. The long-established fields of language arts, social studies, mathematics, and foreign languages, however, often stay close to the stereotyped conception of the secondary school classroom.

Today, however, the conventional wisdom as to staff organization and student grouping is challenged in all curriculum areas. Why all desks facing a teacher, rather than smaller clusters for discussions among students? Why one teacher rather than a team? Why not differentiated staffing? Why 25 to 30 students, rather than listening

groups of 100 and discussion groups of 12 to 18, and carrels for individual study? Why not rooms of many sizes? Why students of a
common age, rather than diverse ages? Why dependence on a
blackboard, when technology ranging from overhead projectors to
computers has become available? Why the inherent limitations of a
classroom, when a wider world exists outside the school? Why walls at
all? Why a bell clamorously signaling the end of a fifty-minute period,
when many learning activities require more or less time than this
sacred interval? Why a single period for a single subject, when interdisciplinary problems cry out for study? Why not options as to grades,
rather than insistence on letter grades for all?

In recent years proposals for new ways of curriculum organization
have been developed at the secondary school level. New groupings are
created as late childhood and early adolescence meet in the middle
school, and as secondary education extends into the junior college
years. Nongraded approaches cut across formerly sacrosanct grade
lines and group together the junior high school grades or the senior
high school years. Team teaching abolishes teacher isolation and
brings together teachers of diverse backgrounds and abilities to share
with groups of students. Lectures, films, recordings, and television
programs are heard and/or seen by students gathered in large groups.
Quiet reigns in carrels and corners and at machines where the student
learns as an individual. The arbitrary boundaries between subjects give
way as problems that cut across subject matter lines are studied and
acted upon in core and block-time programs.

The past decade has been a time when such approaches have been
described in books and magazines and tested in pilot schools. The task
of the contemporary innovator includes not only creation and testing
of new forms of organization but also finding more effective ways to
disseminate them into the broad stream of American secondary education. A goal of the innovators is the enhancement of the motivation of
more individual learners through varied approaches.

This issue pertaining to effective organization is examined in
chapter 9, "How Should Learning Be Organized?" by J. Lloyd
Trump and Gordon F. Vars.

TEACHING STRATEGIES

*How can secondary education best mobilize and use instructional resources
and processes for learning experiences for youth?*

Gutenberg ushered in a revolution in communication. No longer was it necessary to depend upon person-to-person communication or upon tablets chiseled in stone. Now movable type could multiply the spread of the message.

Education has embraced the written word almost to the point of identification of education with literacy; early Americans often referred to education as "book-learning." Until well into the twentieth century, the task of the teacher was to conduct young people into the world of books.

But the twentieth century is a time of revolution in communication. Not only does the printed word proliferate, making real Ecclesiastes' observation that "of making many books there is no end." New media have developed, such as radio and television. Acting has escaped the bounds of live actors and limited audiences; now millions simultaneously see the actor's movements and hear him speak his lines as the masses go to the movies. Platters spun and were supplemented by magnetic tape cassettes. Crude teaching machines developed and have been outpaced by sophisticated computers. Technology has brought a variety of new ways of communication.

Thus the late twentieth century secondary school teacher, though often willingly a prisoner of print, has had the potentiality of becoming the master of a magnificent mix—a mix which includes print proliferated enormously and the new media. The possible repertoire is wide—wide to the point of creating confusion. For a good learning experience with respect to X, should the learner put on the earphones? Or should he look and listen in a darkened room? Should he sit before the console of a computer? Should he pore over a microfilm? Should he be out in the community talking to people? Should he be flipping the pages of a newspaper? Should he be in a library steadily turning the pages of a book? The mix was already rich and growing richer.

In such a setting, questions of teaching strategy became central. Is the established role of the teacher as a presenter of information sufficient? Was an alternative strategy enabling the student to engage in activities and solve problems? Should teachers use the strategy of exemplifying for students what they hoped students would learn? Are there occasions when one type of strategy was called for rather than another? Do differing goals call for differing strategies? And what about the relationships established within a classroom that then characterize the atmosphere within which students and teachers work?

Such questions are fundamental to decision making with respect to mobilization and use of the wide variety of resources and materials becoming available in secondary education and such questions are basic in the development of methodology.

The critical problem of effectively mobilizing and using instructional resources is examined in chapter 10, "Teaching Strategies for Pluralistic Teaching" by Ronald T. Hyman.

ADMINISTERING SUPERVISING IMPROVING

How can secondary education best draw upon all affected groups, whether teachers, administrators, students, official bodies, interest groups, or individual citizens, in administering, supervising, and improving the educational enterprise?

For a long time now we have said that the public schools belong to the people. They do not belong to the teachers or the administrators, although sometimes some teachers and administrators act as though they do. For a long time we have also been saying that teachers and administrators must exert leadership rather than be puppets. But how can we reconcile this role of professional expertise and leadership with the idea that schools belong to the people?

The question grows increasingly complex in a time when, in the immortal words of Jimmy Durante, everybody wants to get into the act. Administrators are better trained and belie the old stereotype of the coach promoted into administration. Teachers see themselves as professionals rather than as people "keeping school;" their organizations, whether the National Education Association or the American Federation of Teachers, move beyond welfare concerns into curriculum. In crisis periods in our national life, the voices of students are raised demanding a say over their lives, as we remember well from the late 1960s and early 1970s. People of the community are being recruited to play a new role in schools as assistants and para-professionals and in communities as helpers and instructors in a period when secondary education involves more interrelationship between schooling and community functions. Individual citizens and groups speak up, whether through the media or in person. All have a deep interest in the outcomes of education and all have some role to play with respect to the educational enterprise.

Obviously, a possibility for the profession is to close ranks and fend off the "outsiders" in the name of professional expertise and leadership. But this has not worked in the past and there is no likelihood that it will work in the future. Furthermore, it evades another bit of folk wisdom, this time that of Carl Sandburg who pointed out that "everybody knows more than anybody." It ignores the American assumptions that the schools belong to the people and that the professionals are their representatives. It also ignores the fact that the secondary school educators need the cooperation of people in the community who have expertise. The new secondary education cannot be contained within the school walls.

It behooves all who are genuinely concerned for education to keep the processes of administration, supervision, and improvement from becoming a giant version of the street game of "king of the hill," in which all attempt to clamber to the top and pull down any who succeed. So we must encourage experimentation to develop leadership in new participants in secondary education. Behind the struggles over accountability, decentralization, student revolt, financing, union power, arbitrary administration, lie the questions of the proper roles of varied groups with respect to the administration, supervision, and improvement of secondary education.

The issues involved in the administration, supervision, and improvement of schools are examined in chapter 11, "How Can Learning Be Fostered?" by Ronald C. Doll.

We turn now to a history of issues in secondary education in the United States. In chapter 2, Robert H. Beck examines the core issues of equalizing the chance for adequate secondary education and of cultural pluralism, both of which have persisted in American education. He also deals with several conjoint issues. These historical issues underlie the nine crucial areas in secondary education today that are discussed in this volume. We then conclude with speculation by Virgil A. Clift and Harold G. Shane on emerging future issues in secondary education.

CHAPTER II

A History of Issues in Secondary Education

ROBERT H. BECK

Introduction

In the history of education all issues with which the writer is familiar have originated in what people have thought desirable for education. Thus, the history of issues in Anerican secondary education involves perceptions of, and sometimes debates on, what is desirable. In this discussion, we shall deal with a few crucial issues, which we shall call *core* issues, plus a very few *conjoint* issues. Both will be discussed in terms of their respective social and cultural milieus, and within broad periods of time.

It is convenient to think in terms of the following four periods or eras: *colonial* (to 1776); *early national* (to 1860); *late national industrial-bureaucratic* (to 1914); and *modern* (post-World War I). The format of the chapter seeks key issues within a social-cultural matrix that moves across these four periods, each of which ends with a war. Wars are points of crisis and, as such, can serve as points of reference in an essay on critical issues. For the most part, the chapter will but nudge the present.

The overarching issue in the unfolding of American secondary education has often been phrased as "equalizing educational opportunity." Unfortunately, the phrase is ambiguous. It rarely has meant offering the same education to all persons of junior and senior high school age. The word "chance" makes the issue more clear. For the ideal has been to make it possible for young people to have a chance for a high school education without being handicapped by the lack of free and accessible schools or by attendance in grievously under-financed schools. The ideal has been a chance for an education without being handicapped by lack of opportunities or by disadvantages related to being female, a member of a low-income family, a member of a minoriity, religious, or immigrant group, or living in a ghetto or rural slum.

This issue of an equal chance really involves a cluster of objectives, some of which have been more or less achieved. The provision of secondary schooling is widespread; religious and other groups can have their own independent or private schools. But many of those who embrace the principle of private schools feel that they should have access to funds supporting public schools. So there is some residual of dissatisfaction, insuring that there will be controversy about secondary education. Nor will that residual only be felt by those dissatisfied with the status quo of public funding of public secondary education. Exposes have come from "revisionists" among students of American educational history—Michael Katz, Colin Greer, Joel Spring, Clarence Karier, and Paul Violas being typical—together with such critics as Raymond E. Callahan, or the Center for Law and Education at Harvard, which, since 1969, has published the series entitled *Inequality in Education*.

A history of issues in secondary education in the United States will be well served by pivoting on the ideal of *equalizing the chance for adequate secondary schooling*. A number of lesser but conjoint issues cluster about this core. Each is associated with the core, yet is independent. The connection is a logical one; the conjoint issues are more specific than the core issue, which is ideological and necessarily vague. For instance, the issue of general education as opposed to vocational-technical training is conjoint, but it is connected with the larger issue of educational opportunity.

Closely tied with the overarching core issue of equal opportunity is another core issue, that of *cultural pluralism*. As has been the case with equality in opportunity, cultural pluralism generally has been held a good thing, but not unreservedly so. With respect to equality in opportunity, there are reservations held by some people who believe limitations are imposed by race, wealth, or even sex. It is only recently that there has been a persistent challenge to Jonathan Swift's remark to a young lady correspondent: "You can never rise in point of learning to the perfection of a school boy." Some who have reservations about equal opportunity still ask: "Are blacks of lesser intellectual potential than whites? Are the poor *poor* because they are naturally lazy?" Similarly, reservations about cultural pluralism cannot be overlooked. For example, does the achievement of a cultural melting pot override the desirability of retaining the cultural markings that come from another nation? Is advanced academic education not "other than" vocational and technical training, but "superior to" that alternative for all, regardless of cultural backgrounds?[1]

A few may examine such concepts as equality of educational opportunity and cultural pluralism and conceive them as middle-level abstractions that might better be subsumed under higher-level abstractions, such as the idea of democracy. Most of us, however, are caught up with such manifestations of cultural pluralism as black nationalism, or Indian control of Indian education, or local control of schools by the immediate community. If we call these conjoint issues, others will call them practical or real. "Immediate" would be a more likely term. We are pressed into dealing with immediate issues. We walk amidst trees and can miss the forest.

This chapter will attempt to relate the conjoint issues themselves as well as to relate them to the higher level of abstraction represented by the core issues. The core issues will be reviewed with an awareness that most have not appeared *de novo*. Not every issue that is modern could also be recognized in its colonial appearance, or in its manifestation in the early national or late national industrial-bureaucratic era. Yet many can be. Cultural pluralism erupted in the tensions of religious groups during the seventeenth and early eighteenth centuries. To be sure, education was affected and one can simply chronicle the immediate effect. But these religious tensions were a crucial component of the concept of cultural pluralism. In the nineteenth and twentieth centuries the core issue of cultural pluralism was involved in the Americanization programs for immigrants in the later national and industrial-bureaucratic era, or, again, in the demands of national, ethnic, and minority groups in modern times.

Cremin writes that midway through the colonial era "the educational institutions . . . constituted a fascinating kaleidoscope of endless diversity and change."[2] Cultural pluralism was not fought, tolerated, or welcomed; it was a fact of life. German Lutherans settled in Pennsylvania, the French Huguenots in South Carolina, and

1. For a brief and cogent review of the matter see Lawrence A. Cremin, *The Transformation of the School* (New York: Alfred A. Knopf, 1961), p. 338 f.

2. Idem, *American Education: The Colonial Experience, 1607-1783* (New York: Harper Torch Books, 1970), p. 479.

English Puritans in New England. In these communities birthrates were high and the deathrates among children low enough so that parents could invest emotionally in their children. And this led to a concern for schooling that complemented other interests in extending education and in such conjoint issues as arose from the realizations that there was a close relationship between education and productivity (which the English Puritans certainly believed), that missionary zeal demanded schooling for those who were to be led to the good life, and that literacy was requisite for participation in public affairs.

The succeeding pages will attempt to keep in tandem historical review and philosophical probing of issues in this country's secondary schooling. Beginning with the colonial era one can see a continuity with what follows the Declaration of Independence and the American Revolution, and those earlier times afford a simplicity that cannot be found again. It is not difficult to pick out threads in the design of colonial stands on education. Yet we will avoid the trap of offering to trace those threads throughout the history of secondary education in postcolonial United States. This cannot be done, for everything that now exists as an issue did not necessarily exist in a simple form in earlier times. Preferable to an evolutionary hypothesis is a looser construction in which one takes advantage of an analysis of what did take place and of the precedents created in order to get a true grasp of later developments.

Issues in Secondary Education in Four Eras
THE COLONIAL ERA

Having said that equalization of educational chances and cultural pluralism are the core issues, one does not thereby deny that there were colonists who thought highly of education as necessary for such causes as religious socialization of the young and religious literacy of the adults or, indeed, the economic and political well-being of the commonwealth. There were colonial undertakings that proposed a single system of education, although these came to nothing. The major thrust, of course, was religious and it was that, together with the economic, that touched secondary education. As we know, both the religious and economic have perdured as significant in educational development from the early seventeenth century to the present. Both have continued to be bound up with a belief in the merits of education.

Even a casual student of American educational history remembers the oft-quoted words of Jefferson: "If a nation expects to be ignorant and free, in a state of civilization, it expects what never was and never will be."[3] Those were thoughts penned in 1816, early in the national era, but the sentiments fitted the earlier years. In his first message to Congress Washington urged the first congressmen to support education: "There is nothing which can better deserve your patronage than the promotion of science and literature. Knowledge is in every country the surest basis of public happiness. In one in which the measures of government receive their impression so immediately from the sense of the community, as in ours, it is proportionably essential."[4]

These declarations of faith came almost a century and a half after the promulgation of the Law of 1647 in the Massachusetts Bay Colony requiring a town of fifty or more householders to appoint a teacher of reading and writing. Towns of one hundred or more householders were to "set up grammar schools, ye masters thereof being able to instruct youth so farr as they may be fitted for ye university." And the university was Harvard College, opened only a decade earlier, in 1636. The religious purpose of the Law of 1647 was evident from its preamble, which stated that it would foil that "old deluder, Satan," whose chief object was "to keep men from a knowledge of the Scriptures . . . by persuading from the use of tongues . . . [so] that learning may not be buried in the grave of our fathers. . . ." Further to thwart the intentions of Satan, those who succeeded in the grammar schools continued on to Harvard,[5] where the object also was to foil Satan, not now by educating parishioners, but by insuring a learned ministry. Conversion of Indians was a parallel hope of the religiously inspired Colonials. Most colonists believed that only those who

3. From a letter to Colonel Charles Yancey dated January 6, 1816, in *The Writings of Thomas Jefferson*, ed. Paul L. Ford, 10 vols. (New York: G. P. Putnam's Sons, 1899), 10: 497.

4. Six years later, in his Farewell Address to the American People (1796), Washington repeated his sentiments. Clarity had replaced the obscurity in his earlier reference to the dependence of democracy on education: "Promote then," he urged his countrymen, "as an object of primary importance, institutions for the general diffusion of knowledge. In proportion as the structure of a government gives force to public opinion, it is essential that public opinion be enlightened."

5. Other colonies soon had comparable colleges. Virginia saw William and Mary open in 1693; in Connecticut, Yale was founded in 1701. In 1746 Princeton, in New Jersey, offered its first class.

believed as their group did could possibly be saved. Those who would not convert either were driven away or schooled. To provide the proper sectarian Christian atmosphere, boarding schools were to be opened for the Indians. The Virginia Company, as early as 1620, planned a "college" at Henrico for that purpose and, as Handlin and Handlin report, "similar schemes were common in the next 150 years, although rarely with any practical results."[6]

But not everyone espoused education, even for religious ends. While the Virginia Company thought about the spiritual well-being of the heathen Indians, Governor Berkeley of Virginia wrote: "I thank God, *there are no free schools* . . . and I hope we shall not have, these hundred years, for *learning* has brought disobedience, and heresy, and sects into the world."[7] The Governor's sentiments were to find a complement in the next century when Alexander Hamilton wrote Robert Morris: "The People are turbulent and changing; they seldom judge or determine right."[8] Nor did Hamilton feel that education could repair that defect of nature.

From the point of view of those in the legislative body of the Massachusetts colony (the General Court) and of those who applauded the Law of 1647, the Latin Grammar School (Boston saw the first opened in 1635) and Harvard College were for an elite from which would come religious, social, political, and commercial leadership. That the rank and file of people should be schooled was not then an issue. Even Jefferson held that general education, education for all, should involve only three years of schooling. After that teachers would cull out the academically promising. For the masses of people there were few chances for schooling. For one thing, there was a great shortage of teachers, a reluctance to spend money on the education of someone else's child, and a belief that only the most rudimentary introduction to the "three R's" was useful.

6. Oscar Handlin and Mary F. Handlin, *Facing Life: Youth and the Family in American History* (Boston: Little, Brown and Co., 1971), p. 51.

7. From "Inquiries to the Governor of Virginia: Submitted to the Lords Commissioners of Foreign Plantations, with the Governor's Answers to Each Distinct Head," in Howard K. Beale, *A History of Freedom of Teaching in American Schools* (New York: Charles Scribner's Sons, 1941), p. 34.

8. Arthur M. Schlesinger, Jr., *The Age of Jackson* (Boston: Little, Brown and Co., 1945), p. 19.

What really broke this barrier of apathy were economic circumstances and opportunity. It was believed that the rudiments of the "three R's," together with elementary Christian doctrine and apprenticeship in a trade, offered the best hope that poor children would become independent and be willing to abide by sacred and secular laws. In the early national period, the trumpet sounded by Mann and others on behalf of public support for a common school attended by all youngsters played on the same themes of economic independence (with 'productivity' now added) and moral uprightness before God and man.

The custom is to think that the broadening of educational opportunity for secondary education was signalled by Benjamin Franklin's academy in Philadelphia (1751), followed by the Samuel Phillips Academy at Andover, Massachusetts, in 1778. The academy is then contrasted with the Latin Grammar School, with its elitist, narrow aim and its instruction in Latin, Greek, the elements of mathematics, and later ancient history and classical literature. But this is to sunder the economic hopes (represented by the academy) from the intellectual *cum* moral purposes (represented by the grammar school). To do so is a misleading oversimplification. Instead, the grammar school and the academy can be better differentiated in terms of careers and social classes. While the study of the classics was thought necessary for the preparation of a minister (and the ministerial career took quite an investment), it was natural that there would be an institution like the Latin Grammar School and that few would attend it. By the close of the colonial era the grammar school had all but disappeared. There was no point in attending unless a young man—and it almost always was a young man—intended to attend college and have a career in a "learned profession," normally the ministry.

But there were many other young people whose careers would languish if secondary education in the seventeenth and eighteenth centuries was limited to the grammar school. There were the poor, whom we tend to forget in our romanticization of the "sturdy" pioneers. "But," Beale reminds us, "the men who made laws and established schools and gave of their prosperity for the education of the poor were well aware of the presence of great numbers of ordinary men . . . they hoped to make poor men obedient, law-abiding, and interested in the maintenance of the Colonial status quo—or, more euphemistically, they wished to 'banish Idleness, advance Husbandrye,' and put down all 'evill discontent.' "[9] Beale was writing about elementary education, but this was also the base upon which the evening schools and the academies were founded. Families could not be relied upon to provide such education through the home, and certainly not if they were impoverished. Also, the English model of the extended, patriarchal family rapidly disappeared in colonial America. A young man did not have to follow the dictates of his father, but could marry and set up house for himself—if he could make a go of it. And ever more strict Puritan injunction did not help in New England any more than religious suasion successfully buttressed the family in other colonies.

Apprenticeship was no more invulnerable. Again, the English pattern dropped away. Fathers in families of English craftsmen had taken in apprentices and were duty bound to teach these voluntary apprentices the three R's as well as a craft.[10] In turn, the apprentices were expected to be obedient in all ways. On the colonial side of the Atlantic, the apprentices came to claim a good deal of independence and masters were more interested in production than in teaching. Shifting responsibility to a school was inevitable. The academy is best remembered as a type of secondary school in the colonial and early national era that catered to the great variety of careers that opened. It was as though the Greek Sophists of the fifth century B.C. had come to life, offering teaching for the new careers of Hellas. Then it was upper class youth who had the leisure to listen to the Sophists. In early America it was chiefly the middle class that was represented in the academy constituency.

THE EARLY NATIONAL PERIOD

In the early national period the common school was trumpeted by men, not a few of whom spoke as the first "superintendents" of state systems of education. While our allusion will be chiefly to two from New England, there were others as worthy of remembrance. Yet the names of the formidable exponents of the common school are not of

9. Beale, op. cit., pp. 32-33. The Massachusetts Law of 1642 directed the officials of each town to ascertain whether parents or the masters of apprentices were attending to their educational duties, viz. that children be trained "in learning and labor and other employments profitable to the Commonwealth," that children were being taught "to read and understand the principles of religion and the capital laws of the country."

10. In voluntary apprenticeship, the terms were negotiated and could include education, but this was not so with apprenticing the dependent poor.

import. What is significant is the concept that schooling was taking form as a public responsibility of the several states.

The flood tide for the academy reached its high point about 1850.[11] It had supplemented the grammar school. When the colleges broadened their horizons, academy students were prepared for college as well as for noncollegiate careers. Grammar schools offered all too few opportunities; the academies offered more. But no one could say that the large increase in the numbers of academies attested to full equalization of education chances. Certainly the poor, the blacks, and Indians were scarcely included, although young women did find a place in the academies.

It is often said that the denial of opportunity by charging fees made the academy less democratic than the public high school. Yet it should be recognized that the public high school was not the first triumph of democracy in offering more educational opportunity; it was in actuality a further step along a path taken by the academy. As Bailyn takes pains to remark,[12] the eighteenth century did not differentiate between public and private. The view taken was more in the Roman tradition, where the citizen was expected to act *in bono publico*. Many private people, without seeking profit, backed academies in "the public interest;" there were many instances of academies being finally supported with public moneys.

For more than half of our history the rudiments of education were thought sufficient for general education. Washington and Jefferson would have been startled to learn that they were thought to endorse the notion of universal education beyond the moral and intellectual rudiments. Although the first high school opened in Boston in 1821, it was another fifty years before the Supreme Court of Michigan ruled in favor of the use of public funds for a public high school. That the matter had to be adjudicated is evidence enough that the issue was highly controversial. It is a myth that America in the early national

11. There were academies, institutes, or seminaries, provided by stock companies, denominational societies or by an individual or group of citizens. By 1850 there were some 6,085 academies, although the count is not certain, enrolling approximately 263,-000 students taught by a staff that numbered more than 12,000. Perhaps as many—or as few—as one in seventy whites attended an academy, which, as Kandel points out, was a proportion that no European country could approximate. See I. L. Kandel, *History of Secondary Education* (Boston: Houghton Mifflin Co., 1930), p. 418.

12. Bernard Bailyn, *Education in the Forming of American Society* (Chapel Hill, N.C.: The University of North Carolina Press, 1960).

period opened doors of educational opportunity to all. The doors were tightly closed to most whites as well as to blacks and Indians.

Although it would have made political sense to involve the federal government early in the support of education, it was not until World War I and the Smith-Lever Act (1914) that there was specific federal aid to a portion of secondary education when effective political support rallied behind vocational education. While Article I, section 8 of the Constitution spelled out the powers of the Congress, the Tenth Amendment clearly asserted that powers not delegated to the United States by the Constitution were reserved to the states, or to the people.[13] We think of the Ordinances of 1785 and 1787[14] as first steps in federal aid to public education. Neither the executive nor legislative branches of government, however, put together these ordinances out of a concern for education. Although few in number, military men in the East saw the occupation of the lands of the Northwest as necessary. Their recommendations of a low sale price and school endowments as lures to settlers were joined by the hope that the sale of the Northwest sections would realize enough money to pay off the Continental debt. The ordinances afforded an opportunity to declare, with rhetorical dressing, that the spread of education was in the national interest. The appeal was to the individual householder who saw schooling as useful to his or her children.

Only after repeated and skillful urging by such men as Horace Mann, Henry Barnard, and Calvin Wiley took effect, did any significant portion of the public back tax-supported education. It is a myth that organized labor championed the public school even in the late

13. The language of the Tenth Amendment is clear: "The powers not delegated to the United States by the Constitution, nor prohibited by it to the States, are reserved to the States respectively, or to the people." This does not rule out the manifestation of federal *concern* for education but it does negate any responsibility. Concern, which is distinct from obligation, has been appealed to repeatedly for the federal protection of civil liberties. Appeal is to Article I, Section 8, the so-called "general welfare clause" of the Constitution, which reads: "The Congress shall have power to lay and collect taxes, duties, imposts, and excises, to pay the debts and provide for the common defense and general welfare of the United States . . ."

14. The Land Ordinance of 1785 was promulgated by the Continental Congress and stipulated that public land in the Northwest, divided into townships comprising 36 sections of 640 acres each, was to dedicate the price of one section in each township as endowment for maintenance of public schools. This policy was reaffirmed in 1787 with the passage of the Northwest Ordinance. The Ordinance read: "Religion, morality, and knowledge being necessary to good government and the happiness of mankind, schools and the means of education shall forever be encouraged." The sentiments were familiar.

national and industrial-bureaucratic era. It did not.[15] Aside from pioneering professional educators, it was chiefly in the ranks of the upper middle-class "tory radicals" that one found those who prized public education, elementary and secondary, during both national eras, early and late.

Such upper middle-class groups as the New York Free Public School Society (1805), organized under the leadership of De Witt Clinton, then mayor of New York City, were notable, if only to dramatize the importance of schooling for paupers. Society members literally took to the streets to round up children of the poor. The effort was no small one. By 1839 there were 20,000 children enrolled in the Society's schools. These were not secondary schools. Nevertheless they demonstrated in action the idea that education was the responsibility of the public. The Society looked to the public for funds. And that is what the school leaders like Mann promoted—public funding.

One of the chief ingredients of the call for support of public education that quickened in the early national era emphasized education of the poor. It was not the idea of poverty that was under attack but what was thought to accompany poverty, especially urban poverty. The settlement houses (only known after 1850) had their forerunners in those commenting on the anarchical life of the slum, the terrible quality of so much city life—and at a time when the growth of the city was matched only by the transformation of industry.

Between 1820 and the Civil War the extension of the communication and transportation networks made a reality out of the nascent concept of nationhood.[16] Without an understanding that the nation was important, very little sense can be made of "nativism," such as Americanization (with all its implications for the immigrants, espe-

15. Jay M. Pawa carefully studied the attitude of labor organizations in the state of New York when public education was debated between 1829 and 1890. If Pawa's findings can be generalized for the United States as a whole, a summary statement of his conclusions should be considered with care. "The results," he writes in his research, "show no evidence to indicate that trade unions had any significant interest in the development or expansion of free schools in New York State . . . When the Workingman's Party disappeared after the 1830s, the trade unions consistently ignored school problems. Occasionally, unions referred to child labor as a threat to their well-being but they did not campaign for compulsory attendance laws." Jay M. Pawa, "The Attitude of Labor Organizations in New York Toward Public Education, 1829-1890" (Ed. D. project, Columbia University, 1964).

16. The point was well made half a century ago by Edward H. Reisner in *Nationalism and Education Since 1789* (New York: Macmillan Co., 1923).

cially those from the south and east of Europe), or loyalty oaths, or fear of non-Americanism resulting from teaching languages other than English, or, indeed, the concept of education as a conservator of the leading national values. The challenge to highly esteemed values threatened by slums and dismal working conditions—to say nothing of child labor—was not overlooked by those who read the calls of Mann and his colleagues for more schooling.

Educational opportunity was also part and parcel of what happened in the early national era. The need for skilled labor carried an obvious message for educators. The first compulsory attendance law made its debut toward the end of the early national era, in 1852. (The last such law was to be enacted by Mississippi in 1918.)

With this in mind, the year 1787 should be remembered not only for its political implications[17] but as the year when the first American factory came into operation at Beverly, Massachusetts. In 1791 the first cotton spinning mill was opened on the falls of the Pawtucket River in Rhode Island. The steamboat made its appearance in 1809; the Erie Canal, which opened in 1825, made possible a journey from Albany to Buffalo in ten days rather than twenty. The steam railroad appeared in 1826. Quickly immigrant labor made the railroad mileage grow. By 1860 thirty thousand miles of rails were carrying agricultural and manufactured products.

Ahead lay the later national *and* bureaucratic-industrial era. Big government and big business were "rationalized." The bureaucracy of which Max Weber wrote, together with the design of the corporate structure, arose at this stage.

While the westward migration held the imagination of men, equally commanding was the growth of cities. Urbanization ran parallel to mechanization and industrialization; blighted tenements were matched by sweatshops and factories that could best be described by a Dickens. Between 1840 and 1870 the population of New York City mounted by fully fifty percent every ten years. Many of the newcomers were immigrants, although there also was a flow from rural to urban areas. By 1900, New York City had a population of 3,437,202, ten times what it had been in 1840. In seven more years the city was to

17. The classic study of economic influences that complemented the political ones was Frank Tracy Carlton, *Economic Influences upon Educational Progress in the United States* (New York: Teachers College Press, 1965). The original edition of this work was published in 1908 by the University of Wisconsin.

add almost another million people, its population soaring to 4,285,-400. At first, Chicago grew even more quickly than New York City. The census for 1840 showed Chicago with some 4,500 inhabitants; the city grew to almost 1,700,000 by 1900. In the next seven years Chicago's rate of growth almost equalled that of New York City, its actual population swelling from 1,698,575 to 2,190,800. The problems of providing school buildings, staff, and equipment within the cities were staggering.

The rural-urban balance shifted as an increasing proportion of the population lived in cities. This did not come about with a rush in the early national era; even at the close of that era, in the decade just before the Civil War, four-fifths of our people were designated as rural in the census. But in a hundred years the nation would be heavily urban.[18]

The shift in the ratio of urban and rural population was more characteristic of the North, where by 1860 there were four times as many cities as in the South, which remained basically agricultural throughout most of the nineteenth century. The plight of the blacks was most poignant in the South where slavery was not negotiable. In the early national period, the education of the blacks and the displacement of the Indians as westward expansion proceeded were not political issues.

Pluralism in the early national period was both national and religious. Ravitch titles the third chapter of her book on the school wars in New York City, "The Irish Arrive."[19] By mid-nineteenth century the Irish were the largest national group in the city. "By 1855," she writes, "more than half the city's residents were foreign-born, and more than half the foreign-born were Irish."[20] The culture in which the high school matured was one in which even an English-speaking minority group like the Irish had a most difficult time because the group was immigrant and Catholic in a culture in which the white Anglo-Saxon Protestant (WASP) dominated and was to dominate. Not infrequently, "For Rent" signs added: "No Irish allowed." (Blacks were later to meet with an even more stinging rebuff in Northern cities.) When Tammany Hall realized that there were too many Irish voters to ignore, and encouraged political participation by

18. Irene B. Taeuber and Conrad Taeuber, *People of the United States in the 20th Century* (Washington, D. C.: Bureau of the Census, December 1971), chapter 2.

19. Diane Ravitch, *The Great School Wars: New York City, 1805-1973* (New York: Basic Books, 1974), chapter 3.

20. Ibid., p. 27.

the Irish, some Protestants responded (1835) with the Native American Democratic Society, "which opposed permitting foreigners to hold office, opposed immigration of paupers and criminals, and opposed the Catholic Church."[21] In their turn the Catholic hierarchy forbade Catholic children to attend the schools of the Free Public School Society; Catholic leaders were afraid that Catholics would lose the religious-moral portion of their cultural identity. Decades later blacks, American Indians, Chicanos, and Puerto Ricans all came to share the same fear of losing cultural identity.

Proponents of a strong central government, or, at least, of a strong state government, have hoped that these provincial fears could be overcome. One wonders if some of the proponents of a statewide system of public schools did not think along these lines, although they did not say as much.

Midway in the early national era education was largely private and the private education was often charitable. As there were more visible poor, fear of them increased. The belief that schools could head off juvenile delinquency and antisocial attitudes, and the desire for practical training were joined in efforts to promote the spread of the high school. Even schooling with charitable motives represented a broadening of educational opportunity. It showed the social concern of those who underwrote the charity; some who lent their support believed that schooling was a public responsibility.

The curriculum is a worthwhile indicator of change in the direction of a greater equalization of chances in education. Until about the time when the first public high school (Boston opened its English High School in 1821) made its appearance, the "common branches" sufficed for "the ordinary duties of life." But after 1821 and before 1860 it was common to find the old course of study supplemented with spelling, geography, history, natural philosophy (including what came to be differentiated as astronomy, physics, chemistry, geology, mineralogy, meteorology), natural history (which included elements of botany, zoology, paleontology and physiology—in a word, today's "life sciences"), physical training, and, sometimes, drawing.[22] Writing of

21. Ibid., p. 30.

22. Willis L. Uhl, "Contributions of Research to Special Methods: Music and Art," in *The Scientific Movement in Education,* Thirty-seventh Yearbook of the National Society for the Study of Education, Part II (Bloomington, Ill.: Public School Publishing Co., 1938), p. 171.

these subject matter additions, Butts and Cremin proposed that: "Generally, such demands for expansion reflected an attempt broadly to educate for citizenship and at the same time to bring the new scientific knowledge to the people. Obviously, they tied closely into the republican ideals and scientific interest which characterized the period."[23]

Not everyone applauded the expansion. Then as later[24] there were negative remarks about "frills," most vocally from patrons of the grammar school's classical curriculum who objected to adding such subjects as English grammar, ancient history, geography, algebra, and geometry. Sounding another note, which would be heard again and again, there were those who felt the public school was atheistic, literally undermining religious faith by being nonsectarian. Horace Mann was hotly taken to task by the Reverends E. A. Newton and M. H. Smith. The former demanded sectarianism in order to prevent skepticism and the latter desired a clear statement that the common schools indeed had a really religious base, "the Ark of God."[25] Both critics preached and wrote in rebuke of such a sentiment as expressed in the most memorable of Mann's Annual Reports to the Board of Education in Massachusetts, the famous Twelfth Report of 1848. Mann told the Board in his report that the common schools were not theological seminaries, "but," he hurriedly added, "our system earnestly inculcates all Christian morals; it founds its morals on the basis of religion; it welcomes the religion of the Bible; and, in receiving the Bible, it allows it to do what it is allowed to do in no other system—*to speak for itself.*"[26]

As one reads the most thoughtful of the histories of American education, one gets the impression that toleration was being defended against intolerant sectarianism. Yet altogether ignored were the positions of Catholics, or any non-Protestants, not to mention such an

23. R. Freeman Butts and Lawrence A. Cremin, *A History of Education in American Culture* (New York: Henry Holt and Co., 1953), p. 213.

24. An excellent source of modern criticism of education is Mary Anne Raywid, *The Axe-Grinders: Critics of Our Public Schools* (New York: Macmillan Co., 1962).

25. Butts and Cremin, op. cit., p. 216 f.

26. Horace Mann, *Twelfth Annual Report of the Secretary of the Board of Education* (Boston: Dutton & Wentworth, 1849), pp. 116-17.

atheist position as was adjudicated in the McCollum Case of 1948.[27] The case for cultural pluralism, in this instance religious pluralism, may have been overlooked by such a liberal as Mann. The history of education, and not only that of the United States, displays the limited sensitivity of most reformers.

The limitation on the vision of visionaries—and Horace Mann was a visionary—should be expected, but apparently it is not. Even historians forget to forgive; they give low grades to those who do not see all that there is to be seen. Let Mann stand for those others who "sold" the cause of common school, elementary first and then secondary, during the early national era. They were indeed "salesmen," and they urged the desirability of having more observant citizens and productive workers. Modern revisionists were to write that this catered to the desires of manufacturers and other employers, as well as of those who added up the costs of delinquency, crime, absenteeism at work, and other ways of falling short as citizen and worker. Such a zealot as Mann oversold because he did not wish young people to be exploited. It is difficult to think of opposition to exploitation as a fault. All levels of education in America have been given, and have accepted, excessive responsibility. In carrying out the responsibility the tendency of educators is to make rhetorical allusions to the benefits of enlightenment. Mann was a master of rhetorical selling and he felt that those who must especially be convinced were the businessmen who had most of the taxable income and political power. Typical is a passage from Mann's Fourth of July oration delivered before the authorities of the City of Boston in 1842:

If . . . every government . . . requires talent and probity for its successful administration; and if it demands those qualities in a higher and higher degree, in proportion to its complexity, and its newness; then does our government require this talent and probity, to an extent indefinitely beyond that of any other which ever existed. . . . It is not enough that a bare majority should be intelligent and upright, while a large minority is ignorant and corrupt. Even in such a state, we should be a house divided against itself, which, we are taught, cannot stand.[28]

27. See the discussion of "Illinois *ex rel.* McCollum *v.* Board of Education: 333 U.S. 203 (1948)" in *The Supreme Court and Education*, ed. David Fellman (New York: Teachers College Press, 1960), chapter 4.

28. *Life and Works of Horace Mann* 5 vols. (Boston: Lee and Shepard Publishers, 1891), 4: 354. Based on an edition compiled in 1865-8 by Mary Mann and George Comb Mann.

For Mann the school was to be the grand "balance-wheel" of society, harmonizing special interests by making them seem secondary to the well-being of all citizens.

It was far from easy to advance the cause of universal education, most certainly at the secondary level. There was a good deal of quiet resistance and some outspoken opposition to the idea that money would have to be spent—and raised by taxation on property. Much of the objection was advanced in the name of liberty. The assertion was that a man had the right to dispose of his property as he would (women who held property independently were few and far between) and, more, that it would be a deprivation of that freedom to tax his property for the education of someone else's offspring.[29] As Mann reported the objection:

The man who has reared and educated a family of children denounces it [public taxation] as a double tax, when he is called upon to assist in educating the children of others also; or, if he has reared his own children without educating them, he thinks it peculiarly oppressive to be obliged to do for others what he refrained from doing even for himself. Another, having children, but disdaining to educate them with the comman mass, withdraws them from the public school, puts them under what he calls "selecter influences," and then thinks it a grievance to be obliged to support a school which he condemns. Or if these different parties so far yield to the force of traditionary sentiment and usage, and to the public opinion around them, as to consent to do something for the cause, they soon reach the limit of expense where their admitted obligation, or their alleged charity, terminates.[30]

The objections to enriching education and thus widening educational opportunity continued to draw fire throughout the century. Charles E. Taylor made the point in a typical way in a pamphlet he published in North Carolina in 1894. "People must not starve," agreed Taylor, "but the public purse may not be drawn upon to feed them on turtle soup and plum pudding. The key to knowledge has been put into their hands by the public schools. If they have taste or aptitude for greater things, they may be left to make their way up."[31] Even the Knights of Labor felt the "people's colleges," as high schools came to be called, were luxurious.

29. Carlton, op. cit., chapter 4.

30. Horace Mann, *Tenth Annual Report of the First Secretary of the Massachusetts Board of Education* (Boston: Dutton and Wentworth, 1847), p. 16.

31. Butts and Cremin, op. cit., p. 369.

Such a reformer as Henry Barnard, Secretary to the Board of Commissioners of Connecticut from 1838 to 1842, knew that little could be expected of education so long as teachers were inadequate to their challenge. Barnard contributed to teacher improvement through the multi-volume *Journal* he edited, through his success in organizing institutes for teachers, and through his other efforts to upgrade the quality of the Connecticut teacher corps, whose members often boarded with the families of their students and were expected, as males, to "discipline" the big boys. There were very few facilities for training except, as Gideonse writes of Connecticut, for a very few private (or select) schools that had "normal" departments, providing a review of common school subjects for young ladies who wished to teach in summer schools.[32] It was to take another half century for the scientific study of education to be even recognizable. Not until the end of the first decade of the twentieth century was it to become a force.[33]

THE LATE NATIONAL AND INDUSTRIAL-BUREAUCRATIC ERA

If the choice were forced, the period between the Civil War and World War I would be a likely candidate for the most interesting one in any chronicle of critical issues in this country's secondary education. Those whose chief concern is with the issue of extension of opportunity in education stress the oft-cited Kalamazoo decision of 1874.[34]

32. If salary is an index of esteem, Gideonse found that in 1838, when Barnard's professional career can be said to have begun, the average monthly salary of a male teacher in Connecticut was something over $15. A machinist might expect a wage of $34 a month, a carpenter about $40, and a bricklayer $48. The salary of women teachers was half that of men. Hendrik D. Gideonse, "Common School Reform: Connecticut, 1838-1854" (Doctoral Diss., Graduate School of Education, Harvard University, 1963).

33. For the early history of the science of education see Guy M. Whipple, "The Contribution of This Society to the Scientific Movement in Education with Special Reference to the Trends in Problems and Methods of Inquiry," in *The Scientific Movement in Education*, Thirty-seventh Yearbook of the National Society for the Study of Education, Part II (Bloomington, Ill.: Public School Publishing Co., 1938).

34. The Kalamazoo decision (Stuart v. School District No. 1 of Kalamazoo, 30 Mich. 69) was handed down in 1874. It often is referred to as the "decision of 1872" (e.g., Kandel, op. cit., p. 263). The bill was filed to restrain the collection of tax moneys "assessed against complainants for the year 1872," but 1872 was not the year of the decision. As noted by Knight and Hall, "This very important case was heard July 10 and 15 and decision was given July 21, 1874." The full decision is given in the Knight and Hall *Readings* "because it presents some very important aspects of American educational history." Edgar W. Knight and Clifton L. Hall, *Readings in American Educational History* (New York: Appleton-Century-Crofts, 1951), p. 544 f.

because it set a precedent by declaring that the use of public funds for the support of the (public) high school was legal. Naturally enough, this decision touched off a spectacular growth of the American high school. The number of high schools increased rapidly from 60 in 1850 to 2,526 in 1890 (and about ten times that number in 1940). In the decade after 1889 the population (age 14-17) in school almost doubled, moving from 357,813 to 695,903. By 1910 this population surged to 1,111,393.

One caught up in the tremendous growth in numbers of public high schools might lose sight of the fact that the Kalamazoo decision did touch on the problem of cultural pluralism, not only on the issue of opportunity. After all, one of the objections to the public taxation proposed by the officials charged with responsibility for Union District No. 1 in Michigan was a nativist fear of the anticipated effects of the teaching of a modern foreign language. The fear was to be encountered by Americans again most dramatically when there was a very widespread objection to the teaching of German in schools during World War I.

The Kalamazoo case became a reality because a group of Michigan citizens brought an action against the Directors of Michigan's School District No. 1. They wished "to restrain the collection of such a portion of the school taxes assessed against complainants for the year 1872, as have been voted for the support of the high school in that village and for the payment of the salary of the superintendent."[35] The presiding judge, Thomas M. Cooley, observed that the true purpose of the bill was to seek "a judicial determination of the right of school authorities, in what are called union districts of the state, to levy taxes upon the general public for the support of what in the state are known as high schools, and to make free by such taxation the instruction of children in other languages than English."[36] The decision of the Court supported the action of the school directors, as shown in the words which conclude Judge Cooley's ruling:

We content ourselves with the statement that neither in our state policy, in our constitution nor in our laws, do we find the primary school districts restricted in the branches of knowledge which their officers may cause to be

35. Reisner, op. cit., p. 455 ff.

36. Ibid., p. 456.

taught, or the grade of instruction that may be given, if their votes consent in regular form to bear the expense and raise the taxes for the purpose.[37]

Judge Cooley declared that the principles holding for the lower school applied with no less force to a higher school. The Michigan decision was followed in Illinois (1879) when the case of *Richard v. Raymond* was resolved with the finding that if the Illinois school law providing for the establishment of high schools under special charters was "constitutional, then the levy and collection of a tax to maintain the school was proper. . ."[38]

With such decisions, it was predictable that the high schools would increase in number. This increase made it possible for a truly state-wide system of public education to be realized. The bureaucratization of education was a foregone conclusion.

Judge Cooley read the Kalamazoo decision of 1874; the panic of 1873 struck a year earlier. Students of American educational history hear of the former but rarely of the latter. The panic of 1873 did have one positive consequence; the following year New York passed its first, albeit ineffective, attendance law.[39] Some sponsors of the law hoped to reduce child labor. Handlin writes of 100,000 children in New York factories alone in the 1870s.

The depression that followed the panic of 1873 led to a widespread demand for retrenchment in schooling. Those whose children were not in a high school were opposed to building more high schools and paying for high school education. Some poor people felt that the spread of high schools was just one more act of oppression because few of their children would attend. Then too, businessmen often blamed the schools for the violent strikes in the manufacturing centers:

They said that the high schools were spoiling good laboring men and turning them into white collar workers or into "walking delegates" and labor agitators. They blamed not only the high school but the entire elementary school curriculum as being entirely too ambitious, and said that it tended to

37. Ibid.

38. 92 Ill. 612, 618 (1879).

39. *Children and Youth in America: A Documentary History*, ed. Robert H. Bremmer, with John Barnard, Tamara K. Hareven, Robert M. Mennel, 3 vols. (Cambridge, Mass.: Harvard University Press, 1971), 2: 1422, fn. 1.

educate children of the laboring class beyond their station in life and then left them unable to realize the interest which such advanced instruction had engendered.[40]

Rather than answering the charges, supporters of high school education counterclaimed that the public high schools would make for social stability and harmony inasmuch as young people of all social classes would learn to live together constructively. The studies of differential treatment based on teacher and administrative responses to social class differences had not yet been made. A pioneering study was to appear in 1922 when George Counts published *The Selective Character of American Secondary Education*[41] which, Cremin feels, "demonstrated beyond the shadow of a doubt that despite ideals to the contrary, high schools were perpetuating glaring inequalities along race, class, and ethnic lines."[42] Counts was to demonstrate the same social class influence five years later in his *The Social Composition of Boards of Education.*[43] The Lynds were yet to publish *Middletown*,[44] a classic which pointed the way for the research that has done so much to sensitize educators to social class influences. That sensitization lodged with the future. It was not generally available to the young, lower-class immigrant.

The fortunes of the immigrants have become the most notorious illustration of a cultural blindspot, which, unhappily, has affected the writing of educational history. The mishandling of the immigrants is documented by Colin Greer in his *The Great School Legend.*[45] To put the problem most simply, our public schools were agencies of socialization. For the "uprooted," as Oscar Handlin calls the immigrant, socialization was "Americanization."[46] Those who were zealous champions of the common and public school, or the private

40. Reisner, op. cit., p. 455.

41. George Counts, *The Selective Character of American Secondary Education* (Chicago: University of Chicago Press, 1922).

42. Lawrence A. Cremin, *The Transformation of the School.*

43. George Counts, *The Social Composition of Boards of Education* (Chicago: University of Chicago Press, 1927).

44. Robert S. Lynd and Helen Merrill Lynd, *Middletown* (new York: Harcourt, Brace & Co., 1929).

45. Colin Greer, *The Great School Legend* (New York: Basic Books, 1972).

46. Oscar Handlin, *The Uprooted* (Boston: Little, Brown and Co., 1951).

school for that matter, did not think that they were either repressing the individualism or undermining the confidence of the immigrants. On the contrary, their battle for the extension of educational opportunity was entered into with the best of motives. But the effects may have been to pander to a "cult of efficiency," as Callahan termed it.[47]

Cubberley illustrated the cultural blindspot as to immigration. While Cubberley, a dean of Education at Stanford University but before that a superintendent of schools, was known for his books on school administration, he is now far better known for his historical study, *Public Education in the United States*.[48] Cubberley was important enough as a chronicler of American education to have the very able Lawrence Cremin honor him in an essay on historiography of American education entitled *The Wonderful World of Ellwood Patterson Cubberley*.[49] This is the Cubberley whom Callahan takes to task for being one of those whose principal objective was to make the administration of American education reflect the "cult of efficiency."

Doubtless Cubberley sought efficiency, but he was far more than an efficiency expert. Basically, Cubberley was an evangelist. Indeed, the "sin of evangelism" is one of the three besetting faults Cremin finds in Cubberley's writing on the course of education in the United States. Cubberley, charges Cremin, committed the sin of evangelism "by seeking to inspire teachers with professional zeal rather than attempting to understand what really happened."[50] Cremin is correct. Cubberley sold the American public school; it was a "hard sell." What Cubberley remembered to tell his readers was how many more schools, students, and teachers there were in each succeeding decade. And the message reached many. Writing of Cubberley's message, Cremin flatly says: "It taught a generation of schoolmen an unflagging commitment to universal education. . ."

"Great books," says Cremin, citing a remark of Lloyd Morris, "are either reservoirs or watersheds; they sum up and transmit the

47. Raymond E. Callahan, *Education and the Cult of Efficiency* (Chicago: University of Chicago Press, 1962), pp. 86–89.

48. Ellwood P. Cubberley, *Public Education in the United States*, rev. ed. (Boston: Houghton Mifflin Co., 1934).

49. Lawrence A. Cremin, *The Wonderful World of Ellwood Patterson Cubberley* (New York: Bureau of Publications, Teachers College, Columbia University, 1965).

50. Ibid., p. 30.

antecedent part, or they initiate the flow of the future. Cubberley's *Public Education in the United States* was such a book. It not only synthesized a wealth of previous scholarship into the now familiar story of the public school triumphant; it professed a vision of American education that proved both plausible and persuasive."[51] The vision Cubberley had blinded him to reality, or to all reality but the opposition to universal public education. It is only as one takes in the magnitude of Cubberley's influence and his reputation among school people that his lapse in the matter of the immigrant—and his proneness to the quantitative record—can be properly appreciated.

Immigration provided the greatest number of students and the greatest opportunity for Americanization the public schools have ever had. Millions of people came to this country. Between 1905 and 1914—the peak of immigration—there were six years in each of which more than a million immigrants came. Except for two years during the Civil War, the flow never was less than 100,000 per year between 1845 and 1930. There were over 36 million immigrants by the time of the Great Depression.[52]

Where did they come from? Handlin begins with 1846, the first year of the great trek.

In Ireland rot destroyed the potato crop. Four and a half million went westward from Ireland. Over four million went west from Great Britain. . . . From what became the German Empire in 1870 came six million. There were two million Scandinavians, five million Italians, set moving by a cholera epidemic in 1887. From the east went some eight million others—Poles and Jews, Hungarians, Bohemians, Slovaks, Ukrainians, Ruthenians—as agriculture took new forms in the Austrian and Russian empires after 1880.[53]

Then there were three million more from the Balkans and Asia Minor: Greeks and Macedonians, Croatians and Albanians, Syrians and Armenians.

51. Ibid., p. 31.

52. Cubberley's book does contain a factual error that can be corrected. The text has it that between 1820 and 1827 the United States received a total of 36,386,381 immigrants (p. 482). Obviously this is a typographical error; the total immigration for those years was 78,600 but the multi-million figure is not quite correct even if one substitutes 1927 for 1827. The cumulative total Cubberley gives was reached sometime between the reports for 1925 and 1926.

53. Oscar Handlin, *The Uprooted*, p. 35 f.

Between 1881 and 1890 there were over 958,000 immigrants from southern and eastern Europe, constituting only 18.3 percent of the intake. In the following ten years the figure rose sharply from 18.3 to 51.9 percent, which represented almost 2 million immigrants. Between 1901 and 1910 there were more than 6 million immigrants from southern and eastern Europe, and these millions made up 70.8 percent of the immigrants in that decade. That was the top of the curve; in the next decade they numbered 3,379,126, or 58.9 percent of the total immigration and 7 percent more than for the years 1891 to 1900.

Handlin describes how the immigrant was uprooted from his home and alienated in his new country. He singles out the Americanization process of the schools for doubtful honors. The schools weaned the young from their parents; the boys and girls quoted the teacher to the parent and saw their parents as alien and unworthy. At the same time, the schools undermined the self-confidence of these young people. In their schoolbooks they saw reflected a life they never knew. And it was only yesterday that black children saw no blacks in their reades; the children of laborers saw no labor in those books; the ghetto youngster saw only the little white house with its middle-class occupants living in a middle-class suburb.

Some revisionists have misinterpreted the views of such reformers as John Dewey and Jane Addams. Dewey's hope that what he referred to as "hyphenated Americans" might finally be accepted as simply Americans, *without* a loss of their cultural heritage, was not asserted out of disrespect for the immigrant. Jane Addams, who knew and incorporated many of Dewey's thoughts in her settlement, Chicago's Hull House (1889), did not wish to suppress the cultural diversith represented by the impoverished immigrant huddled in national groups in the terrible slums of American cities.[54] Nor were Dewey,

54. For a well-balanced and documented study the reader is referred to Clark Chambers, *Seedtime of Reform* (Minneapolis: University of Minnesota Press, 1963). A very reasonable view of Dewey's position is represented by his talk, "Nationalizing Education," found in the *Journal of Proceedings*, the 54th Annual Meeting of the National Education Association of the United States, New York City, July 1-8, 1916. This address is excerpted and commented upon by Normand R. Bernier and Jack E. Williams in *Education for Liberation* (Englewood Cliffs, New Jersey: Prentice-Hall, Inc. 1973). Bernier and Williams state that Dewey held a moderate view of cultural pluralism, and go on to say: "He accepted pluralism as a fact of life but rejected the view that cultural pluralism should be preserved within enclaves of ethnic identity. Revealing an understanding of the problems generated by ethnic diversity, Dewey in this speech and in

Addams, and others who shared their aspirations, seeking to "socialize" in the sense of making tame and obedient workers of these immigrants. The Americanization classes of the schools, the writings of Dewey, the efforts of Jane Addams all were attempts at smoothing the way for immigrants who desperately needed, and desired, the amelioration of the terrors, the mistreatment, and sometimes outright exploitation that they encountered. It was not in a fearful, certainly not in a "holier-than-thou" spirit, that reformers tried to be helpful.

Wesley has singled out the years 1865-1893 as ones in which "the high school had the glorious prospect of becoming the poor man's college, the enricher of culture, the promoter of industry, the school for citizenship,"[55] all of which had been promised by its proponents. The justification for highlighting the years 1865-1893 is that, as Wesley puts it, leaders of the American high school found those were years in which there was a real chance to become a distinctive institution free of European traditions and other hobbles. Business courses were introduced, along with science laboratories, manual training, and both vocal and instrumental music. The objectives Wesley cites evolved with greater precision until, by 1908, the National Educational Association (founded in 1857) posed the issue as one of general education as against preparation for college.[56] This framed one of the most celebrated debates on curricular objectives in the course of American high school history. What made the debate so intense, and pregnant with battles yet to come, was the widely heralded report of the Committee of Ten, appointed by the National Education Association in 1892.[57] So great was the prestige of those who published the Report of

---

his other writings provides a thoughtful defense of cultural pluralism" (p. 164). In fact, Dewey had said to the NEA in New York, "unless our education is nationalized in a way which recognizes that the peculiarity of our nationalism is its internationalism, we shall breed enmity and division in our frantic efforts to secure unity" (p. 187).

55. Edgar B. Wesley, *NEA: The First Hundred Years* (New York: Harper & Brothers, 1957), p. 63.

56. The resolution read: "Resolved that the public high schools should not be chiefly fitting schools for higher institutions, but should be adapted to the general needs, both intellectual and industrial of their students and communities, and we suggest that higher institutions may wisely adapt their courses to this conclusion." Ibid., p. 64.

57. Those who wish to know what went into that memorable discussion are referred to Theodore R. Sizer, *Secondary Schools at the Turn of the Century* (New Haven, Conn.: Yale University Press, 1964).

the Committee of Ten that it was not until after World War I that one could find vigorous professional support for seeing high schools as something other than "appendages of the college."[58]

In the next generation a crucial assumption of the 1893 Committee of Ten was undermined with the downfall of the theory of "formal discipline" and mortally weakened by the scientific study of education. Contributing to destruction of the assumption was the work of Edward Lee Thorndike, whose research on learning showed that there would be "transfer of training" if, and only if, there were "identical elements" in both what *had* been learned and what was *to be* learned.

But it was in what we term the modern era that the decisive turn was taken. In 1918 the NEA Commission on the Reorganization of Secondary Education published its landmark *Cardinal Principles of Secondary Education*, far better known by its unofficial title "The Seven Cardinal Principles," a five-cent, thirty-two page booklet that rose to prominence because of its fundamental nature. As Rome certainly did not fall in 476 A.D., so this publication, designating health, basic skills, home membership, vocations, citizenship, worthy use of leisure, and character as target areas, did not mark a sharp move away from the older college-preparatory studies to a new "life-centered and socially-directed" education. But the way to a new era was unmistakably pointed.

THE MODERN ERA

The modern era in education is more a concept than a chronological fact. It signifies that the educational system has matured. Although there was no "system," in the European sense of a national organization directed by a Ministry of Education, there was a well-articulated format ranging from kindergarten to junior college, with a junior high school becoming clearly demarcated. In 1909 the junior high school made its debut in Berkeley, California. The growth of the junior high school showed that professional educators were becoming more and more interested in the period of development called

58. Wesley, op. cit., p. 66. The Committee was guided by its general chairman, Nicholas Murray Butler, the president of Columbia University, who was not infrequently called "Nicholas Miraculous Butler." There were nine subcommittees of ten members each. College administrators or faculty and headmasters from private college preparatory schools made up three-fourths of the committee members.

adolescence. Adolescence was coming into its own, with the two volumes of G. Stanley Hall's *Adolescence* (1904) in the background.

Professional organization, of which the National Education Association was typical, was joined with ever more sophisticated and well-published study and research. As one consequence of this study, serious attention was given to children and youth. Just as intense has been discussion of the curriculum and method. Three very grave historical moments punctuated the modern era, World Wars I and II, and between them the Great Depression. Each has left its mark on the two macroscopic issues, educational opportunity and cultural pluralism. For the first time ideology became crucial and the ideology with which educators were deeply concerned was that of democracy.

Democracy had been discussed many times in the past, but never with such a real impact on educational theory. The post-World War I era could have been labelled "the era of democracy" rather than the modern era, for it has been exactly that. The fundamental question of what the high school in a democratic society should have for its primary objectives was subjected to continuous review. Reflection was spurred by the depression. Educational opportunity in the area of curriculum was related to democratic values; the general-liberal versus special-vocational (technical) debate made educational headlines. In the name of democracy, teaching methods and curriculum were assessed for their contributions to national needs and as harming or helping with differentiation or educational opportunity for the individual. Was the individual or society to prevail or was it possible to "have one's cake and eat it too"?

If one takes contemporary revisionism as a cue to what sensitive and critical students of education now regard as grievous problems of education in American democracy, a first criticism is that American education has been subservient to the corporation and its quest for efficiency. A close second is the accusation that American education has been characterized by a white Anglo-Saxon Protestant (WASP) syndrome. A third criticism concerns the hold of the professional bureaucracy with attendant harm to minorities and to the rights of students, teachers, and parents.

There have been revisionists, among them Karier, Violas and Joel Spring, who see the management of vocational education as a paramount issue in American high school education. We agree, and not only because there is such a long history to the issue.

In the late nineteenth century, proponents of manual training claimed that it was for the benefit of the "productive, toiling classes" rather than for the "handful of youngsters" destined for the "so-called learned professions." Clearly, American production, in both agriculture and industry, had an increased need for more highly skilled or technically competent manpower. And the schools have responded since the Douglas Commission was formed in Massachusetts in 1905 "to investigate the need for education in the different grades of skill and responsibility in the various industries of the commonwealth."[59] In the next year the National Society for the Promotion of Industrial Education was founded, with Charles A. Prosser stepping into the role of its Executive Secretary in 1912. Two years earlier it was clear that organized labor, equally with the National Association of Manufacturers, backed the idea of vocational training. But by the opening of the twentieth century, manual training had had its day. A turning point in the debate came in 1910, when there developed an impressive convergence of support in favor of a program in preparation for vocations. Intensive lobbying by these supporters led the crusade. Congress gave its blessing. The Smith-Hughes Act was passed in 1917 as the first of many bills granting federal funds to the financing of vocational education at the high school level.[60]

In the 1950s the topic once again gained notoriety when there was sharp reaction to the phrase used by Prosser when he argued for "life adjustment education." The nub of the controversy that followed lay in the differing conclusions that such men as Prosser and Dewey reached as to vocational education. There is little question that Prosser, and those who supported his views, were more down-to-earth. Fifty years earlier the "take-off" stage of technology had increased the pressure on the secondary school to face up to what was required, if anything, by way of a high school response. The needs of the country in World War I and the success of German business and

59. Roy W. Robert, *Vocational and Practical Arts Education*, 3rd ed. (New York: Harper & Row Publishers, 1971), p. 96 f.

60. For the details of, and the ideas involved in, the Prosser-Dewey and Snedden debate, see Arthur G. Wirth, *Education in Technological Society* (Scranton, Pa.: Intext Educational Publishers, 1972).

industry increased the pressure. From one point of view (and certainly) the National Association of Manufacturers was favorable to it), high schools should do more by way of specific preparation for entry into skilled work. Speaking for a much larger group, Prosser saw specific preparation for occupations not only as filling a social need (i.e., as represented by opening opportunities for trained persons or achieving victory in competition for world markets) but also as meeting the personal needs of the large numbers of youth who would not be entering college.

In later years, students of vocational-technical education came to agree that the curriculum Prosser favored was far too specific. Those who had first led in vocational-technical education desired specialized high schools for vocational-technical subjects. But the research of these later students indicated that specificity was ill-advised, for the world of work changed so rapidly that even the needs of manpower were risky forecasts. Thus, the more common pattern became one in which general vocational education was included among the offerings of the "comprehensive" high school. (This is not to say that any of these conclusions were readily accepted or were dominant early in the modern era. Career guidance, now becoming increasingly familiar, was not being debated. Even the specificity in training programs was almost free of scrutiny.)

Dewey claimed that vocational education catered to what businessmen thought were their manpower needs and was not educational in the general or broad sense. Dewey wanted nonacademic work to come alive in schoolrooms but *only* to give students practice in the cooperative behavior required by the modern economy of an interdependent nation—and world. In addition, Dewey wished students to learn through acting out the ways people made a living. The end Dewey sought, it must be said, was not that youth should become more technically proficient but rather that they should develop insight into productive and distributive processes.

Revisionists have criticized Dewey for underwriting cooperativeness. They argued that cooperativeness would develop both obedience and conformism in workers. But historical review will show that obedience and conformism were not what Dewey sought, any more than Prosser desired to have the high schools graduate docile workers. Prosser felt that those who attended high schools should acquire marketable skills. Dewey wished these students to be at home in, but critical of, the modern world, where so much depended upon the application of science to the technology of management, the production and distribution of goods, or the rendering of service.

The debate really is not ended, although it has helped to remake a general-liberal education into a process that has to do with this world and its problems. In its turn, vocational-technical education has found a place in the high school. But it is encompassed in "career education," with emphasis on counseling and exploring rather than simply on the development of marketable skills.

Discussion of vocational education has been characterized by a cultural blindness that was not aware of what was happening to black, Indian, Chicano, or Puerto Rican youth, or of the bias operating against females and the impoverished. The bitterness of the plight of such young people became all too clear when educators thought about equalizing educational opportunity. And it was not a newly told story. Hard data became available at the end of the depression of the 1930s when the American Council on Education commissioned an inquiry into the lot of high school students and graduates. In a moving report, *Youth Tell Their Story*,[61] well over 40 percent of high school graduates were found to be without full-time employment. The plight of blacks was, and was to remain, even more desperate. This reflection would be no happier were it on the fate of Chicanos, Puerto Ricans, and Indians. The most critical finding of *Youth Tell Their Story* was "the necessity of equalizing educational opportunities." The facts in the study "indicate that our present secondary school is still a highly selective institution adapted to the needs of a small minority of our population." Bell goes on to say: "There is grave danger that the public school system, if present tendencies persist, may become a positive force in creating those very inequalities of men that it was designed to reduce."[62]

The blacks are the largest minority group. They illustrate the segregation that so often has characterized American education—and not only secondary education. The blacks had been introduced to this country as slaves, with the customary stigma that has attached to that

61. Howard M. Bell, *Youth Tell Their Story* (Washington, D.C.: American Council on Education, 1938).

62. Ibid., "Preface," ii.

status, reinforcing segregation. The color line has perpetuated this stigma, making it all the more pronounced.

Legal desegregation was struck down in the memorable decision of the U.S. Supreme Court (1954), *Brown* v. *Board of Education*. The court ruled that segregation made for inequality in opportunity and thus it nullified the idea of "separate but equal facilities" propounded by that same court sixty years earlier in *Plessy* v. *Ferguson*. And in 1964 the Congress passed the Civil Rights Act. The effect of this legislation on schooling was assessed in the Coleman report in 1966.[63]

Does the trend seem to suggest greater participation of blacks in American secondary schools? The *Current Population Reports* of the U.S. Bureau of the Census for the decade of the 1960s indicate that enrollment of fourteen- and fifteen-year-old youth increased from 95.9 percent to 98.2 percent while enrollment of sixteen- and seventeen-year-old youth increased from 76.9 percent to 88.8 percent. These figures are not significantly lower than those for whites only. But when we look at the percent of high school dropouts among persons fourteen to nineteen years old (as of 1970), the figure for black males is 15.9 percent as contrasted with 6.7 percent for white males. For black females, the figure is 13.3 percent, while that for white females is 8.1 percent.

This unhappy contrast complements the equally disheartening fact that many minority group families are clustered in urban ghettos. We know too, that the economic status of these families tends to be lower than that of whites. These economic disadvantages cannot be masked as desirable consequences of cultural pluralism. Nevertheless, the history of the black in American secondary education shows an improvement in position. While that is no justification for complacency, or for "benign neglect," there is no reason to counsel despair.

In recent years, equal chances in education and cultural pluralism without a loss of community have been thoroughly aired both in terms of theory and in program after program, many carefully designed and assessed. Despite this, there has been nothing like consensus on the role that formal education should play in social reconstruction. If Jencks is correct,[64] society will have to be recast to reduce the disparity of in-

63. James S. Coleman, *Equality of Educational Opportunity* (Washington, D. C.: U. S. Government Printing Office, 1966).

64. Christopher Jencks et al., *Inequality: A Reassessment of the Effect of Family and Schooling in America* (New York: Basic Books, 1972).

come, a factor more important to a person's chances in life than the extent of his or her schooling. But Jencks's conclusion is disputed. Whether it holds or not, the rhetorical query remains in order: Shall education be thought a significant agency for the attainment of democracy?

The memory of World War I, and experience with the effects of the Great Depression, fostered attempts by progressives and reconstructionists to deal with the query. The pivot of the discussions from the 1920s into the post World War II years was Teachers College of Columbia University and the leader of these discussions was William Heard Kilpatrick. The discussions led to the formulation of a "frontier" position that favored a liberal or "progressive" social philosophy, one which complemented a "child-centered," "progressive education."[65] Opposing positions were taken by "essentialists" such as William C. Bagley, I. L. Kandel, and others. Debate was heated but did not, and has not, reached satisfactory closure. Progressives and reconstructionists have held that one could answer "yes" to Counts's question: "Dare the school build a new social order?"[66] while the essentialists have insisted that the schools have more to do with perpetuation of the culture, with its essential tools and values, than in formulating and propagandizing for designs to be used in its recasting. Perhaps that debate was too global, too little contained. Today, much more specific issues within the province of equality of educational opportunity and the preservation of cultural pluralism (without sacrifice of community) have largely displaced yesterday's exhibits of philosophic give-and-take.

While there is no consensus on the hierarchy of critical issues, it is plain that cultural pluralism is the most knotty of the regnant issues. What of conjoint issues? The most readily subdued conjoint issue is the right(s) of the teacher. If one looks at the many ways in which a teacher has been circumscribed in the past,[67] there is no doubt that the degree to which they now are unfettered is impressively greater than it has been. As teachers have won professional recognition, their

---

65. Cremin, *The Transformation of the School*, p. 228 f.

66. George Counts, *Dare the School Build a New Social Order?* (New York: John Day, 1932).

67. Howard K. Beale, *Are American Teachers Free?* (New York: Charles Scribner's Sons, 1936); idem, *History of Freedom of Teaching.*

freedom has been guaranteed by repeated decisions of state supreme courts and those of the United States Supreme Court. But for the support of the high school teacher under fire there has been no protection comparable to that afforded by the American Federation of Teachers. The Federation was chartered in 1916 by the redoubtable labor leader, Samuel Gompers, and its first charter member was John Dewey.

Now the rights of the student are regarded as a necessary complement to the freedom of the teacher. The prevailing image of the unbaptized young is not that of the "young viper" of Jonathan Edwards in the eighteenth century.[68] Nor do teachers follow the injunction of John Wesley: "Break your child's will in order that its soul may live." As applied to the child and to the adolescent these remarks recall the view of the young person, the unbaptized child, and the adolescent in danger of sinning. But American education in the modern era was to become steadily more informed by the study of the role of emotion in the educative process.[69] A concern with the self-esteem and self-image of the adolescent displaced the older perspective voiced in *Proverbs* 22:15: "Foolishness is bound in the heart of a child but the rod of correction will drive it far from him." The scientific (psychological) study of human behavior has enlarged its influence on American secondary schooling.

Psychological attention to the feelings of youth, combined with the knowledge of the effects of economic forces and social stratification, was complemented by a heightened concern for individualism, even for nonconformity. For centuries the school had stood *in loco parentis* (old English common law so held) and we know that the ideal of parenthood was anything but soft and indulgent. Added to that parental image was the belief that the school board had almost absolute authority. Counts's early study (1927) of the "bias" in the social composition of school boards, a hypothesis which was tested many times subsequently, did not shake the common belief that the Board of Education was *the* law and the school staff only slightly less so. Now

68. Likening unbaptized children to vipers was not uncommon. Whitefield referred to them as rattlesnakes and alligators and the Rev. Philemon Robbins of Branford declared that "As innocent as children seem to be to us, yet, if they are out of Christ [not baptized], they are not so in God's sight, but are young vipers, and are infinitely more hateful than vipers . . ." Sanford Fleming, *Children and Puritanism* (New Haven, Connecticut: Yale University Press, 1933), p. 69.

69. Daniel A. Prescott, *Emotion and the Educative Process* (Washington, D. C.: American Council on Education, 1938).

this authority has been adjudicated.[70] The image of school authority has been allowed to stand but it is fenced about by the recognition of the civil rights of students, with fewer qualifications made in the instance of the young adult.

Today concern for democracy is penetrating secondary school education. There is greater participation by students in the process of learning and governance. A good deal of attention is given each student's interests, as well as his or her strengths and weaknesses. Symptomatic of what is happening is the serious attention being given all phases of counseling. Unquestionably there is also greater participation by the teacher in the operation of a school or school system. The old corporate and military line-and-staff or hierarchical distribution of power is being attacked. Central in today's controversies are our core issues of educational opportunity and cultural pluralism; the opportunity of students considered in all their individuality has a greater chance of being noticed and nurtured. Maximizing the potential of staff is the other side of this same coin.

While the issue of differentiation of school types has just appeared on the educational horizon, it seems likely that some differentiation will take place—but within the public school system. This would be a natural extension of educational concern for equalization of educational chances and recognition of cultural pluralism.

The enlargement of the concepts of participation, communication, and community to include parents, even more particularly parents of ethnic minorities and the poor, has a much more uncertain future. A significant issue in secondary education today would seem to be that of spelling out which groups are to be included in the "community" of those concerned with education and what is to be the nature of this community. Is it to be racially integrated? Are social-class lines to be very modest advantages and handicaps? And what does any commitment made entail by way of practice?

Much of what confronts educators is alive with feelings. Anything

70. For example, see Richard L. Berkman, "Students in Court: Free Speech and the Functions of Schooling in America," *Harvard Educational Review* 40 (November 1970): 567-95; Stephen R. Goldstein, "The Scope and Sources of School Board Authority to Regulate Student Conduct and Status: A Nonconstitutional Analysis," *University of Pennsylvania Law Review* 117 (January 1969): 373-430; the ruling on Tinker v. Des Moines School District, 393 U. S. 503 (1969) where the decision was that student rights were primarily limited by conduct that might persuasively be described as threatening to an orderly school procedure.

approaching successful resolution will call for professionals to become most sophisticated in the application of the social and behavioral studies and to be guided by their own internalized humanism.

CHAPTER III

Fostering Maximum Development of the Individual

ARTHUR W. COMBS

Whatever is done to improve high school education must be related to some conception of the nature of learners and of the learning process. For several generations our thinking about high school education has been based primarily upon behavioristic views of what people are like and how they behave. Those concepts may have been useful guides when high school goals were simpler, curricula were limited, and the pace of societal change was slower. Secondary education of today and tomorrow must be much more complex and geared to the satisfaction of quite different student and societal needs. To meet these demands, new theoretical concepts are required to orient our thinking and to point the way to new techniques and processes designed to meet current needs. Fortunately, such concepts are available in modern humanistic psychology.

Humanistic psychology has come into being over the past thirty years largely in answer to the needs of persons working in helping professions, such as counseling, psychiatry, clinical psychology, social work, teaching, and pastoral care. The concepts provided by perceptual-humanistic theory offer exciting new ways of thinking about the nature of persons and how they behave. The concepts are applicable to a wide variety of modern problems, and they are especially useful for the problems of education. This is not to say that humanistic concepts deny behavioristic ones. Rather, perceptual-humanistic psychology adds to and builds upon behavioristic concepts. In this way it provides educators with a second tool for dealing with current problems.

As Silberman has pointed out, our educational system suffers from "mindlessness;"[1] many goals are sought and practices are followed for

1. Charles E. Silberman, *Crisis in the Classroom* (New York: Random House, 1970).

no really good reasons. Even a cursory glance at modern public school education reveals an incredible number of barriers to growth and learning in the curriculum, administration, classroom programs, and even in the buildings themselves. Hundreds of practices exist for no truly supportable reasons beyond custom and convenience. Hundreds more are justified by outmoded goals or no longer adequate concepts of learning. A truly effective school system must continuously assess itself in light of the very best theoretical bases available. Such review is especially needed when new conceptions of the nature of persons, of behavior, or of learning come into being. This chapter will attempt to outline four such innovations produced by the social and behavioral sciences in recent years and suggest some questions they raise for freeing human potential in the high school years.

Learning as Personal Discovery

A major contribution to modern education from perceptual psychology has to do with its conception of learning. For a very long time we have been living with concepts of learning derived from behavioristic stimulus-response thinking about the problem. In this view, behavior is understood as a function of the stimuli to which people are exposed. Accordingly, learning becomes a matter of conditioning and effective teaching is seen as a matter of skillful manipulation of stimuli. Such a view of learning has been useful in some aspects of education, especially in the learning of fairly simple skills. Applying these concepts to more complex goals has proven far less satisfactory and sometimes even downright misleading.

Perceptual-humanistic psychology sees learning in a quite different way—the personal discovery of meaning. Perceptualists point out that learning always has two aspects: (1) confrontation with some new information, and (2) the personal discovery of its meaning in the student's own being. Secondary education has done very well with the first part of that formulation. Indeed, we are experts at providing people with information and nowadays, with our modern technology, we are able to provide information in greater quantities and faster than ever before. It is in the second aspect of learning that our problems occur. The high school dropout, for example, is not a dropout because he was not told. He is a casualty because he never was helped to discover the personal meaning information might have had for him.

The basic principle of learning in perceptual-humanistic psychology has been stated as follows: *Any information will affect a person's behavior only in the degree to which he has discovered the personal meaning of that information for him.*[2] This means that learning is a subjective matter, having to do with what goes on in the personal experience of the student. Effective teaching in such a frame of reference is not a matter of managing behavior and manipulating curricula; it is a matter of facilitation, of encouraging, and of ministering to processes going on within the student. This principle helps us to understand why so much teaching has little effect on the student. It also points directions in which we must explore to improve the system.

In light of this basic definition, perceptual theory provides us further guidelines for the construction of effective learning situations. It tells us that the facilitation of learning will be dependent upon the provision of three important conditions.

First, there must be an atmosphere which facilitates the exploration of meaning. From research in counseling, social work, and teaching we already know a good deal about such atmospheres. We know, for example, that the exploration of meaning requires a commitment of self to the process. This, in turn, calls for circumstances in which the learner feels accepted and safe, is challenged but not threatened, and is encouraged and helped to risk himself in the encounter with new problems. Exploration of meaning is an active process, proceeding best through problem-solving conditions with continuous feedback to the learner about where he is and where he needs to go next. Limits which define the learning situation must be reasonable, helpful, clear, and stable. Provision must also be made for involvement, interaction, and socialization with other people in a relaxed and comfortable setting, for learning is essentially a social process.

In secondary education today some conditions for effective learning can be created through the provision of proper physical settings, equipment, supplies and the like. Some can also be created through well chosen curricula and various kinds of learning resources and

2. Arthur W. Combs, Anne C. Richards, and Fred Richards, *Perceptual Psychology: A Humanistic View of the Psychology of Persons* (New York: Harper & Row, 1975).

through opportunities to combine classroom and community experiences. Of far more importance than any of these in the creation of atmospheres for learning, however, are the human beings involved in the process. Effective atmospheres for learning are created by people, and nothing is more important in creating or destroying the atmosphere for learning than the interactions among them. It is teachers, principals, supervisors, counselors, superintendents, and community resource people who contribute to or detract from the quality of the atmospheres for learning.

In the past twenty years a whole new literature on helping relationships has provided important new understandings about effective and ineffective relationships immediately applicable to the problems of education. Research at the University of Florida on effective helpers, for example, shows that it is what helpers think is important that is crucial in determining the conditions for learning.[3] Effective helpers are empathic, sensitive people who have a clear understanding of the nature of the people with whom they work, who see themselves in positive ways, who focus on producing facilitative conditions, and who are deeply authentic persons in their own right. How successful we are likely to be in creating effective atmospheres for learning is a direct outgrowth of the philosophy, understanding, and values of the persons charged with creating them. The kinds of atmospheres created will be dependent upon the belief systems of those responsible for establishing the conditions for learning.

Second, given a facilitating atmosphere, the learner must next confront some new information or experience. This is the thing we do best. Indeed, much of our failure in education is probably due to our preoccupation with this phase of the learning process. The educator's usual answer to most criticism is to do some more with information—revise the curriculum, add a course, teach it earlier, teach it more often, provide experience in more vivid form, force the learner to confront it. Attention is almost exclusively focused on the first of the two aspects of learning.

Our attempts to reorganize the secondary school curriculum usual-

3. Arthur W. Combs et al., *Florida Studies in the Helping Professions*, University of Florida Social Science Monograph, no. 37 (Gainesville, Fla.: University of Florida Press, 1969).

ly overlook the fact that meaning does not lie in the information but rather in the experience of the learner. Mere exposure to new information is no guarantee whatever that any learning will ensue. The crucial aspect of confrontation lies not in the skill of the sender but in the experience of the receiver. For all practical purposes, information has not really been provided if the learner did not hear it or could not handle it.

In many junior and senior high schools we now have at our disposal magnificent new devices for providing students with vast amounts of audio and visual exposure by television, teaching machines, movies, recordings, information retrieval systems, computers, and the like. Our new hardware makes possible the provision of information in a quantity and variety undreamed of only a few years ago. With all this, however, we still have blinders imposed by our concepts of what is worthwhile information and our neglect of needed experiences. We still think primarily in academic terms and the techniques we use for providing information are largely restricted to classroom use. We have not yet really accepted the significance of out-of-school experience as a major resource for our high schools.

Third, there must be provisions for facilitating the discovery of personal meaning. The discovery of personal meaning is the crucial aspect of learning, the end product that the creation of atmospheres and the provision of experience are designed to foster. Provision of information or the manipulation of conditions for learning can in large part be done by the teacher with or without the cooperation of the learner. But the discovery of meaning occurs inside the learner and so is not open to external manipulation. Teachers have control over information, but only the learner has control over his personal meanings. Without his cooperation not much is likely to happen. Important as the need for facilitation of personal meaning is, we probably know less about it than any other phase of learning. Some of our best sources for understanding it currently come from such fields as counseling, encounter groups, experiential learning, and the work of creative teachers interested in personalizing instruction.

To facilitate the process of discovery of meaning requires a concern for meaning in high school personnel. Personal experience is subjective rather than objective, affective as well as cognitive, and deals with elements such as human feelings, attitudes, beliefs, understandings, values, hopes, and fears. Concern for such matters often flies in the face of the wide-spread worship of objectivity, of science, and of the contributions of industry characteristic of our society. Typically, we distrust human feelings as bases for action. Affective education is often regarded as "soft," "fuzzy-minded," mystical, or vague. But if learning is truly the discovery of personal meaning, then good teaching must be regarded as facilitation of the exploration of meaning. And we need to get about the business of finding ways of doing it more efficiently.

Since the exploration of meaning is a personal matter, it follows that its facilitation must be highly individual and adapted to the learner's own pace. It will also require the cooperation of the learner, who has to be helped to take major responsibility for his own learning. This individual character of the exploration of meaning is incongruent with much of the organization of secondary schools around subject matter, sequential presentation of information, fixed curricula, and required courses. Ways must be found to make the high school far more spontaneous in its response to its clientele. Historically, teachers have been almost exclusively preoccupied with their role as "directors" of the learning process. In the light of the concepts of learning outlined here, secondary school teachers will need to spend much more time as "facilitators" and "consultants" in the future.

QUESTIONS ABOUT LEARNING THEORY FOR SECONDARY SCHOOL EDUCATION

If the concepts of learning we have been discussing here are valid, they must certainly have far-reaching implications for designing the high school experience. At the very least they require answers to such basic questions as the following:

1. What is the theory of learning on which we predicate our thinking? Is it maximally appropriate for modern goals? Do we truly appreciate the fact that different goals require the utilization of different theoretical models? Or are we preoccupied with looking at learning from only one point of view?

2. What sorts of barriers are we placing in the path of the learner's personal exploration of meaning? Some years ago I asked a class of young teachers, "Why is it you seem so uncommitted? How come you don't get involved in the learning process?" Here are some of the

answers they gave me, pointing out the barriers to their involvement in their classes:[4]

Nobody thinks our problems are important.
Nobody has any respect for our beliefs.
Teachers don't trust kids.
All they want is conformity.
They feed us a "Pablum" diet—it's all chewed over and there is nothing good left in it.
Everyone is afraid to let us try.
Nobody cares about students as people.
It's details, details, details.
Or grades, grades, grades, as though they mattered.
You can't question anything.
The teachers think the only good ideas are all in the books.

Most shocking to me was the following statement on which all these young teachers agreed: *"The things worth getting committed to don't get you ahead in school!"*

What can we adopt about the atmosphere for learning from other helping professions? How shall we go about creating in classrooms and communities a secondary school education that truly fosters the kinds of atmospheres we know are fundamental to the effective exploration of meaning?

3. While the provision of information and experience is the aspect of learning understood best, nevertheless there are still important questions we can ask about the matter. How, for example, can we bring the information and experience we provide more closely in touch with where students are? How can we use our new expertise in ways that not only provide information better, but also truly aid the learner in the discovery of meaning?

4. How can we discover the barriers to the facilitation of meaning exploration inherent in the present system? What has the experience of other helping professions to offer in understanding this problem? How can we truly personalize the exploration of meaning in secondary schools that are responsible for very large numbers of students? What kinds of relationships do we need to establish for the facilitation of

4. Arthur W. Combs, *Educational Accountability: Beyond Behavioral Objectives* (Washington, D.C.: Association for Supervision and Curriculum Development, National Education Association, 1972).

personal exploration? What kinds of attitudes do these relationships call for in school people and how shall we go about facilitating the development of these attitudes in school personnel so that they may find their way into action?

New Concepts of Human Potential[5]

For generations much of our thinking about behavior has concentrated upon human limitations. In that process we have been selling people short, for the outstanding fact about them is not their limits, but their possibilities. People are overbuilt. Humanistic-perceptual psychology tells us that few of us ever use more than a small portion of our possibilities. Even intelligence, we now understand, is open to far more change than we have ever supposed.

Humanistic psychologists are asking not, "What does it mean to be normal or adjusted?" but "What does it mean to be self-actualizing, to operate at the peak of one's highest potential?" This kind of thinking is not being pursued in psychology alone; persons in the health sciences are intrigued with the question of "high-level wellness," that is, what does it mean to be superbly well?[6] These scientific investigations about man's possibilities are crucial for education, for whatever one decides is the nature of the fully functioning, self-actualizing person must also stand as the important goal of education. It is the release of human potential that education is all about.

From research and writing four characteristics of self-actualized persons emerge:

1. Self-actualizing persons have a rich, extensive, and available field of understanding. They are knowledgeable people with a broad fund of understanding upon which they can call as they confront the events of life with which they must deal. Since we have already mentioned some of the implications of this concept in our discussion of learning as personal meaning, we shall not elaborate further on this characteristic here.

2. Self-actualizing persons have essentially positive views of

---

5. For a fuller discussion of the educational significance of these concepts of human potential, see Arthur W. Combs, ed., *Perceiving, Behaving, Becoming: A New Focus for Education,* 1962 Yearbook of the Association for Supervision and Curriculum Development (Washington, D.C.: National Education Association, 1962), p. 256.

6. H. A. Dunn, *Your World and Mine* (New York: Exposition Press, 1956).

themselves. They see themselves as liked, wanted, acceptable, and able. Maladjusted, inadequate persons, on the other hand, see themselves as unliked, unwanted, unacceptable, unable, undignified, unworthy. Much of human unhappiness, maladjustment, poor health, and depravity is a consequence of deprivation, of lack of fulfillment. The crucial role of the self-concept in determining behavior is one of the most important contributions of perceptual-humanistic thinking. From hundreds of researches we now know that the self-concept is an ever present and crucial factor in every person's experience and determines in very large measure the success or failure of his interactions with the world at every moment of his life. It is especially significant as a factor in the learning process and so must be a major factor in thinking about ways to improve educational institutions and processes. Laws of learning as crucial as the self-concept cannot be ignored because they are inconvenient. To do so will only confound our very best efforts.

Important as the self-concept is in the determination of behavior, of even greater importance for education is the fact that the self-concept is learned. People *learn* who they are and what they are from the ways they are treated by the significant persons they encounter in the processes of their growing up. Thus, not only are the outcomes of education determined by the self-concepts of students, but education provides many of the experiences that *create* the self-concept, provided that educational personnel are truly significant in the lives of students—a condition, alas, we have too often failed to achieve.

3. Self-actualizing persons are open to experience. This characteristic of self-actualizing persons has to do with the individual's interaction with the world, sometimes called by psychologists "acceptance." It is the capacity to confront what is, to enter into a transaction with events, to develop new meanings as a consequence. Highly self-actualizing, fully functioning personalities seem able to deal with life with a minimum of distortion. They are able to look at themselves and the world about them openly, without fear and defensiveness. They see themselves and the events about them accurately and realistically.

Openness to experience and acceptance is learned in part from having been accepted. This provides individuals with the security required to explore and test themselves, which in turn makes possible confronting new events with courage and determination. In part, openness is also the product of successful experience in interaction with rich and varied concepts and events. It is a consequence of being challenged rather than threatened. Since schools can no longer hope to provide all students with everything they need to meet the exigencies of the future in so rapidly changing a society as we have created, the production of citizens who are open, responsive, and realistically aware of outside events is an absolute necessity if we are truly to prepare young people for the world in which they must move.

4. Highly self-actualized persons characteristically have deep feelings of identification with other people. The possession of these feelings in turn produces interactions with one's fellows that corroborate and strengthen existing beliefs. Broad feelings of identification, for example, make it possible to put much more trust in others. Relationships with others can then be entered much more openly and freely with an expectation of success. When one is certain of his welcome, he is free to walk more boldly and dares to do or say what other less certain persons could not risk. Because they feel they belong, broadly identified persons establish relationships with other people as though they were members of the family rather than strangers. Such a sense of oneness with others also gives its possessor a deep compassion for other people. The feedback they experience in these interactions is, also, more supporting and enhancing than that of less self-actualized persons.

The world has grown so small that we live, almost literally, in each other's laps. Our society is so complex and interdependent that each of us is utterly dependent on the cooperation of thousands of persons we have never even seen. In such a world the defection of even a single person (like a Lee Harvey Oswald or a Sirhan Sirhan) at a particular spot and time can throw us all into absolute chaos. Deep feelings of identification, of belonging, of oneness are increasingly crucial to our way of life. Alienation is not just a pity—it is a danger to everyone. Identification is learned. It is discovered as a consequence of experience in the process of growing up. A major task of our public schools must be to contribute to the development of such feelings in our youth.

QUESTIONS ON HUMAN POTENTIAL
FOR SECONDARY SCHOOL EDUCATION

As has been pointed out elsewhere, whatever we decide is the nature of the fully functioning, self-actualizing person must, of necessity, become incorporated in the goals of education.[7] If the above conceptions of self-actualization are true, they must become integrated into the goals of schooling and provide the guidelines for innovations and reform. The implications of these concepts for secondary education are so vast they cannot be spelled out here in detail. We can, however, raise some of the questions posed by perceptual-humanistic principles which must be part of our thinking in the design of better high school education.

Here are a few:

1. What shall the high school do to make rich and extensive funds of information available to its clientele? Of the four factors related to potential, this is, historically, the one on which we have usually concentrated attention. To bring our high schools in closer touch with the information explosion and the modern pace of change, the question still must be asked repeatedly.

2. How shall we make ourselves more aware of the self-concepts of students? What practices, goals, regulations, and policies tear down students' self-concepts? And how shall we make the high school experience produce in students positive views of self? What can we do to help students see themselves as persons who are liked, wanted, acceptable, able—persons of dignity and worth?

3. What can high schools do to develop openness to experience? Bigotry, hostility, and defensive, narrow-minded persons are a drag on our way of life. How shall we design a high school experience to encourage open-mindedness, toleration of ambiguity, and problem-solving behavior? How shall we produce persons possessed of clear and supportable values, unafraid to encounter difficulties and willing to grow and change in a changing world?

4. How shall we help students develop deep feelings of identification with ideas and with persons? A frequent complaint of our time is "the alienation of youth." How shall we construct a school in which students feel they belong, where prejudice and bigotry are reduced to minimal levels? What can we do to create a school in which students feel one with each other, have compassion and respect for themselves and their fellows who may differ culturally and individually, and where teachers and students regard themselves as partners in a common search?

7. Combs, ed., *Perceiving, Behaving, Becoming: A New Focus for Education.*

Motivation and Need

We are accustomed to thinking of motivation in stimulus-response terms. In that frame of reference motivation is understood as a question of what to do to get people to perform in the ways we would like. It is essentially a problem of manipulation and control of forces exerted on the learner. This makes motivation an external problem having to do primarily with what is done to the learner.

Perceptual-humanistic psychology takes a different position. It sees the problem as an internal one, having to do with how people feel, think, believe, want, desire, hope, and aspire. These are internal matters having to do with what goes on inside. According to humanistic-perceptual psychology, the basic need of all people in all times and places is the search for self-fulfillment. People do what it seems to them they need to do at the moment of behaving. One needs but look at his own behavior for a moment to become quite keenly aware that that is certainly true of one's self.

THE BASIC NEED FOR SELF-ACTUALIZATION

The basic need of the organism to move toward health is characteristic of protoplasm itself. Even the lowly amoeba moves away from danger and toward food, if it is possible for it to do so. The basic drive of the living organism is toward health, a fact upon which all the helping professions rely. Thus, in the practice of medicine, physicians may remove the barriers to the organism's recovery by an operation, by the destruction of harmful germs, or by building up the organism's resources in one way or another, *but the organism gets well by itself*. Its own basic drives provide the motivating force. Counselors, psychiatrists, clinical psychologists, social workers, and many others in the helping professions are equally dependent upon this basic need. From the experience of persons in these professions it is clear that the organism possesses a basic need for self-fulfillment or self-actualization and the human organism can, will, must, move toward a healthier condition, providing the way seems open to do so.

This conception of human need has enormous implications for education. For one thing, it means that the human organism is not the perverse, contrary object we have so long assumed. Quite the contrary, the basic human need is a drive toward health. This means people are on our side! Students *want* to be healthy, *want* to be effective, *want* to achieve self-actualization just as their teachers, parents, and friends want them to do.

T.HE NATURE OF MALADJUSTMENT

Unhappily, what seems to a person to be fulfilling can become twisted and perverted as a consequence of negative experience. The young criminal, for example, having come to believe over fourteen or fifteen years that "Nobody likes me, nobody wants me, nobody cares about me, I am not able or good for anything" may come to the conclusion "Well, I don't like nobody, neither," and consequently find it fulfilling to punish his tormentors, confound his oppressors, and join together in gangs with others feeling as he does.

Similarly, persons growing up feeling fundamentally inadequate to cope with life may find it fulfilling to defend themselves against life by innumerable kinds of defenses and maneuvers, described by outside observers as neurotic behavior or mental illness. As we have seen in our discussion of self-actualization, some modern theory regards depravity as a function of deprivation or lack of fulfillment. How effectively a person is able to behave will be dependent in very large measure on need satisfaction. Maslow expressed this principle in his "Hierarchy of Needs."[8] He pointed out that human needs exist in a kind of hierarchy, from very basic ones like the need for air, water, and food, up the scale to the need for contact, caring, and successful achievement, to the highest levels of self-actualization. He pointed out also that higher needs cannot be given attention while lower ones are still depleted. One cannot, after all, think nice thoughts about democracy on an empty belly! It is only when basic needs are fundamentally filled that we can·turn our attention to the satisfaction of higher ones.

The person's own basic need for self-fulfillment is so pressing that it cannot be set aside for very long. As an important factor in human growth and learning it can also not be ignored by education. As a matter of fact, the achievement of self-actualization, as we have seen, must become a basic goal of education itself, and whatever system we devise must serve to help young people achieve the maximum of

8. Abraham H. Maslow, *Motivation and Personality*, 2nd ed. (New York: Harper & Row, 1970).

fulfillment. A major goal of education must be to fulfill the basic needs of its students. But even that is not enough. An educational system which only helped its students to fulfill their current needs would fail its responsibilities to our society. Good teaching is not simply helping a child fulfill his current needs; the genius of good teaching is helping the student discover needs he never knew he had.

LEARNING AND SELF-ACTUALIZATION

Learning, we have seen, is a problem in personal discovery of meaning. But this process is motivated by the students' need to know. It does not take a psychologist to convince us that students learn best when they have a need to know. This is a principle which anyone can discover for himself. But, alas, we behave as though the principle did not exist. As Donald Snygg once pointed out, "The trouble with American education is that we are everywhere providing students with answers to problems they haven't got yet!"

More often than not, we have assumed students *wanted* to know, and we have railed at them for their apathy or punished them for failing to learn whether or not they saw any reason to do so. We have also tried in one way or another to create artificial reasons for learning. But artificial motives like grades, examinations, threats of failure, competition, special awards and honors, continue to prove disappointing. Even when such motives are apparently successful it is shocking to discover how impermanent the learning proves to be when the artificial need is no longer present. Apathy, we need to understand, is not a *cause* of behavior; it is *itself* a behavior produced by the learner's failure to perceive a need for exerting himself. Apathy is a product of irrelevance, a consequence of the student's inability to perceive that what is being asked of him has any relationship to his own need for fulfillment. One needs but listen with half an ear to high school youth today to recognize that irrelevance is a major complaint.

A corollary principle with respect to the question of need is the perceptual-humanistic understanding of emotion as an incidental concomitant of relevance. The strength of a person's feeling about any event is a function of the personal meaning of the event to the self. The closer the event to self, the greater is the feeling experienced. What is not relevant to self provokes very little feeling. This understanding of

COMBS 79

the nature of emotion has vast implications for education. If emotion is an indicator of the degree of personal meaning, then the controversy over whether to include affective education in secondary schools is nonsense. If learning is truly the discovery of personal meaning, and if affect is an indicator of the closeness of events to the self, then affective education is not a luxury, but a necessity. A classroom without affect is a classroom where nothing is happening! Affect is an integral part of the process of learning.

QUERIES ON MOTIVATION AND NEED FOR SECONDARY SCHOOL EDUCATION

In the light of these principles concerning motivation and need from perceptual-humanistic psychology, the following are some of the questions we need to ask about high school education:

1. How should we go about helping personnel understand the universal character of the need for adequacy and self-fulfillment? How can we break down the time-honored feeling of antagonism between teachers and students? Research on the helping professions seems to show that one of the major characteristics of effective helpers is a fundamental faith and trust in the human organism. How shall we help teachers, principals, supervisors, community resource people, and others helping personnel in secondary education acquire such basic attitudes?

The rapidity of change in modern society and the information explosion have made it abundantly clear that to meet the needs of our society the high school curriculum must be more rich and varied than ever before. With the diversity of individual and cultural needs it is further apparent that a high school hoping to meet the needs of individuals must not only provide a rich and diverse curriculum; it must also be highly personalized. This calls for a fluidity and capacity for adaptation beyond anything we have heretofore conceived. The idea of a "course," in the sense of a systematic, sequential offering of information would have to be an early casualty in any such adaptation.

2. How shall a high school go about assessing the needs of its students? And having done so, how shall it then adjust itself so as to meet those needs effectively? How, too, shall high schools go about helping their students to discover needs they never knew they had? High schools honestly seeking to serve the needs of students must find

ways of consulting students in formulation of goals and practices. Who else knows better what students need?

3. Surely high schools committed to the idea of creating needs to know before providing information will need to make considerable changes from the orthodox patterns to which we have grown accustomed. Our secondary schools have developed a tremendous reliance on artificial motives for learning. Many of these, like the grading system, for example, are moss-grown with tradition. Others, like the myth of the value of competition as a motive, are deeply engrained in the fabric of society itself. The substitution of an emphasis upon real needs and motives in place of such artificial ones will not be brought about simply or easily. They are too deeply established in the belief systems at every level of the educational structure and the communities in which they exist.

Growth as a Process of Becoming

Perceptual-humanistic thought sees growth as a process of becoming through personal discovery of one's self and his relationships to the world. Information and knowledge are important in this process, as we have seen. But growth must be more than that. As Toffler has pointed out,[9] historically our educational system has had the task of passing on to the next generation the accumulated culture of the past. As a consequence, it has been primarily oriented around subject matter and the learning of basic skills. This was often quite adequate in a simple and stable society. It is no longer enough. Education must now prepare its students for a future, the nature of which can only be dimly perceived. Since education cannot provide students with the answers to problems that cannot even be formulated now, its goal must be the production of intelligent human beings. The production of intelligent persons cannot be achieved by teaching right answers or even right skills. Intelligence is a way of being, a capacity for entering into effective interactions with the world in ways appropriate to the circumstances confronted. It is a creative act. It cannot be defined in advance. If it could, it would not be intelligent behavior but mechanical. Creativity is not achieved by learning right answers. It is achieved by a process of continuous becoming.

9. Alvin Toffler, *Learning for Tomorrow* (New York: Random House, 1974).

The process begins by accepting individuals where they are. This is often a difficult thing for an institution like the school to accomplish with its emphasis on "excellence" and "correctness." One can hardly quarrel with such lofty ambitions. Unhappily, they often result in a paralyzing fear of making mistakes or unremitting efforts to prod the student ever onward and upward to never-achieved goals. Either way the message conveyed to the students is a lack of acceptance for where they are or condemnation for who they are. One needs but look about him to see innumerable examples of attitudes and practices which inescapably convey a lack of acceptance to students. Such insistence that students be who they are not is like going to a doctor who tells you, "Go away and get better and then I will help you."

Growth is a process of becoming, a search for fulfillment and interaction with the environment. It is encouraged by facilitating environments. It is inhibited or killed by barren or antagonistic ones. Education, like gardening, is a problem in cultivation, ministering to life. As Earl Kelley used to point out, "To grow a fine tomato plant you don't stand around and shout, 'Grow, damn you, grow!' What you do is get the very best seed you can. Plant it in the very best ground you have. Surround it with the very best possible growing conditions. Then you get out of its way and you let it grow." Unfortunately, far too many people in education still see the task of teaching as one requiring control, direction, management, manipulation, or a process of stimulus and response motivated exclusively by systems of reward and punishment.

A system truly tuned to processes of growth must constantly adapt itself to the needs of the organism. It is folly to believe such needs can be ignored. Personal needs are inexorable and the organism will find ways to achieve them in spite of the system, if necessary. Ignoring the needs of the learner only confirms the system as irrelevant, and hence as the enemy to be confounded and subverted in whatever ways are possible. A system truly conceiving learning as growth must enter into partnership with students to define goals and plan on strategies to reach them. Such a partnership is particularly necessary at the high school level where students are approaching the independence and autonomy of adulthood. Practices which seem to youth of their age as extending their childhood are bound to be counter productive.

Beginning with the students' own needs, processes of growth must next advance to helping students explore their horizons and confront new experiences. This calls for the widest, richest possible curriculum in a society as increasingly diverse and changing as ours. To accomplish this goal it seems obvious that the high school we have known is a "dead duck." The high school required for our time must be immensely broader and richer in the opportunities it provides for its students. It seems clear that a curriculum sufficiently rich and diverse to meet the needs of complex modern society can hardly be provided within the confines of a "high school plant." The entire community must become the high school laboratory.

The process of becoming also means that students will become increasingly unique as they proceed through the educational experience—if schools are doing their job. Students will be more unlike and individual at the end of the process than at the start. This is a far cry from the early public schools whose primary purpose was to provide youth with common skills. To keep our world running these days requires ever greater and greater diversity of skills and people who use them. For a hundred years teachers in education have called for personalized instruction but we still keep hoping we can find a way to treat our students alike. An educational system that truly comprehends the principle of becoming must face up to the need for real personalization. Real efforts toward education for uniqueness require a fundamental change in fundamental assumptions. Lip service is not enough.

QUESTIONS ABOUT GROWTH
AS BECOMING FOR SECONDARY SCHOOL EDUCATORS

If the process of becoming described in modern humanistic psychology is accurate, secondary school educators need to ask at least the following questions:

1. What are the real assumptions we make about the processes of teaching and organizing our schools? What implications does the shift in objectives from acquiring a precise body of knowledge to producing intelligent human beings have for the high school years?

2. How shall we go about truly accepting students as they are and where they are? What messages are being transmitted to students by our current practices? What changes are needed in our own

assumptions about goals and processes if becoming is truly the nature of the learning process? How can we go about rethinking our time-honored emphases on control, direction, stimulus, response, reward and punishment?

3. How can the high school truly implement the required partnership with students if the principle of becoming is to work? How can we enter such negotiations with open attitudes and minds so that they may have some chance of success? How can we bring about a real comprehension among education planners and leaders of the fact that high school youth today are more adult than a generation ago?

4. Finally, how shall the modern high school truly meet the immensely increased diversity of needs in modern society? How can we truly go about the process of utilizing the entire community as a learning laboratory? What would such changes in thinking require in the nature of high school organization, buildings, grounds, equipment, and services?

Some Implications of Perceptual-Humanistic Psychology for Secondary School Education

Modern perceptual-humanistic psychology points out two fundamental ways in which we can approach the problem of dealing with human beings. One of these is a closed system of thinking in which the expected outcomes are known in advance. Essentially, the method consists in (1) establishing a clear goal, (2) setting up the machinery to achieve it, (3) placing the machinery in operation, and (4) testing the outcomes of the process. This is the "rational," "logical" approach to dealing with human events with which everyone is familiar. It is also hallowed in our society as "the scientific method" and is deeply admired as the "business-like" way responsible for the magnificent successes of our great industries. Its latest expression in education may be seen in the national push for "accountability," "behavioral objectives," "performance-based criteria," and the like.

An alternative approach is an open system of thinking applicable to those situations where final outcomes cannot be precisely defined in advance. The open system is a problem-solving approach to human dilemmas in which emphasis is on finding appropriate solutions rather than on moving toward ends specified in advance. It is a process, rather than an ends-oriented approach, and it is especially suited to broad, holistic objectives and to humanistic outcomes having to do with individual belief systems.

Both closed and open systems of thinking have important contributions to make to our educational processes in high schools. Closed systems of thinking are particularly appropriate, of course, if outcomes can be clearly stated in advance. This is particularly true for the learning of fundamental skills. Much of elementary education is still very much concerned with these ends. The higher one goes in the educational stratum and the more complex the problems students will have to face, however, the more it is necessary to shift our ways of operation from a closed system to an open one. This is especially necessary as we shift from a past-oriented education to an emphasis on life today and in the future.

If we are to meet the challenges of the future, our educational system cannot afford to predicate its action exclusively on closed systems of thinking. High schools committed to growth as a process of becoming must increasingly adopt an open system of thinking for all its problems. This calls for a clear understanding of closed and open systems of thinking and full appreciation of the impact such systems have upon every aspect of educational experience. In the comparison below a few of the more obvious implications are shown in Table 1.

It must be apparent from an examination of the two systems we have outlined that open systems of thinking are far more conducive to growth. This is not to say that there is no place for a closed system of thinking. There is a very important place for the utilization of closed systems, especially for the acquisition of skills or when the management of behavior is the primary goal of the teacher. The management of behavior and the learning of precisely defined goals will always have an important place in any education system. For the larger goals of perceptual-humanistic psychology, an open, problem-centered approach to the learner will be increasingly required. Many of our traditional approaches to high school education have been primarily formulated in closed systems of thinking no longer appropriate for the attainment of modern goals. If human growth is truly a process of becoming, marked by motivation and need, respecting human potential, and concsiving learning as personal discovery, as perceptual-humanistic thinking would have us believe, then high school education

TABLE 1

SOME IMPLICATIONS OF CLOSED AND OPEN SYSTEMS OF
THINKING FOR SECONDARY EDUCATION

Aspects of Secondary Education	Implications of Closed Systems	Implications of Open Systems
Emphasis	Specific behavioral outcomes	Intelligent behavior—capacity to solve problems
	Management of behavior, manipulation to produce specific behaviors	Problem-solving approaches
		Facilitation of processes of exploration and observing
	The industrial model	Helping professions model
Relation to Society	Segregated from society	Deeply involved with society
Goals	Acquisition of specific vocational skills	Diversity in educational programs
	Self-control and self-discipline	Self-discovery and self-expression
	Conformity	Individualism
	Endurance of stress	Capacity for joy
	Personal acquirement	Personal fulfillment
Philosophy	Control and direction	Emphasis on facilitating processes
	Great man philosophy	Democratic philosophy
Curriculum	Oughts and shoulds	Filling and creating needs
	Acquiring information, right answers	Confronting real problems
Students	Passive, follow direction	Active, responsible
	Teachers seen as enemies	Teachers seen as helpers, aids
	Dehumanized, alienated	Involved, committed
	See requirements as of doubtful relevance	See activities as relevant
	To be made, molded, trained	To become, explore, discover

TABLE 1 (continued)

Aspects of Secondary Education	Implications of Closed Systems	Implications of Open Systems
Teacher	Expert diagnostician	Process facilitator
	Total responsibility	Responsibility shared with students and community
	Must be all knowing	Does not always *have* to be right
	Attention on skills	Attention on persons and processes
	Director role—the shaper and shaker	Facilitator, consultant role Friendly representative of society
Uses	Simple goals	Complex goals
	Skills, precise behavior	Holistic understandings, broad outcomes
	Ends clearly known and ways to achieve clear and manageable	Ends not clearly known, solutions to be discovered
	Management goals	Becoming goals

must increasingly opt for open systems of thinking as basic guidelines for improvement and innovation.

We are accustomed to breakthroughs in the physical sciences—those thrilling times when some new theoretical concept makes possible a "giant leap for mankind." But breakthroughs happen in social and behavioral science also and their implications can be equally profound for our human institutions. This is especially true for education, which ought to be the most human of all institutions. Whenever new conceptions of the nature of persons, learning and behavior arise, great new possibilities are opened for educational practice as well. Just such possibilities lie before us in the new conceptions provided by modern humanistic thinking. Of course, there is always a lag between the best we know and its implementation in practice but it behooves us all to reduce that lag to the minimum wherever possible. This is especially true in times like these when our educational institutions are faced with vast new problems and expectations. We are fortunate, indeed, that the social and behavioral sciences are providing us exciting and promising theories at the very moment our changing needs confront us with the necessity for finding more adequate ways to carry out our educational responsibilities. What is needed now is the fastest possible exploration of these new concepts by the widest possible numbers of persons and their translation into practice with the greatest possible dispatch.

CHAPTER IV

Developing and Applying Humane Values

LAWRENCE E. METCALF

Two Views of Man

MAN AS PROGRAMMED ROBOT

We are told today that the teaching of humane values can best be done inhumanely! Two inhumane ways are operant conditioning and pharmacology. A few years ago Kenneth Clark expressed the paradox when he both titillated and shocked an audience of psychologists with the prediction that the day would soon arrive when human behavior would be controlled and modified by chemical means. His listeners, who daily encountered clients plagued by problems of social division and personal disorganization, could not help but be attracted to a solution as simple and direct as swallowing a pill. At the same time, they were troubled by the questions raised by the application of pharmacology to human behavior. Who is to make and distribute the pill? Who will control whom, and for what purposes?

The same dilemma exists for those who find operant conditioning a tempting solution to chaos in classroom or community. A two-class society consisting of the controlled and the controllers will strike many as undemocratic, yet they may wonder how much longer any kind of humaneness can survive the inroads of crime, war, and economic exploitation in an uncontrolled society, and hostility, apathy, and disorganization in an uncontrolled classroom.

Operant conditioning may not be as efficient as pharmacology. But anything that works more certainly than discussion and inquiry is likely to receive serious attention from professionals who must deal each day with people experiencing fear and failure as their lot. Since we cannot go back to the womb, how about refuge in Skinner's box?

Solutions of our problems through pharmacology or operant conditioning are not as right as they may first appear. Their consequences are not what we want. We do want a more humane society, but the consequences of conditioning include an elitist element that omits democracy as the most humane of all values.

Operant conditioning includes a paradox. If people lack an inner life of dreams, visions, and ideals, as operant conditioners imply, and if we are all products of an environment, how do those who are to manipulate us decide what changes to make in our environment? What human behavior is to be encouraged in us by them? Is it even accurate to designate as human any behavior that is stamped in by a ruling class? Is this ruling class different from the rest of us in its possession of an inner life? One is reminded of Jefferson's statement in his first inaugural address: "Sometimes it is said that man cannot be trusted with the government of himself. Can he, then, be trusted with the government of others? Or have we found angels in the form of kings to govern him?" Our secular age does not believe in angels. Must we believe instead in psychologists?

The pill-pushers are not so foolish as to deny to us possession of an inner life. But they share with operant conditioners the problem of justifying their moral presumptuousness. To the extent that any end derives much of its meaning from the means used to achieve it, democratic values cannot be achieved in the way that pharmacologists and psychologists affirm.

Improper use and programming of computers for instructional purposes could compound the problem.

MAN AS CREATIVE RESPONDENT

Behind any theory of learning is to be found an image of humankind. The image that responds blindly to external influence is not the only one available. Isidor Chein suggests an alternative.

. . .Specifically, I suggest, we must choose between two images. The first is that of Man as an active responsible agent, not simply a helpless, powerless reagent. Man, in the active image, is a being who actively does something with regard to some of the things that happen to him, a being who, for instance, tries to increase the likelihood that some things will happen and that others will not, a being who tries to generate circumstances that are compatible with his intentions, a being who may try to inject harmony where he finds disharmony or who may sometimes seek to generate disharmony, a being who seeks to shape his environment rather than passively permit himself to be shaped by the latter, a being, in short, who insists on injecting himself into the causal process of the world around him. If Man is said to respond to his environment, the word 'response' is to be taken in the sense that it has in active dialogue rather than in the sense of an automatic consequence.

The contrasting and prevailing image among psychologists, whose careers are devoted to the advancement of science, and among astonishingly large numbers of those concerned with behavioral orthogenics (guidance, counseling, psychotherapy, and so on) is that of Man as an impotent reactor, with his responses completely determined by two distinct and separate, albeit interacting, sets of factors: (1) the forces impinging upon him and (2) his constitution (including in the latter term, for present purposes, momentary physiological states). Man, as such, plays no role in determining the outcome of the interplay between constitution and environment. He is implicitly viewed as a robot—a complicated constructed and programmed robot, perhaps, but a robot nevertheless.[1]

Operant conditioning, the theory of learning that today dominates most university departments of psychology, accepts the second image of man as reactor and robot. Pharmacology is the major active competitor to operant conditioning. Some observers have predicted that by 1984 the keynote speakers at conventions of professional educators will be pharmacologists. (One can imagine an in-service workshop for teachers interested in creative thinking as a classroom goal. They would study various kinds of creativity pills, rather than design resource units based upon differences between divergent and convergent thinking.) But one wonders whether a pill-created creativity is really creative. Can any response that is automatic, for reasons of physiology or conditioning, deserve to be called creative? Yet evidence is beginning to accumulate that operant conditioning can be used to modify behavior in directions desired by teachers and the community. It is a sure way, and most people are not philosophical enough to worry about side effects of a less desirable character.

Personal Dilemmas and Moral Growth

An alternative to operant conditioning and pharmacology, one that is based upon Chein's first image of man as an active responsible agent, is offered by Lawrence Kohlberg, O. J. Harvey, and other ego

1. Isidor Chein, *The Science of Behavior and the Image of Man* (New York/London: Basic Books, Inc., 1972), p. 6.

development psychologists, as well as by humanistic psychology. Kohlberg's proposal has received the most attention. Its rationale has been developed by him and his students over a period of more than fifteen years. His approach is consistent with Dewey's philosophy of education and theory of learning. The separation of stimulus from response, with one preceding the other, is rejected in favor of the view that one's responses are part of one's stimuli. When one is stimulated, one has already begun to respond. But we do not respond to every stimulus that comes down the pike. Neither do we all respond in the same way to a particular stimulus. The differences need not be explained by reference to differences in conditioning. An alternative explanation is to attribute our differing responses to the varying insights to be found in individuals.

Insights, according to Dewey, result from problem solving which involves hypothesis testing. Kohlberg has studied problem solving at different levels of maturity. He is interested not only in the quality of an insight but also in the reasoning behind it; apparently, he derives this interest from Piaget's early work with the moral judgment of children. Piaget identified two kinds of morality, the autonomous and the nonautonomous. Kohlberg has refined this conception, and describes three levels of morality with two stages at each level. Prior to the three levels is to be found a premoral stage. The successive stages are defined and described in table 1.[2]

In the premoral stage a person lacks a moral sense. There is no understanding of moral principles. Good behavior is determined by a pleasure principle. To be good is to feel well, to be warm, secure, and pleased with one's environment. Everyone begins life in a premoral stage.

Moral growth means to move from a premoral stage through six successive stages that are hierarchically arranged. No stage can be skipped, and one progresses one stage at a time, with occasional slips of retrogression. Most persons do not achieve Stage 6, the most mature stage of moral development.

2. The reader may wish to refer to Richard Graham, "Youth and Experiential Learning," in *Youth*, Seventy-fourth Yearbook of the National Society for the Study of Education, Part I (Chicago: Distributed by the University of Chicago Press, 1975), chapter 9. Graham deals with the application of Kohlberg's developmental scheme to the problem of appropriately matching various types of activities in action-learning to stages of development.

TABLE 1

DEFINITION OF MORAL STAGES

I. Preconventional Level. At this level the child is responsive to cultural rules and labels of good and bad, right or wrong, but interprets these labels in terms of either the physical of the hedonistic consequences of action (punishment, reward, exchange of favors) or in terms of the physical power of those who enunciate the rules and labels. The level is divided into the following two stages:

Stage 1: The punishment and obedience orientation. The physical consequences of action determine its goodness or badness regardless of the human meaning or value of these consequences. Avoidance of punishment and unquestioning deference to power are valued in their own right, not in terms of respect for an underlying moral order supported by punishment and authority (the latter being Stage 4).

Stage 2: The instrumental relativist orientation. Right action consists of that which instrumentally satisfies one's own needs and occasionally the needs of others. Human relations are viewed in terms like those of the market place. Elements of fairness, of reciprocity, and equal sharing are present, but they are always interpreted in a physical, pragmatic way. Reciprocity is a matter of "you scratch my back and I'll scratch yours," not of loyalty, gratitude, or justice.

II. Conventional Level. At this level, maintaining the expectations of the individual's family, group, or nation is perceived as valuable in its own right, regardless of immediate and obvious consequences. The attitude is not only one of conformity to personal expectations and social order, but of loyalty to it, of actively maintaining, supporting, and justifying the order and of identifying with the persons or group involved in it. At this level, there are the following two stages:

Stage 3: The interpersonal concordance or "good boy-nice girl" orientation. Good behavior is that which pleases or helps others and is approved by them. There is much conformity to stereotypical images of what is majority or "natural" behavior. Behavior is frequently judged by intention—"he means well" becomes important for the first time. One earns approval by being "nice."

Stage 4: The "law and order" orientation. There is orientation toward authority, fixed rules, and the maintenance of the social order.

Right behavior consists of doing one's duty, showing respect for authority, and maintaining the given social order for its own sake.

III. Postconventional, Autonomous, or Principled Level. At this level, there is a clear effort to define moral values and principles which have validity and application apart from the authority of the groups or persons holding these principles and apart from the individual's own identification with these groups. This level again has two stages:

Stage 5: The social-contract legalistic orientation. Generally with utilitarian overtones. Right action tends to be defined in terms of general individual rights and in terms of standards which have been critically examined and agreed upon by the whole society. There is a clear awareness of the relativism of personal values and opinions and a corresponding emphasis upon procedural rules for reaching consensus. Aside from what is constitutionally and democratically agreed upon, the right is a matter of personal "values" and "opinion." The result is an emphasis upon the "legal point of view," but with an emphasis upon the possibility of changing law in terms of rational considerations of social utility, (rather than freezing it in terms of Stage 4, "law and order"). Outside the legal realm, free agreement, and contract is the binding element of obligation. This is the "official" morality of the American government and Constitution.

Stage 6: The universal ethical principle orientation. Right is defined by the decision of conscience in accord with self-chosen ethical principles appealing to logical comprehensiveness, universality, and consistency. These principles are abstract and ethical (the Golden Rule, the categorical imperative); they are not concrete moral rules like the Ten Commandments. At heart, these are universal principles of justice, of the reciprocity and equality of the human rights, and of respect for the dignity of human beings as individual persons.

Source: This table typically is "pass-out" material at any meeting addressed by Kohlberg, or one of his students. A printed version may be found in Lawrence Kohlberg and Elliott Turiel, "Moral Development and Moral Education," in *Psychology and Educational Practice*, Gerald S. Lesser (Glenview, Illinois: Scott, Foresman & Company, 1971), pp. 415-16.

KOHLBERG'S SIX STAGES

If one leaves the premoral stage, one enters what Kohlberg calls the Preconventional Level. Stage one, the punishment and obedience stage, is exemplified by children who misbehave behind the teacher's back, or when he is absent from the classroom. In secondary school and college may be exemplified by the student whose cheating on an examination occurs only when he perceives a low probability of getting caught. Such a student may find the obligations of an honor system more than he can handle.

The second stage of this preconventional level Kohlberg calls "instrumental relativism." A brother will not "tell" on his sister, not necessarily out of strong feelings of loyalty, but rather because he may some day want his sister not to "tell" on him. Similarly, a student who takes examinations under an honor system will not tell the authorities about observed instances of cheating, even though such reporting is one of the rules of the system. Jacob has reported a study by Stouffer in which it was found that college students tended not to report cheating if committed by friends. Sixty-six percent would not report on a friend whereas only sixteen percent would not report on a nonfriend. However, any suspicion that the cheating was known to a proctor, or other authority, increased the probability that students would report friends. In that circumstance only twenty-seven percent rather than sixty-six percent would fail to tell on friends. Those students who would not report cheating if committed by friends are usually somewhere within the preconventional level. Chronological age is not a reliable indicator of a person's level of moral development.[3]

The next phase in moral development is the Conventional Level which consists of two more stages as in the preconventional level. The "good boy-nice girl" stage emphasizes conformity to expected social roles with an emphasis upon pleasing significant others. Kohlberg observes that this third stage is the first to recognize good intent as a moral principle. Next is the "law and order" stage. Just as stage three emphasized stereotypical images of behavior, stage four values the existing social order. Patriotism, loyalty to the status quo, and dutiful observance of the established authorities characterize this fourth stage of moral development. Exceptions to fixed rules of morality are not entertained or tolerated. A stage four person may seem to be a stuffed shirt but he is morally more mature than those whose only motivation is to obey rather than suffer punishment.

The highest moral development is to be found in what Kohlberg has called Post-Conventional or Autonomous Level with its two

3. Philip E. Jacob, *Changing Values in College* (New York: Harper and Brothers, 1957), pp. 23-24.

stages, the social-contract legalistic orientation, and the stage of the universal ethical principle. There is an element of relativism at stage five in that law may be changed constitutionally and democratically if it appears rational to do so. The concept of due process is respected and followed. Personal values may suggest a change in the law or the constitution, but the change must be achieved by peaceful and legal methods. Law is not regarded, however, as a fixed rule, as in stage four. If there is moral value to be achieved in a change in rules, in the "rewriting" of a contract, to the person in stage five it would appear necessary to make the change.

Stage six values the universal principle of justice. Justice is an abstract principle and not a concrete rule. The conscience of the individual in accordance with self-chosen principles will help him to ascertain the meaning of justice in a given situation. Equal rights and the dignity of persons are basic to social justice. Although these principles are self-chosen, Kohlberg claims universality for them because they are found in every culture he has so far investigated. There is more than a suggestion in Kohlberg that although cultural relativism may assist intercultural understanding it should not do so at the expense of any universal principle.

KOHLBERG'S APPROACH TO MORAL EDUCATION

In Kohlberg's program of moral education, the discussion of moral dilemmas serves two purposes. The reasoning exhibited by a person as he is confronted with a dilemma enables the trained investigator to determine the person's stage of moral development. A second purpose is moral development itself. Kohlberg believes that a person can progress to a higher level of moral development if the teacher asks the person to practice the kind of reasoning characteristic of the stage just above where he is. For example, an individual who thinks like a stage one person (punishment-obedience orientation) would be encouraged by a teacher to practice the "reasoning" of stage two. A common mistake among secondary school teachers is to conduct discussions several levels above the students' moral background. An equally serious error is to function below their level, as in the case of a high school teacher who urges a stage five or six person not to copy answers from another student "because you might get caught" or "the copied answer might be wrong."

Perhaps a knowledge by secondary school teachers of a student's stage of moral development is more important than a knowledge of his intelligence quotient! Certainly, there is little or no ground for believing that "bright" people are always more advanced morally than the rest of us. However, a relationship between Piaget's levels of intellectual development and Kohlberg's levels of moral development appears to exist. A stage six person in moral development would necessarily have to think propositionally. In other words, his intellectual development would have to be at the level Piaget has designated as "Formal Operations." To be able to think at the level of Formal Operations is a necessary but not a sufficient condition for moral maturity (Stage 5 or 6).

Kohlberg's work also places personal and cultural relativism in a new light. We often hear it said by social scientists that "what is right in one culture may be wrong in another." Margaret Mead's studies of sex and temperament in various kinds of societies are often cited as supportive of this view. However, some people, including some high school students, have taken this view one step further. Devotees of personal relativism may be heard to say, "I wouldn't be caught dead doing what he has just done, but if it's all right for him then I can't condemn him for it." Such a view is exemplified by people who would not practice tax evasion, adultery, or cannibalism, but are quite reluctant to disapprove of these activities. Kohlberg's studies suggest that such people may be morally immature.

Relativism, to Kohlberg, is a phase in moral development. Relativism is a road toward maturity, but it is not maturity itself. A morally mature person thinks in terms of such universals as justice and equality. Kohlberg's view seems to be that cultural relativism can be a tool of intercultural understanding. Yet morally mature people may condemn much that they understand. To put the matter in terms of recent studies of the logic of instruction: an explanation is not the same as a justification.

The subject matter of Kohlberg's moral education program, then, is the personal dilemma, its study and discussion. He conceives a dilemma as a value conflict between good and good, as did Hunt and Metcalf in 1955.[4]   In contrast, high school committees on the teaching

4. Maurice P. Hunt and Lawrence E. Metcalf, *Teaching High School Social Studies: Problems in Reflective Thinking and Social Understanding* (New York: Harper Brothers, 1955), chapters 5, 11-16.

of moral and "spiritual" values too often conceive value conflict as a battle between good and evil. Kohlberg refers to this concept of the moral problem as "the bag of virtues approach." The bag is full of all kinds of goodies put there by loving parents and concerned teachers. The only virtue in Kohlberg's bag is social justice.

A typical example of a personal dilemma is Kohlberg's Heintz case. Heintz's wife is dying. A druggist has in his possession a drug that would cure the wife. His price is higher than Heintz can pay. He does not have enough money, nor can he borrow the required amount. Should Heintz steal the drug? Answers to this question are then classified, using Kohlberg's six stages as a basis.

Rational Value Judgment

RELEVANCE TO KOHLBERG

Kohlberg's writings have been vague as to their prescriptions for teaching. Although his approach has been subjected to various kinds of research, teaching strategies are left up in the air. We receive only the general prescription that teachers should work near to a student's stage of moral development. In several studies it was found that all students could report correctly all stages below as well as the stage at their own level. A few were able to verbalize the stage just above them. Kohlberg's explanation is that such students were on the way into the next highest stage. Working at a proper stage of moral development may call for a high degree of individualized instruction. Just how a secondary school teacher might achieve this with large and heterogeneous classes Kohlberg does not make clear. Nor does he indicate how many dilemmas a student must respond to before he can be accurately classified. .

Kohlberg's cognitive developmental approach is basically rational in nature. In 1971 Meux, Coombs, and Chadwick presented a model for a rational analysis of value judgments that prescribes in considerable detail teaching procedures they believe to be useful.[5] The procedures of analysis as set forth in the 1971 National Council for the

5. Jerrold R. Coombs, "Objectives of Value Analysis," in *Values Education: Rationale, Strategies, and Procedures*, ed. Lawrence E. Metcalf, Forty-first Yearbook of the National Council for the Social Studies (Washington, D.C.: National Council for the Social Studies, 1971), pp. 1-28; Jerrold R. Coombs and Milton Meux, "Teaching Strategies for Value Analysis," ibid., pp. 29-74; James Chadwick and Milton Meux, "Procedures for Value Analysis," ibid., pp. 75-119; Milton Meux, "Resolving Value Conflicts," ibid., pp. 120-66.

Social Studies Yearbook are clear enough to be taught, practiced, and tested. Whether the practice of the proposals of Meux, Coombs, and Chadwick would foster moral growth is a researchable question. In particular, research could ascertain whether systematic and sustained use of these procedures would ease students into higher and higher stages of moral development.

A rational analysis of value judgments is defined by Meux, Coombs, and Chadwick as having the following four characteristics:

1. The purported facts supporting a value judgment must be true or well confirmed.

2. The facts must be genuinely relevant for the person making the judgment. Facts have relevance to a person when he has strong positive or negative feelings toward them. Statements that appear to him to be rather bland are not likely to be relevant.[6]

3. Other things being equal, the greater the range of relevant facts taken into account in making a value judgment the more adequate the judgment is likely to be. A person who makes his judgment of the Vietnam War, using only the factual claim that the war was a civil war, is guilty of narrow reasoning if other factual claims would be equally relevant.

4. Finally, his judgment will rest upon one or more value principles, each of which is acceptable to him (a very personalistic criterion).

The Meux, Coombs, and Chadwick view of rationality does suggest that a rational person is likely to introduce universal principles into his moral reasoning. At the same time, a rational person may also rely upon some kind of moral relativism.

Although their fourth characteristic could be interpreted entirely in relativistic terms, it could also be claimed that a person who makes a value judgment rationally will tend to rely upon universal value principles. A failure to do so would possibly be interpreted as a failure to carry rational value analysis far enough. This "explanation" smacks too much, however, of circular reasoning. "Rational moralists use uni-

---

6. This criterion ought to be particularly important to any humanistic psychologist who would condemn a rational model as "logicalistic," "inhumane," or "forced and artificial." Is rationality a humane value? Can we be democratic without being rational? Note that the four criteria for a rational value judgment deny the wisdom of separating cognitive and affective domains. Both cold logic and unrestrained feelings are dismissed as impractical alternatives.

versal principles. If they don't, they haven't been rational."

A similar example of circular reasoning is to be found among some advocates of value clarification, a position that is sometimes accused of ethical neutrality. If the clarification process is carried far enough, it is said, a rational person will come to see that some values are clearly superior to others. Yet clarifiers cannot clarify interminably; there is an all too human tendency to terminate the use of clarifying processes as soon as the person "in charge" feels that the client has been sufficiently "clarified." Both value analysis as represented by Meux, Coombs, and Chadwick and value clarification as represented by Raths, Harmin, and Simon[7] need to be researched without recourse to begging the question. One kind of research would develop the conceptual differences, if any, between clarification and analysis, and compare the two approaches as to their effectiveness in promoting moral growth.

SOME FALSE ISSUES

Alienation, personal disorganization, social conflict, and the accumulation of scores of unsolved social problems testify to the existence of a widespread and deep-seated crisis in values and institutions. Because the crisis is both personal and social, it appears in the secondary school counselor's office, the teacher's classroom, and the larger social arenas. The older practice of preparing separate lists of personal and social problems has become dysfunctional. We now believe that the two are opposite sides of the same coin. Likewise affective and cognitive domains are different aspects of the same mental events.

A rational value analysis falls short of its aim whenever it neglects the social origins and effects of a personal conflict. Therapy and instruction join hands when a teacher encourages students rationally to recognize social conflicts to which they have been insensitive. Without rational analysis of the social origins of value conflicts, students often do not know why they are unable to cope with common personal pathologies. They can be part of a problem without knowing what the problem is.

Many humanistic therapists deplore the emphasis on rational analysis, particularly in those highly personal areas which Hunt and

7. Louis E. Raths, Merrill Harmin, and Sidney B. Simon, *Values and Teaching* (Columbus, Ohio: Charles E. Merrill Publishing Company, 1966).

Metcalf have designated as "closed." The more important the issue the less desirable is rationality, seems to be their slogan. Supportiveness and catharsis are offered as viable alternatives to thinking, rather than as necessary conditions.[8]

RELEVANCE OF ELLIS'S RATIONAL-EMOTIVE THERAPY

Albert Ellis is one therapist who openly favors a rational consideration of personal conflicts. In his work as a marriage counselor he relied at first upon direct, common sense discussion. Later he turned to psychoanalysis as a deeper form of therapy. After several years of training and practice, he concluded that the psychoanalytic system did not work very well with his clients. He now employs what he calls "rational-emotive theory." Rational-emotive therapy (RET) locates personal difficulties in the *beliefs* a person has about himself and his behavior. It assumes that people are organisms that value. Consciously or not, they rate things as to their worth. Among their major values is a desire to survive and to be relatively happy while surviving. They also want to get along with members of their social group, and to have intimate relations with a few members. Behavior that serves these four goals they view as rational and that which sabotages their attainment as irrational.

Rational-emotive theory includes three elements: (1) the Activating Event or Activating Experience, (2) a person's Beliefs about the Activating Event or Experience, and (3) the Emotional Consequence of the Activating Event or Experience. Ellis believes that the emotional response following the event is not really a response to the event, but rather to one's beliefs about the event. He calls these elements the A-B-C of personality. Ellis puts it as follows:

> More specifically, if you feel depressed or suicidal at point C, after you have been rejected for a job or a love relationship at point A, your rejection does *not* cause your depression. Rather, it is your *beliefs* about this rejection, at point B. And, normally you are first strongly holding a rational Belief (rB)— e.g., "I don't like being rejected; how unfortunate that I have been; it's really a

8. A relevant discussion of this issue may be found in Hunt and Metcalf, *Teaching High School Social Studies*, chapter 9. Another excellent reference is James Chadwick, "Procedure for Personal Interviews," in *Values Education: Rationale, Strategies, and Procedures*. Appendix, pp. 168-76.

drag!"—that results in an appropriate feeling of sorrow, irritation, and annoyance. But you are also holding an irrational Belief (iB)—e.g., "It's *awful* to be rejected; I *should not* have got myself in this position; what a worthless slob I am for arranging this!"—that results in your inappropriate feeling of depression, anxiety, and perhaps rage at your rejector. Your first set of beliefs is rational because, in accordance with your basic value system of *wanting* to stay alive, be happy, live well in your social group, and relate intimately to a few selected members of that group, it *is* dislikeable, unfortunate, and disadvantageous for you to be rejected; and you'd *better* feel appropriately saddened about this poor state of affairs. Your second set of beliefs is irrational because it isn't awful (that is, *more than* disadvantageous) for you to be rejected; there's no reason you absolutely *should* or *must* not have been rejected (even though *it would have been better* if you were not); and you are not a worthless slob, but at worst an individual with some slobbish *traits* when you are rejected.[9]

Ellis goes on to say that rational beliefs help one to correct one's behavior, whereas the irrational beliefs encourage one to mope, to give up, to feel helpless, and to continue the practice of those Activating Experiences that place in jeopardy the values of survival and happiness. Therapy consists of understanding that certain beliefs are irrational, and then of practicing over and over again more rational beliefs.

Thomas Szasz, in his discussion of mental health, claims that the belief that certain problems in living are indicators of mental illness is misleading. Mental illness, he says, is a myth. The behaviors that are designated as *sick* are real enough. They do exist. Rather than regard them as illness, a metaphor that confuses the facts, we should perceive them as unsuccessful responses to value conflict. Szasz claims that "mental illnesses are, for the most part, *communications* expressing unacceptable ideas, often framed in an unusual idiom."[10] It has long been held that psychotics and neurotics are trying to tell us something. The Szasz metaphor is only one example of those analyses that trace "mental illness" back to sociocultural origins.

In any event, value education, as here conceived, has both instructional and therapeutic effects. The teacher in the secondary school

9. Albert Ellis, "Rational-Emotive Theory," in *Operational Theories of Personality*, ed. Arthur Burton (New York: Brunner/Mazel, Publishers, 1974), pp. 311-12.

10. Thomas S. Szasz, *Ideology and Insanity* (Garden City, N.Y.: Doubleday & Co, Inc., 1970), p. 19.

classroom and the counselor can share in the same enterprise. Teachers of humanities and social sciences can expose students to the conflicts of the culture and the personal dilemmas that represent individuals' expression of those conflicts. Counselors can come at the same conflicts in much the same way—through rational value analysis. A model of value analysis and supporting procedures will be discussed next.

Teaching Rational Value Analysis

Value analysis distinguishes between a judgment of fact and a value judgment. Most philosophers make the same distinction. A few do not; they argue that all judgments are the same. That dispute is not the subject matter of this chapter. The author simply wishes to state that the conflict exists, and to indicate where he stands in respect to it. The value analysis position argues that rational value judgments have a backing that consists of facts and criteria. For instance, it is one thing to say that Car X has reliable brakes (reliable brakes having been defined operationally) and quite another thing to say that good cars must have reliable brakes. Of course, no one is going to call any car good simply because it has reliable brakes. Everyone demands other or additional criteria. Economical operation, safety, beauty, easy and inexpensive maintenance, roadability, high trade-in value—these are only a few of the features people expect to find in a "good" car. People who expect such features may differ in how much importance they give to each criterion, and therefore do not always agree in the value judgment made of a particular car. People who are equally rational may disagree. And people who agree are not necessarily rational!

The value analysis model that makes this distinction between facts and criteria makes use of concepts such as rating, value judgment, value object, value term, valence, relevance, and value principle.[11] A value judgment is defined as the rating of an object according to its worth. A value term is the term used to express a rating of a value object. A factual statement about a value object, sometimes called a description of the object, has valence if the person making the value judgment has strongly positive or negative feelings toward any description he has made of the value object. If a full or partial descrip-

---

11. These terms and their relationship to one another are discussed by Meux, Coombs, and Chadwick in the previously cited Forty-first Yearbook of the National Council for the Social Studies.

tion of a value object lacks valence, it will also lack relevance. (It may be useful at this point to refer to the definition of a rational value judgment on p. 98.)

It is possible to illustrate the above concepts schematically, as in figure 1.

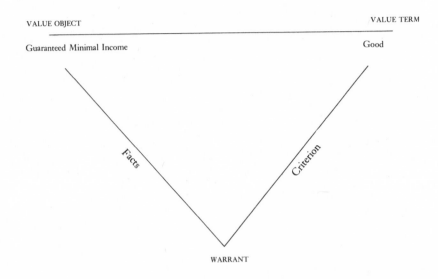

Fig. 1. A simple value model

In figure 1 the value object, guaranteed minimal income, is rated with the value term, good. If the rater were asked to give reasons for his rating, a complete answer would refer to facts (a description of the value object) and the criteria used to justify use of the value term, good. Raters who disagree in their ratings (value judgments) may do so because they do not agree either on the facts, or on the criteria, or both. How a teacher should proceed when disagreement is present depends on what *kind* of disagreement it is.

For instance, the author recalls an occasion on which students could not agree in their rating of guaranteed annual income. He had assumed that there would be disagreement over criteria. In this case, however, the students accepted the same criterion, namely, economic incentive. But they disagreed factually over the consequences of a guaranteed annual income. Some thought it would undermine incentive; others thought that incentive would be bolstered. They agreed that incentive was a good criterion. The appropriate teaching strategy in these circumstances, at least initially, would have been to engage students in a search for a factually adequate theory of economic motivation, and to avoid the addumption that all policy disputes are normative in nature. Making an assumption that is wrong commonly leads to employing a wrong teaching strategy.

Sometimes students will present an incomplete basis for a rating, one that is entirely factual. If one or more criteria are needed, this incomplete rating should be filled out by the teacher, or the class. For instance, in the case of the economic incentive discussion cited above, a complete syllogism would include:

A policy that bolsters economic incentive is a good policy.
The policy of a guaranteed annual income would bolster economic incentive.
Therefore, a guaranteed annual income is a good policy.

However, the above example is too simple to be real. Ordinarily, a policy will have many consequences, and not all of them will have the same valence. Some of the consequences will be favorably rated, others negatively. This problem of mixed consequences requires use of a value principle that expresses a selection among conflicting criteria. An older way of putting it is to say that we should "weigh" our values. The following example illustrates the problem and its solution:

(Fact) The war in Vietnam is primarily a civil war.
(Criterion) One nation ought not enter into the civil wars of other countries.
(Fact) U.S. withdrawal will result in a substantially reduced rate of killing.
(Criterion) It is wrong to kill or cause a large number of killings.
(Fact) U.S. withdrawal would reduce the level of civil strife in the U.S.
(Criterion) A stable, peaceful society is a good thing.
(Fact) U.S. withdrawal would free U.S. resources which could be used to cope with pressing social problems in the U.S.
(Criterion) It is desirable for a society to have resources available to handle pressing social problems.
(Fact) U.S. withdrawal would result in a repressive, communistic society in South Vietnam.
(Criterion) Illiberal societies are undesirable and immoral.
(Fact) The U.S. has committed itself to defending South Vietnam against takeover by the communists.

(Criterion) A nation ought to honor its commitments.
(Fact) U. S. withdrawal would be construed as a sign of weakness and lack of desire.
(Criterion) A nation ought not let others think it is weak or irresolute.[12]

In this illustration the evaluator has four reasons for withdrawal, and three for staying in. Because the various reasons are not likely to be given equal weighting, he cannot settle his problem by a simple four-to-three vote. He might decide in favor of withdrawal by formulating a complex value principle such as: "a nation ought not be involved in a civil war to save another country from a repressive government if that involvement increases the level of killing in the war and diverts the nation's attention from pressing social problems."[13] Some one else might decide against withdrawal, using as his complex value principle "a nation ought to honor its commitment to oppose repressive societies and ought to avoid appearances of weakness, even though it represents intervention in a civil war, increases the war's kill rate, increases civil strife at home, and delays solutions to important domestic social problems." Both evaluators are equally rational if they observe the standards on p. 98. Rational raters can rationally disagree. This is why reflective thought cannot guarantee in advance particular value conclusions, though many people participating in a school community seem to assume value conclusions can or ought to be guaranteed. Only operant conditioning can presently claim to guarantee particular value conclusions, and we have already indicated our disagreement with the attendant conditioning process and the accompanying image of mankind as reactor and robot.

Today's Value Crisis—Its Global Nature

As indicated before, personal value conflicts can be better understood if traced back to the large social conflicts of the day. Today these social conflicts are now largely global, or planetary, in nature. In the recent past, it became customary in secondary school teaching to view many of the problems of the local community as national problems; their solution was seen as requiring national action, usually

12. Coombs, "Objectives of Value Analysis," in *Values Education: Rationale, Strategies, and Procedures*, ed. Lawrence E. Metcalf, pp. 16-17.

13. Ibid., p. 17.

by the Federal Government. Many such problems remain, but a host of new problems have developed, global in nature and beyond the capacities of any nation-state, or alliance of such states.

A growing literature is addressed to the problems of Planet Earth. A recent textbook in political science by Harold and Margaret Sprout is significantly entitled *Toward A Politics For Planet Earth.*[14] A new area of scholarship called "World Order Studies" has emerged at the university level. Courses and curriculums in war/peace studies, international studies, and conflict resolution have been developed on the secondary and college levels. Those teaching this kind of content are numerous enough to band together in an organization called the International Studies Association which has subsections on peace and on other problem areas.

Many neuroses of the future probably will come from an international environment. Man in the twenty-first century, if he is to enjoy mental health, will have to be a transnational person with commitments to supranational institutions as he searches for solutions to the problems of McLuhan's *Global Village.*[15]

FIVE GLOBAL PROBLEMS

What are the global problems, and what makes them global? Mention will be made of only five, although there are many more. One of the global problems is ecological imbalance, and air pollution is just one aspect of this problem. Air pollution is a global problem simply because pollutants will not stay put. They have the habit of drifting about with the winds; pollution that originates in Tokyo can later hover over Los Angeles. If any city in the United States achieved a perfect clean air policy, it would not be long before air pollution would once again become a problem. Neither local governments nor the national government can effectively legislate against Japanese pollution, and in turn, the Japanese cannot protect themselves against American-made pollutants. There is no world government to step into

14. Harold and Margaret Sprout, *Toward a Politics for Planet Earth* (New York: Van Nostrand and Reinhold Co., 1971).

15. Marshall McLuhan and Quentin Fiore, *War and Peace in the Global Village* (New York: McGraw-Hill Book Co., 1968).

the breach. The earth may be physically unified, but it is politically fragmented. All that the United Nations is empowered to do is what it is now doing—setting up and operating monitoring stations that can report to the world's peoples whether pollution in any part of the world has reached a level alarming enough to be called an international emergency.

Another global problem that threatens both human survival and happiness is war. Because there is no effective defense against nuclear weaponry, particularly those that have been "MRVed," reliance has been placed by nations on a theory of mutual deterrence. This theory places a nation's security in the hands of the other side. Misperception or a willingness to call a bluff can mean Armageddon. Once the level of arms reaches the dimensions of overkill, a continuation of the arms race does not make sense. More warheads decrease rather than strengthen the security of those who participate in such competition. Citizens would have nothing to lose by unilateral disarmament up to a point and they would gain by major reductions in taxation. Yet in the absence of some other security system such as world government, no nation seems willing to relinquish mutual deterrence and increasing overkill which is presumed to offer some sense of security, albeit a minimal and highly expensive kind.

The growing gap between rich and poor nations together with the tendency of rich people in any nation to become richer constitutes a third global problem. Poor nations are unable to lift themselves by their own bootstraps. The amounts of capital required to attack effectively the twin problems of economic development and human welfare exceed the resources of many nation states. Not even regional authorities seem adequate. Bilateral or multilateral solutions will probably have to be supplemented or supplanted by world solutions that take on a supranational character. A World Bank or world food reserve that depends upon the political decisions of the nation-state system is bound to fall short of an adequate solution.

The absence of democratic government and the violation of human rights by many governments, democratic or not, are the fourth and fifth of our major global problems. At least two-thirds of the national governments are authoritarian. Not to have a voice in making decisions that affect everyone is to invite widespread alienation.

Millions have concluded that the head of state is not their friend, and that governments are more or less tenanted by liars. Even the democratic nation states often violate the rights of women because they are women, of children because they are children, and of nonwhites because they are not white. True, in a nation such as the United States the individual whose rights are violated by the city of Chicago, or the state of Mississippi, may turn to the national government for redress. But citizens of the United States, or of any other country, have no place to turn once national alternatives are exhausted. The only World Court in existence does not have compulsory jurisdiction over the affairs of any nation state. The United Nations Declaration of Human Rights is simply that—a declaration. Meanwhile, human rights are being violated and those who prate the most about national sovereignty have nothing to say about the sovereignty of the individual.

Counselors and other therapists usually do not think of such world problems when they ponder the personal problems of their clients. But they will have to learn to relate the social setting to personal problems. Classroom teachers in secondary schools are more likely to instruct their students in national rather than world problems. Whether the problems studied in this nation's classrooms are national or global, the teacher conceives himself as an instructor and does not see himself as a therapist. (In fact, he may have been told, as part of his education, that emotional problems cannot be solved by intellectual means.) But secondary school teachers will have to learn to relate the world and the nation, instruction and therapy. The procedures of rational value analysis question the conventional assumptions that separate the personal from the social, the national from the global, and instruction from therapy.

If a discussion of the personal dilemma of Heintz can foster moral growth, why cannot a similar result be achieved by discussion of large global problems that can become personalized through being related to the student's concerns? Consider the following scenario:

The White House has *conclusive* evidence that several hundred nuclear warheads aimed at each of the major cities in the United States have been launched from overseas bases. The evidence is completely convincing that the Soviet Union is the offending nation. Within fifteen minutes, cities, industries, and people will be obliterated. At least half the population will be killed, and roughly three-fourths of the industrial capacity of the United States destroyed. The President of the United States orders retaliation, and hundreds of nuclear warheads are fired at targets in the Soviet Union. Did he do the right thing?

Whenever this scenario has been tried out with junior high school students the large majority of students immediately endorse retaliation as morally right. They want to get even. According to the scenario, half of them will not be around to enjoy their vengeance, but that seldom acts as a deterrent. When the teacher asks, "Would you still favor retaliation if you and your parents were tourists stopping off in Moscow?" the first glimmer of reflection appears. Prodded by further questions, their discussion takes on all the excitement and meaning of any moral discourse.

Bruner has reported the same power of value-oriented discussion of personalized alternatives and choices:

> . . . I took a group of fourteen-year-olds to see Peter Ustinov's *Billy Budd* on film. The intensity of the discussion of moral philosophy on the way home convinced me that we have overlooked one of the most powerful allies in keeping alive our engagement in history, in the range of human life, in philosophy. Drama, the novel, history rendered with epic aids of its patron goddess Clio, are all built on the paradox of human choice; on the resolution of alternatives. They are in the best sense studies in the causes and consequences of choice. It is in their gripping quality, their nearness to life, that we can, I urge, best make personal the dilemmas of the culture, its aspirations, its conflicts, its terrors . . . [16]

If teachers and counselors will apply rational value analysis to the personal manifestations of a cultural crisis that is now worldwide, and make this application under experimental conditions, we may learn to deal with some of the unsolved problems of education as to values. Secondary educators have long believed in teaching the humanities. They have long believed in teaching the policy sciences and studying social problems. But we have not always seen the relevance of such content to moral growth and mental health. That relevance is becoming more clear. We now have some substantial understanding of actual down-to-earth teaching procedures for the analysis of value-laden content. These procedures are teachable, and it is possible to ascertain the effects of their use.

The only negative factor is lack of time. The race between educa-

16. Jerome S. Bruner, *Toward a Theory of Instruction* (Cambridge, Mass.: The Belknap Press of Harvard University Press, 1966), p. 162.

tion and catastrophe is still on. Whether we can make it into the twenty-first century may well depend on how fast and soon we can turn around the way people think about moral problems. Unfortunately, the prospect that this can be done fast and soon is bleak.

CHAPTER V

Coping With Social Realities That Threaten Survival

WILLIS W. HARMON

The paramount social reality is that the technologically advanced nations of the world are approaching one of the great transformations of human history. Even a few years ago it would have been necessary to hedge that statement with tentativeness and qualification. At this point few would question it. In this chapter we undertake the delineation of this transformation—its salient characteristics and the choice of responses—and the identification of the most important implications for education.

One caution as we begin. Even though it is convenient to speak of "the coming transformation," we in no way mean to imply that this future is predictable or that the circumstances attending such a transformation are beyond some rational guidance. In other words, we need always to remember to talk in terms of *alternative* future contexts for education and to test contemplated actions against more than one such context. This point will be emphasized again later on.

Varieties of Societal Problems

At the surface level of observation, this nation and the world are beset by numerous societal problems such as poverty, crime, racism, pollution, unemployment, inflation, drug abuse, social disruptions, famine, threat of nuclear war, and the like. Experience with attempts to deal straightforwardly with these problems indicates that such direct measures are partial solutions at best.

Thus price and wage controls offer temporary relief from inflation, but in the end may leave us worse off than before. Urban renewal programs aimed at improving housing conditions for the poor seem to have worsened the neighborhood environment for a large fraction.

111

Welfare regulations instituted to improve the lot of ghetto children have apparently contributed to weakened family structure. Minimum wage laws intended to aid unskilled workers have become a factor in their unemployability. Legislation and programs dedicated to the reduction of inequalities of opportunity between the races seem to have heightened interracial tensions.

The reason for such unsatisfactory consequences may be intrinsic. Perhaps these manifest problems are in some sense symptoms of underlying conditions that are more pervasive and less easy to objectify. As in the much-noted medical analogy, where the primary concentration has been on the removal of one symptom, the exacerbation of another has too often resulted. If this be the case, it is not an accident that planned social measures have produced results that are the opposite of those intended by their well-meaning sponsors.

Thus we come to suspect that there is a second level of viewing the ills of the society. Analysts who take this tack have argued that the miseries of the poor, the injustices experienced by minorities, the violence committed by the criminally disaffected, and the ravages of the environment can in the long term be alleviated only through basic changes in the institutions of the society, in built-in power distributions, in the traditional roles into which people are indoctrinated, in the time-hallowed structures and processes. They hold that for the problems of poverty, crime, discrimination, civil disorder, pollution, and environmental degradation should be substituted the problems of altering institutions and roles so as to incorporate less economic and political injustice and to be less productive of hypocrisy, intolerance, racism, and greed; of creating incentive and regulatory structures so as to reduce exploitation of persons and environment; of restructuring social programs so that they do not depend upon persuading people to act against their own perceived special interests.

But others, especially in recent years, have come to note that there is yet a third level of problems with respect to which those of the second level stand in the relationship of symptoms. This is the level of the most basic assumptions, attitudes, and felt values held by the individual and institutionalized in and promoted by the culture. When this level of the social structure gets out of consonance with reality, difficult and thoroughgoing transformation may be required. This appears to be where we are now.

To urge that these third-level problems press for attention is by no means to argue that the other two levels should be ignored. The physician who diagnoses a patient's surface symptoms as having organic, immediate causes and still deeper psychogenic origins, does not withhold symptomatic relief just because he perceives the underlying problem to be one of basic attitudes toward life. Let us avoid a psychological reductionism that claims if everyone would experience the right religious conversion, or undergo successful psychotherapy, the problems of the world would solve themselves.

To focus attention on the third-level problems is not to overlook the possibility that making the changes in institutions and roles toward which the second-level problems aim may very well be among the best ways of fostering third-level change in basic beliefs and attitudes. For individual personality comes into being, grows, functions, and alters through interpersonal relations within social institutions.

As we examine the dilemmas facing society we shall keep the primary focus on the United States—on the United States as part of a world system, to be sure—but we shall be describing the problems in the particular form they assume in this nation. For Sweden or Japan or France it would be somewhat different, and for Russia or East Germany more different still. Most nations of the Third World would be looking at some of the problems from the other end of the telescope, so to speak. But if a systemic change is required, as we assert, all parts of the system will be affected. We shall not be unduly parochial if we concentrate on the form this change may take in our own particular part of the system.

Also, we shall have little to say here about the threat of nuclear war. This problem will and must be pursued by the world's diplomats and statesmen and be studied in our schools. But there can be little assurance of avoidance of nuclear conflict as long as the fundamental dilemmas remain, system performance is worsening, and partial system breakdown is a realistic expectation. This space can be best used, not in discussing alternative approaches to nuclear arms control, but in trying to clarify why both diplomatic and technological approaches to removing the nuclear threat are probably futile. An analogy may explain. Imagine a marriage counselor faced with a warring man and wife, each of whom has taken to sleeping with a loaded pistol under the pillow. It would not be a very fundamental approach to the problem to attempt to persuade them they should switch to butcher knives.

Four Basic Dilemmas

Let us then focus on four basic dilemmas of the industrialized world. These dilemmas subsume many of the recognized societal problems. Because they are, or appear to be, unresolvable as long as the system retains its present structure and underlying premises, they point up the need for transformation. Society's complete inability to resolve them, individually or together, constitutes a large part of the personal malaise that manifests itself in feelings of alienation and despair, in alcoholism and drug abuse, in vandalism and crime and is one of the components contributing to that complex plague of inflation and unemployment.

THE GROWTH DILEMMA

The first of these is the growth dilemma. On the one hand, industrialized nations—capitalist or socialist—need continued economic growth for a viable economy; on the other hand, it becomes more and more clear that they cannot live with the consequences.

This dilemma is by now widely discussed, with frequent reference to "limits to growth"[1] and the need to achieve a "steady-state economy."[2] A continued high rate of technological and economic growth brings worsening problems of the "new scarcity"—of materials, of energy, of natural fresh water, of arable land, of habitable space, of the ability of the natural environment to absorb the waste products of industrialized society, and of the resilience of the planet's life-support systems to absorb insult. This scarcity, stemming from the fundamental planetary limits, differs from the "old" scarcities of food, clothing materials, shelter, game, and farmland, which were so successfully solved by expanding geographical and technological frontiers. The "new scarcity" will require basic cultural and institutional change for its resolution.

The reason that growth is such a perplexing dilemma is that there are a host of reasons why a sudden decrease in growth rate would be disastrous. Unemployment and economic depression are the most ob-

1. Dennis L. Meadows et al., *The Limits of Growth* (New York: Universe Books, 1972).

2. Herman E. Daly, ed., *Toward a Steady-State Economy* (San Francisco, Calif.: W. H. Freeman, 1973).

vious. Then too, if growth slows there will be social tensions associated with increased pressure for redistribution of wealth and income, a pressure for a "bigger piece of the economic pie" that was less in evidence when the pie was expanding more rapidly. Also, the poor nations of the world will oppose any changes in growth that interfere with their own freedom to industrialize as fast as they choose or can.

The dilemma reaches its sharpest definition around the issue of energy. Presently, national energy demand in the United States is rising at a rate of 4 to 5 percent a year, corresponding to a doubling time of around fifteen years. If wasted energy (for example, through poor building insulation, inefficient automobiles, energy-wasteful industrial practices) were conserved, the doubling time could be increased to twenty or perhaps twenty-five years. But the demand still doubles, and doubles again, again, and again. Energy is so inextricably linked to industrial productivity and to Gross National Product (GNP) that growth in the use of energy could not be lowered further without lowering economic growth—unless a radical restructuring of the society brings about much more energy-frugal behavior patterns and industrial production methods. But the environmental and social costs of increasing domestic energy production to meet this exponentially increasing demand are unacceptable, and the economic and political costs of meeting it through purchased foreign oil are unacceptable. The full magnitude of our predicament is only now coming into our consciousness.

THE CONTROL DILEMMA

A second dilemma is that relating to technological control. It has become clear that we have now, or could develop soon, the power:

1. to change to an immense extent the characteristics of our physical environment, and the plant and animal population of the biosphere;
2. through biological and genetic engineering, to modify indefinitely the characteristics of individual human bodies or of the evolutionary development of the human race;
3. to alter to a tremendous extent the social and psychological environment, including people's mental and emotional characteristics;
4. through weapons of mass destruction, to annihilate large segments of the human race and devastate large areas of the earth; and
5. to change significantly, in many other ways, the kind of world to be handed on to the next generation.

The recent formation of the Office of Technology Assessment as an arm of the Congress indicates awareness of the growing need for some sort of social guidance of technology, to anticipate and assess side effects and future consequences, direct and indirect, and to regulate technological development and application in the light of needed guidance and probable consequences. The recent battles over supersonic air transportation and the current clashes over the form and amount of nuclear power production are harbingers of more such controversies to come.

Two brief examples will illustrate how lack of such foresight in the past has contributed to our present dilemmas. Unguided application of the technologies of automobile manufacture and highway construction has led us to an extremely energy-extravagant system of transportation that is now proving to be very costly to alter. Foresight would have dictated that, at the least, public urban transportation might have been kept operative. More dramatic is the example of the excessive growth of the present world population, largely the consequence of massive technological interventions in the areas of medicine and public health.

There is increasing recognition of the need for assessment of future technological impacts and for some sort of societal control. Yet it is not clear that such control can be imposed and the interests of the overall society can be protected against those who would derive individual benefit from application of new technologies, without jeopardizing the basic characteristics of a free enterprise, democratic system.

THE DISTRIBUTION DILEMMA

The industrialized nations will find it costly in economic terms to move toward a more equitable distribution of the earth's resources. However, not to do so may be even more costly. As the less developed nations modernize and begin to demand their share of scarce materials, including minerals and fossil fuels, this pressure may become a major threat to world stability. The achievement of a level of existence in accord with fundamental human dignity for the world's nearly three billion poor does not appear possible without continued economic growth in both developing and developed nations. And yet, as earlier noted, economic growth on the pattern of the past poses an undeniable threat to the environment and to the health of man. Agricultural methods that are highly dependent on fossil fuels for agricultural and food transporting and processing machinery, and on fossil feedstocks for fertilizers and pesticides—to the point where the food on the table involves more fossil energy than solar energy—prove increasingly costly in environmental terms and in social terms (since they force peasants off the land into crowded cities with high unemployment); yet they seem necessary to keep up with the demands of rampant population growth. The expectations and demands of the lesser developed world may well come at such a pace that they could be met only by a drastic lowering of the material standard of living in the rich nations. Yet if they are not met the likelihood of accelerating world instability seems high.[3]

THE WORK DILEMMA

The fourth dilemma may be the most perplexing of all, partly because we have kept it from our awareness so successfully. The dilemma is that while possession of a societally supported work role seems essential to the individual's healthy development and sense of self-esteem, yet the economy (at least in the capitalist nations) seems increasingly unable to provide enough satisfactory work opportunities.

To be sure, the employment statistics and survey data are equivocal with regard to the seriousness of unemployment and worker discontent. Yet we are clearly seeing the beginning of a chronic shortage of meaningful social roles brought about by the combination of automation and cybernation, together with limitations on expansion by the "new scarcity" condition mentioned above. The evidence strongly suggests that by 1930 the thrust for efficiency and productivity, for replacement of men's muscles and brains by machines, had brought about a potential labor force in this country far greater than that needed to conduct the necessary activities of the society. Furthermore, division of labor has been carried out to the point where many

3. The omission of population problems from this list of basic dilemmas may be puzzling. Population increase is, of course, a relentless driving force tremendously aggravating the four dilemmas being listed. However, even if world population densities could somehow miraculously be arrested at their present levels, the four more fundamental dilemmas of industrial society would still remain. Population excesses with all their attendant problems, serious as they are, do not represent as fundamental a system paradox as the four listed.

jobs are reduced to tedious and stultifying boredom. That meaningful work opportunity has come to be considered an increasingly scarce commodity is attested to by concern over underemployment, rising worker complaints over boring tasks, inflated job-entry requirements, forced early retirement policies, featherbedding and make-work policies, and generation of jobs through arms races and "pyramid building."

Lack of a satisfactory work role (for example, as employee, self-employed, housewife, student) can result in personal disintegration.[4] Competition for jobs exacerbates racial and intergroup conflict. Unemployment fears constitute a barrier to dealing with problems of environmental pollution and waste of natural resources. Economic needs may be met with welfare payments or other income maintenance, but this does not take care of the need for satisfying and valued social roles and the psychological aspects of employment. The inability of the economy to provide enough satisfactory work roles to go around (except perhaps at completely unacceptable levels of inflation) is a serious flaw.

The End of the Industrial Era?

The four dilemmas described above are basic to the industrial system as we have known it. They are, in fact, *the ineluctable consequences of its successes*. Simultaneously, of course, we have to deal with an assortment of other problems not obviously related to these four dilemmas. Some of these are, although less apparently, aspects of the same dilemmas—the world food problem and massive urban poverty in the poor nations are partly a consequence of the impact of medical and agricultural technology, bringing death control without birth control and elimination of the peasant role without creation of substitute roles. Others appear to be symptomatic of increasing stress accompanying the unresolved dilemmas—for example, increasing violent crime and mental illness, social alienation, and some aspects of inflationary pressure. Still other problems appear to be the consequence of poor decisions—for example, the contribution to inflation of the Vietnam war and our failing to tax ourselves for this war, or the contribution to energy shortage from failing to deregulate natural gas

4. James O'Toole, Chairman, *Work in America*, Report of a Special Task Force to the Secretary of Health, Education, and Welfare (Cambridge, Mass.: MIT Press, 1973).

prices and failing to build sufficient facilities such as oil refineries. We focus on the four dilemmas because, although some other types of problems could be patched up within the present system structure, it seems likely that the fundamental dilemmas are in fact unresolvable without major systemic change.

Let us explore further what that assertion may mean, and on what it is based. It is convenient to employ the word "paradigm," which appears more and more frequently in recent years with an expanded meaning. Paradigm, originally essentially a synonym for "pattern," has come to mean the basic way of perceiving, valuing, thinking, and doing associated with a particular vision of reality.[5] The four fundamental dilemmas of our time are intrinisic to the paradigm of the industrial era.

The basic paradigm that has dominated the industrialized world is characterized by: (1) industrialization through organization and division of labor; (2) development and application of scientific method; (3) wedding of scientific and technological advance; (4) progress defined as technological and economic growth; (5) man seeking control over nature; positivistic theory of knowledge; (6) acquisitive materialism, economic-man image; (7) emphasis on individualism and free enterprise; and (8) few restraints on capital accumulation. (The last two would have to be modified for the nations with centrally controlled economies.)

This paradigm leads to striving toward such goals as efficiency, productivity, continued growth of production and consumption, and ever-increasing technological-manipulative power over the physical and social environment. This eventually results in processes and states (for example, extreme division of labor and specialization, technological unemployment, artificially stimulated consumption, planned obsolescence and waste, exploitation of common resources) that end up counteracting human ends (for example, enriching work roles, resource conservation, environmental enhancement, equitable sharing of the earth's resources).

The result of goals and processes that counteract human ends is a growing and massive challenge to the legitimacy of the present industrial system. It manifests itself in a variety of ways, among the most

5. Thomas S. Kuhn, *The Structure of Scientific Revolutions* (Chicago: University of Chicago Press, 1970).

obvious of which are the consumer movement, the environmentalist movement, youth dissent, women's liberation, old people's movement, deteriorating attitudes toward business, and demands of labor for job enrichment and industrial democracy.

A sustained challenge to the legitimacy of an institution is in the end the most potent of social change forces. It brought about the change from monarchial to democratic governments, in spite of the fact that it was the kings who had all the resources, wealth, and military might. It brought about the dissolution of the imperialist colonial system. We could be witnessing the beginnings of such a challenge to the industrial-business system.

We have argued that the unresolvability of society's fundamental dilemmas within the industrial-era paradigm suggests that this paradigm, with its technological imperative and its high value on the materialistic goals of efficiency, productivity, growth, and consumption, must give way to another. Viewed historically, the two centuries or so of the industrial era have been a step to some sort of post-industrial, equilibrium society. Present monetary, economic, political, material shortage, and social crises can best be viewed as symptoms of the approaching transition period.

To aid in grasping what this implies, consider the formulation shown in table 1, where the five premises on which the industrial era has been based (in this somewhat oversimplified view) are listed in the left-hand column. These premises are no longer viable; their replacements may be something like those shown in the right-hand column.

The industrial-era premises are so interwoven in all aspects of modern culture and social institutions that they cannot alter unless there is a thoroughgoing systemic change, a shift of the whole social paradigm. Because lavish and expanding energy and materials usage are so intimately involved in the old goal of material progress with its growth-and-consumption ethic, the institutional change implied by such a shift of fundamental premises is profound and threatening. The threat is not imaginary. Severe economic transition pains seem almost inevitable.

The challenge to the legitimacy of industrial-business system a-rises only in part because of the system's manifest inability to make satisfactory progress toward human goals, even when these are described

TABLE 1
Industrial-era Premises and Possible Replacements

Industrial-era Premise	Substitute Premise
1. Human beings find work (labor) repugnant and seek to escape from it. (Meanwhile they work, and work hard, for a variety of reasons, including the Protestant ethic.)	1. Human beings seek meaningful activity and meaningful relationships to the society. Man thrives not on pleasure but on challenge. Access to a satisfactory social role is a fundamental political right.
2. Energy is and will remain cheap and plentiful.	2. Here to stay is the "new scarcity" of energy, materials, natural fresh water, arable land, habitable surface area, capacity of the natural environment, and resilience of life-supporting ecological systems.
3. Thus it makes sense to industrialize production of goods and services —to organize and subdivide work and replace human labor by energy-driven machines.	3. Thus the outputs of the economy must be thought of as goods and services *plus* satisfying social roles.
4. Problems of scarcity can be successfully solved by expansion of geographical frontiers and the accomplishments of science and technology.	4. Pushing back geographical and technological frontiers will not alone resolve the problems of the "new scarcity;" movement toward some sort of "frugal society" is required.
5. The "central project" of the society is material progress—making things and generating "services" at an ever-increasing rate, all of which consumers, with a potentially insatiable demand, can be taught to want or "need."	5. A new "central project" must be found, capable of enlisting the energies and inspiring the commitments of society's members. It will no doubt emphasize quality of life, spiritual as well as continued technological development, and awareness of man's role in the evolutionary development of consciousness on the planet.

in its own terms. The challenge arises also in part because of changing value emphases in the society. We need now to look at the possibility that current value changes reflect a deeper, long-term change in the culturally dominant image of man.

Changing Images of Man

What is a useful meaning for this phrase "culturally dominant image of man?" Clearly, if we attempt to be too precise it will turn out that no culture, nor even any individual, carries around a unique and specifiable image of man that determines behavior, social roles, and institutions. Yet, equally clearly, in some sense a particular society at a particular historical time tends to see man-in-the-universe in a way that distinguishes it from many other societies. As noted in the preceding section, an aspect of the industrial paradigm has been an image in which man is largely activated by economic motivations, sufficiently so that whether the economic variable happens to symbolize at the moment his survival need for food or his self-actualization need for a vacation in the country, his economic behavior and the functioning of the economic system will be fairly dependable and predictable. Other societies and social groupings have placed more emphasis on other kinds of motivations, such as the social force of tradition, tribal loyalty, patriotism, identification with the common welfare, moral righteousness, and the search for truth.

To clarify the concept, contrast the following five competing images of man which have to some extent coexisted in this society in recent decades:

1. *Man as mechanism* with physiologically based motivations, responding to stimuli in his environment as these impinge upon his physical sense organs, hence ultimately predictable by a much more sophisticated science than is presently available
2. *Man as conditioned animal* with instinctual energies and desires modulated by such subconscious processes as repression, resistance, transference, etc., which result from social conditioning
3. *Man freely choosing* with self-awareness of his condition, endowed with reason, intentionality, and a valid sense of value
4. *Man as God's creation*, possessed both of human freedom and moral responsibility to seek God's will through revelation and to act accordingly
5. *Man as transcendental Being*, as having "the Divine within," a "true Self" or "Atman" or "Oversoul," awareness of which the individual may come to have through experiencing altered consciousness, thus recognizing it to be one with "Brahma," the "divine Ground"

Human society is not yet past battling bitterly over which of these or other candidate images is the "true" one. Nonetheless more and more awareness grows that reality is too rich to be fully expressed in any one image or metaphor. Just as physicists once learned the folly of fighting over whether light is waves or particles, coming to see these as complementary metaphors, so we are gradually learning that such well-worn dichotomies as free will versus determinism, physical ver-

sus spiritual, and science versus religion are really only expressions of
the tension between complementary metaphors.

Still, to whatever extent one such image of man can be said to be
dominant in our culture, it is a valid and important question whether
that dominant image of man seems to be changing.[6] For surely if it is,
that will affect all aspects of the social culture. Education above all is
fundamentally based on an image of man's basic nature, his process of
development, and his ultimate relationship to the universe around him.
Obviously the findings of scientific research influence society's image
of man (for example, the researches that led to various evolutionary
hypotheses), but so also does the prevailing image shape the choice of
scientific inquiries and the way they are carried out. The concepts of
democracy and free enterprise, legal and governmental structures and
processes, the definitions of criminality and how it is dealt with, treatment of the poor and the handicapped—all stem from the underlying
image of man.

What are the evidences of change at this basic level, the implicit
image of man-in-the-universe that undergirds the whole social
paradigm? The evidences are not conclusive, to be sure. They may
conveniently be grouped under three headings:

1. Observable cultural changes such as swelling interest in self-
    realization, metaphysical, psychic and arcane literature and discussion
    groups; survey and poll data on changing values and attitudes toward a
    "new naturalism," especially among certain elite groups such as
    students and corporate executives;[7] the "consciousness-expanding" ac-
    tivities of the "human potential" movement ranging through yoga,
    meditation, body awareness, dream interpretation, psychic
    phenomena; numerous other cultural indicators (books read, voluntary
    associations, themes of plays and motion pictures, "New Age" sub-
    culture) showing greatly increased interest in and tolerance for the
    transcendental, religious, esoteric, occult, suprarational, mystical, and
    spiritual
2. Awareness of need for a new social paradigm—of the inadequacy of
    the growth-and-consumption ethic of business-dominated affluent
    society for political guidance and for commanding the deepest loyalties
    of the society's citizens, of the apparent unresolvability of contem-

6. O. W. Markley, *Changing Images of Man* (Menlo Park, Calif.: Stanford Research
Institute, 1974).

7. Daniel Yankelovich, *The Changing Values on Campus* (New York: Washington
Square Press, 1972).

porary societal dilemmas in the present paradigm, of the extent to which positivistic science had debunked transcendental values on which Western civilization had been based

3. Developments within science supportive of a more transcendental image of man

This third area requires further examination. Developments within science today suggest a new legitimation of, and new interest in, systematic scientific exploration of subjective experience, varied states of consciousness, religious beliefs and mystical experiences, meditative insight, psychic phenomena, and occult mysteries. This came about in a curious way during the mid-sixties. Scientists had been cautiously edging toward it for many decades, of course. Scientific exploration of various previously taboo areas had been legitimated—hypnosis, sleep and dreams, unconscious processes, and creativity (formerly termed "inspiration"). Parapsychology had been in and out of favor, but never fully accepted. Then a remarkable discovery was made. Subjective inner states have measurable physical and physiological correlates—rapid eye movement, galvanic skin response, muscle tensions, electroencephalogram components, and electric and magnetic field components. Furthermore, when these indicators are picked up by sensors and returned to the body as input signals (biofeedback) all sorts of involuntary bodily processes and states can be brought under voluntary control. Here was a new basis for legitimation of studies of man's inner world of experience—scientists feel more secure when they can observe pointer readings—and a whole new kit of tools besides.

One crucial experiment by Puthoff and Targ, if substantiated, provides powerful evidence of the universality of telepathic-clairvoyant capacities and of the almost complete repression of awareness of this source of knowledge.[8] The experiment depends upon the discovery that if a stroboscopic light at around fifteen flashes per second is shined in a subject's eyes, a characteristic alpha component appears in his electroencephalogram. In the Puthoff-Targ experiment two remotely isolated subjects are used. The light is flashed in one subject's eyes and the other is asked to guess whether, in a given time

8. Harold E. Puthoff and Russell Targ, "Information Transmission Under Conditions of Sensory Shielding," *Nature* 251 (October 18, 1974): 606. More detail is available in a later paper by the same authors, "A Perceptual Channel for Information Transfer over Kilometer Distances," to be published in the Proceedings of the Institute for Electrical and Electronic Engineering (1975).

interval, the light is on or off. He is unable to guess better than a
chance basis, but the telltale alpha voltage component appears. Thus he
apparently knows at an unconscious level with certainty, in an ex-
trasensory way, when the light is in the other person's eye, even while
he is denying such knowledge to his conscious mind. Such demonstration of the repression of knowledge of paranormal abilities would help
to explain the erratic nature of experimental results in this area, and
also the irrational quality of some of the debates.

Even though these new studies have not progressed very far as yet,
we can already infer something about which direction they will push
the image of man. Wherever the nature of man has been probed deeply,
the paramount fact emerging is the duality of his experience. He is
found to be both physical and spiritual, both aspects being "real" and
neither fully describable in terms of the other. At various times and
places the spiritual or the material has been temporarily dominant, and
on rare occasions for brief historical periods there appears to have been
a wholesome balance. The area of psychic phenomena occupies a
peculiar place in that the term refers to experiences that have no conceivable "physical" explanation, yet fit quite comfortably into the
complementary image where spirit is "real." (A useful analogy may be
seen in physics where certain photoelectric effects have no "explanation" in terms of the wave image of light, while the electron
microscope is "unexplainable" through a particle model of electrons.)

The extent of the potential impact on the scientific world view is
suggested by the following list of characteristics of empirical science.
The scientific paradigm, until recently, has tended to imply:

1. The only conceivable ways in which man comes to acquire knowledge
   is through his physical senses and perhaps through some sort of
   memory storage in the genes.
2. All qualitative properties are ultimately reducible to quantitative ones;
   that is, color is reduced to wavelength, hate and love to the chemical
   composition of glandular secretions, etc.
3. There is a clear distinction between the objective world, which is
   perceivable by anyone, and subjective experience which is perceived
   by the individual alone, in the privacy of his own mind.
4. The concept of the free inner person is a prescientific explanation for
   behavior caused by forces impinging upon the individual from his environment interacting with internal tensions and pressures
   characteristic of the organism. "Freedom" is behavior for which scientists have not yet found the cause.

5. What we know as consciousness or awareness of our thoughts and feelings is really only a side effect of physical and biochemical processes going on in the brain.

6. What we know as memory is simply a matter of stored data in the physical organism, strictly comparable with the storage of information in a digital computer. (Thus it is impossible for a person to "remember" an event that happened to someone else, in a different lifetime.)

7. The nature of time being what it is, there is obviously no way in which we can obtain foreknowledge of the future other than by rational prediction from known causes. (Thus it is impossible for anyone to "remember" an event happening three weeks hence.)

8. Since mental activity is simply a matter of fluctuating states in the physical organism, it is completely impossible for this mental activity to exert any effect directly on the physical world outside the organism. (Thus reports of levitation or other psychokinetic events have to be nonsense or trickery.)

9. The evolution of the universe and of man has come about through purely physical causes, through random mutations and natural selection. There is no justification for any concept of universal purpose or teleological urge, either in the evolution of consciousness or in the strivings of the individual.

10. The individual does not survive the death of the organism, or if there is any sense in which the individual exists on after the death of his physical body we can neither comprehend it in this life nor in any way obtain knowledge regarding it.

The reason psychic and consciousness research is such a bitterly contested battleground is that the data in these areas challenge *all* of the above premises. Yet it was on the basis of these premises, in effect, that the increasingly prestigious scientific world view was able, in the past, to dismiss as of secondary consequence the religious, aesthetic, and intuitive experiences of man and hence to erode the value postulates based in those subjective experiences.

The transcendental component of human experience, which positivistic scientists set out to debunk, formed an essential basis for American ideals and institutions. "The very deepest goals for Americans relate to the spiritual health of our people . . . for ours is a spiritually based society."[9] The symbolism of the Great Seal of the United States on the back of the dollar bill is perhaps the most potent

9. President's Commission on National Goals, *Goals for Americans* (Englewood Cliffs, N.J.: Prentice Hall, 1960), p. 1.

reminder that the structure (the unfinished pyramid) is not complete unless the transcendent all-seeing eye has the capstone position. It is clearly in a transcendental sense that all men are created equal. The institutions of representative democracy are predicated upon a belief in spiritually free citizens possessed of a valid sense of value. The free-enterprise market system assumes a transcendental "invisible hand" to insure that the individual microdecisions in pursuit of self-interest will add up to satisfactory social macrodecisions. Thus, much of high social import hinges upon the issue represented in the ten premises above.

The challenging image of man, then, involves a "new transcendentalism," within which science on the one hand, and the humanities and religion on the other, are seen as two complementary inquiries illuminating the physical and psycho-spiritual aspects of man's nature.

Growing out of this "new transcendentalism" comes a pair of complementary ethics which are most congenial to the kind of transformation we postulated earlier as being necessary for the resolution of contemporary societal dilemmas. One of these is an "ecological ethic;" the other a "self-realization ethic."

The "ecological ethic" involves recognition of man as an integral part of the natural world—hence inseparable from it and from its governing processes and laws. It fosters a sense of the total community of man, a joining in partnership with nature in modifying ecological relationships and the future of the planet, and a relating of self-interest to the interests of fellow man and of future generations.

The "self-realization ethic" asserts that the proper end of all individual experience is the further evolutionary development of the emergent self and of the human species, and that the appropriate function of social institutions is to create an environment that will foster that process. This ethic would guide the society toward a restructuring of social institutions to satisfy the individual's need and desire for self-determination and for full and valued participation in the society.

These two ethics, the one emphasizing the total community of man-in-nature and the oneness of the human race and the other placing the highest value on development of selfhood, are not contradictory but complementary—two sides of the same coin. Together they encourage both cooperation and wholesome competition, love and individuality. Each is a corrective against excesses or misapplication of the other.

To thus state the derived ethics from the new image of man is to risk overlooking that it is the form and strength of the inner dynamic giving force to these ethics that is of import. The ethics as abstract principles have been around for many centuries. But only for brief periods in relatively small societies have they ever been institutional ized as the dominant guiding principles.

The Coming Transformation?

We have identified thus far two main forces that seem to push for systemic transformation. One is the growing realization that without such systemic change the most fundamental societal dilemmas are un-resolvable. The apparent tradeoffs (for example, unemployment ver-sus inflation, energy versus environment) can only grow more in-tolerable within the industrial-era paradigm. The reason is that all the serious societal problems now are directly or indirectly the conse-quence of the successes of the industrial paradigm, hence they are un-likely to be solved by more of the same.

The second force is a changing perception of man and his place in the universe, a change in the felt, intuited, internalized metaphysic of the society. This appears most tellingly in the suspension of disbelief (for example, with regard to the possible values of mystical experience and meditative insight, the possibility of psychic phenomena that do not have "physical" explanations and of time-honored religious truths that neither have "scientific" explanations nor fit into rational philosophical conceptualizations). This increased cultural tolerance for mystery gives a new legitimacy within the official truth-seeking scien-tific institutions for systematic exploration of inner, subjective ex-perience, and that in turn assures that the change is not just a passing fad or superficial value shift.

Together these two forces suggest the possibility that a transfor-mation of the whole-system paradigm may be underway. We might compare it with two other historically recent transformations—the In-dustrial Revolution and the Copernican Revolution.

The Industrial Revolution involved profound institutional change; on the other hand, it itself depended upon previous institutional in-novations, particularly the great trading companies and the economic structures of capitalism, both originating over two centuries earlier. There were accompanying value changes and life-style changes, but the main impetus came from innovations in production methods. (In-terestingly enough, some of the most important initial advances seem to have been prompted by a fuel shortage—of firewood.) The innovations were characterized by apparent advance on some fronts, and regression on others (most notably quality of life). There were bitter opposition and attempts to resist change by some elements.

The Copernican Revolution centered around innovations in society's truth-seeking system, both with regard to method of inquiry and to questions addressed. Accompanying the profound change in beliefs and values were important institutional changes. There were bitter opposition and attempts to resist change by some elements, and a traumatic transition period.

Both these "revolutionary" transformations are within the time span (about 800 years at least) of what Kahn has termed the basic "long-term multifold trend" of Western civilization. Kahn lists the following items in this multifold trend:

1. Increasingly sensate (empirical, this-worldly, secular, humanistic, pragmatic, manipulative, explicitly rational, utilitarian, contractual, epicurean, hedonistic, etc.) cultures
2. Bourgeois, bureaucratic, and meritocratic elites
3. Centralization and concentration of economic and political power
4. Accumulation of scientific and technical knowledge
5. Institutionalization of technological change, especially research, development, innovation, and diffusion
6. Increasing military capability
7. Westernization, modernization, and industrialization
8. Increasing affluence and (recently) leisure
9. Population growth
10. Urbanization, recently suburbanization and "urban sprawl"—soon the growth of megalopoli
11. Decreasing importance of primary and (recently) secondary and tertiary occupations; increasing importance of tertiary and recently quaternary occupations
12. Increasing literacy and education and (recently) the "knowledge industry" and increasing role of intellectuals
13. Innovative and manipulative social engineering—i.e., rationality increasingly applied to social, political, cultural, and economic worlds as well as to shaping and exploiting the material world. . .
14. Increasing universality of the multifold trend
15. Increasing tempo of change in all the above[10]

10. Herman Kahn and B. Bruce-Briggs, *Things to Come: Thinking About the Seventies and Eighties* (New York: Macmillan Co., 1967), pp. 6-7.

To this list one could add additional components of the multifold trend that seem more important today than they did a few years ago: (1) increasing scale of environmental impact of human activities; (2) increasing rate of use of "nonrenewable" natural resources of minerals and fossil fuels; (3) movement toward a single world economy with closely linked worldwide economic institutions; and (4) increasing gap between rich and poor populations.

The transformation we are postulating involves a significant departure from that trend. It entails, as we have seen, both profound institutional change and a shift in the basic image of man-in-the-universe from which the values and goals of the society derive. Thus it may share some of the characteristics of both the two earlier transformations mentioned above. In a sense it is more fundamental than either.

This is a sobering eventuality to contemplate. History gives us little reason to take comfort in the prospect of fundamental and rapid social change and little reason to think we can avoid the accompanying threat of economic decline and disruption of social processes considerably greater than anything we have experienced or care to imagine. If indeed a fundamental and rapid change in basic perceptions and values, roles and institutions, occurs, such a chaotic and disruptive period seems inevitable as the powerful momentum of the industrial era is turned in a new direction, and as the different members and institutions of the society respond with different speeds.

This discussion would not be complete without consideration of the reasons the postulated transformation might *not* take place. Basically there are two. One is that the two forces we have identified—the press of dilemmas and the "new transcendentalism" in the culture— may prove to be not nearly as strong as we have assumed, and the momentum of the "long-term multifold trend" may turn out to be durable, bring us a future something like Daniel Bell's "post-industrial society"[11] but plagued with increasingly vexing social and environmental problems. The second reason might be that the two forces for transformation are indeed present in strength, but the resistances to change may prove to be too strong, in which case the society might continue on a decline without recovering.

These sources of resistance are several. Most deeply rooted is individual and cultural resistance to change in fundamental perceptions

11. Daniel Bell, *The Coming Post-Industrial Society* (New York: Basic Books, 1973).

and premises. If indeed there exists a basic wrongheadedness with regard to institutions (in that those found suitable for the building up of a vast technological-industrial apparatus are inadequate to the humane use of the new Faustian powers) and a basic wrongheadedness with regard to the dominant image of man (in that he is persuaded that he is less than he discoverably is), then experience suggests that disclosure of this wrongheadedness will be resisted mightily. The phenomenon is well known in psychotherapy, where the client may resist and avoid the very knowledge he most needs to resolve his problems. A similar situation probably exists in society. There is suggestive evidence both in anthropology and in history that a society tends to hide from itself knowledge that is superficially threatening to the status quo but may in fact be badly needed for resolution of societal problems.

Institutions have rigidity and inertia, and tend to perpetuate the values and premises that have been built into them. Thus, for example, economic institutions that have long been guided by a concept of exploiting the environment for economic gain through the "outputs" of goods and services would tend to resist reorientation toward enhancement of the environment and acting as though the creation of meaningful social roles were one of their most important "outputs." Furthermore, this resistance is not without realistic justification. The whole society behaves more or less as an integrated organism, and a particular institution that attempted to move more rapidly than the rest of the system could accept would find itself in deep trouble.

Anxiety over change toward an unknown future is reflected in irrational and unconsciously motivated behavior opposing that change. If there is not sufficient understanding of the necessity for change and vision of a positive future that is both desirable and reachable, a society may make quite the wrong responses to the challenges it faces. It is somewhat like the situation of a woman finding herself undergoing the physiological changes associated with childbirth and, never having heard of pregnancy nor being able to envision the ultimate outcome of the process, tenses up because of her anxiety and does just those things that make the experience more traumatic.

Implications for Education

We want finally to examine some educational implications of the foregoing considerations. These will be under four headings: theory of education, institutionalization of education, educational research, and demands and constraints.

THEORY OF EDUCATION

Suppose the new paradigm as delineated earlier were to gain in acceptance. What would this imply for the theory of education? The most obvious reorientation is toward more emphasis on self-discovery and consequent development of a wholesome self-image. Since self-discovery cannot be taught in the usual sense of the word, this suggests a radically different role for the "teacher" (or facilitator).

Theories of human development would require much reexamination. To the familiar arguments about the relative influences of genetic endowment and social conditioning in explaining individual differences (nature versus nurture) would be added a third element, an individual character essence.

It would seem self-evident that the breadth and magnitude of human capabilities and resources far exceed present levels of realization, and that the primary limitations on the actualization of potentialities are the individual's own negative beliefs, his limited self-expectations. It would be assumed that unconscious processes comprise a major portion of significant human experience (perceiving, learning, thinking), and that developing access to these processes (in their creative aspects even more than their repressive aspects) is a central task of all education. Access to unconscious processes would be understood to be facilitated by attention to feelings and emotions, and by visual imagery; hence interpersonal sharing, art and music, and creative experience would be given more significant roles in education.

It would also seem self-evident that the manifest factors that influence the learning process (cost per student, student/teacher ratio, systemic reinforcement, physical environment, behaviorally defined objectives, subject material organization, and the like) are probably much less determinative in the end than a host of subtle factors that are difficult to get at in operational terms and hence typically overlooked (for example, teacher expectations, basic esteem for the students as persons, enthusiasm for methods used, congruence of stated and non-verbal messages, implicit contracts between student and teacher, student self-images and expectations).

INSTITUTIONALIZATION OF EDUCATION

Implicit in the new paradigm is the proposition that all institutions of the society are, in an important sense, educating institutions. Furthermore, education is the paramount function of society. Robert Hutchins describes "the learning society" as one that will have transformed "its values in such a way that learning, fulfillment, becoming human, had become its aims *and all its institutions were directed to this end*. This is what the Athenians did . . . They made their society one designed to bring all its members to the fullest development of their highest powers . . . Education was not a segregated activity, conducted for certain hours, in certain places, at a certain time of life. It was the aim of the society . . . The Athenian was educated by the culture, by Paideia."[12]

The individual will have several careers during his lifetime, but not because they are forced upon him by job obsolescence in a technological-industrial megamachine madly careening out of control and ever faster. Rather, it will be because it is in this way that he best realizes his own potentialities and maximizes his own fulfillment. But institutional changes will be required to accomodate to more or less continuous education throughout life, with particularly intense learning activity during periods of career change. These changes may come about partly, for example, through new kinds of collaborative arrangements between educational institutions and industrial and commercial organizations, or by the emergence of wholly new kinds of private-sector institutions with diversified goals.

One needed institution among others with an educational function is some sort of ecoplanning network with units at local, regional, national, and world levels. At national and world levels, focus should be on available future alternatives for all aspects of the well-being of man and nature for at least two to three decades ahead, and on the actions that need to be taken to avoid intolerable and to reach desirable futures. At regional and local levels, there need to be two functions served—a technical and brokering activity, staffed by professionals and charged with illuminating available alternatives, and a policy-formulating activity that involves public officials and participating citizenry. Examples of areas of concern are: land use policy (which

12. Robert M. Hutchins, *The Learning Society* (New York: Praeger, 1968).

valleys shall be inundated by dam building or filled in with solid waste, which estuaries filled in, what rich farmland covered with shopping centers and subdivisions); development policy (human, social, and ecological—not just economic and technological—including incentives for population redistribution for de-urbanization); implementing man-nature ecosystem designs; strategic assessment of future problems; strengthening the ability of local governments to implement rational, future-oriented planning; gradual reorientation of the powerful business system so that its actions are better aligned with the overall welfare and hence it regains its endangered legitimacy.

The "unneeded people" problem was earlier identified as one of the key dilemmas of the late industrial era. A large fraction of persons engaged in learning and ecoplanning roles, and the frequent "recycling" of persons undergoing career change will take the stigma off the recycling of those which the modern industrial state shunts out of the productive mainstream, often irretrievably—those labeled "technologically disemployed," "elderly," "unemployable," "dropout," "poor," "delinquent," "criminal," "deviant," and "mentally ill." Appropriate emotional support and reeducational opportunity will be the assumed responsibility of widely distributed public, private, and voluntary organizations, rather than the charge of a huge welfare bureaucracy that dispenses "income maintenance" but cannot offer useful and meaningful roles.

EDUCATIONAL RESEARCH

Educational research in the new paradigm would put a great deal of emphasis on such topics as stages of psychological and social development; resistance and repression as phenomena in the learning process; roles of expectations, suggestion, and images; kinds of consciousness; origins of human value commitments; interpersonal dynamics. Much less research emphasis would be placed on matters relating to the imparting of subject matter, techniques of skills training, and measurement of cognitive achievement.

One of the most significant differences from the past would be the high priority given systematic exploration of subjective experience, including especially those deepest experiences from which the basic value commitments and noblest visions of human civilization have sprung. This would be not in a reductionist sense, "explaining" them in terms of something else, but rather in the intuitive aesthetic sense of coming better to understand them in their own terms. Several characteristics of such research derive from the nature of its focus.

For one thing, it is tolerant of many alternative metaphors. It does not insist, for example, that all human behavior should be explained in terms of any particular model. It allows for levels of explanation and levels of awareness, accommodating to the fact that humans do behave in some respects like conditioned automata, but they partake of the godlike as well.

Educational research is essentially a moral inquiry. It can never escape, only conceal, the fact that education is always directed toward some end. The fact that in the past we may have thought it possible to study the educational process without regard to what was being taught itself betrays a value commitment with the most profound consequences.

Research must be participative. To be sure, one gets a certain kind of knowledge from pursuing the paradigm wherein there is an "experimenter" who knows what is going on, and a "subject" who is deceived or kept in ignorance. Much of academic psychology has followed this model. But a much different picture emerges when the researcher says, "Come, let us explore together. By sharing our innermost experiences let us find what is universal to man."

Finally, we should note that the distinction between educational research and other areas will to some extent become more blurred. The educational enterprise is guided by the goals of the larger society; its problems are reflections of the problems of the society; the demands made upon it by the society arise from those problems. The problems of unequal educational opportunity cannot be separated from either the external structure that perpetuates inequities, nor from the deeply unconscious cultural prejudices that participate in subtle ways in the sustaining of those inequities. An essential type of research, which we have not learned to do very well at all, is research on the whole social organism as an entity—what state it is in, where it is trying to go, what paths are open, and how the process of choosing takes place.

DEMANDS AND CONSTRAINTS

And so, to sum up what has been said in the foregoing, the society, including its educational institutions, will somehow have to cope with realities which threaten its survival as a civilization. Much depends upon what is the correct interpretation of present crises. They may be, like many problems of the past, solvable by new organizations and new technologies. Until recently this has been a fond and widely held hope. We have advanced a different interpretation, namely that the dilemmas faced by the technologically advanced nations of the world, and the particular form those dilemmas assume in the United States on the occasion of its 200th birthday, are signs of the decreasing workability of the industrial-age paradigm, essentially because its successes have brought us to a fundamental crisis point. The already visible signs of partial breakdown will become more frequent and more severe. Either the whole social organism will undergo a transformation to a profoundly different paradigm, one more satisfactory in human terms and ecological consequences, or the attempt will fail and the breakdown will become more complete.

The next few years will reveal whether or not this transformational hypothesis holds up. If it does, then the period just ahead will be one of severe trauma for the whole society, its educational institutions included. The demands made on education will be next to impossible to meet because it will be asked to do what only the social organism as a whole can do. The constraints will be severe, both because of catastrophic economic decline and inflationary breakdown of the financial structures, and because of extraordinarily high anxiety levels.

Yet in the broader sense education is our only salvation—education of ourselves toward fuller understanding of the evolutionary leap mankind struggles to effect and of the requirements for a successful transformation. All we have learned in psychotherapy suggests that it is at the precise time when the individual most feels as though his whole life is crashing down around him, that there is the greatest likelihood that he may accomplish that inner reorganization which constitutes a quantum leap in his growth toward human maturity. Perhaps it is also like that with societies.

CHAPTER VI

Utilizing Man's Experience: The Quest for Meaning

ARTHUR W. FOSHAY

Introduction

In this chapter, we shall examine the ways man's experience is made available to the young, with special attention to the fact that the official version of what is most meaningful in man's experience is offered in school. In systematic school instruction, knowledge is offered in three forms. The confusion of these forms with one another explains in some degree the feeling of meaninglessness many high school students associate with formal school learning. They take what they can, but many of them consider nonformal experience to be more meaningful than school experience. From our consideration of this situation, certain recommendations pertaining to formal school instruction will emerge.

Man's experience comes to us in many forms: as organized knowledge, often in the form of disciplines; as myth, as metaphor, as lore, as "conventional wisdom," as mores, as customs, as rituals, as superstitions. All of these forms of experience find their way into organized education, but most of the attention of the curricularists is given to organized knowledge, and in the secondary schools to that knowledge organized into school subjects which more or less reflect academic disciplines.

To say this is not to ignore the importance of the other forms through which man's experience is reflected in schools, or the sometimes conflicting implications of experience, say, with school athletics and with the classroom experience in English. One receives conflicting ideas of the heroic from the football field and *The Red Badge of Courage*, or from a school election and the reality of public elections as reported on television or studied in a social studies class.

There is a profound difference, sometimes overlooked, between systematic and incidental knowledge. Incidental knowledge is picked up in the course of daily life. Some of it has high impact, such as witnessing an arrest, or an accident, or one's family coming apart. Some of it is covert, like the barrage of distorted experience portrayed in the mass media. Some of it is an accumulation of practical experience, like learning to shop at a store. But all such experience is sporadic and uninterpreted, and most of it is private, unvalidated by social reference.

In contrast, school subjects are offered systematically, and they are socially validated and interpreted. Systematic experience differs from incidental experience in its depth. At a time in the discussion of education when it has become popular to emphasize the concealed messages conveyed by incidental experience with the organization of the school and the impact of community life outside of schools, it is important for us to remember the fundamental difference between systematic and incidental experience. Systematic instruction, at its best, seeks to explain events by looking behind them. Incidental experience presents only the events themselves. Systematic instruction can examine causes; incidental experience tends to be superficial.

It is the unique function of the school, and other types of formal education, to offer systematic experience. It is this offering that justifies having formal educational institutions. It is in the field of systematic knowledge that we exercise deliberate control. Although the incidental experience of school may be in conflict with the systematic offering (e.g., mathematics is sometimes offered in such a way as to engender fear and dislike of the subject), it is to that which is systematic that we as school people ought to devote most of our efforts, and it is to systematic knowledge that this chapter is addressed. We will leave to others the problem of the inconsistencies between systematic and incidental learning.

How shall we think of systematic experience, offered in school? What shall be our conception of man's experience, so offered? It is our purpose here to examine three such conceptions, and to consider their consequences in the curriculum.

Three Types of Knowledge

There are three types of knowledge offered in formal education: (a) knowledge about findings (what has been discovered, or "is known"), (b) knowledge of the processes and sources needed to establish findings, and (c) knowledge of techniques. Let us consider these three types of knowledge.

KNOWLEDGE OF FINDINGS

The findings, or "facts," that have been established are what most people consider learning, and they occupy most of what is offered in school. A long-established tradition of schooling demands of us that we offer that which is certainly true—and what is certainly true is what has been found out. That is why most laymen think of teaching as presentation—witness the disastrous "teaching" on educational television during its early years—and most of us feel "taught" when we have been told. Knowledge of findings passes for erudition. The textbook, indeed the very idea of a textbook, perpetuates the idea that to know these findings constitutes learning. By "findings" we mean all information presented authoritatively: "facts," for example, the Earth is almost round; "principles," for example, "power corrupts . . . ;" and "rules," for example, "don't write a double negative." The tradition with respect to findings is to present the world and everything in it as ultimately lawful and factual in character. Science is its idol—that is, that version of Science which the layman has heard of, the findings— not science as it is understood by scientists, a process of painstaking inquiry. To be a learned person, according to this overwhelmingly dominant education tradition, is to be able to recite. To be trained is to be able to do. (See "Knowledge of Techniques," below.)

KNOWLEDGE OF PROCESSES AND SOURCES

The knowledge of processes and sources is what makes theorizing, or thought, possible. But the tradition of secondary education gives such knowledge a relatively minor place in the curriculum. It appears, however, when students are required to write essays in which they put forth and defend what is for them an original idea. It appears in science teaching when a student is required to develop a hypothesis to explain some event in the physical world. It appears in the social studies when a student is asked to attempt an explanation of a societal event, such as the origins of the Civil War. It appears very prominently in the arts, when the student is asked to develop his own statement in one of the arts media (though not, typically, in music). It appears at all those places in the curriculum where the student is required to develop his own statement, design, or hypothesis.

It is worth noting that the principal emphasis of the major curriculum development projects of the fifties and sixties was on knowledge of processes and sources to foster theorizing and thought. The modern projects, following the lead of the Physical Sciences Study Committee, focused on processes and sources as the main content of the offering. These projects sought to build knowledge in the students of modes of inquiry, not merely knowledge of findings. In order to conduct inquiry, one must of course make use of findings, and the one encompasses the other. These projects, however, have often been reduced to knowledge of findings—sets of facts and rules—or to technique (see below). Thus their basic meaning has been distorted and their importance reduced. Moreover, since the evaluation devices in widest use continue to emphasize facts and findings as against reasoning, the newer projects are too often mis-evaluated. Tests of reasoning in some fields have been developed, but the objectives they measure are not widely accepted by a public and a corps of school people still dominated by the tradition of teaching facts and findings.

KNOWLEDGE OF TECHNIQUES

A technique is a set procedure for doing things which, once mastered, requires no further thought or information. One learns a technique as a means to an end—to get jobs done, not for the sake of theorizing. To operate a typewriter, one need not know how to design one, nor need one be acquainted with communications theory. To drive an automobile, one need not be an automotive engineer. While some knowledge of linguistics might help one with grammar, no such knowledge is needed to write according to the rules.

Useful and important as technical knowledge is, it is no substitute for knowledge of sources and processes—the "know why." That is why the captain of the aircraft is in charge of the engineer. Knowing how is absolutely essential, but it is not the same as knowing why.

Another dominant tradition of the school is to deal with know-how, that is, to reduce as much as possible to technique. To the degree that we can teach the general public how to do things, the public thinks we have been successful. So, sadly, do many educators. Know-how is certain, predictable, true, like facts and findings. We seek to reduce almost all learning to skills; most operational learning theory is concerned with skill learning: memorizing, learning manual skills, and the like.

The technician is a doer, and thus fits well into that aspect of the American tradition that emphasizes action rather than words. It is very satisfying to command a skill, perhaps because the feedback from one's efforts is so fast. Mastering a skill yields intrinsic satisfaction; it is socially rewarded, too, since one can be "useful." Without technique little can be accomplished.

For all these reasons, we tend to reduce to technique as much as possible of what we offer in school. Technique is tangible, it is rewarding, and it is personal.

Types of Knowledge and Subject Matter

These three types of knowledge are not usually distinguished from one another. Certain difficulties arise from the failure to do so. For one thing, the failure to distinguish processes and sources from technique leads to a reductionism in which students memorize paradigms (i.e., techniques) for conducting inquiry, thus failing to make discoveries of their own.

MATHEMATICS

The memorization of paradigms is essential for some purposes. Mathematics, for example, depends on sets of logic. At the secondary school level, solving problems mathematically appears to consist of matching existing paradigms to the given problem—an act of memory. In general, the closer a field is to mathematics, the more appropriate are such acts of memory. Mathematics, which is often considered the highest order of thinking, is for most students simply knowledge of the first type described above—knowledge of facts and findings.

The analysis of a problem into its mathematical components, in order to permit the search for the appropriate paradigm, is thinking. But "doing" mathematics is not. It is perhaps the failure of mathematics teachers to face the implications of the form their subject takes, and to teach in ways appropriate to this form, that accounts for the widespread failure of mathematics teaching and the dislike this subject has engendered among students at the secondary school level.

ENGLISH AND SOCIAL STUDIES

As one leaves mathematics, our second type of knowledge—knowledge of sources and processes—becomes more prominent in high school education. English and social studies compete to be the least elegantly conceived of the subjects we offer at the secondary school level. By their very ambiguity, they most invite invention by students. Students are required, when these two subjects are offered in ways true to their nature, to make use of primary source materials and to devise their own ways of interpreting them. That is, they are if the teacher invites such usage and interpretation. It is when the two subjects are reduced to knowledge of findings—in this case, given "facts" and canned interpretations—that the subjects are aborted, have relatively little impact, and are often disliked by students who see little relationship between such subjects and the real world. When English and social studies are reduced to facts, findings, and techniques, they become "merely academic."

It is interesting to consider what has often happened to English when it is combined with social studies: it becomes technique. Students are asked to write well, technically, about social studies content. The English curriculum is thus aborted, since literary meaning is left out, and becomes merely academic. To be merely academic is to fail to generate meaning.

The generation of meaning has not been seen as a principal purpose of study in the secondary school. Such schools, under private auspices, are still called "preparatory schools," that is, schools that prepare students for the higher learning, where meanings finally emerge as the core of study.

However, when those who really shape the disciplines offered in the secondary schools took a hard look at the offering during the fifties and sixties, it was precisely the lack of meaning they criticized. To offer physics as a set of findings, the Physical Science Study Committee said, was to misrepresent physics. The same criticism was made of the other offerings in science; in mathematics the same criticism led to the more recent emphasis on processes and concepts, as against the memorizing of paradigms.

TECHNICAL SUBJECTS

Technique as such occupies a large and unhonored place in the secondary school curriculum. Courses in the shops and in office practice are not exploited for their deeper career meanings, except by an occasional gifted teacher. They are frequently not respected.

This lack of respect arises from the system of prestige that is associated with the types of knowledge we have been discussing. The American comprehensive high school, one of our American social inventions, has never recovered from its beginning as a preparatory school—a school for budding gentlemen, about to be honed and polished into their proper role at the university. Such people, traditionally, either postponed hard thinking or left it to others. They saw no need to master any useful skill other than the (unrecognized) pure technique in the service of academic learning in the fields traditionally recognized as constituting learning. They left the mastery of useful skills to the working classes, thus projecting into the comprehensive high school the class structure of an earlier time. This class structure remains in the high school to this day.

The prestige system of the comprehensive high school reflects the values and mores of the nineteenth century. It is expressed by the notion of "solid" subjects—the most academic, with the humanities and the sciences competing for the summit—and the other subjects, variously called "practical," "technical," or "vocational." This situation places the contemporary comprehensive high school in conflict with its own times. The class structure implied by the prestige system of the high school is no longer characteristic of American society. The distribution of power in the United States no longer matches the education system—if, indeed, it has since 1870. The emergence of big business, big labor, and big government have wholly altered the genteel tradition, which is preserved in only a few pockets in contemporary America.

The students sense this. Increasingly, they view traditional academic studies as a meaningless game to be played against teachers. The teachers reinforce this view by reducing academic "solid" subjects to facts, findings, and techniques, thus avoiding meaning. Yet the school in its official reward structure also denies respect to the doers of the "practical," "technical," and "vocational" subjects. The whole system, the students feel, is without meaning or justice. They turn it into a race for grades, or they reject it.

Some schools have responded, spottily, to this situation by introducing, for instance, courses in film, black studies, and politics. Such a response is inadequate; it reflects the confusion we have been describing here.

What is needed is a system of rewards that acknowledges the three-fold nature of knowledge we teach; which honors facts and findings for what they are—but no more; which insists that sources and processes be universally taught in the school offering; which recognizes the satisfactions, the dignity, and the value of technique— without confusing the three.

The Confusion of Types of Knowledge

The confusion of the three types of knowledge is at the root of the problem. The spotty responses of the secondary schools to the disaffiliation of many students do not confront the problem, nor do they confront the genteel tradition of the school for the inhibiting force it is, nor the problem of the relevance of the school's offerings to life as students think it is lived.

The confusion of fact with technique has been alluded to. Let us explore it further. In order to teach, one must make things easily understandable. This can be achieved via various methods, from presentation to discovery. However it is attempted, though, it must be achieved, or learning will be temporary and trivial, if it takes place at all. Facts and findings are easy to grasp: a mnemonic device will serve (as St. Wapernicl served an earlier school generation to remember the then United States cabinet officers). One can get quite far on the basis of sheer memory. Even the shards of memory can make one seem informed. Remember πr^2? Remember what it is for? Such formulas become useful anchors while one is studying a subject, and students make progress because they know them. To be able to recite the names of the United States presidents is to have a framework for the placement of events important to us. However, students are tempted to take formulas, frameworks, "facts," paradigms, and rules to be the stuff of knowledge because they serve well while one is groping for mastery of a subject.

To reduce knowledge to facts and findings is, in a sense, to technify it. The great confusion we convey to the public begins at this point. We too often merely technify school subjects, either by reducing them to a set of nonunderstood rules to be followed, or by reducing them to facts and findings to be recited.

The key term is "nonunderstood." To understand something is to be able to give reasons for it, or to be able to reconstitute it from its primary elements. Understanding, so viewed, is the prerequisite for interpretation, and interpretation is the ultimate objective of learning.

It is our failure to teach the ability to interpret that haunts us. Men make progress, personally and collectively, according to their interpretations. It is "know why" that governs us.

"Know why" is what general education seeks to develop. It has been a long time since there has been a widespread discussion of the purposes of general education at the secondary school level. We have pursued goals in the shorter range: college admission, the acquisition of "fundamental" skills, job preparation. It is time to reconsider the larger purposes of the secondary school. The feeling of meaninglessness that afflicts students and teachers need not continue, if we will but direct our attention to the matter of meaning and the achievement of meaning.

Types of Knowledge and the Pursuit of Meaning

All education that is offered at the secondary school level should be infused with the pursuit of meaning. The difficulty with facts and findings and with technique is that they are insufficient to the achievement of meaning. Meaning is to be found in the examination of sources and processes, the second of the three kinds of knowledge discussed earlier. Moreover, the study of sources and processes encompasses both findings and techniques. We shall argue here that only in the study of sources and processes is a general education to be found.

GENERAL EDUCATION

Let us consider "general education" further. The general education of the well-educated consists of concepts and terms of wide applicability, which make it possible to confront the buzzing confusion of the world in such a way as to bring about a degree of order. These concepts and terms have to be earned. They cannot be taught as facts and findings, for their application to fields other than those in which they appear will not be practiced by the student if they are so offered. To earn them, one must make constructs out of primary information.

Such concepts and terms are to be found, ordinarily, deeply embedded in organized knowledge. They form the ordinary vocabulary of the educated.

What are these concepts? Let us examine a few illustrations. Take, for example, the idea of *composition*. It arises most obviously in the arts. One composes a picture, or some music, one choreographs a dance, one attempts to structure a play, and so on. In school, written essays used to be called "compositions," and so they are. But the term is not to be found on the surface of the arts. The surface consists of existing works. No, to earn the term "composition," one must attempt to compose: to write music, or at least to organize a performance of it; to make an art object, to write an essay. But the term has wider applications. The step from composing an art object to developing a scientific experiment is short, if one is to believe those scientists who discuss theorizing as an art. One can, with profit, take the planning of a lesson and its execution as an event with a dramatic structure, and it has so been taken. What about the composition of a political body (i.e., an examination of its basic structure), or of a school, or a corporation? It seems farfetched to some to take an organization as an art form, but contemporary students of human organization take it that way frequently. To consider the organization as an arrangement of forces in tension leads to rich interpretations—richer, some would say, than taking them as input-process-output mechanisms, and richer, because human beings act according to the arts as well as according to the dictates of cold logic.

Let us take another term, *interaction*. The term arises in several fields. It arises, notably, in the elementary grades in one of the widely used new science curricula, the Science Curriculum Improvement Study (SCIS). There, young children learn that substances and objects interact according to their properties, and many children move rather quickly to the application of the idea to human behavior—they earn the right to observe that people interact, too. A little later they will discover that political entities, economies, art forms, and ecosystems all interact.

There are many others: the notions of *fact, legend, myth*, all from history in the first instance; the notions of *life, adaptation, development, cell*, all arising in biology; the notions of *ratio, set, correlation, geometric progression*, all from mathematics. Every subject in school that permits inquiry contributes its peculiar generalizable concepts.

Such terms as these, and many others, form the vocabulary of thought, of speculation, of problem-solving, and of interpretation. They offer ways of dealing with unsorted experience, and are the groundwork for a general education.

It is in the making of meaning that meaningfulness is to be found. It is not the events, but the interpretation of events, that constitute the core of meaningfulness in every field we offer in the secondary school. Let us examine what this generalization implies for several of the standard school offerings.

We will begin, not with the academic subjects, but with the technical offerings, for the problems are very severe in this field.

THE QUEST FOR MEANING AND POLYTECHNIC EDUCATION

The "vocational subjects," or what Conant called the "marketable skills," suffer from the prestige system of the comprehensive high school, as has been noted above and in many other places. The problem arises in part from the self-selections of students into these fields. Those who do not intend to prolong their educations (and they are in the majority) naturally seek the most explicit preparation for entrance into adult life they can find, and this appears to them in the form of vocational subjects—shop training, office practice, typing, and in some schools specific trades, such as printing, work with clothing and other fabrics, and so on. What is taught in such subjects are the entry skills for various occupations.

One of the difficulties with this offering is that it quickly becomes obsolete, as techniques change in the real world. High schools do not keep their equipment up-to-date because it is too expensive. Teachers drift out of touch with current technical developments in their teaching fields.

The polytechnic schools in Europe, including those in the socialist countries, have shown how this problem may be overcome. They deal not only with entry-level skills (which are indeed "marketable" for a short time), but also with the underlying concepts that give rise to the skills. They exchange some degree of "know how" for "know why." In other words, they deal with meanings. Students who learn to repair electronic devices learn more than a smattering of the theory, or the physics, underlying the devices. Students who learn to service automobiles learn the physics of the various systems that an automble employs. This is done at some length, in programs that have such explanatory knowledge as their principal objective.

What is proposed here is that technical education be considerably upgraded—that it deal with the sources and processes that underlie "marketable skills," and that these skills be offered only in the presence of such basic knowledge, as consequences of it. Much of the entry-level skill training should be left to be learned on the job; it is the entry-level skills that change most markedly with the invention of new equipment and production systems, and, ironically, it is those whose training has been focused on these entry skills who are most vulnerable to such changes.

Let us put it briefly: pride in work is a function of sources and processes, not of facts and findings alone or of technique alone. The pianist who tunes his own piano finds greater satisfaction in playing it than the one who knows nothing of how the instrument works. The famous European craftsman of earlier generations knew his craft in depth. Hence the excellent quality of his work. It is a depth knowledge of technical processes that we urge here as the core of technical education.

Let us take another underrated field—physical education. Contemporary leaders in the field call for fundamental study of body movement (kinesics) as the core of the field. Education in sports has not been considered adequate by these people for nearly a generation. Yet we continue to confuse physical education with athletics, with the result that high school graduates either seek further athletics (perhaps as professionals) or, as in the great majority of cases, drop the field altogether, considering it as mere meaningless play. As is true in the technical fields, if basic knowledge of body movement were the core of the subject, and if athletics were seen as a consequence of this basic knowledge, the likelihood that people would continue their interest in the way their bodies function would be increased, and the health of the nation would be improved. We do not continue interest in body movement, and public health statistics reflect it.

In the arts, at the high school level, the record is dismal. We continue to restrict the offering in the graphic and plastic arts to the talented; our offerings in poetry and drama are either nonexistent, or, again, offered by chance and chiefly to the talented. In music, the emphasis on public performance gets in the way of serious study of what is fundamental to the art—composition and analysis.

This sad state of affairs is not, and never was, universal. There have always been a small number of teachers of the arts who took their students into the knowledge of sources and processes. Some progress is being made at the elementary school level through the development of arts curriculum projects such as the Aesthetics Education Program at CEMREL (formerly Central Midwest Educational Laboratory, now CEMREL, Inc.) in St. Louis, and the programs supported by the JDR III Fund (so named after its founder, John D. Rockefeller III), plus the projects supported by some of the state Councils on the Arts. Such projects have so far had little effect on the high school arts offering, however, and art continues to be, in the main, an offering for the talented. The Arts, which could lie at the core of general education, which could have such a civilizing effect on masses of students, continue to be left to a small elite, who are viewed by the majority to be at play.

THE QUEST FOR MEANING AND ACADEMIC FIELDS

The academic subjects are more obviously susceptible to the approach advocated here, as has become clear during the past decades. To "think like a physicist," or a member of one of the other scientific disciplines, has been translated into concrete programs. The same is true of the newer social studies programs. It has always been true of the graphic and plastic arts programs at the secondary level, with their studio emphasis, though with the drawbacks mentioned above.

The academic programs least responsive to the approach through primary sources and processes have been English and foreign languages, which have remained comparatively untouched by the curriculum reforms of the fifties and sixties. Despite the emergence of linguistics as a potentially transforming influence on the teaching of writing, the writing program continues to be offered essentially as it has been, with an emphasis on form at the expense of substance. The same formal emphasis continues to dominate the teaching of literature, with the consequence that we have a nation of non-book-readers. "If you had as few bakeries as you have book stores," a Frenchman once said to me, "you would starve."

Yet in writing and in literature, more obviously than in other fields, one struggles with meaning. When one reads, one enters into an encounter with an author. What were the alternatives he had available? Why did he do what he did? What are the meanings of one's personal encounter with his work, how did he go about it, how might it be interpreted, on what basis should it be evaluated? These are the principal questions professional critics raise, and they could be made familiar to high school students. Alas, programs in literature that take the critic's discipline as the core of the search for meaning are very rare.

Essay writing is at the heart of the search for meaning. Most of the writing we see and take seriously is in this genre. But serious essay writing is only rarely required in school: the statement of a generalization, a consideration of its implications, the mustering of evidence for it and against it—all this gives way to purely formal considerations: paragraph structure, grammar, length. Good essay writing is difficult; if one grasps it, one can enter into meaningful encounters with influential essays, such as those that appear in the more serious magazines and newspapers. Those who have mastered the genre have an undue influence over the rest of us. Their influence would be reduced to its proper proportion if more of us had grasped the discipline, and could counter persuasive argument through analysis of the essayist's reasoning.

The most neglected literary form at every level is poetry. It is the poet who pushes language to its limits. It is through the reading and writing of poetry that one may approach real mastery of the verbal aspect of experience. There are exceptional high school English teachers who understand not only the formal aspects of poetry, but also its sensuous, technical, and expressive aspects. However, poetry is typically left to be mysteriously "appreciated," and is in large part ignored, except by the handful of those who read the slender books that appear, often at a loss to the publisher, and the occasional poems that are published in the more intellectual magazines. This need not be, but to change it would require a massive re-education of the nation's English teachers, and a massive readjustment of the prevailing public attitude toward poetry, especially as held by school administrators. The prospects are gloomy.

Except for such technical changes as the aural-oral approach, little has been done in the teaching of foreign language that makes the study of the field a quest for meaning. It remains an exercise in decoding. There are several reasons for this. For one, we do not allow enough time. It has been demonstrated repeatedly in Europe that even in the presence of neighboring countries and many residents and tourists who speak another tongue, it takes approximately six years to acquire reasonable facility in a foreign language, and much longer to acquire fluency. We try to do it, using essentially the same approaches used in Europe, in two or three years. Small wonder that most of our students acquire only a bare reading knowledge!

If we took the learning of a foreign language as part of the student's quest for meaning—if we took the sources and processes approach to teaching in this field—it would be transformed. To decode is to seek translation, not to seek meaning. To begin with the simplest sentences, and then to stress grammar and vocabulary, is to seek definitions, not significant interpretation. The trouble with "schoolboy French" is that it is trivial French. The entrance requirement for studying a foreign language, as things stand, is at least a year of meaningless activity. That is why it takes so long to gain fluency, and that is why the great majority of our students fail in their pursuit of foreign language.

The alternative is to begin, and to continue, with material that is importantly meaningful, leaving grammar to arise as it will. Such material could be from popular magazines that deal with matters both comprehensible and important to students; for some, it would begin with poetry; for some, with drama; for some, the newspapers. It would be "oral-aural," but that technique would be subordinated to the attempt to interpret what had been heard or read. The constant emphasis would be on fluency. Foreign language would be learned by students much as they learned their native language, but more intensively and with a greater emphasis on meaning appropriate to the student's maturity. The complaint of foreign language teachers, that they must spend the first year teaching their students English grammar, would become irrelevant.

THE QUEST FOR MEANING AND THE COMMUNITY AS EDUCATOR

There remains for our consideration the movement just now beginning to gather momentum: the use of the community as educator. Beginning with the Parkway experiment in Philadelphia and the Metro experiment in Chicago, continuing with the City as School experiment in New York and less publicized programs in other cities, an attempt is being made to confront students with the uninterpreted experience of real life, together with seminar-like attempts to interpret it. The experiences are various, including child care, participation in a political campaign, work in a broadcasting studio, work in the distributive occupations. Experience in these and the many other settings is incidental in character; to give it systematic meaning, teachers are leading students to make interpretations of it, to seek connections between academic experience and the actual world, and (very importantly) to "try on" such experience for its career possibilities. As these programs mature, one can imagine that the school walls will become more permeable to the community, and that working with students, both in and out of school, will come to be seen as a regular part of the working life of adults. If that is achieved, the view of education as a lifelong affair will seem only a short step further.

Summary

We have considered here three types of knowledge that are offered in the secondary school: knowledge of facts and findings, knowledge of sources and processes, and knowledge of technique. An attempt has been made to place each of these types of knowledge in a reasonable relationship with the others. The confusion between technique and facts and findings, and the subordination of knowledge of sources and processes, has been seen to reduce the meaningfulness of what is offered in the secondary school.

Since knowledge of sources and processes incorporates the other two types of knowledge, it has been argued that this type of knowledge should be sought in all the offerings at the secondary school level, including the emerging community-as-educator approach, in which the community and its institutions are used as educational resources.

The key to the present argument is that high school students, like all other people, demand that their activity have meaning. If they cannot see the meaning, they will withdraw (psychologically or physically) or make up meanings for it—such as the race for grades or game-playing with teachers. Much of the disaffiliation of students that plagues high school teachers arises from this failure to approach high school teaching as a quest for meaning. Yet many secondary school teachers succeed in doing so. In their example lies our hope for a better secondary school future.

CHAPTER VII

Where Should Learning Take Place?

VERNON H. SMITH AND ROBERT D. BARR

Where should learning take place? On an airstrip? At an aquarium?
In an artist's studio? In a computer center? At a drug crisis center? In a
hospital? In a hotel? At a medical center? In a museum? In a national
monument? In an office building? At a Playboy Club? In a railroad
station? On a showboat? In a storefront? In a TV studio? At a theater?
In a Victorian mansion? In a warehouse? On wheels? At a zoo? These
are a few of the settings for alternative schools and action-learning
programs currently in operation.

Introduction: Standardization vs. Diversification

Any list of events that affected, and are still affecting, secondary
education during the past quarter of a century would have to include
the National Science Foundation Act (1950); the Supreme Court decision in *Brown vs. the Board of Education of Topeka* (1954); the con-
solidation of school districts from over 100,000 at the end of World
War II to fewer than 20,000 today; the National Defense Education
Act (1958); the Conant report, *The American High School Today*
(1959), which urged the improvement of programs for the academically talented, supported the concept of the comprehensive high school,
and suggested the graduating class of at least one hundred as the
minimum for effective high school size; the Bruner report, *The Process
of Education* (1960), which was concerned with the development of
cognitive skills through new curricula; the national curriculum projects of the 1960s; the Elementary and Secondary Education Act
(1965); the establishment of the National Foundation for the Arts and
the Humanities (1965); and the performance-accountability movement of the late 1960s, including National Assessment. One of the
cumulative results of all these efforts was the increasing standardization of American secondary schools.

That major unsolved problems in secondary schools remained while standardization increased is obvious to lay persons and professional educators. For instance, each year for more than fifteen years (1958-74) over one million youth have dropped out of school before high school graduation.[1] This situation is projected to continue at least through 1980, indicating that secondary education of all American youth is still far from a reality.

Concern about standardization and about the problems that it had created grew in recent years. There was a growing demand for local community control of schools, particularly in large school systems. There was an increasing concern that the emphasis on academic and cognitive development was resulting in neglect of other areas of development, particularly the affective (emotional), the moral, and the social. Some laymen and educators felt that the schools—buildings, regulations, and procedures—were increasingly based on industrial-technological models that failed to provide settings conducive to learning and growth. Others objected to the monolithic structure of public education, in which children and youth were typically assigned to one school without choice. If the psychology of learning indicates that different people learn in different ways and at different times, why, they asked, are all the children in one neighborhood assigned to one school and then segregated by age within that school?

By the late 1960s there were sporadic reactions to standardization efforts: an increased interest in small nonpublic schools—free schools, freedom schools, communal schools, and in some parts of the country, white academies; a move toward open education sparked by the success of British infant schools and concentrated largely but not exclusively at the elementary level; a community school movement in some cities; the development of optional alternative public schools; and an increase in out-of-school learning experiences (action-learning) as an integral part of secondary education. All of these reactions, but particularly the last two, raise the issue: Where should learning take place? This chapter will focus on the emerging pluralism in schools, settings, and experiences in secondary education.

In 1973, more than a decade after the publication of *The American*

1. National Center for Educational Statistics, "Estimated Fall Enrollment in Fifth Grade Compared with High School Graduates Eight Years Later: United States, 1950-58 to 1974-82" (Washington, D.C.: U.S. Office of Education, Revised April 1, 1973), p. 1.

High School Today,[2] three national reports on secondary education appeared: *The Greening of the High School,*[3] *The Reform of Secondary Education,*[4] and *Youth: Transition to Adulthood.*[5] Another was prepared in 1974: "The Report of the National Panel on High Schools and Adolescent Education."[6] These four reports have several common elements. They all differ dramatically from Conant's 1959 report. Where Conant advocated comprehensiveness and the strengthening of the academic curriculum, these reports of the 1970s advocate diversity, pluralism, and more attention to the total development of all youth— emotional development, the development of social responsibility, and vocational (or career) preparation, as well as cognitive and academic development. All four reports are critical of the ways that secondary schools isolate youth from the world outside the school and of the ways that the schools segregate youth from adults and from other school age groups.

All four reports indicate the need for alternative schools, settings, and programs, and the need for action-learning experiences outside of schools but still as integral parts of secondary education. The National Commission on the Reform of Secondary Education urges that "Each district should provide a broad range of alternative schools and programs so that every student will have meaningful options available to him."[7] The Panel on Youth of the President's Science Advisory Committee states that "diversity and plurality of paths to adulthood are important for the youth of any society,"[8] and advocates placing

2. James B. Conant, *The American High School Today* (New York: McGraw-Hill, 1959).

3. Ruth Weinstock, *The Greening of the High School* (New York: Educational Facilities Laboratories, 1973).

4. B. Frank Brown (Chairman), National Commission on the Reform of Secondary Education, *The Reform of Secondary Education: A Report to the Public and the Profession* (New York: McGraw-Hill, 1973)

5. James S. Coleman (Chairman), *Youth: Transition to Adulthood*, Report of the Panel on Youth, President's Science Advisory Committee (Washington, D.C.: U. S. Government Printing Office, 1973).

6. John Henry Martin, "Chairman's Digest," Panel on High Schools and Adolescent Education, Office of Education, mimeographed (Washington, D.C.: U. S. Department of Health, Education, and Welfare, April 1974).

7. Brown, *The Reform of Secondary Education*, p. 109.

8. Coleman, *Youth: Transition to Adulthood*, pp. 145-46.

youth in different roles from the student role, which will involve "learning through action and experience, not by being taught."[9]

The development of alternative public schools and the development of action-learning programs are efforts to answer the questions: Where should learning take place? What is the optimal size for the secondary school? What is the role of the schools in the transition from youth to adulthood? Alternative schools and action-learning programs differ significantly from previous reform efforts. They are not intended to replace conventional education or the standard secondary school. They are available by choice for those families, those teachers, and those administrators who want different learning environments and different learning experiences. Since they are available by choice, they are not compulsory for all youth, and they do not require consensus within the community.

The development of alternative public schools and the development of action-learning experiences are based on three simple concepts: (1) that students, parents, and teachers should have choices among learning environments and learning experiences; (2) that different people learn in different ways; and (3) that schools should not be isolated from the "real" world outside.

Alternative Schools and Settings

The alternative public school movement started with Philadelphia's Parkway Program in 1969. Parkway was probably the first secondary school designed to be available by option to every student in its community and designed to use the total community, the city of Philadelphia, as a learning environment. The optional public school caught on quickly. By 1974-75, five years after Parkway's inauguration, there were at least a dozen types of alternative public schools operating in several thousand communities and enrolling at least half a million students, elementary and secondary.

The optional alternative public school seems to be an educational "idea whose time has come." In 1971 Neil Postman wrote, "All of the reforms that will take place in education in the next decade will have their origins in the alternative school movement."[10] In 1973, Mario

9. Ibid., p. 146.

10. Neil Postman, "Alternative Education in the Seventies," *The Last Supplement to the Whole Earth Catalog* (March 1971): 41.

Fantini said, "The development of public schools of choice is the only major movement in American education today."[11]

In 1973 the Fifth Annual Gallup Poll of Public Attitudes Toward Education reported almost two-thirds of the respondents favored alternative schools. "People in cities of medium size seem particularly favorable to the alternative schools idea."[12] Over 60 percent of the parents and over 60 percent of the adults with no children in the schools and 80 percent of the professional educators responding favored alternative schools.[13]

In 1974 after at least seven years of funding public and nonpublic alternative schools, the Ford Foundation produced a report on alternative schools with this final statement: "The point has been made that alternatives are necessary and can work educationally. Whether they continue and multiply now depends more on school systems' own initiatives than on external assistance."[14]

And in 1974 the North Central Association of Colleges and Schools published standards for the approval of optional schools with this introduction:

In recent years the concept of educational choice (optional schools, alternative schools—call them what you will) has penetrated deeply into the American system of education. It seems likely that in the foreseeable future many different types of schools will exist side by side within the total educational structure, each designed to meet a different set of specified learning and living needs of young people. These schools will be complementary in effort and thrust, helping American education redeem its long-term commitment to the fullest education of every child. . . . Widespread educational options—the coexistence of many types of alternative schools and programs—should strengthen American education as a whole.[15]

11. Mario D. Fantini, in a speech at Vancouver, B.C., August 21, 1973.

12. Stanley Elam, ed., *The Gallup Polls of Attitudes Toward Education 1969-73* (Bloomington, Ind.: Phi Delta Kappa, 1973), p. 175.

13. Ibid., p. 164.

14. *Matters of Choice: A Ford Foundation Report on Alternative Schools* (New York: The Ford Foundation, 1974), p. 35.

15. *Policies and Standards for the Approval of Optional Schools and Special Function Schools 1974-1975* (Chicago: North Central Association of Colleges and Schools, 1974), p. 1.

ALTERNATIVE SCHOOLS:
WHAT ARE THEY? WHERE ARE THEY?

An optional public school is usually developed in response to some perceived educational need within its community. As a result, every alternative school is unique in its program, in its setting, or in its relationship to the community outside the school. But there are some common types into which the majority of optional alternative public schools would fit.

Open schools. Open schools provide individualized learning experiences organized around interest or resource centers throughout the building. Interest in open education has been growing because of its popularity in Great Britain and because of recent developments in the psychology of learning, including humanistic psychology.

The St. Paul Open School, housed in a refurbished warehouse, enrolls over 500 students, kindergarten through grade twelve. The school is organized around seven learning and resource areas: art, music-drama, humanities, math-science, industrial arts, home economics, and physical education. Each area has a library-resource center, space for quiet study, space for group and individual projects, and large open spaces.

The Brown School started in the former Brown Hotel in downtown Louisville in 1972, then moved into the remodeled Brown Office Building next door. The school has an enrollment of 400 students in grades three through twelve. The Brown school is an open multicultural school with its student population evenly divided between blacks and whites.

Both the Brown School in Louisville and the St. Paul Open School serve as voluntary integration models within their communities. Both have long waiting lists of applicants, indicating that these schools and this form of voluntary integration are well accepted by their communities.

Schools-without-walls. Schools-without-walls provide learning experiences throughout the community and much interaction between the school and the community so that the conventional barriers between the school and the community are broken down.

The Chicago High School for Metropolitan Studies (Metro) opened in February, 1970, just a few months after Philadelphia's Parkway Program. Metro's 350 students in grades nine through twelve are chosen by lottery to reflect the ethnic, racial, and socioeconomic makeup of the city; each year there are hundreds more applicants than there are spaces available. Metro's headquarters is housed on two floors of a downtown office building, but students have choices among over a hundred elective courses offered all over downtown Chicago. A student might select Television Production at NBC, Creative Writing at Playboy, Marine Biology at the Shedd Aquarium, or Animal and Human Behavior at the Lincoln Park Zoo.

Community High School in Ann Arbor has its headquarters in a fifty-year-old former elementary school. Over 400 students in grades nine through twelve are enrolled in over 300 courses out in the community. Conventional courses meet in the school building. Students who want courses not offered at Community High may enroll for these in other Ann Arbor high schools. Hourly shuttle buses transport Community High students throughout the community.

Sometimes there is confusion over open schools, schools-without-walls, and the *open space plan*, an architectural concept referring to school buildings without, or with very few, interior walls, providing large open spaces for flexible use. While some open schools, including those described in St. Paul and Louisville, do operate in open space buildings, many do not. Open education can be implemented in a traditional school building by rearranging facilities to make conventional classroom areas into resource centers.

Learning centers. Learning centers provide a concentration of resources in one location available to all students in the community. Some learning centers are complete alternative schools. Others provide learning experiences for part of the student's day or part of the school year. Historically, the vocational or technical high school with its special courses and special equipment was an early form of the learning center.

The St. Paul Public Schools have developed a network of learning centers that contribute to the voluntary integration of St. Paul students of varied racial, ethnic, and social class backgrounds. These include a New City School Learning Center (senior high), the Junior and Senior High School Performing Arts Learning Center, the Junior High Automotive Transportation Learning Center, plus six elementary learning centers. All students are assigned to their home schools for basic education. Students may elect to spend part of the school day (usually a half day) during one quarter of the school year (nine weeks) in one of the learning centers. Voluntary participation in this program is above 90 percent. All students are bussed from the home schools to the learning centers.

The Resource Center for Environmental Education (TREE) is in the Federal Hall National Monument in New York City, jointly sponsored by the Learning Cooperative of the Board of Education, the National Parks Service, and Museums Collaborative, Inc. Students are released from their regular schools one day per week to attend environmental workshops at the Center, where they study the natural and man-made environment of New York City.

Magnet schools. Magnet schools provide opportunities for students to specialize in depth in a particular interest area. Originally, some magnet schools were elite and open to very few students in a community. For instance, the Bronx High School of Science in New York City accepted only the top science students in the city. Today many magnet schools are available by choice to those students who are interested.

Houston has two magnet schools in operation: the High School for the Performing and Visual Arts and the High School for the Health Professions. The high school for the arts had its first graduating class in 1974 and had more National Merit Scholarship finalists per capita than any other Houston high school. The High School for the Health Professions is part of the Texas Medical Center in Houston. The school was founded by the Houston Public Schools and the Baylor College of Medicine "to help relieve the critical shortage of health personnel in Texas and to offer Houston students an alternative education."[16]

Educational parks. Educational parks provide a variety of programs and sometimes several different schools on one location, part or all of which may be available by choice to all of the students within the community. While most alternative public schools tend to be smaller than their conventional counterparts, the educational park is an exception. It usually enrolls a large number of students and is frequently the community's largest educational facility.

The Skyline Center in Dallas, a fourteen-acre building complex on

16. "Fostering a Healthy Interest," *Nation's Schools and Colleges* 1 (September 1974): 17.

an eighty-acre campus, is open to students from any high school in Dallas. The Center has three main divisions: Skyline High School, the Career Development Center, and the Center for Community Services. The Skyline Center provides learning facilities and experiences which would not be feasible in every high school—an aircraft hangar and airstrip, a computer center, and courses in Greek and Swahili.

Grand Rapids' Educational Park started in 1967 with federal funds, but is now supported by the regular budget of the school district. It combines the educational park concept with the school-without-walls, the school-within-a-school, and the learning center. Classes meet at the Park, in a senior high school, in a junior college, in an art museum, in a civic theater, and throughout the community. Over 1500 students are enrolled, most of them part-time juniors and seniors from the other high schools in the community. It too offers aviation and Swahili, plus over forty other courses and independent study experiences not available in the regular high schools.

Continuation schools. Continuation schools provide programs for students whose education in conventional schools has been, or might be, interrupted. They are one of the oldest forms of alternative public schools. After the Civil War and on into the first part of this century, some cities developed evening high schools for children and youth who were full-time workers in factories and for adults who had not completed high school.

Today's "dropout centers" and "street academies" are usually small schools housed in vacant stores or houses in locations that make them convenient for students who have dropped out of school and wish to resume their education but not to return to the conventional school. A "re-entry program" may be just an office somewhere in the community where a counselor is available to aid dropouts who wish to return to the regular school. "Pregnancy-maternity centers" provide continuing education for pregnant school-age girls who do not wish to remain in their regular schools. Each year nearly a quarter of a million school-age girls, married and unmarried, become pregnant. At present few school districts provide for their continuing education. Directors of pregnancy-maternity centers report a decrease in pregnancies among girls over fifteen and an increase in pregnancies among girls age eleven to fifteen.

The Metropolitan Youth Education Center with four locations in Denver and nearby Jefferson County has served over 20,000 students, all dropouts, since it opened in the fall of 1964. Graduates from Metro have entered colleges throughout the country.

Park School in Grand Rapids serves pregnant girls from several school districts in Kent County, Michigan. The school, located in a hospital, provides opportunities to continue regular course work plus additional courses in child care and nutrition. At times when girls are unable to attend school, homebound instruction is provided. Nearly 200 girls choose to attend Park School each year.

Multicultural schools. Multicultural schools provide a curriculum based on cultural pluralism and emphasize ethnic and racial awareness. They usually serve a student body from various racial and ethnic backgrounds. Some bilingual schools would fit in this category.

Agora is a multicultural high school in Berkeley with an enrollment of 125 students in grades ten through twelve, about one-third black, one-third Chicano, and one-third white. Multicultural events involving all students are scheduled throughout the year. The curriculum provides traditional subjects, multicultural subjects, and other innovations, including Harlem Renaissance, Chicano Studies, Black Seminar, Modern and Afro Dance, Math Games, Black Drama, American Folklore, Women's Studies, Chess, Mexican Folk Dance, International Cooking, and Human Awareness.

Environmental schools. Environmental schools provide a curriculum and learning experiences focused on the environment and environmental concerns. Instead of separate basic subjects, the fields of mathematics, English, social studies, and science may be integrated as they relate to specific environmental projects.

The Zoo School in Grand Rapids is an environmental school for sixth graders that meets all year in space provided at the John Ball Zoo. The students study the environment on the zoo grounds and throughout the community. The program, available by choice, is also designed to help the students make the transition from elementary school to junior high school.

Free schools. Free school is a term that has been used to describe a variety of small nonpublic schools, but there are also free schools within public education. The free school provides opportunities for students and teachers to determine and plan the curriculum and learning experiences with freedom from conventional constraints. In Minneapolis the Southeast Free School started in a church basement. The West Philadelphia Community Free School, a model for public alternative school systems (PASS),[17] has several locations in former residences and other available space throughout the community, with no more than 200 students per house. This high school program is nongraded and individualized with basic courses offered in the houses and with electives throughout the community.

Schools-within-schools, satellite schools, and mini-schools. Any of the various types of alternative schools described above could be found as schools-within-schools or as satellite schools. A school-within-a-school might be housed in a few classrooms, a wing, or a separate floor of a conventional building. A satellite school is at a separate location but maintains administrative ties to the larger "home school." The term mini-school is sometimes used for schools-within-schools, satellite schools, or learning centers.

Cooperatively developed alternative schools. Another approach to the alternative school is the school that is cooperatively developed and operated by several nearby school districts. In Hartford (Conn.), Philadelphia, and Kent County, Michigan, several school districts have joined to develop alternative schools.

Shanti (a Hindi word meaning "the peace that surpasses all understanding"), a school-without-walls serving the greater Hartford region, is cooperatively supported by the Hartford Board of Education and school boards in seven surrounding districts. Shanti, with an enrollment of 100 students, is housed in part of Hartford's former railroad station. Gene Mulcahy, director, explained that the school chose the station "because it is an exciting, romantic and centrally-located facility."[18]

The complex of alternative schools. The complex has several optional alternative schools housed together in one building, and usually under one administration. Haaren High School in New York City; Quincy II in Quincy, Illinois; and New School in Cleveland Heights, Ohio, are high schools which consist of a number of alternative schools or schools-within-schools. The conventional program may or may not exist as one of the alternatives. The impetus for this diversification within the large high school has come primarily from a dissatisfaction

17. Aase Eriksen and Joseph Gantz, *Partnership in Urban Education: An Alternative School* (Midland, Michigan: Pendell, 1974), p. 5.

18. Robert Bickford, *Hartford's Union Station and Union Place* (Hartford, Connecticut: Knox Parks Foundation, 1974), p. 11.

with the large bureaucratic organizational structure of the comprehensive high school. Some secondary educators feel that the smaller, simpler structure of the schools-within-a-school provides an atmosphere more conducive to learning and teaching.

This classification of alternative schools is meant to be illustrative but not exhaustive. There are certainly other types of alternative schools in existence. For instance, we know of one optional public school based on behavior modification and of two individualized continuous progress elementary schools. Recently a few fundamental elementary schools have been opened because some parents felt that conventional schools had gotten too far away from "the basics," and they demanded this option.

WHAT ARE THE CHARACTERISTICS OF ALTERNATIVE PUBLIC SCHOOLS?

While each alternative public school has been developed in response to specific needs within its community, most of these optional public schools have common characteristics:

1. As previously stated, the school provides an option for students, parents, and teachers. Usually the choice is open to all, but there must be a choice for some. Consequently, the alternative public school has a voluntary clientele.

2. The school population reflects the ethnic, racial, and socioeconomic makeup of the entire community.

3. The school has as its reason for existence a commitment to be more responsive to some perceived educational need than the conventional secondary schools are.

4. The school usually has more comprehensive goals and objectives than its conventional counterpart. While alternative schools are concerned with developing basic skills and preparing students for college and vocations, they are also concerned with improving self-concepts; developing individual talent, creativity, and uniqueness; understanding and encouraging cultural plurality and diversity; and preparing students for various roles in society, such as consumer, voter, critic, parent, and spouse.

5. The school is more flexible, and therefore, more responsive to planned evolution and change. Since the alternatives are being developed in the age of

accountability, they rely on feedback and formative evaluation in developing and modifying curricula and programs.

6. The school is usually smaller than the comprehensive secondary school. The median enrollment in alternative public schools is under 200.

7. Because they are smaller, alternatives tend to have fewer rules and fewer bureaucratic constraints on students and teachers.

8. The school provides students and teachers with opportunities to participate in decisionmaking on the school's program and on their individual roles within the school. The result is both more choice and more responsibility for each individual.

Some alternative schools do not have all of these characteristics. Many conventional schools have some of these characteristics. But, in general, these characteristics indicate that the optional alternative secondary schools do differ in significant ways from their conventional counterparts.

The total impact of the optional schools on the school system is even more significant than the different characteristics we have pointed out. Each optional school, by being responsive to particular learning needs, helps to create a total school system that is more responsive to the needs of its community. The ultimate goal within any community is to provide every family with meaningful educational choices. When the school district provides multiple options, as in Berkeley, Grand Rapids, and Minneapolis, the conventional school becomes one of the options and benefits by a clientele that comes by choice rather than by compulsion.

WHAT ARE THE RESULTS?

Today's comprehensive secondary school evolved gradually over a period of more than a hundred years. The optional alternative public schools are new on the scene, and their diverse character will probably change constantly as they develop in the next quarter of the century. Perhaps it is premature to suggest results, but here are some observations on developments to date.

Both students and teachers report that the optional schools are more "humane" than the conventional secondary school that they attended or taught in previously. At least part of this feeling is attributable to the smaller size of the alternative school. Most alternative schools have fewer than 200 students. Most of these teachers and students have come from schools that enrolled over a thousand students. Inhumaneness may be related to size. Certainly a school for several thousand must have more rules and constraints than a school for one hundred. In many optional schools, students and teachers know everyone in the school by name.

Both teachers and administrators report that students and their parents are more loyal to, and more cooperative with, a school that they themselves have chosen. Teachers prefer to choose their schools too. Administrators and teachers report a preference for working with a student population that is voluntary rather than compulsory.

In those places where alternative schools have been in operation for a few years, there is usually a waiting list of applicants. In some communities, hundreds and even thousands of students apply for the alternative schools each year, indicating a real community acceptance of the optional school.

Most alternative public schools have been subjected to some form of evaluation, usually the same modes of evaluation used in the conventional high schools in the same school district.

How do the students who attend alternative schools fare? Where standard measures of achievement such as test scores and college admission are applicable, they show that alternative school students perform at least as well as their counterparts in traditional school programs, and usually better. Attendance rates almost without exception exceed those in regular schools.[19]

Most alternative high schools send a higher proportion of their graduates on to college than the regular high schools in the same district. After Parkway's first two classes had graduated, John Bremer, then the director, reported, "Every student who had applied to college had been accepted, most of them by their first choice."[20]

Whether the factors involved are humaneness, size, or the different environment, principals of alternative high schools report less absence, less truancy, and less vandalism than conventional high schools in the same districts.

19. *Matters of Choice*, p. 6.

20. John Bremer and Michael von Moschzisker, *The School Without Walls* (New York: Holt, Rinehart & Winston, 1971), p. 178.

Action-Learning

THE NEED FOR ACTION-LEARNING

Earlier in this chapter four national reports were identified that recommend directions for change in public secondary education during the years immediately ahead. All of these reports recommended the development of action-learning opportunities to complement existing public school programs. In addition to the reports already noted, the National Association of Secondary School Principals has also become increasingly active in this area. In 1972, NASSP published a conference report entitled *American Youth in the Mid-Seventies*, which focused on action-learning.[21] More recently NASSP held a Wingspread Conference on action-learning and published a report.[22] The National Commission on Resources for Youth was organized to encourage the development of action-learning programs and to disseminate information on exemplary programs.

The recommendations for action-learning programs have grown out of a number of common concerns about public education, such as the following:

1. James Coleman has argued that the information-rich environment of the contemporary multimedia society has rendered the "information-giving" function of schools obsolete.[23] Many others now urge that the role of schools must be redefined in order to utilize the resources of the community.

2. Far from assisting youth in the process of moving toward maturity and adulthood, schools may be retarding this process. Some observers believe that schools invariably give students little responsibility and few opportunities for making decisions, and that secondary schools continue to deal with youth as irresponsible children. Yet, simultaneously, youth has changed in a dramatic fashion. Society in fact seems to be "dejuvenilizing" our youth.[24]

21. *American Youth in the Mid-Seventies*, Conference Report of the National Committee on Secondary Education of the National Association of Secondary School Principals, November 30—December 1, 1972 (Reston, Va.: National Association of Secondary School Principals, 1972).

22. "Action-Learning," *Bulletin of the National Association of Secondary School Principals* 58 (November 1974): 1-80.

23. James S. Coleman, "The Children Have Outgrown The Schools," *National Elementary Principal* 52 (October 1972): 16-21.

24. For an interesting recommendation for action-learning as a method of assisting youth in their transition to adulthood, see Maurice Gibbons, "The Australian

3. Schools today have a tendency to isolate youth and increasingly separate them from significant contact with older adults, other than parents and teachers. Some concerned critics believe that schools have contributed to the "decoupling" of the generations and acted as "social aging vats."

4. In the past it has been assumed that all formal education should take place in a single institution, the school. Today it is recognized that there are many different kinds of learning. Each may suggest, or even require, a particular setting. Some require classrooms, but not all.

5. The social needs of our communities are becoming increasingly acute; crisis situations grow out of our major dilemmas. Many would argue we can no longer permit the schools to segregate the rich resources of youth and energy from the needs of the day. Neil Postman has put it this way:

America's towns and cities need all the help they can get, and, in my opinion, most of them can no longer afford to lock up their youth in school buildings for twelve years. It is clear that adults need help in creating livable communities, and the great curriculum question of the seventies is: How can we use the energy, intelligence, and idealism of the young for purposes of social reconstruction?[25]

ACTION-LEARNING PROGRAMS

A growing number of public schools throughout the country have already organized action-learning programs. In some instances it has been young people themselves who have initiated the programs outside the school day.[26]

Learning in the great outdoors. The utilization of a natural setting as a learning environment has grown rapidly in recent years. School districts across the country are beginning to utilize the geographical assets of their areas through hiking, back-packing, bicycling, canoeing,

---

Walkabout: A Model for Transition to Adulthood," *Phi Delta Kappan* 55 (May 1974): 596-602.

25. Neil Postman, "The Ecology of Learning," *English Journal* 63 (April 1974): 63. For a proposal for a national conscription for all youth to perform action-learning as a public service, see Theodore Sizer, *Places for Learning, Places For Joy* (Cambridge, Massachusetts: Harvard University Press, 1973), pp. 113-114.

26. An interesting proposal concerning action-learning is made by Richard Graham, "Youth and Experiential Learning," in *Youth*, Seventy-fourth Yearbook of the National Society for the Study of Education, Part I (Chicago: Distributed by the University of Chicago Press, 1975). In this chapter Graham seeks to correlate various types of work experience with the stages of moral development defined by Lawrence Kohlberg.

spelunking, and camping experiences. Many of the programs are being developed for students who have not succeeded in academic learning and traditional classrooms. The programs have also attempted to use the cultural neutrality of the outdoor environment as an ideal place for confronting and reducing racial antagonisms.

A wilderness program was developed at Northwestern Junior High School in Battle Creek, Michigan, in 1972-73 to alleviate racial and class conflicts among students. The program was not only endorsed enthusiastically by students, teachers, and parents; the school also experienced a 75 percent decrease in discipline referrals of a racial nature.

The Brown School in Louisville, Kentucky, is a public school alternative with an equal racial mix of black and white students on the basis of voluntary enrollment. Finding that school classrooms were not the best place to try to deal with racial antagonism, the school staff developed a weekend outdoor camping program, especially designed to confront black and white students with entirely new situations. Students and staff found the experience to be extremely productive in the area of racial understanding. So the students developed their own proposal for a school camp and are approaching foundations in a search for funds.

The Cambridge Pilot School in Massachusetts taught inner-city youth who were lacking in academic skills the techniques of outdoor education and then used these students as guides and teachers for more academically able students. The self-concepts of the target students improved.

In Grand Rapids, Michigan, a week-long camp-out on Isle Royal culminates a series of weekend camping experiences. The camp-out serves as an external reward which encourages students to work on basic educational skills in the school's behavior modification program. Thus the camping program is designed to motivate academic learning.

Probably the best known outdoor education program is Outward Bound, with headquarters in Denver, Colorado. Outward Bound has assisted schools throughout the country to develop programs that involve both students and teachers in outdoor situations where they are faced with seemingly impossible tasks that call upon the maximum in personal reserves and individual perseverance.

Learning in unfamiliar cultures. A number of schools have

developed action-learning programs that immerse school age youth in cultures different from their own. Students at East High School in Denver have harvested beets with migrant workers, worked in welfare agencies, served food in soup lines, spent weekends on a Navajo reservation, lived with Mexican families, and collected garbage with city sanitation workers. All such activities are recognized with high school social studies credit. In Lincoln-Sudsbury Regional High School near Boston, students lived for five weeks with black inner-city families while working in social agencies. The inner-city experience was followed by five weeks in remote rural settings in Connecticut and Nova Scotia where they worked on farms, in dairies, at maple syrup factories, and at organic food cooperatives.

Learning in service agencies. One of the most practical and potentially valuable action-learning experiences involves the use of secondary school students as volunteers in various community agencies and programs. Students volunteer their time and energy to work in hospitals, homes for the aged, drug centers, mental health clinics, and other social agencies. Some students have even organized their own agencies and offer services within their communities. In Adams City High School in Colorado, students leave school to work as tutors and teachers for second and third graders, thus providing elementary teachers with needed assistance. The Yorkville Youth Council in New York City is another program that uses adolescents as teachers and tutors. Student volunteers in Marion, Indiana, have become an important part of the staff at the local Veteran's Administration hospital.

A number of drug programs throughout the country use high school students as counselors; some of these programs have been planned, developed and are operated completely by high school age students. The National Commission on Resources for Youth, Inc. has identified four exemplary crisis drug centers utilizing student volunteers.[27] Project Community in Berkeley, California, attempting to fill the need left by "a faltering church and seriously ailing school," has programs of human growth and understanding, and cross-age-group learning programs. "Number Nine" in New Haven, Connecticut, is a crisis center that was designed, initiated, and implemented by youth. "Encounter" in New York City is a nonresidential drug center

---

27. Mildred McClosky with Peter Kleinbard, *Youth Into Adults: Nine Selected Youth Programs* (New York: National Commission on Resources for Youth, Inc., 1974).

designed to help people to cope and survive, despite easy availability of drugs on neighborhood corners. Another program in New York is "Compass," a residential drug program. All of these programs, and many more like them, represent efforts of today's youth to deal with their problems by helping one another.

Perhaps one of the most dramatic examples of the potentiality of youth volunteers was provided by the Community Medical Corps, organized in the Bronx of New York City. In the early 1970s, a group of medical students recruited 110 high school students from 14 to 17 years of age to assist in screening children in local tenements for traces of lead poisoning. The students were put through a rigorous orientation session, given white medical jackets, and put to work canvassing neighborhoods and conducting blood tests. By the end of a summer program, the students had seen over 3,000 children and taken over 2,000 blood samples. Over 2 percent of the children tested were found to have dangerously high levels of lead poisoning. The following was written about the program:

High school age youngsters had proven that they could be depended upon to do difficult work. Many of them had come into the program originally with an awe of doctors and what they did. By the end of the summer, the directors reported, "We had kids telling the doctors what to do. They had assisted with blood taking hundreds of times and knew the job as well or better than any doctor." The kids who worked here, all of the 110 kids, know more about lead poisoning than most doctors.[28]

As a result of the program, many students are now determined to become nurses, teachers, social workers, and doctors. The program exemplifies the fact that adolescents thrive on significant, meaningful work.

Learning in the professional community. Internship programs have proven to be one of the most popular action-learning experiences. While many internship programs have a career or vocational emphasis, a large number of such programs emphasize social and academic areas. Students are moving into the professional community, working with leaders in private business, government, social agencies, cultural centers, and serving just about anywhere that professional men and women are at work. A student from Herricks High School in New

28. Ibid., p. 91.

York City worked for one day each week at a research center studying with a doctor researching formations in the blood. In Webster Groves, Missouri, high school students work half-days in offices throughout the city and change positions three or four times each school year. In Grand Rapids, Michigan, students work in local courtrooms and government offices and even in mortuaries. Often these internship experiences are the core learning experience for youth. They usually take place during eleventh or twelfth grade, and usually run for an entire semester. The Brown School in Louisville has developed a program where students can complete all their academic requirements by the end of the eleventh grade. This enables interested seniors to spend a year full-time in one or more internship positions.

While an increasing number of schools of all kinds are establishing social internships in their local communities, there are two national programs that have been organized to assist local schools in developing effective internship programs. Located in New York, the Executive High School Internship Program has developed a network of school districts in six states which participate in student internship programs. The program enables juniors and seniors to take one-semester sabbaticals from their regular studies to serve as special assistants to federal commissioners, judges, museum curators, and other senior executives. The students spend four days per week in the internship, and plan and conduct weekly seminars. None of the participants is paid, but all receive credit. A similar organization that offers schools assistance in establishing internships is Dynamy, Inc., located in Worcester, Massachusetts.

Learning from the past. A number of schools have involved secondary students in action-learning projects that focus on preserving local history and folklore, reconstructing past cultures, or recording oral history. Students in the Atlanta Public Schools' Independent Study Program spend three months away from school and gain full credit for work at an archeological dig preserving remnants of an ancient Indian culture. In Brooklyn, New York, students attempted to refute historians' contentions that residents of Weeksville, a black community in nineteenth century New York, were "drunken, shiftless, and lived in shacks." Students worked in the midst of the demolition that preceded a Model City construction. They searched through foundations, in cisterns, wells and attics, behind mantelpieces, and between walls, looking for evidence of the Weeksville community. Material the students discovered indicated that many members of the black community lived in permanent and comfortable homes, dressed well, read extensively, and attended school. Some of the new information that the students found has been used by *Encyclopaedia Britannica.*

In Grand Rapids, Michigan, a group of high school students investigated, wrote, and did the layout on a book about their city, which was published and adopted by the public schools as a textbook.

In Rabum Gap, Georgia, an English teacher encouraged students to go on collecting tours through Appalachia, gathering knowledge about the folklore and culture of the area. The students recorded how to build log cabins, how to weave baskets, how to make traps and so on. The student activities have attracted such high interest that their findings are now recorded in a number of major publications under the title of *Foxfire.*[29] Similar enterprises have also been developed by Alaskan students, Sioux Indians, Flathead Indians, Navajo Indians, and high school students in several states, all of whom started their own publications focusing on local folklore and culture.

Learning in construction and urban renewal projects. Students have also entered into action-learning projects designed not only to be financially rewarding, but also to be focused on beautifying and renewing their communities. In Denver, Colorado, a group called "Creative Urban Living" has negotiated contracts totalling more than a quarter of a million dollars to build and refurbish houses, replace several blocks of city sidewalks, and construct several mini-parks for the city. The students keep records on banking, payrolls, bills, loans, and insurance, and even publish a newsletter. In Canton, Ohio, high school students have worked for twelve years in a Candlelight Youth Corps, renovating houses of the handicapped, the elderly, and the blind. Students also built a house and two duplexes and sold all three. Similar construction projects have been formed in Mollala, Oregon, in LaPuente, California, in Indianapolis, Indiana, and in many other school districts throughout the country.

In Minnesota, a group called Teen Corps organized 350 teenagers to provide volunteer labor to worthy projects around the state. The students built five summer camps for mentally retarded youth, a home

29. Eliot Wigginton, *The Foxfire Book* (New York: Doubleday, Inc. 1973).

for juvenile delinquents, a social center at a migrant worker camp, and an inner-city park. In Sacramento, California, volunteers visit welfare recipients' homes, screen cases, and assist in refurnishing and repairing houses.

Learning on the road. A few schools have organized traveling learning experiences that combine academic study with on-site visitation and experience. St. Paul Open School students have traveled to the Dakota Badlands and to the Gettysburg Battlefield to combine geological and biological study with study of culture and history. In Lake Geneva, Wisconsin, a group called the American Essence Traveling School offers a program for high school seniors and postgraduates in which young people spend nine months crossing the United States by rail, highway, footpath, inland waterways, and even wagon trails. The program is designed as an in-depth immersion in America's heritage in the hope that the participants will gain a deeper commitment to the future based on a personal awareness of the past. Many schools, of course, have much less ambitious programs of weekend travel and summer experiences.

Learning in the political arena. Encouraged by the student activism of the late 1960s and early 1970s and armed with the right to vote at age eighteen, some high school students have moved forcefully into the political arena. Students of East High School in Denver went to Greenwood, Mississippi, to assist in voter registration. The Connecticut Citizens Action Group, the first state affiliate of Ralph Nader's Center for the Study of Responsive Law, provided a model for youth participation in communities all across the United States. The students in Connecticut have conducted a statewide survey of food prices, developed an Earth Platform for election campaigns, and lobbied state legislators for a disposable bottle tax. And all this has been done after school and on weekends, without school credit. In other states, students are participating in a pool of volunteer workers to gather information, conduct surveys, and then utilize their information to influence voters, candidates, and legislators.

Another program that involves students in action-learning in the political arena is the Washington, D.C., Street Law Program. Offered as a high school course, the program is built around sixteen law students from Georgetown University who teach the "street law" courses. The courses use discussion groups and special projects, and culminate with students conducting a simulated trial with a federal judge chairing the proceedings. Both the high school students and the law students earn credit for this work. The program has become a model for such courses in other school districts.

Learning in the world of work. Career and vocational education offer almost unlimited opportunities for action-learning; an added incentive for secondary educators is that such programs are supported by federal funds. The Office of Education has developed an Experimental Based Career Education that is much more than a terminal program for noncollege bound students and that is a far cry from on-the-job training. Experimental Based Career Education defines careers broadly to mean "one's progress through life" or "life paths"—not a restricted nine-to-five segment of life. The program enables students to complete the last two years of high school by participating in extensive experiences, independent and group study, and many activities. Graduation requirements are based on survival competencies rather than course completion, a significant development.

One of the Office of Education programs is located in Tigard, Oregon. The program enables students to leave school during the last two years for action-learning. During this time students attend no classes. They demonstrate their competencies in things it is assumed most Americans should know in order to function effectively in their daily lives. Each competency is judged by a specific community adult. Another impressive career education program is found at Skyline Center in Dallas, Texas. In a school staffed by professional teachers and craftsmen and utilizing skilled professionals throughout the community, students may survey as many as twelve career opportunities during one year.

An important action-learning program that has been in operation for a number of years is the National Junior Achievement Program. In this program, students use consultants from the business community to assist them in organizing a business, producing and marketing a product, and generally participating in the entire range of experiences associated with running a business.

ACTION-LEARNING: SOME RESERVATIONS

While there is currently an increase in interest in action-learning, some cautions should be mentioned. The following are major concerns to be taken into account:

1. Action-learning poses extremely difficult scheduling problems

because the programs of public secondary schools were not designed to provide community-based learning. Consequently, action-learning often has been scheduled as supplementary to regular classroom work, or as a component for one particular course, or as independent study. Some schools provide semester-or-year-long "sabbatical leaves." Some proposals for action-learning have moved in the direction of "high schooling without high schools" by advocating alternatives to school rather than alternative schools. Few schools have been able to operationalize Edward Meade's suggestion that the schools act as a "broker for sending youngsters to and from the 'real world of experience.' "[30]

2. The matter of legitimacy must still be raised. Many question whether or not these programs really belong in schools even though the research available on action-learning is generally favorable.[31]

3. Many of the action-learning programs described earlier are very expensive. This poses a difficult problem. One response is that of the National Commission on Resources for Youth, which recommends that all action learning should be financed through student projects to earn funds.

4. The most difficult problem of all may be the question of availability of opportunity. All of the programs that have been described are small; some are only pilot projects. What happens if all students—or even a major proportion of students—are to be involved? The organizational and administrative problems are mind-boggling. The added problem of finding available opportunities outside the school is also formidable.

5. The question of accountability is a difficult one. A number of state departments of education have begun to develop guidelines and accept credits for action-learning. Sometimes credit is tied to existing courses, tied to hours of participation, or dealt with in an ad hoc manner. Yet much work is still to be done in the area of organization and administration if action-learning programs are to be carefully monitored and evaluated.

30. Weinstock, *The Greening of the High School*, p. 33. (A good example of a school acting as a broker is the Action Learning Center, Niles Township High School, Skokie, Illinois.)

31. Alexander M. Moore, "Evaluation and Action-Learning Programs," *Bulletin of the National Association of Secondary School Principals* 58 (November 1974): 65-74.

The Future: A Diverse Array of Settings for Secondary Education

American secondary schools have entered a period of transition—from the large monolithic comprehensive school to a total educational structure that will include the comprehensive school along with a pluralistic realm of different and usually smaller optional alternative schools, each designed to be responsive to the learning and living needs of youth; from the isolated adolescent community to the community-centered education designed to bridge the gaps between academic learning and action-learning; from an institution with basic responsibility for cognitive education to an institution with basic responsibility for the transition from adolescence to adulthood.

Currently very few students are involved in alternative public schools or in action-learning programs, probably not more than two to five percent of the total public secondary school enrollment. It is difficult to predict how fast communities will move to make alternative and action settings available to larger proportions of secondary school youth. Because many of the alternative schools and action-learning programs have been developed very recently, it is even more difficult to predict which types of alternative schools and action-learning programs will eventually become integral parts of secondary education. But it is not difficult to predict that secondary education in the remainder of this decade and this century will continue to move toward a pluralistic array of opportunities for learning.

CHAPTER VIII

What Should Be Taught and Learned through Secondary Education?

WILLIAM VAN TIL

The question to which this chapter is addressed can be phrased in many ways. Herbert Spencer expressed it as "What knowledge is of most worth?" To Robert S. Lynd, it was "Knowledge for what?" To the contributors to a yearbook of the Association for Supervision and Curriculum Development it was "What shall the high schools teach?" and to the authors of a later ASCD pamphlet, "What are the sources of the curriculum?"[1]

However phrased, it is the same question—the question of content, the curriculum, the appropriate learning experiences, what is to be taught and to be learned. It is an inescapable question that recurs in many versions throughout the ages. The answers differ with the era.

The discussion in this chapter is limited to what Beck has termed "the modern era" in chapter 2 of this volume—the period in American education from World War I on. The selection is not arbitrary; the modern era in American education began with a milestone report in the development of secondary education in this country, that of the Commission on the Reorganization of Secondary Education, usually called simply the Seven Cardinal Principles.[2] A watershed in the

1. Herbert Spencer, *Education* (New York: Appleton-Century-Crofts, Inc., 1875); Robert S. Lynd, *Knowledge for What?* (Princeton, N.J.: Princeton University Press, 1939); *What Shall the High Schools Teach?*, 1956 Yearbook of the Association for Supervision and Curriculum Development (Washington, D.C.: distributed by the Association for Supervision and Curriculum Development, NEA, 1956); Association for Supervision and Curriculum Development, *What Are the Sources of the Curriculum? A Symposium* (Washington, D.C.: Association for Supervision and Curriculum Development, 1962).

2. Commission on the Reorganization of Secondary Education, *The Cardinal Principles of Secondary Education*, Bulletin no. 35 (Washington, D.C.: U.S. Bureau of Education, 1918).

evolution of secondary education in the United States became evident in the early twentieth century and the report on the seven cardinal principles marks the crest of that watershed.

The Watershed in Secondary Education

On the side of the watershed called past, lay an America oriented to agrarian and rural ways, complacent about racism, taking for granted that women's place was in the home, relatively innocent of world affairs, turned inward to family and local community events, confident of a better future tomorrow. On the side of the watershed called future, lay an America becoming increasingly urban and industrial, marked by racial strife and the emergence of black consciousness, rejecting male domination through challenges by suffragettes of the teens of the century and by liberated women of the 1970s, fighting declared and undeclared wars abroad in the uncomfortable role of a world power, engulfed by broad social problems of energy, environment, population, depression, and inflation; and visibly shaken and unsure in an age of anxiety and alienation.

On the side of the watershed called the past, there existed a secondary education for a few, a situation marked by substantial inequality of access to educational opportunity, whether measured by class, racial, ethnic, or sex dimensions. On the side of the watershed called future, there was to emerge secondary education nominally open to all, yet blocked by actual inequalities in treatment based on class, racial, ethnic, and sex factors.

On the side called past, a secondary education for Americanization through melting pot techniques attempted to standardize young Americans regardless of their backgrounds. On the side called future, a secondary education was to develop for a stubbornly pluralistic society in which immigration from Europe was to be supplemented by internal migration of blacks, native American Indians, and people of Puerto Rican and Mexican-American stocks.

On the side called past, secondary education relied heavily on academic instruction through the separate disciplines. On the side called future, secondary education quested for relevant and meaningful learning by youth through disciplines, interdisciplinary study, and action-learning.

On the side called past, secondary education assumed that the better road to vocational competence was the indirect path of a traditional education. On the side called future, secondary education attempted to create more vocational programs, to mix schooling with work experiences, and to develop career education.

On the side of the watershed called past, the four-year high school of the 8-4 system had developed. On the side of the watershed called future, there was to emerge the junior high school of the 6-3-3 educational ladder, born in 1909 and destined to grow rapidly from the 1920s on, and the middle school of the 4-4-4 and 5-3-4 alternatives destined to appear in the late 1960s. On the side of the watershed called past, secondary education prepared selected young people for college entrance; in 1900, 6.4 percent of persons seventeen years old graduated from high school. On the side of the watershed called future, the middle, junior, and senior high schools were to attempt to educate almost all of the American young people, whether college-bound or not; by 1972, 75.1 percent of persons eighteen years old graduated from high school.[3]

On the side of the watershed called past, reports conceived secondary education as separate subjects to be juggled for better college entrance preparation, earlier college entrance, and closer articulation between high school and college. Note the names of the committees submitting reports after 1893: Committee of Ten on Secondary School Studies, Committee on College Entrance Requirements, Committee on Economy of Time in Education, and Committee upon the Articulation of High School and College.[4] On the side of the water-

---

3. Bureau of the Census, U.S. Department of Commerce, *Statistical Abstract of the United States, 1974* (Washington, D.C.: Government Printing Office, 1974), p. 132.

4. The reports submitted by the first two of these committees were published for the National Education Association under the titles *Report of the Committee of Ten on Secondary School Studies* (New York: American Book Co., 1894) and *Report of Committee on College Entrance Requirements* (Chicago: University of Chicago Press, 1899). The Committee on Economy of Time, appointed by the National Educational Association in 1911, made four reports that were published as yearbooks of the National Society for the Study of Education: *Minimum Essentials in Elementary-School Subjects—Standards and Current Practices*, Fourteenth Yearbook, Part I (Bloomington, Ill.: Public School Publishing Co., 1915); *Second Report of the Committee on Minimal Essentials in Elementary-School Subjects*, Sixteenth Yearbook, Part I (Bloomington, Ill.: Public School Publishing Co., 1917); *Third Report of the Committee on Economy of Time in Education*, Seventeenth Yearbook, Part I (Bloomington, Ill.: Public School Publishing Co., 1918); and *Fourth Report of the Committee on Economy of Time*, Eighteenth Yearbook, Part II (Bloomington, Ill.: Public School Publishing Co., 1919). The Committee upon the Articulation of High School and College, chaired by Clarence D. Kingsley, made several

·shed called future, came reports that conceived secondary education as related to objectives and purposes, principles and problems,
individuals and society. The future was ushered in by the 1918 report
of the Commission on the Reorganization of Secondary Education.

THE SEVEN CARDINAL PRINCIPLES

The Cardinal Principles report recommended that the content of
secondary education be based on the present and prospective lives of
young people, a heretical idea from the point of view of those who saw
the high school as designed simply for college entrance. To the Commission, secondary education existed to deal with:

1. *Health.* Health needs cannot be neglected during the period of secondary education without serious danger to the individual and the race. The
secondary school should therefore provide health instruction, inculcate health
habits, organize an effective program of physical activities, regard health needs
in planning work and play, and cooperate with home and community in
safeguarding and promoting health interests. . . .

2. *Command of fundamental processes.* Much of the energy of the elementary school is properly devoted to teaching certain fundamental processes,
such as reading, writing, arithmetical computations, and the elements of oral
and written expression. The facility that a child of 12 or 14 may acquire in the
use of these tools is not sufficient for the needs of modern life. This is particularly true of the mother tongue. . . .

3. *Worthy home membership.* Worthy home membership as an objective
calls for the development of those qualities that make the individual a worthy
member of a family, both contributing to and deriving benefit from that
membership. . . . The coeducational school with a faculty of men and women
should, in its organization and its activities, exemplify wholesome relations
between boys and girls and men and women. . . .

4. *Vocation.* Vocational education should equip the individual to secure a
livelihood for himself and those dependent on him, to serve society well
through his vocation, to maintain the right relationships toward his fellow
workers and society, and, as far as possible, to find in that vocation his own
best development. . . .

reports, including the "Report of the Committee of Nine on the Articulation of High
School and College," National Education Association *Journal of Proceedings and Ad-
dresses* 1911: 559-66; "The Report of the Committee on the Articulation of High
School and College," NEA *Journal of Proceedings and Addresses* 1912: 667-73; and the
"Third Report of the Committee on the Articulation of High Schools and Colleges,"
NEA *Journal of Proceedings and Addresses* 1913: 489-91.

5. Civic education. Civic education should develop in the individual those qualities whereby he will act well his part as a member of neighborhood, town or city, State, and Nation, and give him a basis for understanding international problems. . . .

6. Worthy use of leisure. Education should equip the individual to secure from his leisure the re-creation of body, mind, and spirit, and the enrichment and enlargement of his personality. . . .

7. Ethical character. In a democratic society ethical character becomes paramount among the objectives of the secondary school. Among the means for developing ethical character may be mentioned the wise selection of content and methods of instruction in all subjects of study, the social contacts of pupils with one another and with their teachers, the opportunities afforded by the organization and administration of the school for the development on the part of pupils of the sense of personal responsibility and initiative, and, above all, the spirit of service and the principles of true democracy which should permeate the entire school—principal, teachers, and pupils. . . .[5]

More than half a century later, the reader may find some of the earlier phrasing archaic, with words like "race" and "inculcate" now having different meanings than intended by the original authors. But, despite the lapse of more than half a century, the central idea that the overall objectives of a secondary school must relate to the present and prospective lives of young people, rather than to traditional subject matter categories, shines through and is neither archaic nor obsolete.

Again and again, later studies and reports have testified to the wisdom of the authors of the Seven Cardinal Principles report in reconceptualizing secondary education. This is the case whether the reader turns to reports on youth in the 1930s, or the reports of the Progressive Education Association in the 1940s, or the reports of the Educational Policies Commission in the 1930s to 1960s, or the compensatory education movement in the 1960s, or the contemporary criticisms of public secondary education in the 1970s.

Sources of Content of Secondary Education

But to urge that secondary education should relate to the present and prospective lives of young people and to suggest seven cardinal principles for secondary education only opened, rather than closed, the debate. For over a half century of the modern era in education,

5. *The Cardinal Principles of Secondary Education,* pp. 11-15.

educators have debated the question of the best source or sources for the secondary school curriculum.

Four ways of conceptualizing secondary education have emerged. To some educators, the curriculum should be based on the needs, interests, and wants of the individual learner. To a second school of thought, the curriculum should be based on the demands of society and the imperative social realities of the times. To a third group, the curriculum should clarify value alternatives and educate for a democratic way of life. To a fourth way of thinking, the curriculum should teach the structure of the disciplines through a process of education that emphasizes principles and relationships and the ways of inquiry employed in the various disciplines.

Though many participants in the debate on the sources of the curriculum have stressed one of these sources and have sometimes appeared to deny or only grudgingly admit others, they (or those who followed them) have frequently qualified their positions by recognizing that the curriculum should be based on the interaction of several sources, although they held their chosen source to be paramount. Many contemporary educators have come to reject such oversimplified dualisms as youth problems versus societal reform, needs of learners versus subject matter, or value orientation versus improvement of the social order. In effect, participants in the debate have increasingly recognized that secondary educators must bear more than one source in mind simultaneously.

NEEDS OF LEARNERS

In the modern era of American education, William Heard Kilpatrick was the philosopher of education most identified with emphasis on the needs of the learner. He became famous with his project method, based on student experiences, which involved the learner in problem solving marked by analysis, judgment, discussion, and evaluation. In his writing there recurs emphasis on pupil involvement and student-centered learning through purposeful activity and intrinsic motivation. "We learn what we live," he reminded us. To Kilpatrick, the enemies of learning were extrinsic motivation, memorization, rote learning, and meaningless formal instruction purveyed through the Alexandrian approach. (He traced the genesis of traditional education to Alexandria in ancient Egypt where education became identified with mastery of the books in the great library.)

Yet Kilpatrick, even though historically identified with the needs approach and insistent on beginning with the interests of the learner, did not deny the importance of social and value orientations. In the 1930s, a time of worldwide depression and the rise of Hitler, Kilpatrick increasingly stressed the importance of dealing with social problems in the schools while avoiding indoctrination. He steadily saw the school as a value-oriented agency for the development of character and personality.

Lawrence A. Cremin has documented the needs and interests orientation of many early progressive school leaders of the 1920s.[6] Yet, as the Progressive Education movement matured, the books sponsored by its several commissions avoided the oversimplifications of the child-centered and youth-centered school. In the 1930s, the progressives increasingly recognized the necessary interaction of the individual learner and the social setting. "Needs," in the volumes of the Commission on Secondary School Curriculum, became "personal-social needs," testifying to the indissoluble bonds between the individual and society.[7] The reports of the Eight-Year Study by the Commission on Relation of School and College of the Progressive Education Association in the early 1940s also emphasized the personal-social nature of needs. As one of these volumes pointed out:

> While needs may be chiefly personal or social in *origin* they cannot be considered as completely personal or social in *nature*. Whatever the origin of the need may be, it has both personal and social aspects. In some cases, such as the need for "self-assurance," the personal element is dominant yet it cannot be attained except in situations involving the social environment. Indeed the need for self-assurance would not exist expect for the interaction of the individual and the social environment.[8]

6. Lawrence A. Cremin, *The Transformation of the School* (New York: Knopf, 1961).

7. Commission on Secondary School Curriculum, Progressive Education Association, *The Social Studies in General Education* (New York: D. Appleton-Century Co., 1940); idem, *Language in General Education* (New York: D. Appleton-Century Co., 1940); idem, *Mathematics in General Education* (New York: D. Appleton-Century Co., 1940); idem, *Science in General Education* (New York: D. Appleton-Century Co., 1938); idem, *The Visual Arts in General Education* (New York: D. Appleton-Century Co., 1940); idem, *Reorganizing Secondary Education* (New York: D. Appleton-Century Co., 1939).

8. H. H. Giles, S. P. McCutchen, and A. N. Zechiel, *Exploring the Curriculum* (New York: Harper & Brothers, 1942), p. 8.

The Progressive Education Association reports also emphasized values. For instance, *Exploring the Curriculum* said:

The nature of the society and the values held by society determine to a great extent the character of the needs that are social in their origin. We cannot determine needs from a study of society and adolescents as they *are* but must take into consideration the values we hold to be most worthwhile. The individual *needs* growth and development, but the direction of that growth is to be determined by the ideals of the culture.[9]

When the progressive educators spelled out their program, they utilized subject matter from the broad fields of the curriculum, as the titles of the books published by the Commission on Secondary School Curriculum testify: *The Social Studies in General Education, Language in General Education, Mathematics in General Education, Science in General Education,* and *The Visual Arts in General Education.* They did not restrict their experimentation to core curriculum or common learnings programs alone. Some of the finest school programs of the progressive education era, however, did stress interdisciplinary problem-centered study that cut across the boundaries of subjects and broad fields.

At a later time, the outstanding proponents of the needs and interests doctrine have been the members of a group variously described as the "romantic," "sentimental," "radical," or "compassionate" critics. (The latter term more accurately describes the concern of the group for the lives of children and avoids negative semantic connotations.) A loosely organized alliance of kin spirits, the compassionate critics include John Holt, Herbert Kohl, James Herndon, George Dennison, Jonathan Kozol, Neil Postman, and Nat Hentoff. Holt, for instance, said in 1964:

Behind much of what we do in school lie some ideas, that could be expressed roughly as follows: (1) of the vast body of human knowledge, there are certain bits and pieces that can be called essential, that everyone should know; (2) the extent to which a person can be considered educated, qualified to live intelligently in today's world and be a useful member of society, depends on the amount of this essential knowledge that he carries about with him; (3) it is the duty of schools, therefore, to get as much of this essential knowledge as possible into the minds of children. Thus we find ourselves trying to poke certain facts, recipes, and ideas down the gullets of every child in school, whether the morsel interests him or not, even if it frightens him or

9. Ibid., p. 9.

sickens him, and even if there are other things that he is much more interested in learning.

These ideas are absurd and harmful nonsense. We will not begin to have true education or real learning in our schools until we sweep this nonsense out of the way. Schools should be a place where children learn what they most want to know, instead of what we think they ought to know. The child who wants to know something remembers it and uses it once he has it; the child who learns something to please or appease someone else forgets it when the need for pleasing or the danger of not appeasing is past.[10]

The same viewpoint was elaborated upon by Jonathan Kozol in *Death at an Early Age* in 1967.[11] Yet it is apparent from Kozol's account of his dismissal by the Boston Public Schools that, rather than his needs orientation, it was his interest in teaching about the United Nations and in using a socially-oriented poem by Langston Hughes, "Ballad of the Landlord," which triggered his dismissal. A few years later, in 1972, Kozol graphically repudiated dependence on basing the curriculum exclusively on a child-centered and youth-centered orientation. He wrote scornfully of alternative school teachers who were "determined that poor kids should make clay vases, weave Indian headbands, play with Polaroid cameras and climb over geodesic domes."[12] His perception of a good school had become:

> In Roxbury, Massachusetts, on Leyland Street, a beautiful Free School, nourished and sustained by eloquent young parents and good teachers, discovers that several of its children are in grave medical danger as a consequence of lead poison in the peeling paint and crumbling plaster of the nearby tenement houses. They canvass the neighborhood, enlist physicians, fire broadsides at the press. . . . Forty children in the neighborhood turn out to have been poisoned by the lead paint. . . . The school itself becomes the scene of medical examinations for all children, not just those who are the members of its student body. . . . The liberal press does one or two brief stories. . . . The courts do little . . . the city agencies still less . . . in the winter, a child in Roxbury dies of lead-paint poison. . . . The Free School is in the midst of true and human confrontation with the real world of exploitation and oppression that the law, the rental patterns and the medical profession constitute.[13]

10. John Holt, *How Children Fail* (New York: Pitman Publishing Co., 1964), pp. 174-75.

11. Jonathan Kozol, *Death at an Early Age* (Boston: Houghton Mifflin Co., 1967).

12. Jonathan Kozol, "Free Schools Fail Because They Don't TEACH," *Psychology Today* 5 (April 1972): 32.

13. Jonathan Kozol, *Free Schools* (Boston: Houghton Mifflin Co., 1972), p. 52.

His conception of a desirable Free School was one which included the basic disciplines, especially reading. As he saw it, "Harlem does not need a new generation of radical basketweavers. It does need radical, strong, subversive, steadfast, skeptical, rage-minded, and power-wielding obstetricians, lab technicians, defense attorneys, building code examiners, brain surgeons."[14]

As practitioners translated the ideas of the compassionate critics into practice through alternative schools, the importance of social realities and of disciplinary and interdisciplinary content became increasingly evident to many of them; they modified the earlier emphasis on needs and interests alone.

SOCIAL REALITIES

Just as William Heard Kilpatrick symbolized a philosophy of education that stresses the needs and interests of learners and yet had room for other referents, so George S. Counts in the modern era symbolized a philosophy which stressed social realities yet which did not rule out all other referents. Counts, a pioneer in social reconstructionism, was acutely aware of the social problems of the decade in which he reached the apex of his influence, the 1930s. He called for a curriculum which would grapple with the social realities on the international and domestic scenes, including Hitler's fascism and the Great Depression. He urged the school to throw its potential strength into the struggle to build a new social order. He electrified a depression-era conference of the Progressive Education Association with his address entitled "Dare the School Build a New Social Order?"[15]

Firm though Counts was in his conviction that the curriculum must deal with social issues, he acknowledged the importance of the needs of the learner. But to Counts, needs alone were not enough of a basis for a genuinely progressive program of education.

Counts was intent on the necessity for youth to live by the social values of democracy. So vigorous was his advocacy of social realities and of the values derived from the democratic tradition that his opponents constantly accused him of indoctrination, a charge in which he gloried rather than for which he apologized. All education involved

14. Kozol, "Free Schools Fail Because They Don't TEACH," p. 114.

15. George S. Counts, *Dare the School Build a New Social Order?* (New York: John Day, 1932).

imposition of values, he argued; the important thing was to give young people a vision of the possibilities which lie ahead. The teacher's own beliefs as to societal problems and desirable values should be unmistakable.

As to the place of the disciplines, he took for granted the established structure of the secondary school curriculum, while especially emphasizing the challenge of using such subjects as history to create a better society.

In our own era in which human survival is threatened by war, famine, pollution, energy depletion and other man-made plagues, the social reconstruction viewpoint is by no means dormant. For instance, Theodore Brameld proposed in 1970 a curriculum model based on a "moving wheel." The rim represented man's predicaments and aspirations—his value dilemmas and hopes. The hub represented a central question dealing with problems and issues—the social realities of our times. The spokes represented areas and courses bearing directly upon the central hub question—the disciplines and interdisciplinary studies to be employed.[16]

In twentieth century curriculum making, many attempts have been made to focus the curriculum on social processes and functions. Not all have reflected the zeal for reform of the social reconstructionists; influential formulations have often emphasized the social demands of the surrounding society. For instance, in the modern historical era Hollis L. Caswell and Doak S. Campbell argued in their influential 1935 book, *Curriculum Development:*

> Study of group life shows that there are certain major centers about which the activities of individuals and the plans and problems of the group tend to cluster. These centers, which may be referred to as social functions, tend to persist and to be common for all organized groups. . . . Since these centers or social functions represent points about which real life activities tend to gather and organize, it is considered reasonable that a curriculum which is concerned with guiding children into effective participation in the activities of real life may appropriately use these social functions as points for emphasis and orientation in outlining the curriculum.[17]

A curriculum program adopted in the state of Virginia, developed

16. Theodore Brameld, "A Cross-Cutting Approach to the Curriculum: The Moving Wheel," *Phi Delta Kappan* 51 (March 1970): 346-48.

17. Hollis L. Caswell and Doak S. Campbell, *Curriculum Development* (New York: American Book Co., 1935), pp. 173-74.

with the aid of Caswell, specified these social functions: Protection and Conservation of Life, Property, and Natural Resources; Production of Goods and Services and Distribution of the Returns of Production; Consumption of Goods and Services; Communication and Transportation of Goods and People; Recreation; Expression of Aesthetic Impulses; Expression of Religious Impulses; Education; Extension of Freedom; Integration of the Individual; Exploration.[18]

Henry Harap proposed similar functions of living: Living in the Home; Leisure; Citizenship; Organized Group Life; Consumption; Production; Communication; Transportation.[19]

Yet these curriculum theorists did not repudiate the importance of needs and interests. Caswell and Campbell wrote: "Interests, then, do not represent passing fancies or whims. They are deep-lying attitudes, developed through experience, which largely determine the intensity and consecutiveness of efforts and the tendency to engage in particular activities in the future. They are, when so conceived, a most important element in the educative process."[20]

Nor did the social functions thinkers repudiate values. Harap said, "We take our cue for the organization of the curriculum from our basic concept of the aim of education which emphasizes the continuous improvement in the quality of individual development and group living. We, therefore, cannot escape the responsibility of going to democratic life for the principle of organization."[21]

Subjects and areas, contended this group, should be permeated with concern for the social functions. For instance, health should be a major concern of such areas as physical education and the biological sciences. Problems related to consumption of goods and services should be stressed by several fields, such as mathematics, home economics, business education and the social sciences.

The social functions approach is still advocated today. For instance, Edward G. Olsen, an experienced community school leader, called in the 1970s for a "life-concern-centered" curriculum to deal

18. Ibid., pp. 178-83.

19. Henry Harap, *The Changing Curriculum* (New York: D. Appleton-Century Co., 1937), p. 96.

20. Caswell and Campbell, *Curriculum Development*, p. 211.

21. Harap, *The Changing Curriculum*, p. 81.

with fundamental life concerns and problems of living: Securing Food and Shelter; Protecting Life and Health; Exchanging Ideas; Adjusting to Other People; Sharing in Citizenship; Controlling the Environment; Educating the Young; Enriching Family Living; Appreciating the Past; Meeting Religious Needs; Engaging in Recreation; Enjoying Beauty; Asserting Personal Identity.[22]

Spokesmen for schools of thought which stress social realities, whether they be social reconstructionists or advocates of studying life functions and problems of living, often point out that their proposals are not denials of the importance of the needs of learners or of the significance of value-oriented learning or of the usefulness of disciplines and interdisciplinary study. They regard other curricular referents as necessary. But they stress the primacy of the social source of content for the curriculum.

VALUES

The views of philosopher of education Boyd H. Bode serve as a useful point of departure for demonstrating that some philosophies of education in the modern era conceive values as central in curriculum making. Bode believed that the central task of education was to clarify the nature of the democratic way of life and its competitor, the authoritarian way of life. He summarized his views in two small but cogent books, *Democracy as a Way of Life*,[23] which argued the case for democracy as the necessary value structure for modern American education, and *Progressive Education at the Crossroads*,[24] which criticized the Progressive movement for undue emphasis on the needs and interests of learners. For Bode, the meaning of the democratic way of life must be clarified through the entire curriculum:

The school, therefore, is clearly under the obligation to show that democracy is a way of life which breaks sharply with the past. It must not merely practice democracy but must develop the doctrine so as to make it

22. Edward G. Olsen, "Enlivening the Community School Curriculum," *Phi Delta Kappan* 54 (November 1972): 177.

23. Boyd H. Bode, *Democracy as a Way of Life* (New York: Macmillan Publishing Co., 1937).

24. Boyd H. Bode, *Progressive Education at the Crossroads* (New York: Newson & Co., 1938).

serviceable as an intellectual basis for the organization of life. . . . The idea of democracy, consequently, cannot be disposed of by dealing with it in a separate course and at some fixed point in the curriculum. . . . The school is, *par excellence*, the institution to which a democratic society is entitled to look for clarification of the meaning of democracy.[25]

Unlike the philosophers Kilpatrick and Counts, who supported the needs and the social realities positions respectively, Bode sharply rejected certain other referents in curriculum development. He was especially critical of the needs position, even when reconceived as personal-social needs. For instance, in *How We Learn*, he said that the Progressive movement ". . . seems unable to get its mind off the individual pupil long enough to reflect on what it is that it is trying to do. . . . With reference to the question of controlling ideals, however, it has scarcely achieved sufficient intellectual respectability to be classed as a movement at all."[26] Consequently when *Reorganizing Secondary Education*, a key publication of the Commission on Secondary School Curriculum of the Progressive Education Association, appeared, he condemned it, writing, "We are invited to take part in a good old-fashioned quest of needs, with no nonsense of philosophy about it. . . . Is it the function of philosophy to clarify and define needs, or are needs to be located and defined independently? We cannot have it both ways."[27] A fellow philosopher, V. T. Thayer, a moving spirit in the several reports of the Commission, responded to this criticism with an interaction position: "Consequently, while we agree with Bode in holding that interests and wants cannot be guided, refined or clarified without resort to philosophy, we also hold that philosophy will bake poor bread indeed if it formulates its standards, its ideals, its frames of reference without regard to the wants and the desires and the peculiar circumstances of man. That is, what holds true of the man, holds true with appropriate adaptations to the child and the youth."[28]

Contemporary exponents of a values analysis position have been less rigid with respect to curricular referents than was Bode. For in-

25. Bode, *Democracy as a Way of Life*, pp. 94-95.

26. Boyd H. Bode, *How We Learn* (Boston: D.C. Heath & Co., 1940), p. 50.

27. Boyd H. Bode, "Needs and the Curriculum," *Progressive Education* 17 (December 1940): 534-35.

28. V. T. Thayer, "V. T. Thayer Replies," *Progressive Education* 17 (December 1940): 540.

stance, Maurice P. Hunt and Lawrence E. Metcalf, while holding that the task of the school is to help young people clarify their values, simultaneously indicated that the way to throw light on values is to consider what they term the "closed areas" in American discourse.[29] Typical of today's closed areas are capitalism and communism, sexual behavior, drug addiction, student dissent, the black revolution, workings of the CIA, and the like. In chapter 4 of this volume, Metcalf advocates the use of personal as well as social dilemmas in value analysis. Exponents of values advance few objections to teaching disciplines and to interdisciplinary studies in the secondary school curriculum if the content emphasizes the use of the method of intelligence and if the curriculum deals with the "closed areas" and with personal and social dilemmas.

STRUCTURE OF THE DISCIPLINES

In the half century which followed the publication of the Seven Cardinal Principles report, the traditional approach to secondary education had many practitioners. The conception of a secondary school curriculum devoted to teaching separate subjects was taken for granted by many educators as a self-evident truth which required little justification or examination. When justifications were cited they often were expedient, such as the requirement by colleges of a pattern of Carnegie units for college admission. When theoretical defenses were advanced, they were often based on a notion of training the mind, which reflected an obsolete faculty psychology, or on purveying a "cultural heritage" amorphously defined with little or no explication of how one chose what was significant from accumulated knowledge.

In the 1960s an intellectually defensible case for studying the separate disciplines was made by Jerome S. Bruner and his followers through the theory of the structure of the disciplines. The Bruner school of thought differentiated the disciplines approach from the miscellaneous accumulation of knowledge characteristic of formal traditional education. In *The Process of Education*, Bruner urged that: "the curriculum of a subject should be determined by the most fundamental understanding that can be achieved of the underlying prin-

---

29. Maurice P. Hunt and Lawrence E. Metcalf, *Teaching High School Social Studies* (New York: Harper & Row, 1955).

ciples that give structure to that subject."[30] Philip H. Phenix called for understanding of how scholars in the various disciplines conducted their inquiries; he pointed out that each discipline has its characteristic methods that distinguish it from other disciplines.[31] In essence, the "structure of the disciplines" advocates asked for stress on principles and relationships and on methods of inquiry, rather than for accumulation of a smattering of knowledge.

As the projects in separate subject fields developed during the post-Sputnik era, the scholars in discipline-oriented projects often rediscovered three insights fundamental to contemporary education. They recognized that motivation was essential if individuals were to learn and that the importance of the drives of the learner could not be minimized. They recognized that, in value-oriented education, problem solving was preferable to inculcation. They recognized that many of the fundamental social problems and dilemmas of mankind could not be dealt with in separate compartments but instead required interdisciplinary study. So the structure of the disciplines proponents moved beyond a position which initially paid insufficient attention to needs, values, or social realities. They found that the concerns of earlier twentieth century progressive educators must be taken into account, even as did Charles E. Silberman who described in *Crisis in the Classroom*[32] how he moved from a highly intellectualized academic view of education to a recognition of the importance of the questions raised by his progressive predecessors in education.

The evolution of the thinking of the theorists of the structure of the disciplines and the practitioners of the projects in the disciplines is exemplified by the reconsiderations of Bruner a decade after publication of *The Process of Education*. First in a speech to the Association for Supervision and Curriculum Development and later in an article in *Phi Delta Kappan*, Bruner recognized that dependence on study of the structure of the disciplines alone was insufficient for a comprehensive educational program. He wrote:

The movement of which *The Process of Education* was a part was based on a

30. Jerome S. Bruner, *The Process of Education* (Cambridge, Mass.: Harvard University Press, 1960), p. 31.

31. Philip H. Phenix, *Realms of Meaning* (New York: McGraw-Hill, 1964), p. 332.

32. Charles E. Silberman, *Crisis in the Classroom* (New York: Random House, 1970).

formula of faith: that learning was what students wanted to do, that they wanted to achieve an expertise in some particular subject matter. Their motivation was taken for granted. It also accepted the tacit assumption that everybody who came to these curricula in the schools already had been the beneficiary of the middle-class hidden curricula that taught them analytic skills and launched them in the traditionally intellectual use of mind. Failure to question these assumptions has, of course, caused much grief to all of us.[33]

In his reconsideration, Bruner proposed a dual curriculum which would deal not only with "the standard topics" (apparently the disciplines approach) but also with "immediate and compelling concerns." Bruner summarized:

In a recent article. . . I proposed that it is possible to conceive of a Monday-Wednesday-Friday curriculum covering the standard topics, and a Tuesday-Thursday and indeed Saturday way of doing things in which immediate and compelling concerns are given the central place—activism? Let them on Tuesdays and Thursdays prepare "briefs" in behalf of their views, make a case for things they care about. Let them prepare plans of action, whether they be on issues in the school, on the local scene, or whatever. What is important is to learn to bring all one's resources to bear on something that matters to you now. These are the times for the migratory questions that wander on long after their answers are forgotten, just because they are great questions.[34]

Thus, by 1971 Bruner had come to the recognition that the structure of the disciplines approach was not in itself a complete answer to the curriculum problem. Indeed, he suggested: "I believe I would be quite satisfied to declare, if not a moratorium, then something of a de-emphasis on matters that have to do with the structure of history, the structure of physics, the nature of mathematical consistency, and deal with it rather in the context of the problems that face us. . . ."[35]

INTERACTION OF SOURCES

Variations on the foregoing viewpoints on the sources of the secondary school curriculum have been heard throughout more than a

33. Jerome S. Bruner, "The Process of Education Revisited," *Phi Delta Kappan* 53 (September 1971): 19.

34. Ibid., p. 20.

35. Ibid., p. 21.

half century since the publication of the Seven Cardinal Principles report. In broad terms, the child-centered view (with its secondary corollary, a youth-centered view) dominated the educational dialogues of the 1920s. In the social crisis of the 1930s, the debate over the social order, sparked by the social reconstructionists, held the center of the educational stage. The period of the 1940s saw a revival of concern for the values by which Americans should live, typified by the United States Office of Education stress on zeal for democracy and the projections of a better postwar society. In the late 1950s, theorists and project practitioners fostered the study of the separate disciplines. The social turmoil of the 1960s was reflected in the compensatory education movement on behalf of the socially underprivileged. In the late 1960s the compassionate critics emphasized the needs and interests of the learner. Alternative transitions to adulthood, involving action-learning and expanded work opportunities, were proposed in the mid-1970s.

So the pendulum of education continued to swing. Yet claims to exclusive dominance of one curricular source became less extreme. While spokesmen for the varied interpretations of the sources of the curriculum usually insisted on the importance of one favored referent, many spokesmen, as we have shown, conceded the legitimacy of other sources.

During the modern era, an occasional major report represented an interaction position, rather than exclusive dedication to one single source of the curriculum. For instance, in 1938 the Educational Policies Commission published *The Purposes of Education in American Democracy* which described four classifications of objectives. The objectives of self-realization were: the inquiring mind, speech, reading, writing, number, sight and hearing, health knowledge, health habits, public health, recreation, intellectual interests, esthetic interests, and character. The objectives of human relationship were: respect for humanity, friendships, cooperation, courtesy, appreciation of the home, conservation of the home, homemaking, and democracy in the home. The objectives of economic efficiency were: work, occupational information, occupational choice, occupational efficiency, occupational adjustment, occupational appreciation, personal economics, consumer judgment, efficiency in buying, and consumer protection. The objectives of civic responsibility were: social justice, social activity, social understanding, critical judgment, tolerance, conservation, social application of science, world citizenship, law observance, economic literacy, political citizenship, and devotion to democracy.[36]

Supportive of the reconciliation of viewpoints that stress needs, social realities, values, and disciplinary-interdisciplinary studies was John Dewey. Though often misinterpreted by disciples who quoted him in support of their chosen referent, Dewey steadily held to interaction among several curricular sources. Just as he rejected either-or dualisms that posed in opposition theory or practice, school or society, general or vocational education, Dewey rejected false forced choices among curricular sources. For instance, his *Experience and Education*, written in his later years, clearly repudiated a child-or youth-centered school that rejected social problems.[37] In the same volume he also called for educators to develop a new progressive organization of subject matter.

Perhaps in the closing quarter of the twentieth century an educationally pluralistic view that recognizes the interaction of several sources of the curriculum will prevail. Perhaps we will recognize and learn to implement a secondary education concerned with the needs of youth as perceived by the humanistic psychologists, the analysis of values as recommended by the philosophers, the social realities of our times as reported by the students of sociology of education, and the uses of meaningful disciplinary and interdisciplinary knowledge as developed by the scholars.

Major Clusters of Content

If secondary educators do accept a pluralistic conception of the interaction of sources of the curriculum, programs of secondary education will have to include and to stress major clusters of content or centers of experience which grow out of the interacting sources: needs of learners, analysis of values, social realities of our times, and meaningful bodies of knowledge. The sixteen centers of experience

36. Educational Policies Commission, *The Purposes of Education in American Democracy* (Washington, D.C.: National Education Association, 1938), pp. 50, 72, 90, 108.

37. John Dewey, *Experience and Education* (New York: Macmillan Publishing Co., 1938).

listed below are suggested by the author as highly important in a balanced and significant program of secondary education today:

War, Peace, and International Relations
Overpopulation, Pollution, and Energy
Economic Options and Problems
Governmental Processes
Consumer Problems
Intercultural Relations
World Views
Recreation and Leisure
The Arts and Aesthetics
Self-Understanding and Personal Development
Family, Peer Group, and School
Health
Community Living
Vocations
Communication
Alternative Futures

Obviously, the above clusters of content are not proposed for eternity; as new developments within the interacting sources require new adaptations, the clusters of content should change.[38] The suggested list of centers of experience represents no particular rank order of priority.

The suggested clusters of content merit careful consideration whether secondary education takes place in alternative or comprehensive secondary schools, in senior high or intermediate schools, through the community or within the school walls. They should be taken into account whether secondary education proceeds through separate subjects or interdisciplinary approaches, through action-learning or academically oriented instruction, or through any combination of such approaches.

38. For earlier listings of centers of experience, see William Van Til, "Exploring Educational Frontiers," chapter 1 in *Leadership through Supervision*, 1946 Yearbook of the Association for Supervision and Curriculum Development (Washington, D.C.: Association for Supervision and Curriculum Development, 1946), pp. 15-16; and William Van Til, Gordon F. Vars, and John Lounsbury, *Modern Education for the Junior High School Years* (Indianapolis, Ind.: Bobbs-Merrill, 1967), pp. 261-71.

Each center will be discussed below through a sequence of four paragraphs that will relate each cluster of content to social realities, values, needs, and ways of organizing knowledge.

War, peace, and international relations. International problems of war and peace are crucial to the survival of the human race. Overkill is no longer the monopoly of a few great powers; steadily, the new capacity to destroy through nuclear weapons moves into the hands of smaller nations too. Military expenditures expand, though the world seeks understandings, deténtes, and peaceful relations through the United Nations and the negotiations by world powers.

Ways of living of the varied nations of the world must be studied if international understanding is to prevail. Long gone are the days when international studies could be limited to western Europe. Now the values of such powers as the Soviet Union, China, and the bloc of Arab states must be understood. The nationalistic ambitions of countries in Africa, Asia, and South America must be reckoned with.

In the late 1960s American (and world) youth graphically demonstrated how important to them were the world's problems of war and peace. The undeclared war in Vietnam and throughout Southeast Asia contributed to youth dissent and anger on an unprecedented scale. Wars are fought by the young and no one knows this better than the young people themselves. Problems of military service and establishing a lasting peace are high among the genuine concerns of young people.

In such a setting, secondary education in America must deal with war, peace, weaponry, nationalism, imperialism, gaps between developed and underdeveloped nations, blocs, alliances, conflicting world views on the international scene, and the like. The social studies, language arts, world languages, and the several arts can make contributions to international understanding. Cross-disciplinary studies of world areas and dilemmas offer another desirable opportunity to teach about war and peace and international relations.

Overpopulation, pollution, and energy. In the 1970s people and their leaders began to sense that the interrelated problems of overpopulation, pollution, and energy depletion were creating a crisis for human survival comparable to global war. On the world scene there appeared grim manifestations of famine and hunger, poisoning of land and air and oceans, and oil shortages. Population soared, especially in the un-developed lands. The headlong rush to industrialism gouged the earth, fouled the air, and killed life in rivers, seas, and oceans. Meanwhile the limits to growth grew nearer as the developed nations used up much of the earth's resources even before the underdeveloped nations had their opportunity to exploit nature's bounty.

One such problem as overpopulation, pollution, or energy deple-tion is deadly enough; the problems occurring in interrelation are deadlier still. The value choices involved are delicate and complex; policies adopted today can haunt tomorrow.

The concern of American young people for this cluster of problems is apparent. They enlist in campaigns to save the environ-ment and improve the surrounding ecology. Many of them demonstrate their support for population controls in their personal family planning. They are aware of the necessity for conserving energy and often more willing to forego material goods than their elders. For youth is keenly aware that they are the inheritors of decisions with respect to the three interrelated problems.

Potential contributors to the study of these problems in the second-ary schools include disciplines within the sciences, mathematics, physical education, home economics, the social studies, and the language arts. The three interrelated problem areas and the attendant growth dilemmas might also be attacked through interdisciplinary ap-proaches.

Economic options and problems. In America, the economy soured in the early 1970s. Inflation combined with economic stagnation and produced a hybrid, stagflation. The classical economic assumptions did not work automatically in an economy rigidified by oligarchic price maintenance, closely protected profits, collective wage demands, and fixities built into government budgets.

In an inflationary setting, those who lived by the work ethic were penalized and those who followed the philosophy of the grasshopper were rewarded. In a recession-depression setting, inequalities in in-come distribution became increasingly apparent as unemployment grew. Possibilities as to systems of production and distribution within a democracy ranged from free enterprise to socialism and involved different assumptions as to the good life, the nature of man, and human behavior. Analysis of choices had to extend beyond economic factors alone and into philosophical, social, and psychological realms. So questions of values became inescapable.

Economic trouble hits youth particularly hard. In economically depressed times, the proportion of young people unemployed exceeds that of the general population; the problem is particularly acute for black and Puerto Rican and Chicano youth, for their rate of unemployment is greater than that of the rest of the youth population. Young people are necessarily caught up in the work and distribution dilemmas.

The need for studying economic relationships through the discipline of economics and through interdisciplinary social education approaches becomes increasingly apparent in the economically troubled 1970s.

Governmental processes. Though civic education has long been a major objective of American education, political and governmental developments in the 1970s demonstrated that the nation had far to go to achieve the informed and active citizenry envisaged by Thomas Jefferson and Horace Mann. In the post-Watergate atmosphere, cynicism was widespread; whether personally involved or not, all politicians had been tarred by the Watergate brush. Disillusionment combined with apathy; in the elections of 1974, with the entire House of Representatives and one-third of the Senate up for election, only 38 percent of the electorate bothered to vote.

The jungle values of exploitation on behalf of predatory vested interests challenged the values inherent in the American dream of a free self-governing citizenry. Ends-justify-means philosophies were blandly accepted in high places in American life. The hope of using governmental institutions for social welfare and human enhancement was threatened by the cumbersomeness and lethargy of bureaucracy. Were venality and indifference so entrenched that Americans could no longer depend on their political and governmental processes to help create a better society? Study and action in politics and government offered many opportunities for value analysis.

Though opportunities for the young to participate in the political and governmental process had been increased through lowering of the voting age to eighteen, it remained an open question in the mid-1970s whether youth would take advantage of its potential to make a difference. While there was evidence of the persistence of youthful idealism, there was evidence too of youth apathy and escape into privatism within an apolitical youth culture. Perhaps a new emphasis on action-learning might teach the young how to count in their communities.

The challenge not only involved the social studies but also such broad fields as the sciences, the language arts, business-vocational education, and the varied art areas. At issue were questions of the potentiality of the common man to govern himself democratically and to achieve his potential through individual and group action.

Consumer problems. Choosing, buying, and using goods and services has become increasingly complex in the United States. Not only has there been an increase in the variety of goods and services available. Not only does the problem of shoddiness and even harmfulness of products persist. The added element in consumer education is, as Harman puts it in chapter 5 of this volume, "the 'new scarcity' of energy, materials, natural fresh water, arable land, habitable surface area, capacity of the natural environment, and resilience of life-supporting ecological systems."

Consuming always involves value choices; each time a person buys, he or she is casting an economic vote. But now that vote represents more than an expression of personal idiosyncratic preference. Now the consumer's choice often represents a decision which preempts goods and services that will be needed by the immediate descendants of the consumer. We have come grudgingly to the recognition that resources are finite and that reliance on the ingenuity of technology to solve all of our energy problems is a great gamble. So consumer education must now involve value decisions as to life-styles. Thoreau once advised his countrymen to simplify; now the advice may be mandatory if we hope for human survival.

The new issues are of major concern to contemporary young people. Behind many of the youth challenges of the later 1960s was a criticism of the overly materialistic patterns of their elders. Youth responses in the form of communes and simplified "greenings of America" may have had their ludicrous overtones, yet the gropings reflected the recognition by young people that happiness could not simply be measured by a quantitative standard measuring one's volume of possessions.

The field of consumer education embraces many broad areas of the secondary school curriculum, notably home economics (not for females only), industrial arts (not for males only), business education, mathematics, the social studies, and the choice-making as to reading and viewing inherent in the language arts. Consumer education also affords an opportunity for interdisciplinary studies.

Intercultural Relations. That human beings in the world and in our nation are of differing racial, religious, national, and socio-economic backgrounds suggests the desirability of inclusion of human relations education in the school curriculum. The additional fact that relationships among people of such varied backgrounds have been characterized by discrimination, prejudice, hostility, and outright violence makes intercultural education imperative. Though we are all aboard spaceship Earth, some passengers receive highly differential treatment. Being black or white, Spanish-speaking or Anglo; being of native American Indian or of varied European stocks; being Catholic, Jew, Protestant, or unchurched; being of one or another of the social classes—all factors initially and sometimes permanently beyond the young person's control—make a difference in the life Americans lead.

One of the great tests of a nation's values is how it treats its varied group members. The historic values of democracy simply cannot be reconciled with discrimination. Nor can Christian-Judaic religious ethics be reconciled with racism. Nor can equal justice under the law be reconciled with preferential treatment based on ethnic differences. Nor does the objective quest for truth by science validate master race theories.

Young people of minority group backgrounds find their daily experience permeated with problems of human relationships; strategies as to human relations, such as desegregation-integration and identity-separatism, involve difficult decisions. Majority group white youth, however WASP their backgrounds, also encounter intercultural relationships; actual or vicarious encounters with people of diverse backgrounds are inescapable.

There is no field of the secondary school curriculum which is unrelated to human relations education. The need for a massive renaissance of intercultural education in a multi-ethnic society is urgent. Interdisciplinary approaches drawing upon such fields as language arts, the social studies, and the biological sciences hold promise.

World views. The world view of the democratic way of life that relies upon the use of the method of intelligence by the common man competes with the world view of authoritarianism that relies upon fixed answers determined by elite groups. This fundamental cleavage carries over into the affairs of nations, religions, philosophies, and institutions.

A variety of value orientations persist and new world views develop. Nations ally themselves into blocs based on ideologies and interests, such as the Western democracies, the two major Communist blocs, the Arab oil bloc, and the Third World nations. Long-established religions such as multi-denominational Christianity, Judaism, Buddhism, Hinduism, and Islam, attempt to maintain and extend their spheres of influence. Schools of philosophic thought set forth their assumptions and their principles and attempt to refute each other's claims. Newer industrial institutions replace older agrarian-based ways of organization.

Individual young people grow up within the world views that are dominant in their particular culture. As they mature, they grow increasingly curious about the basis for the assumptions, principles, and beliefs that have been their social inheritance; their curiosity extends to the world views of others who choose to differ from the world views they have acquired. Thus, opportunities to teach about divergent ways of conceiving the life of mankind emerge.

Secondary education provides many opportunities for the study of world views via, for instance, the study of national and world literature through the language arts, the study of a variety of civilizations through the social studies, the study of knowledge accumulated through the sciences, the recognition of varied art expressions through the humanities, the world languages through foreign language study. Cross-disciplinary studies of comparative cultures, religions, philosophies, and institutions provide opportunities for high school youth to understand and improve their own socially inherited world views and to understand and respect the world views of others.

Recreation and leisure. The Bible reminds us that man shall not live by bread alone. Nor should mankind live by the bread of social problems alone, however necessary these may be for human survival. A vital area in the social experience of modern Americans is the use of recreational and leisure time. For in a developed nation like ours, people have substantial free time; the nature of our industrial system has mandated a reduction of work time. Even the most task-oriented moonlighters in the United States have more free time than their ancestors had.

Contemporary recreational and leisure opportunities necessitate value choices. For instance, "spectatoritis" vies with participation. Participation is frequently praised for concomitant gains such as mental and physical health that accompanies taking part in games and sports, tours and travel, and the like. Spectatoritis is often maligned as simply an obsessive fixation on the omnipresent television set. Yet a spectator can watch and appreciate the best performances the contemporary world can provide. A reader of books is a spectator, yet at the same time can be a mentally active participant. A viewer of a movie is a spectator, yet simultaneously can be a participant whose experience is being expanded. Perhaps more important than whether one's recreational time is characterized by the supposed passivity of spectatoritis or the supposed action of participation may be the extent to which the potential capacities of the person are stretched by the leisure experience.

That youth is actively expanding experiences in leisure and recreation is so apparent that the point need not be amplified here.

In secondary education, recreation and leisure have frequently been regarded as the province of the physical education specialists. Their contribution is not to be deprecated, yet we might well maximize the additional contributions of a variety of fields of the secondary school curriculum. To cite one among many, consider the potential contribution of the language arts with its long-established emphasis on reading and its newly established emphasis on communications media.

The arts and aesthetics. For civilized man, the use of one's time reaches its apogee in the arts. It is no accident that civilizations throughout history have had their music, fine arts, drama, and poetry and prose. Through the arts, mankind expresses creativity and moves beyond a pedestrian life.

The arts encourage the humane values of self-expression and creativity. Admittedly, the arts are most significant to the individual when the person participates in shaping the clay, playing the role, evoking the music, mobilizing the words. Yet not to be deprecated is the art experience of the art consumer who looks or listens and enters into the mood and the spirit of the art product. To be prized are the communication with the painter and sculptor in the gallery, the hush as the curtain goes up, the mood created by the music, the shock of recognition of kin experience in the presence of a printed page.

The fascination of the young with the arts has been repeatedly demonstrated. Even our too frequently dull and routine approaches to the arts often fail to turn off the eagerness of the young to create or to react to the creations of others. Young people are frequently most alive when encountering art experiences.

A substantial portion of the high school curriculum exists for the cultivation of art experiences under such titles as music, fine arts, home arts, and aspects of industrial arts. The field of language arts, at its best, goes far beyond teaching the mechanics of communication; language arts instruction can foster creative participation and absorption. If in high school education we could learn to blend art experiences into cognitive intellectualized studies, we might make the arts even more integral in the lives of the young. We might teach young people that there are other ways of expressing ideas than via speech and writing alone. We might encourage them to communicate their insights through painting, dramatizing, dancing, composing, and a host of creative activities in various fields and in interdisciplinary studies.

Self-understanding and personal development. There is abundant social justification for the inclusion of self-understanding and personal development in the secondary school curriculum. After all, the social order is no stronger than the units which comprise it—individual persons; the struggle for a better society must begin in the hearts and minds of individual human beings.

Fundamental in a democratic philosophy of education is respect for the worth and dignity of each individual. If the worth and dignity of the individual is to prevail, the individual must have faith in his or her own personal worth and dignity. To attain a desirable self-concept the individual must struggle for self-understanding and must cope with the inevitable problems which impede personal development. Therefore, if schools are to foster a democratic philosophy which values the individual, the secondary school must help young people to come to terms with themselves.

Concern for self-understanding and personal development is conspicuous among the needs of young people. Early and late adolescence are times when the young are seeking to know who they are, and who they might become. Adolescence is a period when the young are trying to come to terms with a bewildering rapid physical development, accompanied by emotional, intellectual, and social perplexities. Consequently, a variety of personal problems arise, typified by the area of human sexuality. If the schools ignore personal needs, these become a hidden agenda for the young person, to the detriment of learning whatever the school blandly assumes that individuals are learning. Meeting the personal needs of the learner is a prerequisite to an individual's learning much else.

Though guidance staffs have rightly staked out a major claim to dealing with the personal problems of youth, this area of content is too important to be left to a supporting service alone and unaided. All broad fields of the secondary school curriculum are potentially strong contributors to youths' quests to know themselves. For instance, the language arts field can draw on vast resources by way of literature and creative writing; the social studies can interrelate social and personal problems and dilemmas; the sciences can include psychology. Highly helpful can be what Kimball Wiles called "analysis groups," sessions not bound by the limits of subjects or fields, in which students talk through their personal problems and decisions with their peers and with a sensitive adult.

Family, peer group, and school. One of the paradoxes of secondary education is that much more instruction is provided concerning such institutions as government and industry than instruction concerning family, peer group, or school. Yet the immediate environment in which the high school student lives has a pervading influence on the lives of youth. Surely, social understanding of the student's surrounding milieu—the home and the family, peer group members with whom the individual must closely relate, and present and prospective schooling—is essential if students are to become acquainted with social realities which they recognize as actual.

Since the student must daily make decisions within the home-friends-school environment, opportunities for value education are abundant. How should one live in these immediate environments? What makes for good relationships with the many people encountered? What are the possible consequences of contemplated plans for the future?

Since the home-friend-school complex of relationships is immediate and inescapable, this cluster of content ranks high among the expressed needs of youth. Students of highly varied backgrounds and of a wide range of intelligence are apt to recognize the relevance of such discussions and inquiry.

In the usual high school program, home economics often plays a significant role with respect to family and peer groups. Other broad fields occasionally touch on family and friends but seldom extensively explore these topics. Learning about education is frequently neglected. Core and orientation programs in junior high schools sometimes deal with home, school and friends. Yet still more focus on the immediate environment in which youth lives is needed if secondary schools are to be realistic.

Health. Despite its famed technology, the United States is a considerable distance from the top level of developed nations in its health program. Once again it is a case of having the know-how and potentiality but failing with respect to social arrangements. Despite elaborate equipment, Americans fail to provide sufficient medical care for all of the people at a reasonable cost. It is not simply the lower income groups and the minorities who are shortchanged; the cost of private medical care pinches the middle classes too. Inadequacy of health care is a perennial American problem which looms large in any appraisal of social deficits in America.

A nation's health has sometimes been accorded high priority because of the relationship between good health and defense against foreign enemies. Draft rejections statistics have led to crusades for better health programs. But surely civilized people can recognize a higher social justification for good health than the presence or threat of the scourge of war. Simply put, is there not a higher quality of life in a society where good health is prized than in one in which poor health is prevalent? Disease, crippling, malnutrition, and poor health care wear no uniforms yet are life's deadly enemies.

That young people often behave as though they assume they could never be ill, injured, or dead is a reason to include, not neglect, health education in the curriculum. True, the problem of motivation is more difficult when one does not attribute a need to oneself. Yet young people can often be reached through appeals to their feelings for fellow human beings.

Two broad fields have an especial responsibility for fostering good health: physical education and the sciences. Physical educators rightly recognize the challenge in the chosen name of their organization: physical education, health, and recreation. The sciences include biology which, rightly taught, can foster understanding and improvement of health. Yet too often health appears to be an afterthought in secondary school programs. A greater impact on the personal and social aspects of health could be achieved if the study of health as a total pervasive problem were a fundamental part of a general education which crossed disciplinary lines.

Community living. Save for hermits, humankind, whether primitive or cosmopolitan, lives in communities. People must produce, distribute, and consume goods and services. They must communicate their messages. They must work out the organization of their group life; for instance, they must protect lives and property. They must agree on ways of governing themselves or else be subject to the governance of others. They must control their environment and conserve their resources. They must develop institutions to facilitate exchange of ideas, to educate their young, to meet their religious needs, to foster their artistic expression, and to use their leisure time.

Their interrelationships are fraught with value choices. What version of the good life should we strive for? What image of humankind should guide us? The abstractions become translated into practical decisions in respect to the functions of living named above. The choices become real in business and industrial organizations, in labor and agricultural groups, in governing bodies, in specializations in the community.

Steadily the interest of the adolescent in the community expands. He sees that many of the home, peer group, and family relationships which have absorbed him because of their immediacy are community influenced. The world "out there" with its procedures and taboos, its customs and expectancies, becomes increasingly recognized as important to the individual. To understand community life, and in time to change it in desirable directions, becomes a concern of youth.

In the usual high school curriculum, the social studies area has the primary responsibility for helping youth to understand and participate in social living. But, in a school which seeks relationships to the community, social education cannot stop at an area boundary. Consequently, fields such as the sciences, language arts, business education, and home economics, use the community for the application of the insights developed through these areas. Yet the characteristic structure of the subject-by-subject secondary school curriculum is such that comprehensive study of the community and its functions is difficult and participation in the life of the community through action-learning becomes well nigh impossible. So support grows for community education programs that cross subject boundaries and involve experiences in the community marked by action-learning. As community problems, such as those of the inner city or the rural slum, grow more vexing, the need for tapping the reservoir of youth energies grows more imperative.

Vocations. Among all social realities, it is the field of vocational orientation and preparation which has achieved highest recognition in the secondary school curriculum. Today high school educators are bombarded by advocates of career education, vocational education, and making the occupational transition to adulthood. If anything, secondary educators may need to guard against a possible over-vocationalizing of the curriculum.

Value considerations are prominent in instruction related to vocations. Not only are there long-established problems, such as reasonable vocational choices based on dependable data. Today the rationale of the work ethic itself is being questioned; the relative importance of work in a person's total life is being reexamined by social critics in an age that suspects that materialism is a dead-end road. Meanwhile, one segment of the population, youth from families living on welfare, finds little opportunity to experience the prevalent work ethic; to such young people any debate about the work ethic is academic.

Despite challenges to or inexperience with the work ethic, so strong is the prevalent emphasis on work in the United States that the vocational area continues to be of very high importance to the large majority of young (and older) people. Preparation for a job is often perceived as the basic reason for attendance at school. School, as youth frequently views it, is to train you for a job, help you "to do better" than your family, provide you with a higher income than if you lacked a diploma or a degree. "Practical" is often a good word in youth's lexicon, while "theoretical" and "abstract" are bad words.

In recognition of the importance of vocations in contemporary American life, secondary education sets aside a substantial proportion of time for "the third environment," namely work. Part of the curriculum is identified by its title as vocational, such as business education, industrial education, distributive education, agricultural education, and home making. Separate schools exist, whether broadly labeled vocational or indicating through their titles particular trades and occupations. And even the curriculum areas less identified as vocational by their titles are currently urged by United States Office of Education proposals to gear their offerings to career education. The high school reform proposals of the mid-1970s, typified by Coleman's *Youth: Transition to Adulthood*,[39] call for still more emphasis on the world of work, whether within or beyond the aegis of secondary schools.

Communication. Despite the deprecation of the three R's by those who contend that modern technology, such as television and electronic calculators, has rendered them obsolete, the ability to read, write, and handle mathematics remains important in communicating with people in today's pattern of social realities. To be a competent member of society today one must possess not only rudimentary skills but also a degree of mastery. Much of our knowledge is still set down in the form of words and symbols. Rather than minimize the relative importance of the three R's, we would be more sensibly employed in teaching them well while also recognizing the value of using the newer media of communication. We would be foolish people indeed if we ignored either the force of the tide of the new technology or the persisting power of the enduring underlying waves of earlier skills and media. Of course we need skills beyond the original three R's. But teaching the new basics need not imply discarding the old basics.

Whether the communication skills are old or new, they frequently communicate concerning matters of right and wrong, good and bad. This is as true in today's secular society as when the Puritans inter-

39. James S. Coleman, Chairman, *Youth: Transition to Adulthood*, Report of the Panel on Youth, President's Science Advisory Committee (Washington, D.C.: U.S. Government Printing Office, 1973).

preted the function of reading as that of enabling people to read and interpret the Bible. Value analysis is still essential. That today's communication media advance conflicting messages through commercials, propaganda, manipulated statistics, and attempts to shape public opinion, heightens the need for the development of reflective thought applied to all communication.

A caricature of youth portrays resistance to learning the three R's as the student celebrates the end of the school term or an unanticipated "snow day." The criticism inherent in the caricature might better be directed to unimaginative routine methods of instruction by teachers. In a classroom that relates both the skills and the new media to the young person's living experience, rather than simply teaching skills as something apart from reality, the process of communication via mathematics and language arts can become integral to meeting the needs of youth. In the hands of the creative teacher, communication processes can become vital to the solution of problems and perplexities faced by youth in modern society.

The curriculum area that has the major responsibility for teaching two of the original three R's and the uses of new media is the language arts. Yet the truism that every teacher should be a teacher of oral and written communication is sound. Team relationships between language arts teachers and teachers of other curricular areas hold promise and do not threaten the additional responsibilities of language arts teachers.

Alternative futures. Consider a twelve-year-old who is about to enter a secondary school in 1976. About half of this youngster's life will be lived in the twenty-first century! By the end of the twentieth century he or she will be only thirty-six years old. Some hardy specimens will still be alive into the second half of the twenty-first century. To confine study of social realities to the past or even to restrict such study to the present, would be to shortchange today's twelve-year-old by depriving him or her of the opportunity to learn about the alternatives that lie ahead.

Contemporary futurists do not predict that any single fixed future pattern will inevitably emerge. Instead, they emphasize that alternative futures must be projected and examined. Some of the alternative futures are preferable to others; some are highly desirable while others are repugnant. Consequently, study of alternative futures forces secondary school students to examine their values. They can no longer conceive their value choices simply as abstract preferences; they come to recognize the power of daily operational decisions in shaping alternative futures.

The twenty-first century can no longer be conceptualized as an era inhabited by people vaguely termed posterity. It becomes that segment of time in which the individual will live most of his or her life. Today's value-related decisions on energy, pollution, population, the economy, and the like, take on real significance when an individual recognizes that what people do today will help shape a highly personal tomorrow in which the individual will live, sharing whatever triumphs, dilemmas, or disasters lie ahead. Whether academically inclined or not, young people can see the relationship of alternative futures to their own lives and thus contemporary problems take on greater meaning.

Teachers of all subjects in the secondary school curriculum might profitably relate their instruction to alternative futures. Their potential gains would include more meaningful subject matter and a more motivated student group as students consider, for instance, alternative futures in the arts, in the sciences, in literature, and in society. But the most exciting approach to alternative futures is interdisciplinary study through which youth, with no holds barred, can envision the full sweep and range of the possible futures in which they may live.

Possible Curricular Organizations

While each of the above clusters of content is desirable in a well-rounded secondary education, schools will probably continue to differ in the relative emphasis they will place on each center of experience. For instance, while specialized vocational schools exist it is realistic to expect heavier emphasis on the vocational component of the above list in such schools. One might realistically expect that an alternative school that focuses heavily on the environment might especially stress the overpopulation-pollution-energy cluster of content. Similarly a comprehensive high school in an inner-city area might quite understandably judge communication to be an aspect of the curriculum deserving highest priority. While such differences are to be anticipated, a broad coverage of the centers of experience is desirable if a secondary school is to achieve an education based on needs, social realities, values, and knowledge. The total omission of one or more of the components of the list would serve neither the individual student nor American society.

We might well anticipate too that the forms of curricular organization adopted for implementation of these clusters of content will continue to be varied. No doubt the traditionally organized high school program will continue to implement these clusters of content through incorporating them in whole or in part in the separate curriculum areas and in disciplines within these areas. Thus we might expect to find certain of the clusters of content incorporated within disciplines in the areas of the social studies, the sciences, the language arts, mathematics, the several arts, the business-vocational subjects, physical education, and world languages. Other schools might emphasize certain of the centers of experience in more integrated teaching through, for instance, social studies instruction that interrelates social studies disciplines or subjects. Still more experimental forms of organization will use and extend core, team, humanities, and similar interdisciplinary and cross-disciplinary approaches to some of the clusters of content.

However the curriculum is organized, it is reasonable to anticipate that recognition of the importance of the centers of experience cited will grow in a relevant late twentieth century secondary education based on the interaction of social realities, needs, values, and meaningful bodies of knowledge. Reconsideration of the content of secondary education seems inescapable in the years ahead. Let us welcome reconsiderations, rather than resist them.

CHAPTER IX

How Should Learning Be Organized?

J. LLOYD TRUMP AND GORDON F. VARS

A cartoon prominently displayed in countless school administrators' offices shows two recumbent figures, one of whom says, "One of these days we've *got* to get organized." The message of this chapter is that organization—the fitting together of all the elements necessary for an institution to achieve its purposes—is truly a major factor in the success of any program of secondary education. We will especially consider the domain of secondary education and, in particular, curriculum organization, staff organization, other structural elements, and patterns to enhance motivation.

The Domain of Secondary Education

The extent of the domain of secondary education involves questions of the boundaries between elementary and secondary education, between secondary education and higher education, and between learnings provided in schools and learnings provided by the community and the home. Between elementary schools and senior high schools lie junior high schools and middle schools. Between senior high school and the upper years of college lies post-secondary education in community and junior colleges. The typical youth is educated by school, family, and community. What then is the domain of secondary education?

JUNIOR HIGH AND MIDDLE SCHOOL

The junior high school movement that began near the turn of the century brought about a separate intermediate institution in secondary education. The resultant junior high schools usually embraced grades 7, 8, and 9, although there were variations from state to state, from community to community, and sometimes even within the same school system. Although proposed as a transitional institution, neither

214

elementary nor secondary in character, many junior high schools became little more than imitation high schools. Thus, most communities ended up with essentially six years of elementary education followed by six years of secondary education usually carried on in separate junior and senior high school buildings.

The middle school movement which began in the mid-1960s also aimed to establish a truly transitional unit, uniquely different from either elementary or secondary education. Most proposals have been for a middle school unit consisting of grades 6, 7, and 8 or grades 5 through 8. Whether this new organization will develop the unique characteristics its proponents advocate, or whether it, in turn, will become another imitation high school for still younger students remains to be seen. If the latter occurs, the boundary between elementary and secondary education, now usually regarded as the beginning of the seventh grade, will have shifted down to grade 4 or 5.

The arguments for one form of intermediate institution as opposed to another have been examined elsewhere.[1] To date, neither logic nor research give unequivocal support for any particular clustering of ages or grade levels during the intermediate years. In most school districts, these matters are determined primarily by the capacity of available school buildings and current trends in enrollment, rather than commitment to a particular form of intermediate school organization. This situation suggests that educators might well cease the grade grouping argument and get on with the task of providing learning experiences appropriate for whatever age, grade, or maturity levels happen to be housed in a particular unit.

The intermediate level program requires that the curriculum, staff, and school environment be especially suited to young people going through "transescence," to use a term coined by Eichhorn to connote the transitional years that surround puberty.[2]

Theoretically, these provisions could be made in elementary, middle, or junior-senior high schools. As a matter of fact, each of these types of institution is likely to have a different atmosphere and identity, which in turn influence the educational program. For example, cir-

1. John H. Lounsbury and Gordon F. Vars, "The Middle School: Fresh Start or New Delusion?" *National Elementary Principal* 51 (November 1971): 12-19.

2. Donald H. Eichhorn, *The Middle School* (New York: Center for Applied Research in Education, 1966), p. 3.

cumstances may make it difficult for a seventh grade teacher to meet his young students' needs if he is teaching in a junior-senior high school, where status is accorded the senior high school athlete, scholar, or student leader. If, on the other hand, that seventh grade teacher seeks to serve transescents in an elementary school, one designed primarily for children, he may find himself limited by schedule, facilities, lack of staff specialists such as guidance counselors, and a program emphasis on teaching the basic skills. Inevitably and inexorably the "label" of a school, its public image, and its major clientele influence, both overtly and unconsciously, the general nature of the program. Thus a case can be made for a separate institution for transescents, although its most desirable boundaries cannot be set with certainty.

One possible solution is to have coinciding school environments, as suggested years ago by Anderson.[3] He proposed overlapping nongraded institutions embracing the equivalents of grades K-7, 6-10, and 8-12. Transfer from an elementary to an intermediate or middle school could take place at any time over a two-year period, and would depend upon the individual's academic progress, physical maturity, and sociopsychological status. Similar considerations would determine when the student was ready to move into a high school type of learning environment. Under such an arrangement, there would be no hard and fast boundaries between elementary and middle or between middle and high school education, but rather a truly articulated educational program.

A logical extension of this idea is to replace the concept of a graded school with a continuous progress program similar to but more sophisticated than the system that existed in this country prior to the middle 1800s when the graded system was imported from Prussia. Students in those days came to school when they were not needed for work on the farms, continuing their school work from the point where they left it previously. The continuous progress idea today permits students to progress at their own pace, freed from the necessity of spending nine months in one grade. A professional decision rather than arbitrary rules uniformly applied determines whether the school serves

3. Robert H. Anderson, "The Junior High School," *Architectural Record* 129 (January 1961): 126-31.

a given student better by keeping him or her with age mates or permitting advancement to a higher level where other students may be older.

Larger school systems may establish alternative institutions serving approximately the same age ranges but with different learning environments. For example, Middle School X would offer an especially warm, supportive, child-centered environment for slow-maturing students or those for whom transescence presents particular difficulties. Middle School Y would cater to the early maturing youth, offering both social and academic challenges that are geared to children who are advanced physically and intellectually but yet lacking in years of experience. Middle School Z would concentrate on the academic studies and give relatively little attention to students' person-social development, testing the dubious but often-stated assertion that the best way to help young people through adolescence is to ignore it. A better arrangement would be to have alternative environments within the same school building so that a student under guidance could transfer easily if he found himself too far out of step with his peers.

SECONDARY EDUCATION AND HIGHER EDUCATION

Controversy over what is secondary and what is higher education is less pronounced than over the issue of elementary *versus* middle *versus* secondary. Although in California grades ten through fourteen are sometimes housed in one public school facility, the predominant arrangement throughout the nation is to terminate high school education at grade twelve and to consider grades thirteen and fourteen to be part of higher education. Community colleges and junior colleges have tended to pattern their programs after four-year colleges and universities, even when they occupy the same building as a high school.

Increasingly, students enrolled in high schools are taking college-level courses as the continuous progress idea gains acceptance and the rigid separation between secondary and higher education decreases in significance. Independent study programs and flexible schedules in high schools facilitate the process.

The transition in philosophy and program between high school and college has not been as marked as that between elementary and secondary, hence there has been less concern over how education in grades thirteen and fourteen is labeled. Higher education usually represents a continuation of the specialization of instruction begun in the high school years.

SCHOOLS AND COMMUNITIES AND HOMES

The question of domain here is: What learnings should take place in schools and what should be learned in the community and at home? Learning has long occurred in homes, but since that domain had numerous drawbacks, society for centuries has operated institutions called schools. There have always been conflicts over the areas of responsibility of these two institutions. Use of the community as the third learning environment also has a long history. In this century the vocational education movement in the United States, given impetus by the Smith-HughesAct of 1918, emphasized increased use of the community. Over the years there has been more heat than light in the controversy over the respective domains of the three locales, largely because of the differences in what happens in the three places.

It is generally assumed that the school should be responsible for learnings that homes and communities do not provide, or else do not provide as well as the schools. Unfortunately, professional educators who operate schools have not themselves seen those distinctions clearly. For instance, some educators obviously believe that some school-initiated learnings are acquired better at home than at school or else they would not assign homework. But what kind of academic learning goes on in a noisy home with omnipresent television and a telephone available for peer interaction?

Use of the community as a learning environment has been stifled at times by the schools' insistence on providing replications or substitutions in school buildings. For example, for teaching auto mechanics, extensive shops often have been included in secondary school plans. Yet it is needlessly expensive for schools to install and maintain the up-to-date equipment that garages need to serve their customers. On the other hand, homes have been ineffective in teaching students how to drive automobiles safely and skillfully, so the school has to assume some of that responsibility. Similarly, it would be overly expensive, and indeed senseless, for schools to establish large "make-believe" department stores rather than to develop cooperative relationships with stores in the community for young people preparing to earn their living in merchandising.

Whether schools should serve as custodial institutions for students who no longer wish to attend is another current debate. Keeping students off the streets by forcing them to attend school may do damage to other students who want to learn in the school. It may also keep the students who do not wish to be there from learning in another environment that would suit them better. But educators and laymen have long supported universal public education, struggled to extend equal educational opportunities, and campaigned against students dropping out.

In 1973 the National Commission on the Reform of Secondary Education, established by the Charles F. Kettering Foundation, included among other recommendations that the formal school-leaving age should be dropped to age fourteen.[4] This proposal does not imply that learning stops at age fourteen but does urge that secondary schools should not be responsible for providing education for all students beyond that birthday. Rather, the report urges that students should have the opportunity to seek learning elsewhere and not be required by law to attend school.

We believe a better solution is to provide more individualized programming for secondary school students under the guidance *and monitoring* of teacher-advisors and professional counselors as demonstrated in a longitudinal program developed by the National Association of Secondary School Principals in a national project to improve schools. This program, as described later in this chapter, allows students under guidance and systematic reporting to spend considerable amounts of time in locations other than the school building. A combination of continuous progress, flexible scheduling, and curriculum alterations makes it possible for teacher-advisors to monitor each student's progress and needs to make the program work.

Also needed to make such a proposal work are more alternative schools, more alternative programs within each school, and a wide array of action-learning possibilities, as described in chapter 7. Orchestrating such a variety of options and helping each young person and his parents to make wise selections is a challenging task for the professional educator. It should not be left to chance or to the whim of an inexperienced youth.

It is difficult to justify any arbitrary age for the termination of compulsory education, be it fourteen or seventeen, or any other age.

---

4. National Commission on the Reform of Secondary Education, *The Reform of Secondary Education, A Report to the Public and the Profession.* (New York: McGraw-Hill Book Company, 1973), pp. 133-37.

The transition from full-time education to full-time employment should be a gradual one, varying in each individual case. Ultimately education must be accepted as a total effort of society, extending from the cradle to the grave, with formal schooling representing only a small portion of the process.

Curriculum Organization

One basic issue is whether the curriculum should be organized at all. Under such headings as "open education," "free form education," and "the free school," some persons argue that students should be completely free to choose what they will learn. Educators may offer and suggest, the argument goes, but they should not require students to participate in any particular learning experience. Other persons believe that reaction to the oppression and uniformity found in too many secondary schools today is hardly sufficient justification to embrace the other extreme, completely unstructured or "disorganized" education, except as an occasional diversion from the required learning activities. If one accepts the position that responsible adults must select and organize a portion of a student's learning, the form of organization becomes an issue.

Next comes the question of required versus elective learning experiences. Many schools still follow the pattern proposed more than three decades ago in *Education for All American Youth.*[5] In this plan the common learnings, which are emphasized in the early years, are diminished gradually through the years of secondary education. During the middle school years, required common learnings might make up a little more than half the program, whereas in senior high school student choice under guidance would predominate.

Today's schools usually organize the curriculum into courses measured in Carnegie Units, which typically require nine months to complete. A more rational organization would look at the question of required and elective learning as a three-way distribution: essential, special interest, and career.[6]

Every student should be required to achieve *essential* learnings in

5. Educational Policies Commission, *Education for All American Youth* (Washington, D.C.: National Educational Association, 1944).

6. On establishing priorities for curriculum improvement, see J. Lloyd Trump and Delmas F. Miller, *Secondary School Curriculum Improvement*, 2nd ed. (Boston: Allyn and Bacon, Inc., 1973), pp. 22-24 and 435-36.

the cognitive, affective, and psychomotor domains (in all of the areas of human knowledge). These common learnings should include widely diversified content. Unfortunately, the required curriculum is usually determined by experts in the various fields, who naturally are over-committed to the importance of their specialty. The identification of what is needed for everyone needs much more input from educators who are not specialists in a single subject field, as well as from adults outside the professional field of education. This kind of analysis is best done at the level of the local school district under the guidance of curriculum specialists. Ultimately we may reach some defensible national guidelines.

A second curriculum division provides for students who have a *special interest* in a particular topic or subject area but who are not viewing the area as a potential career. This division has sometimes been called the "hobby level." Both new and already existing special interests of students should be cultivated; the school should make every effort to interest students in learning more in all of the curriculum areas than they think they need at the moment.

The third part of the curriculum is that which is essential at the *career* level. Obviously, preparation for a career requires competence and interest in a subject beyond either the level that is required of everyone or the hobby level. Occupying a relatively small portion of the curriculum in the intermediate years, specific career preparation becomes increasingly important in senior high school and post-high school education.

Within any of these divisions, curriculum organization usually is conceptualized in two dimensions, horizontal and vertical, referred to by curriculum specialists as "scope" and "sequence." *Scope* refers to the array of experiences to which schools expose students within the same time frame. Thus the scope of a school program usually is defined by the variety of courses or units available during any one year, semester, or other designated period of time. The scope of each course or unit includes the ideas, skills, issues, and the like, with which the segment deals. *Sequence* refers to the order in which the school presents these ideas, experiences, courses, or segments to the students.

SCOPE

Defining scope in terms of subjects, such as English, biology, fine arts, and the like, continues to be the dominant approach in secondary schools today. This pattern, which copies the departmental structure of the university faculty, has the weight of tradition behind it. Students, teachers, and parents have relatively congruent notions of what is included in an English or mathematics course, especially if it bears a more specific title, such as "American Literature" or "Algebra II."

This form of organization has a number of competitors, most of them designed to counteract the compartmentalization of thinking that may come from departmentalizing the curriculum. Frequently secondary schools reduce departmentalization through a broad fields approach that divides the curriculum into such areas as the language arts, the social studies, and the sciences. Yet each broad field is compartmentalized.

Although terminology changes from time to time, the basic curriculum alternatives to compartmentalization have changed little since the experimentation of the 1930s with correlated subjects, unified studies, and core.[7] Time for these curricula may be arranged in conventional periods, in a large block-of-time, or in periods of varying length under a flexible schedule. Courses may be taught by one teacher per class or by a teaching team.

Correlated subjects. Since life is a seamless web and school subjects are largely arbitrary divisions of mankind's experience, overlapping of subjects is inevitable. Correlation is the deliberate attempt to capitalize on this overlap to reinforce student learning. Two or more courses are organized so that their contents run parallel. For example, if a history and an English teacher have the same students, the English teacher may deal with stories and poems related to World War II, while the history teacher covers the major events of this period. If the same students are also taking physical science, that teacher could deal with the science of nuclear energy, which played such a decisive role in the conflict. Two teachers may get together on a major written assignment, one teacher judging it in terms of English expression, while the other looks primarily at the content.

Successful correlation requires that teachers have ample time to plan together. An interdisciplinary team format facilitates the required continuous collaboration. The major difficulty with this approach is

7. William Van Til, Gordon F. Vars, and John H. Lounsbury, *Modern Education for the Junior High School Years*, 2d ed. (Indianapolis: Bobbs-Merrill, 1967), pp. 171-96.

keeping separate courses on the same timetable. Moreover, one course or the other may have to be taught in a less-than-optimal sequence to make it correlate with the other.

Unified studies. When two or more courses are fused into one course, eliminating the problem of timing, the result is called unified studies. In a humanities course, for example, teachers draw upon concepts and learning materials in literature, history, art, music, and philosophy using whatever content best meets the specified objective. A program made up of unified studies demands even more teacher collaboration than one using correlated subjects, since all team members design the new curriculum cooperatively. This kind of interdisciplinary program requires extended class periods, which are provided by doubling or tripling the number of periods (the block-time approach) or by assigning the course a large number of mods in a modular schedule.

Fusing subjects in a unified studies program may make the content more relevant or life-like, thus further reinforcing skills through application to a variety of learning experiences. On the other hand, fused subjects lose their identity and whatever logical sequence might seem appropriate when they are taught separately.

Core. Core is a quantum leap beyond unified studies, since it is based on a different approach to curriculum building. Instead of correlating or fusing the separate subjects, core is based directly on problems and concerns of young people as they grow up in contemporary society. Subject matter is brought in as it is needed to examine the problems. Core programs vary in the amount of direct student input in the selection of problems for study.

In "structured core," the teaching staff, after examining the needs of the learner, contemporary social realities, major values and organized knowledge, designs a set of broad problem areas or centers of experience to serve as a basic framework for the course. Certain centers of experience may be required of all core students at a certain grade level, or they may be merely suggested starting points for the teacher's planning with a particular class. In any case, the center of experience is broad enough to allow for considerable input from students in selecting specific questions for study, methods of approach, and evaluation procedures. In other words, teacher-student planning is a vital part of the teaching process in a core class, even when the problem area to be investigated is decided in advance by the staff.

In "unstructured core," each class and its teacher(s) is free to design its own curriculum, usually applying criteria such as the following in selecting units for study: (1) the unit must be worthwhile in the eyes of both students and teacher; (2) there must be adequate instructional resources for its study; and (3) it must be of interest to most of the students. Here, again, cooperative planning is the basic process, the important role of teacher guidance being symbolized by the all-important hyphen in the phrase *teacher-student planning*.

Core requires even more planning time than unified studies, and the staff must be willing to subordinate concern for covering conventional subject matter in favor of designing learning experiences focused on problems.[8] Even if the staff opts for an unstructured core, continuous attention must be given to grounding the program in student needs *and* social realities *and* values *and* appropriate knowledge.

In their current efforts to "humanize" or "personalize" education, many educators are unwittingly "re-inventing" the core curriculum. Unfortunately, in their zeal to make education responsive to the feelings and concerns of students they run the risk of repeating the excesses of the extreme child-centered wing of the Progressive education movement. Core educators learned long ago that curricular and instructional decisions cannot be turned over completely to students if schools are to meet their concurrent obligations to society and to the scholarly community. Those who wish to give student problems and concerns a more prominent place in the curriculum would do well to consult the literature on core, which spans five decades and embraces extensive experience.[9]

SEQUENCE

On the vertical dimension, the conventional age-graded curriculum is being challenged by a number of nongraded or continuous progress plans. All these approaches aim to break the learning sequence into

---

8. See *Core Today: Rationale and Implications* (Kent, Ohio: National Association for Core Curriculum, 1974); Gordon F. Vars, ed., *Common Learnings: Core and Interdisciplinary Team Approaches* (Scranton, Pa.: International Textbook Co., 1969).

9. Gordon F. Vars, "Curriculum in Secondary Schools and Colleges," in *A New Look at Progressive Education*, Yearbook of the Association for Supervision and Curriculum Development (Washington, D.C.: Association for Supervision and Curriculum Development, 1972), pp. 233-55.

steps smaller than a full-year course, so that failure to master any one set of learnings does not necessitate repeating a year or even a semester of instruction. Also, the learner, regardless of age or year in school, may work through these sequences at his or her own rate, taking up in September where he or she left off in June. Having opted to develop a nongraded curriculum, the curriculum designer must decide the number of sequences to be established.

The *single sequence* approach is typified by linear programmed instruction. The assumption is that there is one best sequence for learning a particular set of concepts or skills. The learner is led through this sequence a small step at a time, is reinforced for his correct responses, and is forced to repeat only those parts he misses. Linear programming can be a powerful tool when used appropriately, such as for instruction in basic skills. Secondary school students, however, may become bored and restive when their learning is so closely controlled.

The *multiple sequence* or branching design provides optional pathways, all leading to accomplishment of the same goal. Learning is broken down into small bits as in linear programming. Control of the learning sequence remains in the hands of the curriculum designer but the student is not "led by the nose" quite so closely. Computer-based systems represent quite sophisticated applications of this approach.

The *variable sequence* design places control of the sequence in the hands of the student on the assumption that no specific order is best for studying the material. The curriculum usually is divided into units of subject matter considerably larger than the segments of programmed learning but smaller than a semester or year-long course. Minicourses are a popular approach, usually embracing six to nine weeks of instruction on a particular topic, theme, or problem. Some schools break the curriculum into even smaller units and present them through learning packets that require anything from a few hours to several days for the student to complete. Occasionally the school exercises control over the sequence by setting prerequisites for certain minicourses or learning packets.

The curriculum designer must decide how crucial the matter of sequence is in learning a particular set of skills, concepts, or generalizations. Experts do not agree on any one best sequence for learning even such basic skills as reading and mathematics. Therefore, the single-sequence approach would appear to have little application in secondary education, except in some highly technical training tasks, such as electronics. Branching programs, provided that the alternative paths make allowances for individual differences in learning style, might be useful for remedial instruction in areas such as reading and mathematics. Foreign language instruction, too, might be taught effectively by offering multiple sequences. Laboratories for language learning make this approach feasible. As students grow in capacity and experience, they should exercise ever-increasing options under professional guidance. Hence, variable sequence designs should be the norm in most secondary curricula.

In both scope and sequence, curriculum organization should vary according to the nature and purposes of the learning being provided. The school may provide certain common learnings through an interdisciplinary team or core program, while essential basic skills are developed through one or more continuous progress sequences. Special interests and career preparation may be provided through electives, minicourses, independent study, and student activities, each utilizing whatever curriculum design the staff considers most appropriate. In curriculum, as in most things of life, there is no one best design for learning.

Although both the scope and the sequence of the curriculum should make allowances for individual differences, a student should not work by himself during most of the school day. Peer interaction is extremely important for the social and emotional health of young people. In the model that follows, although most of the *curriculum* is individualized, *instruction* provides ample opportunities for the student to work with others in groups of various sizes.

Staff Organization

Although traditional staffing patterns still predominate, schools are turning more and more to differentiated staffing in recognition of the variety of functions that need to be carried on and the different types of persons needed to help young people.

In a model disseminated by the National Association of Secondary School Principals, the *people* involved in interacting with learners include a differentiated instructional staff, a differentiated counseling staff, and a differentiated staff for supervision and management. Differentiated staffing makes obsolete the usual staffing ratios, such as one teacher for each 25 students, one guidance counselor for each 300, and one principal for the entire school, aided by varying numbers of assistant principals, usually one for each 750 to 1,000 pupils or major fraction of that number.

One plan for a differentiated instructional staff, advocated by Trump and others for many years, is based upon studies of what roles teachers perform in schools. Available for each teacher in the school, but not necessarily assigned to each teacher, should be an average of twenty hours per week of services by instructional assistants, ten hours per week of clerical assistance, and five hours per week of service from general aides.[10]

Instructional assistants work under the supervision of teachers in various study/work centers in the school and throughout the community. Some instructional assistants, usually parents of the school's students, also aid students in their study and work at home. Teachers need to provide all of these assistants with adequate guidelines and also to supervise their work with varied degrees of closeness, depending on the location of the assistants and what the teachers expect them to do. The work of *clerical assistants* includes typing, keeping records, tabulating data and preparing reports, and is also under the supervision of teachers. These clerical activities now take as much as one-third of the time that teachers spend in schools without clerical assistance for teachers. *General aides* assist teachers by getting materials out, putting them back, supervising the cafeteria and performing other tasks where neither specific knowledge in a subject field nor clerical skills are essential. All of these persons who assist teachers should be carefully selected, trained by the staff, supervised, and evaluated by the staff under programs developed by the school's supervisory team.

The differentiated counseling staff includes teacher-advisors with roles markedly different from teacher roles in conventional homeroom or advisory groups. (What teacher-advisors do is described in another section of this chapter.) These advisors are supervised by professional counselors who are freed from routine work related to attendance, discipline, making out student programs, and the like—tasks that others perform. Each professional counselor supervises the work of ap-

10. J. Lloyd Trump, *Images of the Future—A New Approach to the Secondary School* (Washington, D.C.: National Association of Secondary School Principals, 1959.), pp. 19-22.

proximately twelve teacher-advisors who, in turn, are responsible for monitoring the progress of 300 to 350 students. Thus, a school of 1,000 or so pupils would have three professional counselors who supervise three clusters of twelve teachers each and the 300 to 350 students that each cluster of twelve teachers advises.[11] An assistant principal in this school of 1,000 students would supervise two counselors and their teacher-advisors, meeting with them regularly, while the principal would supervise the other counselor and the teacher-advisors assigned to that person.

The other members of the guidance staff are specialists who assist, as needed, all of the above groups and persons involved: psychologists, psychometrists, speech pathologists, audiologists, and other technical and clerical assistants. Whether these persons are full-time or part-time specialists depends upon the size of the school and the system.

The differentiated staff for supervision and management that we recommend is based on the conviction that the present concept of the principal as "jack-of-all trades" is unrealistic and ineffective. Since the most important responsibility of a school principal is the continuous effort to improve the quality of learning and teaching, in the setting of the local school and community, we suggest staffing that makes this goal possible.

Principals now spend much of their time and energy on tasks for which they are not prepared effectively and that could be done better by persons who have special training to perform them. We have recommended in other publications[12] the following staff and functions, with the number of persons varying with the size of the school. The principal needs to spend three-fourths of his or her time on instruction and one-fourth in general supervision of the other staff persons. Assistant principals should spend all of their time working with teachers and students on the improvement of instruction. There should be one such assistant principal for each 1,000 students in a school or major fraction of that figure.

Other functions are performed by four persons: the building ad-

11. J. Lloyd Trump, and William Georgiades, *The Teacher-Advisor Role*. Filmstrip with sound and descriptive pamphlet (Washington, D.C.: National Association of Secondary School Principals, 1973).

12. J. Lloyd Trump, "Principal Most Potent Factor in Determining School Excellence," *Bulletin of the National Association of Secondary School Principals* 20 (March 1972): 3-9.

ministrator, the external relations director, the personnel administrator, and the activities director. These positions would be full-time in a school of 2,000 pupils; in a school one-half that size two full-time persons would perform the tasks indicated here. The *building administrator* greets visitors, sees salesmen, looks after the condition of the building, and the like. The *external relations director* handles school finances and public relations, working with various individuals and groups in the community as well as with the central office, the state education department, regional accrediting agencies, and other external bodies. The *personnel administrator* works with juvenile and welfare agencies in the community, supervises the general program for dealing with students and staff, and performs related functions. The *activities director* is responsible for all of the entertainment and athletic programs of the school as well as the varied program of extra-curricular activities. These staff persons do not have the identical training that principals and assistant principals are provided through the usual courses in school administration and supervision; instead, they are especially prepared for the jobs assigned to them.

The emphasis in the training of principals and assistant principals is on improving the quality of instruction. They work closely with unit, team, or "house" leaders or the chairmen of the curricular departments of the school, who in turn aim to improve the selection of content and methods of teaching and learning.

Other Structural Elements in Education

Learning in a school also depends on how *time* is used; the *student groups* that are assembled at various times and places for different learning activities; the kinds and numbers of *spaces* that are provided in the school *facilities*, in the community, and in homes; how *money* is spent and the *consequences* of expenditures in money and time; the procedures that the school devises to provide *options* for students in *evaluation*; the *duration* of school sessions; and the *alternatives* that are provided in the utilization of program and people resources in a school for *instructional organization*.

We emphasize certain features here because neglect of any one of these aspects of *structure*, just as in the case with *people* and *programs*, will limit the potential success of the services that the school provides for students.

TIME

How time is used tells us much about an individual. How time is organized and utilized tells us much about a secondary school. It is both unrealistic and ridiculous to assume that learning for all persons requires the same number of minutes per week in all subjects. The concept of ringing bells every fifty minutes or any other standard length of time has been criticized for many years.[13] The needs, talents, and interests of individual learners should be taken into account in determining how much time each one of them will need in any given kind of activity.

Obviously, some group meetings have to be scheduled at specified times. But the number of these meetings usually can be much fewer than at present, leaving the major amount of time in a school at the disposition of each teaching team. With more mature students, greater responsibility for time utilization should be delegated to the student himself, working under the general supervision and direction of his teacher advisor and more directly under the staff member in charge of the particular area in which the student has agreed to study at a given time.

STUDENT GROUPINGS

The conventional secondary school arranges most student activities in standard groups of approximately twenty-five to thirty persons. If the number is smaller, the school worries about the cost; if the number is larger, the concern is whether extra chairs or desks can be crowded into a standard-sized classroom.

Completely different concepts as to the grouping of students are needed. So far as study is concerned, the number of pupils working at a given time may vary from one to an indefinite number. Some learning activities are best developed by the student working alone as a single individual. More frequently three or four students may work together around a table or in an area. At other times, however, groups of a different size may be assembled, according to the type of learning activity. For group problem solving and practice in discussion skills, the groups typically should be about twelve to eighteen. Much larger

13. J. Lloyd Trump, *And No Bells Ring*, black and white sound film with narration by Hugh Downs (Washington, D.C.: National Education Association, Distributor, 1960).

groups may be assembled to hear a teacher, a community member, a student presentation, or to view films or television programs. This kind of large-group instruction for specific purposes may occur either in the school or in the community. Most schools have found that groups of approximately 100 or so are easier to manage than extremely large groups.

The point is that the size of any group or the number of pupils that are assembled at any time should relate specifically to the purpose of the learning and teaching under way. When size and number are recognized as related to learning and teaching it would appear that the usual classroom size of twenty-five to thirty is not the right size for anything! A group of twenty-five to thirty is too large for discussion, unnecessarily small for presentations, and inappropriate for individual study and small group work.[14]

SPACE AND FACILITIES

Every student should be able to find a place in the school building where he or she can work happily and effectively. That requirement necessitates a variety of learning spaces. Each space should be comfortably heated, lighted, acoustically satisfactory, and well maintained. Since some students listen and view better than they read, a variety of materials to aid in learning should be available.

Teachers also need similar kinds of arrangements. Yet many schools do not provide a private and well equipped place for teachers to study and work. Every teacher needs his own office, not large, but adequate. The same situation applies to members of the supervisory-management team.

A school needs a variety of spaces for independent study with an equally wide variety of supplies and equipment if individual needs are to be served. Schools also need a variety of places for students to meet in small groups. Also needed is a teaching auditorium quite different from the theater-like auditoriums that many schools provide. A teaching auditorium provides close contact between the listeners and the presentation.

Obviously, then, the spaces that are provided in schools must vary in size. Schools have approached the solution to this problem in

14. J. Lloyd Trump and Dorsey Baynham, *Focus on Change—Guide to Better Schools* (Chicago: Rand McNally, 1961), pp. 24-33.

various ways during the past two decades. First came the adoption of operable walls, so that teachers could open or close walls whenever needed. Then came the modular concept that makes it possible to vary the size of teaching spaces, perhaps even by remodeling over a weekend. The wide-open "loft" plan also is popular.

In large schools, space should be arranged so that students do not feel lost in the mob. Room clusters or pods facilitate the organization of "houses" or schools-within-a-school, an important means of giving each student a manageable number of peers and staff with whom to identify and interact.

The more imaginative school administrators and architects now are designing buildings with a variety of spaces in them. Students move about these buildings in accordance with their need for one kind of space or another. Such buildings are acoustically and aesthetically more satisfying than either schools with cavernous open spaces or those with operable or movable walls that are not acoustically satisfactory.

The typical older building may get in the way of student learning; many of the newer buildings are no more than neutral in this regard. We need schools with a variety of spaces that contribute positively to teaching and learning. Today there is too little relationship between the amount of money that is spent and the constructive contribution that buildings make.

Educational facilities change as a school's ideas grow. Facilities must be warm, beautiful, exciting environments that say something positive to the students, teachers, and supervisors who live and work there. And we must always remember that all learning does not occur in a place called a school building. The responsibility is to relate the total learning environment—school building, community, home—to the educational program of each individual in it. Schools increasingly are using the community as study environments, as chapter 7 has pointed out. As this trend continues, school buildings and grounds may be smaller than they are now and thus more economical.[15]

MONEY AND CONSEQUENCES

One hopes that ultimately the organized teaching profession of this country will advocate spending money *differently* rather than simply spending more of it on conventional activities and programs.

15. An excellent school designed along these lines is the Bishop Carroll High School, Calgary, Alberta, Canada.

Determining the consequences of the expenditure of money is an essential ingredient in improving the use of money. Having agreed on the goals of learning in any school, the question should always be: What are the learning outcomes of the money that is being spent? Is it wise to spend money on data processing to print out the same kind of report cards? Might it be a better expenditure of money to use data processing to assist in monitoring the progress of students? Computers can keep track of a wide variety of educational objectives in order to produce data that would be used by professional teachers in diagnostic and prescriptive teaching. Similarly, we might ask whether it is wise to spend money on data processing to make the same kind of schedule or to assign pupils to the same kind of classes.

OPTIONS IN EVALUATION

Options also should be available in the field of evaluation. Rather than argue about whether all schools should give all students, A, B, C, D, F grades, P-F grades, no failing grades, or no grades at all, school staffs should provide options in progress reports just as they provide options in other aspects of schooling.

Educators do need to know at any time precisely where a student is in working through a nongraded sequence of required learnings. They need to know progress toward cognitive, affective, and psychomotor objectives. These needs call for criterion-referenced, highly individualized evaluation and record keeping. On the other hand, each school needs to know how its students' performance compares with others. This calls for some norm-referenced evaluation. Rather than argue whether a school should utilize criterion-referenced evaluation strategies or norm-based strategies, school staffs should use both, plus comprehensive records of each individual's productivity.

DURATION OF SCHOOL SESSIONS

The time that schools are in session also influences learning. Is there any reason to expect learning to take place only between the hours of nine and three each day, or from September to May or June? Yet, some of the proposed arrangements for year-round schools suggest dubious replacements: turn learning on for eighteen weeks and then forget about it for three! And do we think students learn only Monday through Friday, or from ages six through eighteen?

Schools should always be available. With advice and with supervision, high school students should be able to drop in and drop out of school with a reasonable degree of freedom. William Wirt said it very well many years ago in a booklet entitled *The Great Lockout in America's Citizenship Plants:* schools should never be closed and students should be able to learn at any time.[16]

ALTERNATIVES IN INSTRUCTIONAL ORGANIZATION

Throughout this discussion we have emphasized the value of the individual student, his or her needs, concerns, and unique potentialities. The degree of individualized learning that operates in any school is directly proportional to the number of options that the school provides under systematic guidance and supervision. If options are to contribute to individualized learning, someone in the school must constantly monitor the progress of each student through diagnosis, prescription, implementation, and evaluation. The aim is to help each student discover his own interests and talents and to capitalize upon them to the maximum degree possible.

The role of the teacher-advisor. A school needs arrangements whereby every student is known by someone who does not have to consult a file before talking to the individual, parents, prospective employers, or to college representatives about the student's total educational situation. A humane school, among other things, is a place where every human being is known, cared for, and valued by at least one other person. A teacher-advisor for each student is needed. Classroom teachers know pupils in their classes but mainly as students of the subject they teach, unless the student is either exceptionally "good" or exceptionally "bad." A teacher-advisor has sufficient data to work with the student in diagnosing problems that he or she faces and in analyzing the successes or failures that the individual is experiencing.

The students assigned to a given teacher-advisor should represent two or more of the grades or age levels in the school and the teacher-student relationship should extend over several years. It is always possible for the guidance counselor or the administrator in charge to make changes when it is in the best interests of either a given student or of a given teacher.

16. William A. Wirt, *The Great Lockout in America's Citizenship Plants* (Gary, Ind.: Printed by students of Horace Mann School, 1937.)

Placing decisions about programs and procedures in the hands of a teacher-advisor rather than a guidance counselor, assistant principal, or principal, represents a basic but necessary departure from present practice for most schools. It is essential because counselors and principals simply do not have the time and knowledge to make adequate decisions: the number of students with which they have to deal is too large. The teacher-advisor has the time and the authority to do something constructive about helping each student in the school.

Incidentally, this assignment changes the role of the teacher. The teacher-advisor no longer is interested only in the subject or broad field he or she teaches, but now becomes interested in all of the educational opportunities that the school affords, because advisees are involved with all of them. The advisor receives reports and has contacts with all aspects of the students' educational program in the school, in the community, and in the home. This development is wholesome for teachers. It does not detract from their specialized interests in the subjects or broad fields they teach; in fact it improves their teaching because they now see what they teach in relation to all of the other learning opportunities that the school provides.

Improving social attitudes and performance. While it is true that the central focus in organizing teaching and learning is on the individual student, a second element also is essential. Society depends for its survival both on the quality of the individuals who make it up and also on their willingness and competence to cooperate effectively for the general welfare of the total group. The strength of a group comes from the vigor and self-adjustment of individuals in it. Social sensitivity, cooperation, and appreciation of group needs and goals are essential. The school needs to organize a specific program to develop both individual and group skills.

The core curriculum is a time-tested vehicle for developing individual and social values and competencies. Other interdisciplinary programs such as unified studies or humanities also have some potential in this regard, provided that these objectives are definitely built into the curriculum.

In schools that retain the departmentalized pattern, we recommend that groups of ten to fifteen students be assembled regularly to discuss matters of personal and social concern to them. Such "analysis" groups help in bringing home the relevance of the problems studied in all the curricular areas. Groups of ten to fifteen students are large enough to represent divergent values and points of view yet small enough to permit an effective group process to take place. Although techniques of group discussion may be taught in regular classes, they need to be practiced in dealing personally with experiences that the students are having currently in school, in the community, and at home.

Evaluation of these activities comes through the use of observation ratings, sociometric devices, attitude scales, personal essays, diaries, and the like. The proof of success lies in changes in student skills, attitudes, values, and knowledge—in short, the functioning of students as total human beings.

Organizational Patterns to Enhance Student Motivation

The procedures followed in many schools to motivate pupils are too often inadequate. We refer to such practices as: ability grouping, the "self-sufficient" classroom, conventional grading and reporting policies, and the system of rewards and penalties that emphasizes constant threats and seldom produces rewards that are meaningful to different kinds of students. Even teacher-student planning may fail to motivate students if it is overly dominated by teachers or if students "play the game" and do what the teacher had in mind anyway.

Ability grouping is practiced on the presumption that students are competing with students of similar ability or past achievements. In point of fact, ability grouping merely camouflages differences among students, leading both teachers and students to stereotype and stigmatize students in both the "high" and the "low" groups.

A self-sufficient classroom can be the scene of excellent learning experiences. Too often, however, the one-teacher-per-classroom approach has grave limitations: teacher-dominated discussions, limited supplies and equipment, separation from the home and community, grading and reporting policies that doom in advance some students to average and below-average grades or that provide rewards that are interesting only to academically oriented and talented students. Students need the emotional security that comes from extended association with a teacher-advisor, but most of them also need the stimulation and variety provided by a teaching team.

The basic interests of students are in their "real world," that is, the present in time and space. For many, five years ago is ancient history.

Motivation relates to the students' present environment, often extremely limited for ghetto youth, only a little wider for the wealthier suburbanite, and, in both cases, influenced by television and other mass media. The typical teacher's purposes mostly are in a "make-believe world" as far as pupils are concerned. So motivation requires that the teachers utilize the pupil's real world of time and space to arouse his interests, if the "make-believe world" is ever to become real to the student.

Many factors affect motivation. Required learnings must be right for each pupil, neither too difficult nor too easy. Suggested learning activities must be clearly explained, and the student must be told how he may judge accurately whether or not he has accomplished the specified goals. The student should complete the work at his own pace.

Motivation also requires that a student may relate to and learn from the teacher who can best help him. In a good school a student can relate to a variety of teachers, to instructional assistants in the school and in the community, and to teacher-advisors, guidance counselors, administrators, media specialists, and other adults. Frequently among his teachers may be another student who understands a concept or skill and can explain it better than an older person.

Motivation requires an individual schedule that permits each student, with the advice and consent of his teacher-advisor, to spend different and varying amounts of time in diversified study and work centers at the school and in the community (with, by the way, transportation provided).

Students should constantly be bombarded in all areas of knowledge and activity by the most exciting presentations the school can produce to stretch the students' minds and, hopefully, to snare them into doing more and better independent study. These presentations can be made by teachers, by other students, by people from the community, by films, television, and other audio-visual devices, by challenging magazines and newspapers, by thought-provoking bulletin boards, and so on, in a variety of settings.

The evaluation and reward system that the school provides also influences motivation. The possibility of obtaining a high grade is motivation for some, but not for all. While it may be unwise to abolish A, B, C grades completely, it may be equally unfortunate to insist that all pupils receive letter grades. Some students may be motivated by a monetary reward, the privilege of working in the community, the privilege of spending some time with snacks provided in the school's social room, the privilege of a field trip, some recreational time, and so on. A variety of rewards are needed in a school.

The emphasis in evaluation must basically be with comparisons related to the student's own past achievements. He also needs, however, to understand his scores on standardized or norm-based tests as well as his progress in reaching certain criteria set by the school or by himself. The school staff also needs to record the achievement of each student in independent study, even if the product might have been insignificant. What was done by that student belongs in his record. And his records are now open to his parents.

The availability and kinds of study materials also affect pupil motivation. Large libraries and large multi-purpose resource centers may overwhelm students and contribute to a loss of interest, because students may have difficulty in finding what they need or want. Supplemental resource centers, perhaps arranged by subject areas or clusters of related subjects, may be more useful for some students. Since the resources in the community may be superior to those in a school, they should be utilized and made readily accessible.

Motivation requires subtle, but continuous, adult supervision of students. Too often, the open-campus, unstructured-time concept is anti-motivational, because unscheduled time is viewed as free time. Accountability of the right kind is required; chaos destroys interest and shows that the school personnel really does not care about the individual.

A school needs a variety of motivational arrangements if pupils are to meet and work together. For instance, some students will be turned off by overly-supervised, artificially-quiet study areas. Other students will be equally turned off if the atmosphere is noisy and chaotic. So schools need a variety of places, all under supervision, so that students may choose quiet or less quiet places. Since students also study and work at home and in the community, the school should be extremely careful in making assignments that are to be completed in those two locales; the school personnel should decide which locale is best for certain kinds of learning, then make assignments and recommendations accordingly.

Conclusion

Diversity and flexibility are key concepts in organizing learning experiences. The secondary school is a multipurpose institution, providing essential common learnings, special interest experiences, and career preparation. Students, too, are diverse in maturity, learning style, ability, and life goals, to name but a few of the factors to be considered. Staff members also are different, and communities vary in what they expect of their schools.

With such diverse purposes, clientele, staff, and patrons, the secondary school must offer a rich array of organizational alternatives, and it must be prepared to modify curricula, staffing patterns, student groupings, time, space, facilities, and even intangibles such as school climate whenever needs change. Yet secondary schools must have enough stability and order to provide the psychological security essential to us all.

Organizing secondary schools to provide the right mixture of order, flexibility, and diversity is a major challenge that educators must constantly confront and resolve. The continuous analysis of the effects of various organizations of learning provides data for further prescriptive actions in the never-ending search for better ways of serving the diverse needs of the students, teachers, and the community.

CHAPTER X

Teaching Strategies for Pluralistic Teaching

RONALD T. HYMAN

Teaching Strategies
ROOTS AND DEFINITION

The concept of strategy and the use of strategy are ancient and have been with us in teaching for centuries. In reply to Meno's request to teach him, Socrates sets up a demonstration. In this demonstration Socrates wisely interrupts himself after each critical step in his strategy in order to comment on what has happened so that Meno will not miss the importance of each step. Furthermore, during the interruption Socrates introduces the next step in the demonstration so as to guide Meno in observing Socrates, the master strategist.[1]

Socrates understands what his strategy is, knows its various parts, and has a keen insight about teaching it to others. Hence, he proceeds one "step" at a time in his demonstration and points out the essence of his "step by step" procedure before and after each step. By this demonstration for Meno, Socrates shows his mastery of teaching on two levels, teaching and teaching how to teach. On each level he uses a different strategy. An explication of these different strategies follows in this chapter.

Indeed, the very word "strategy" is derived from the Greek word for "general." A Greek *strategos* devised a careful plan so as to lead his men successfully in achieving their goal of winning. In time, the word "strategy" came to apply generically to endeavors where a leader uses a plan involving a series of steps. So as to have an explicit referent for

---

1. Ronald T. Hyman, *Ways of Teaching*, 2nd ed. (Philadelphia: J. B. Lippincott Company, 1974).

the word "strategy" as it applies to teaching, we will use the following definition: *Strategy is a carefully prepared plan involving a sequence of steps designed to achieve a given goal.*

The current rise in interest in teaching strategies stems from two movements that gained popularity in the 1960s. The first, the curriculum reform movement, is commonly associated with Bruner and his followers.[2] Educators sought new ways to revitalize teaching in the schools. They were aware that there was more than one way to teach. The educational literature of the 1920s, 1930s, and 1940s had called on teachers to shift their emphasis and approach. Yet one way still predominated across the country. With the design of new curricular projects from nursery school through graduate and professional school came the pressing need for a variety of teaching approaches. That is to say, the conception of a particular project demanded a particular teaching strategy or strategies. Teachers could not implement the "new curriculums" unless they adopted teaching approaches in harmony with the projects.

The second movement, the study of verbal interaction in the classroom, is commonly associated with Flanders, Smith, Bellack, Gallagher, Aschner, and Hughes, among others.[3] This movement arose as a result of the desire by educators to know more about what teachers actually do in the classroom, rather than what they should do. Related to this study of verbal interaction were the concurrent movements in (1) philosophy, which set out to describe the uses of ordinary language, and (2) educational research, which set out to delineate at least the groundwork for a theory of teaching.[4] These educators realized from their descriptions of the verbal interaction in classrooms that a common and uniform approach to teaching persisted, despite the enthusiastic requests for and the acceptances of alternative strategies. They further recognized the need to specify clearly the teaching strategies that could serve as alternatives to the existing patterns of classroom interaction.

2. Jerome S. Bruner, *The Process of Education* (Cambridge: Harvard University Press, 1960); idem, *On Knowing* (Cambridge: Harvard University Press, 1962).

3. Ronald T. Hyman, ed., *Teaching: Vantage Points for Study*, 2nd ed. (Philadelphia: J. B. Lippincott Company, 1974).

4. Ronald T. Hyman, ed., *Contemporary Thought on Teaching* (Englewood Cliffs, N. J.: Prentice-Hall, Inc., 1971), Parts I and II.

It is significant that many of the educators who subsequently delved into the development and popularization of alternative teaching strategies were precisely those who were closely associated with one of the two foundation movements mentioned above. For example, Taba based her prescriptive strategies on her descriptive studies of thought processes in the classroom.[5] These strategists' efforts, therefore, are an outgrowth of previous work, rather than a superimposed trend or an opposite trend appearing out of context and springing full grown from the heads of educational faddists.

TYPES OF TEACHING STRATEGIES AND THEIR RATIONALES

There are three main types of teaching strategies, classified and named according to the essential activity of the teacher: exemplifying, enabling, and presenting. Each type has its distinctive characteristics, rationale, advantages, and disadvantages. Let us examine these three strategies closely.

The three names for the strategies are deliberately stipulated. First, the name of each strategy offers a capsule idea of the teacher's intent and activity when utilizing that particular strategy. Second, the names are couched in plain and clear English in order to facilitate comprehension and to avoid confusion and vagueness. Third, names are new so as to eliminate associations teachers have with previous labels for strategies that are identified with a particular group of people, curriculum project, or philosophy.

Several more common labels are therefore missing. Take the case of "heuristics," a word of Greek derivation, which was a popular term in the 1960s. Most classroom teachers did not and still do not understand that word. What is worse, the term "heuristics" misleads many teachers, for it often appears as a synonym for "discovery" teaching. But discovery is generally designated as the goal of the student, not the teacher, and hence the teacher does not receive help and clues about what the *teacher* should do when following the exhortation that he should engage in heuristics or discovery teaching. So, "heuristics" and "discovery," as strategy names, as well as the terms "didactics,"

---

5. Hilda Taba and Freeman F. Elzey, "Teaching Strategies and Thought Processes," in *Teaching: Vantage Points for Study*, pp. 483-500.

"guidance," "modeling," and "expository," among others, are absent from our description of possible strategies.

THE PRESENTING STRATEGY

At this time, the best known strategy in its various forms is the presenting strategy. Most teachers consciously use the presenting strategy more than enabling and exemplifying. The lecture and recitation belong to this type of strategy, in which the teacher sets forth the information to be received and learned by the student. Usually the teacher does this orally; occasionally he does so in writing. The teacher can be a live person or a substitute in the form of a textbook, film, recording, or computerized program. The student receives and processes the information presented in order to understand the message transmitted to him. Sometimes the message is a general idea or belief. At other times the message sent by the teacher is a group of specific information units. The student then either particularizes the general message or generalizes from the specifics. He may do so through the aid of some check-up questions prepared by the teacher, but he does so mainly through his own efforts. Often the teacher particularizes or generalizes for the student. The student then relates his new learning to his own life and acts upon it in the future in situations related to it.

The presenting strategy is based on the following ideas: (1) that the teacher knows what information the student needs to know; (2) that the teacher is himself familiar with the needed information; (3) that the teacher can effectively transmit his message containing the information to the student; (4) that the student can cope with the highly symbolic nature of this strategy (symbolic in that the teacher's message comes mostly through oral channels); and (5) that the student can particularize and generalize from transmitted messages, relate the teacher's messages to his own life, and act on symbolically derived learning.

In the presenting strategy the teacher is the more active participant, physically, cognitively, and emotionally. He selects the information, organizes it, presents it, and re-presents it in an effort to be clear and comprehensible, and questions the student in order to be sure that the student is following him. The teacher is the diagnostician, selector, organizer, synthesizer, presenter, questioner, and examiner. The student is mainly a receiver and relater in the classroom. Usually the student is expected to act on his new learning out of class, rather than in class in connection with the presentation. The physical, cognitive, and emotional load of the student is not nearly as great as that of the teacher.

The greatest single advantage of presenting is its "generational" efficiency. Through this strategy, each generation of students can benefit easily from its predecessors. Were it not for our ability to learn through symbolic crystallization and transmission of information, each generation would be forced, so to speak, to rediscover slowly on its own how to make a fire, how to make a wheel, how to write, how to calculate, how to cure diseases, how to build bridges, how to make telephones, and so forth. The teacher who presents can teach about many topics in a short period of time.

Other advantages of the presenting strategy are related to its generational efficiency. Because they are not significantly taxed physically, cognitively, and emotionally, students can devote themselves to several teachers and their messages simultaneously. The low expenditure of energy allows the students to study longer and hence receive more messages. The presenting strategy also suits many students who do not feel ready to study on their own, or who do not have the resources available to do so, or who prefer to listen to an experienced, knowledgeable person.

The disadvantages of presenting are equally apparent. Many students simply do not have the cognitive ability to cope with the symbolic nature of the transmitted messages. Therefore, their ability to understand, relate, and then apply the messages is limited. Such students learn little through this strategy. Furthermore, since most of the decisions and tasks dealing with the information come from the teacher, the student may not even be interested enough to exert the necessary effort to receive, perceive, relate, and apply the message. That is, the message may not be meaningful to the students because they are not sufficiently involved with it. When meaningfulness and interest are lacking, the students often do not exert the cognitive attention and energy needed to perceive, to particularize, to generalize, to relate, and to apply the message. If "forced" to do these tasks by the teacher through extrinsic rewards, threats, tests, or check-up questions, the students may become hostile. On the other hand, teachers fear that without such extrinsic and coercive techniques the students may quickly forget what they have learned. Such means and such results have their own well-known limitations that need no further comment here.

The second type of strategy is enabling. The enabling strategy is not widely used in schools even though recent educational literature is replete with urgings and guidelines. The reasons for this situation are several and complex. For one thing, the teacher needs more sophistication, experience, desire, and involvement with students to teach as an enabler than as a presenter. Discussion, brainstorming, laboratory activities, and problem-solving projects belong to the enabling strategy.

In the enabling strategy the students engage in some activity, most often under the supervision of the teacher. Generally and preferably the activity concerns a problem to be solved. The teacher need not participate in the activity, although in terms of his understanding of both the students and the activity he gains by doing so. If he does participate with the students, he must continually remember that his task is to "enable" the students, not to solve the problem for them. He must encourage and allow them to take the lead as he facilitates their activity. Preferably, the teacher and students select the activity together, although either can do so alone.

The activity may not arise from a problem facing the students but rather from interest or curiosity or as part of an everyday ongoing activity. For example, students may be interested in knowing about the moon as it orbits the earth. They begin to read about previous investigations, observe the moon with a telescope, read the accounts of the astronauts, perhaps even interview or correspond with the astronauts, and calculate further movements of the moon and their effect on Earth. Then the teacher and students recount or report on the essential particulars of the activity in order to be fully aware of them and to understand them. The students then generalize from the specifics to some abstract idea on their own. The students then apply the generalization they have learned to their lives in and out of the classroom in the future.

If the activity arises from a problem to be solved, then the teacher and students clearly formulate what the problem is through definition and analysis. They offer a hypothesis that serves as the basis for the subsequent collection of relevant data. They analyze and try to explain the data. They test the hypothesis to see if it indeed solves the problem. If they do not accept the hypothesis, they then formulate another hypothesis. If need be, they might even reformulate the problem situation so as to clarify it. Once a tested hypothesis is accepted, they apply what they have learned to their lives in and out of the classroom in the future.

The teacher's role in the enabling strategy is obviously not to perform the cognitive tasks for the students. Rather, it is to enable the students to generalize from the particulars of the activity, to formulate and test hypotheses. The teacher enables the students by directing them in the processes involved in learning from their own activities. He enables them to interpret their own experiences through helpful, appropriate questions and suggestions. Since the teacher's intent is to enable, he does not ask questions in a quizzing tone but in a helping tone. The teacher steps in, makes suggestions, and asks questions only when it is necessary to enable the students to proceed on their own.

The enabling strategy is based on the following ideas: (1) that students learn skills, knowledge, and beliefs meaningfully through activities they are involved in themselves; (2) that students probably will act on generalizations and tests hypotheses with which they have been actively concerned themselves; (3) that there is intrinsic motivation to learn and remember what is learned when activity arises out of interest, curiosity, or a problem; (4) that the teacher can enable students to learn to think analytically and creatively by suggesting, prodding, challenging, and leading, since he cannot meaningfully abstract an idea for the student or apply an idea to the students' lives; and (5) that students perform cognitive tasks well and with significance when they are physically, emotionally, and cognitively involved in activity.

In the enabling strategy, the teacher is not necessarily as physically active as the students. The teacher may participate with the student in the activity, although this is not essential. It may be pedagogically advisable, however, for the teacher to participate so as to establish a good relationship with the students, to be aware of the particulars of the activity from which the students will generalize, and to be aware of the ramifications of the problem situation as well as the hypotheses formulated. If the problem faces both the teacher and the students, then of course the teacher must participate.

The advantages of the enabling strategy are several. First, students learn willingly, enthusiastically, and meaningfully when they have an active, relevant stake in the teaching situation. The students learn generalizations and solutions to problems because they have been involved integrally themselves. Second, in a problem situation the solving of a pertinent problem is itself a reward; it removes feelings of perplexity, distress, and obstruction and it brings a sense of success and satisfaction. Third, with practice the students learn how to benefit from an activity or problem situation because they have learned how to proceed to generalizations and acceptable solutions. Fourth, there is, therefore, little or no need for extrinsic reward because of the overall intrinsic reward of becoming an able person. Ability, as a result of enabling, is its own reward.

The disadvantages of the enabling strategy center on the degree of sophistication required of the teacher. The teacher needs to understand the processes of generalizing and problem solving as well as the developmental status of the students relative to these processes. He needs to be insightful so that the activities of the students are pertinent and have potential for meaningfulness. He must be able to restrain himself from doing the tasks of the students when he sees that he can do them better and faster himself. He must be able to allow the students to fail in generalizing or solving a problem and to encourage them to learn from their experience as they try again with additional help. In short, the teacher must constantly keep in mind that his task is to *enable* the students to learn.

Because the enabling strategy relies on activity that is meaningful and because it is not possible for the teacher to know in advance what will be all the particulars of that activity, it is difficult to plan in great detail. In the short run, at least, this strategy is time consuming since it requires the development of activities and problems so as to create a solid foundation upon which to build. It takes time to generate many potentially fruitful particulars and to formulate hypotheses. Since the teacher must follow the flow of the activities that are meaningful, devote considerable time to the activities and their outgrowths, and schedule loosely rather than follow a tight plan, it is virtually impossible in most teaching situations to "cover" a given area of study exhaustively and systematically. Furthermore, since the aim is to enable the students to think critically (analytically and creatively), it is difficult for most teachers to test and assess the learning of the students.

THE EXEMPLIFYING STRATEGY

The third strategy, exemplifying, is the least used by teachers. Teachers do not often consciously and deliberately exemplify what they aim toward so that the students will learn through the teacher's exemplification. Teachers may at times exemplify certain skills, such as how to spell correctly, and certain moral beliefs, such as being honest. But they do not exemplify many other important skills and beliefs. In general, teachers do not strategically engage in exemplary action in order to learn new information, new skills, and new beliefs so that their students can observe and learn from their doing so. Currently, teachers usually do not deliberately and consonantly use the exemplifying strategy as much as they use the presenting and enabling strategies.

This is not to claim that teachers never exemplify particular behaviors. In whatever a teacher does, he is exemplifying something to his students. Much of what teachers exemplify, however, is unintentional and nonstrategic. Worse yet, much is inconsistent or dissonant with the explicit aims and verbal statements of the teachers. This unintentional exemplification is part of the hidden agenda or unstudied curriculum in schools. The hidden agenda is impressive in its extent and the unstudied curriculum is often the one that students learn, remember, and act upon in the present and future.

The exemplifying strategy is particularly suited to the teaching of skills, processes, and values. With this strategy the teacher shows the student, for example, how to hammer, how to repair a flat tire, how to establish testable hypotheses, how to conduct research, how to arrange data so as to make generalizations, how an honest person acts, how a person respects other individuals, and how a fair person acts. By exemplifying, the teacher allows the students to see for themselves the consequences of all these actions as well as how to perform them.

This strategy also is suited to teaching facts and generalizations. Obviously, a teacher cannot exemplify a fact or explanation or principle in the same way he can exemplify a skill or manifest a value. But a teacher can demonstrate and thereby have his action serve as a particular instance of a general case for the students to witness. The teacher is using the exemplifying strategy in such a case, although technically he is demonstrating rather than exemplifying. He is deliberately demonstrating a fact or generalization as part of the exemplifying strategy.

In the exemplifying strategy, the teacher sets up or builds upon a situation, appropriate in time and place, that has the potential for him to exemplify what he intends for the students to learn. He arranges the necessary materials. He clarifies for himself the concepts, the skills and processes, and the beliefs involved in the forthcoming activity as best he can foresee them. Then, after he has thought out what he will do, the teacher engages in the activity publicly. The students may participate with the teacher if the activity is a joint one or one that focuses on a common concern. The teacher exemplifies what he wants the students to learn in his action and the students watch him. Sometimes, as in cases of creative works, such as a poem or painting, for example, the students may see only the finished piece, but not see the teacher actually handling the pencils and brushes, although it is preferable that they do. The teacher may or may not comment on his activity as he goes along. The students relate what they see and learn to their own lives and act on what they have learned in similar situations in the future.

The exemplifying strategy is based on the following ideas: (1) that students learn from watching a model and imitating it; (2) that students learn from concrete and meaningful examples in the classroom, just as they have done all along from the first minutes of their lives; (3) that the teacher does not necessarily verbalize or, at least, needs only minimal verbalization as an accompaniment to strategic exemplification; (4) that it is only natural and sensible for the teacher to exemplify a harmony among objectives, verbal action, and nonverbal action since the students learn from him as a model in any event; and (5) that many students respond better to the primarily nonverbal model exemplified by what the teacher does than to the verbal language spoken by the teacher.[6]

Exemplifying is primarily a nonverbal mode of teaching. The

6. See the last part of the essay by R. S. Peters, "Education as Initiation," in *Philosophical Analysis and Education*, ed. Reginald D. Archambault (New York: The Humanities Press, 1965), pp. 87-111, for the value of shared experiences with someone already initiated into a given area.

teacher may, if he chooses, comment verbally on what he is doing as a means of reinforcing his point or assuring himself that he is communicating his message to the students. This is what Socrates did with Meno, as mentioned earlier. But, even if we argue that at some point the teacher *must* necessarily comment on his actions, the nonverbal aspect is still the essential one.

The advantages of the exemplifying strategy relate to this nonverbal element. First, many students, but especially the young and the inexperienced ones, whatever their ages, can learn from a nonverbal message but have difficulty with a verbal, symbolic one. For example, in teaching generalized conservation to young students, researchers found that only the exemplifying procedures, and not conventional or verbal explanation, were effective with disadvantaged Mexican Americans.[7] Second, the exemplifying strategy continues a communication form that is prominent in life outside the classroom. Much of what people learn in life they learn by imitating the nonverbal examples they see about them. We learn how to eat, talk, and walk, for example, by imitating the deliberate and nondeliberate examples of other people. To learn from examples is a natural way of life for people, including students. These two advantages are put succinctly in an old limerick:

> There once was a person named Beecher
> Successful, effective, great teacher.
> "I'll tell you the key:
> What I teach them is ME,
> I serve as a model, not preacher."

Third, via the exemplifying strategy the teacher has an effective means of concretizing the abstract values, principles, and processes he wishes to teach. Teachers are wary of verbalizing abstract points in simple terms, and rightfully so, since many times their efforts only result in further symbolic complexity. The exemplifying strategy offers a way of avoiding this trouble.

Fourth, the exemplifying strategy elicits from students action they are capable of performing but for some reason are not doing at the time. When a teaches exemplifies an activity, he encourages students to

7. Barry J. Zimmerman and F. Susan Ghozeil, "Modeling as a Teaching Technique," *Elementary School Journal* 74 (April 1974): 440-46.

draw on their repertoire of abilities to perform new actions. The new actions are now more likely to occur than before.[8]

Fifth, the exemplifying strategy, because it continues a natural and deep-seated way of learning, forms a bridge between school and society. This bridge brings meaning to the teaching situation as it relates that situation to other life activities. It shows that the teacher is a real person engaged in real activities.

Sixth, the use of the exemplifying strategy serves to motivate the teacher. No matter which strategy the teacher uses, he benefits when he teaches. The acts of preparing, organizing, clarifying, and reclarifying all benefit the teacher as well as the students. There is indeed truth to the popular adage that a good way to learn something is to teach it to others. But the exemplifying strategy benefits the teacher more than the presenting and enabling strategies. The teacher gets caught up in the situation more easily and quickly when he exemplifies. The activity can serve as a springboard for future activity outside of teaching, since the distinction between the teaching activity and his other life activity quickly fades away.

The case of Harry Kemelman serves to support this point. Kemelman, a teacher of English at Boston State College, was teaching a class in advanced composition and trying to show his students "that words do not exist in vacuo but have meanings that can transcend their usual connotations, that even short combinations can permit a wide variety of interpretations." Kemelman got caught up in his attempt at making inferences and projections and then finally sat down himself to write a story based on his own thinking. The result was a detective short story featuring Nicholas Welt, a professor who solved problems by pure logic. Out of the Nicky Welt series of stories Kemelman developed a series of books featuring Rabbi David Small. Kemelman achieved public acclaim with his detective novels beginning with *Friday the Rabbi Slept Late*, winner of the Mystery Writers of America "Edgar" for the best first mystery novel of the year. Kemelman has commented that "Rabbi David Small can be said to be the son of Professor Nicholas Welt" who "was born in the classroom."[9]

The disadvantages of the exemplifying strategy begin with the dif-

8. Ibid., 442.

9. Harry Kemelman, *The Nine Mile Walk: The Nicky Welt Stories* (New York: G. P. Putnam's Sons, 1967), pp. 9-12.

ficulty of setting up a teaching situation where the teacher can smoothly and comfortably exemplify the skills, values, and principles he wishes the students to learn. If the situation appears odd, the effect of this strategy will decrease. Second, once he has established an appropriate teaching situation, it is hard for the teacher to determine to what extent he is communicating his message to his students. The teacher may think he is exemplifying a skill or value to the students yet the students may not be perceiving the intended message. If and when the teacher checks with students, he may spoil the smooth flow of nonverbal activity and remove the desired subtlety of the communication.

Third, it is difficult to measure the learning of the students based on the exemplifying strategy. Since any exemplified activity has multiple dimensions that the student can witness and learn, it is difficult to test precisely what and to what degree the student has learned. The testing issue is important to teachers who desire to or are required to test their students.

Fourth, the student may find it difficult to observe the teacher intimately over a sustained period of time, to extract the essential elements of the activity for emphasis and learning, and finally to apply the exemplified, nonverbal message to his own situation. This disadvantage exists today in large measure because under current practices students simply do not have enough classroom experience in learning from the exemplifying strategy.

TEACHING STRATEGIES AND TONE

Whenever one teaches, a certain tone or climate is created, whether or not one desires it. The teaching tone concerns the relationships established between the teacher and the students and grow out of the verbal and nonverbal interaction between the teacher and his students. The teacher manifests certain attitudes toward the students, and the students manifest certain attitudes toward the teacher. They do so whether they intend to or not, whether they are aware of the attitudes or not.

The teacher and students seldom talk to each other about the tone that exists during the teaching activity. Students may talk to other students about the cold and aloof atmosphere in Smith's room or how friendly and relaxed they feel with Jones. Teachers may talk to each other about how they relate to a particular student or group of students. Some teachers and students, however, apparently are unable to articulate the differences in tone from situation to situation. Nevertheless, that teachers and students feel the tone and react to it is evidenced by their actions. Observers can sense this intangible tone by listening to the talk and perceiving the activity taking place.

In the past two decades a number of researchers have studied teaching climate. They have offered several instruments for measuring tone based on various concepts. Rather than choose and present one such instrument here, we instead simply offer the basic concept that tone can be described on a positive-negative continuum. The concept of positive-negative tone seems to be common in some form to virtually all the instruments for measuring tone. Anyone who wishes further specificity can select his own fuller, more detailed set of concepts in accordance with his preference.

Generally, it is the teacher who sets the tone of the teaching situation. Although some people would like to claim innocence in regard to establishing a climate, research repeatedly shows the teacher to be responsible for setting classroom climate. By virtue of his position, the teacher has substantial power to establish the climate he chooses. For some teachers, however, the establishing of tone is not a deliberate act. Tone simply flows out of the activities chosen by the teacher as leader of the class. Recognition of the teacher's responsibility for the classroom climate, whether deliberately created or not, is essential to knowledgeable teaching.

The concept of positive-negative tone applies to all three teaching strategies. It is possible for a teacher to use the presenting strategy with a large group of students and establish a positive tone in the room. Another teacher might create a negative tone. Although it might seem otherwise on the surface, even with a small group of students a teacher can utilize the enabling strategy is such a way as to create a negative rather than a desirable positive tone. With the exemplifying strategy, the teacher can also be positive or negative.

The positive end of the tone continuum can be described through a cluster of words that give meaning to it, such as warm, patient, accepting, supportive, and encouraging. The negative end of the tone continuum also can be described through a cluster of words such as cold, impatient, rejecting, hostile, ignoring, and harsh.

The many advantages of teaching with a positive tone have been well set forth in chapter 3 of this volume. Among the advantages, a positive tone encourages students to learn by fostering (1) understanding between the teacher and students; (2) respect between people; (3) clarifying experiences between teacher and students; (4) helpful interaction among students; (5) a pervasive momentum to carry the classroom activities forward; and (6) further learning of the material at hand.

The disadvantages of teaching with a negative tone are several. A negative tone discourages students from learning by destroying the students' motivation. It does not reinforce accomplishments by the students. Nor does it lead to mutual respect and shared activity between teacher and student.

TEACHING STRATEGIES AND GOALS

The three teaching strategies, presenting, enabling, and exemplifying, also relate to other aspects of teaching, including a key aspect, goals. Strategies relate to goals and do so in such a way as to give added meaning to both the strategies and the goals.

It is possible to categorize the goals of teaching in several ways. One convenient, understandable, and yet simple way is to consider the three-fold nature of goals. First, some goals of teaching are social in nature. With such goals, teachers focus on the social, political, and economic elements of life. The teacher aims to help the student understand life about him and to be able to participate as a member of a society now and in the future. School teachers are not teaching students to live a totally solitary life. In line with this social nature of goals, the teacher teaches appropriate skills and processes, values, and knowledge.

Other goals of teaching are personal in nature. Here the teacher focuses on the student as a person. The teacher aims to help the student understand himself and develop his individual interests and talents. The teacher fosters personal growth, which includes the psychological, aesthetic, and metaphysical dimensions of life. Each student is a unique person experiencing his own particular way of life; at the same time he is a member of a large society and several small groups. In line with this personal nature of goals, the teacher teaches appropriate skills and processes, values, and knowledge.

Still other goals of teaching are intellectual in nature. Here the teacher focuses on knowledge and thinking. The teacher aims to teach the student how to gather information and process information so as to gain knowledge. The teacher helps the student to perform various cognitive operations such as remembering, generalizing, analyzing, and synthesizing. The teacher's aim is to teach the student to think critically and reflectively for himself as the student gathers and processes information in various ways. In line with this intellectual goal, the teacher teaches appropriate skills and processes, values, and knowledge.

Each of the three strategies can be used in attempting to achieve each of the three types of goals. A teacher can use the enabling strategy, for example, to achieve either the social, personal, or intellectual goals as he teaches the appropriately selected skills and processes, values, and knowledge concerned with the topic at hand. One could specify, perhaps, combinations of strategy and goal that are more desirable than others. But that is not the point here; to specify desirable combinations we first need to establish guidelines and determining factors. The point is, rather, that each strategy potentially can apply to each goal, and when it does, it offers something particular to the situation.

INTERRELATIONSHIPS OF STRATEGIES, TONE, AND GOALS

These three dimensions of teaching (strategies, tone, and goals) are not opposed to each other. On the contrary, there are interrelationships among them. In graphic form (figure 1) the relationships are shown as a cube that contains eighteen possibilities resulting from the intersections of strategies, tone, and goals as achieved through teaching appropriately selected skills and processes, values, and knowledge. For example, one intersection is *exemplifying* strategy with a *positive* tone for a *social* goal. Another combination is the *enabling* strategy with a *positive* tone for a *personal* goal. Still another possibility is the *presenting* strategy with a *negative* tone for an *intellectual* goal. The purpose of this graphic representation is to show clearly that strategies interact with goals and tone in various combinations. True, some combinations may be more desirable and others less so.

A teacher who examines his own teaching activity with this cube in mind now has a way of organizing his self-reflection. The teacher might ask himself, "Am I using the presenting strategy with a social goal as well as with an intellectual goal?" "If not, how can I plan for initiating this new combination?" "At what points in the school day do I and can I use the exemplifying strategy?" "Do I really create a positive tone with a personal goal?"

Supervisors of secondary school teachers as well as college professors of secondary education who refer to this cube have a way of observing and helping teachers. They can use the cube as an initial point of departure in discussing variety and pluralism in teaching. For instance, if professors find that their students know about and utilize only the presenting strategy no matter which goal they seek, the college staff members might well re-examine their preparatory courses and student teaching experiences. If supervisors observe that their

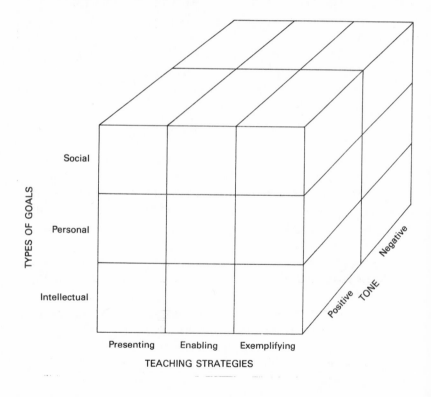

Fig. 1. Relationships between teaching strategies, tone, and types of goals

teacher are ignoring some goals because a favored strategy does not seem to achieve such goals, then they have an excellent point of departure on which to base future discussions and workshops.

This cube, showing the combinations of strategies, tone, and goals, therefore serves a double purpose. First, it offers a frame of reference for observing and analyzing current teaching along three critical dimensions. Second, it offers a guideline for choosing future activities so as to bring about a wholesome pluralism in teaching.

Obviously, every educator will prescribe and encourage teachers to strive for a positive tone. No one will seriously suggest that we teach with a negative tone. Hence, as a guideline for future activities, an educator will choose from the nine combinations of strategy and goal and positive tone. The analyst and the prescriber of teaching situations will need to consider other elements in addition to strategies, tone, and goals, such as philosophy of education, psychological framework (behavioral, psychoanalytical or humanistic), budget, physical environment, and student characteristics. Nevertheless, the need exists for a wholesome pluralism in teaching within the nine combinations of strategy, goal, and positive tone. It is urgent to foster pluralism in education if the secondary school is to be a viable, influential institution in the future.

The Need for a Wholesome Pluralism in Teaching

Our society today is complex. Just a few people flee to faraway villages, farms, or mountain retreats. The rest of us, virtually all of us, continue living in a high speed, highly interdependent, highly mechanized, highly electronic, and highly organized life. As a result of such a life we all resemble our neighbors in many ways. Yet, we quickly assert that we are significantly different from them, that we are individuals. Perhaps we are correct in our assertion that we are individuals; perhaps we are not. Perhaps we know we are similar, but the claim that we are not reflects a need we feel to resist the ongoing homogenization of people that results from common influences such as mass television, mass advertising, and mass bureaucratic government.

In either case, whether we *are* different from our neighbor or whether we *need to feel* different in order to cope with the complex life we lead, today's educators need to provide varied approaches to schooling so that individualization will prevail. If not, mass schooling will contribute to, rather than help resolve, the troubles and pressures secondary students feel just prior to attaining such significant rights as the right to vote, the right to marry, and the right to work full time as young adults.

The need for pluralism also arises because we know that students learn differently. Some learn quickly, some do not; some learn well alone, some do not; some thrive in small groups, some do not; some learn to perform complicated psychomotor-cognitive skills, some do not; and some learn happily and well from a presenting strategy while others learn best from an exemplifying or enabling strategy. That is to say, just as we need a pluralism in regard to programs (such as manual occupational preparation or fine arts specialties) so, too, do we need varied approaches to teaching so as to serve our students better.

The importance of treating students differently is stated pointedly by Tobias when he compares birds with pupils in a short fable. The hero of the story offers this advice to his fellow citizens in order to attract birds back to their town. "Not all birds are alike just as all pupils are not alike. Birds have to be fed differently just as children have to be taught differently. The woodpeckers must have their suet and the sparrows their grain. The chickadees prefer to dine in the trees while the mourning doves keep to the ground to feed."[10]

The need for pluralism also results in part from the undesirable effects of relying on only one form of one strategy. Currently, according to the research on classroom behavior, the presenting strategy in the form of the recitation clearly persists as the dominant strategy today.[11] The recitation has been common for many years despite attempts in the past few decades to get teachers to change. (Many educators have been urging teachers to use the enabling strategy in the form of the "problem-solving" method of the 1930s and 1940s and the "discovery" method of the 1960s). If anyone doubts the prevalence of the presenting strategy, he need only visit several schools on his own to be convinced that the researchers have been reporting data accurately.

10. Jerachmiel Tobias, "The Teacher and the Birds," *Contemporary Education* 45 (Fall 1973): 77.

11. James Hoetker and William P. Ahlbrand, Jr., "The Persistence of the Recitation," *American Educational Research Journal* 6 (March 1969): 145-67.

Connected with the persistence of the recitation is the low level of student participation in the language of the classroom. There is a definite correlation between the strategy used by the teacher and the level of student participation. Each teaching strategy involves the students at a different level of language participation. Study after study reports the overwhelming dominance of the teacher over the students in classroom talking. Research indicates that not only do students speak less often than the teacher, but they also speak just a few words at a time when they do speak.[12]

This low level of student participation is of significance since recent research shows the positive relation between language and thought. As people talk, they think. For this reason, discussion often brings about the remark by a participant, "I never thought of that before." Active participation in the classroom through talking and writing fosters and creates new thought experiences for the students. Barnes, who studied language interaction in secondary schools, put the significance of language this way: "It is when the pupil is required to use language to grapple with new experience or to order old experience in a new way that he is likely to find it necessary to use language differently. . . . This would suggest that the low level of pupil participation in these lessons, if they are at all typical of secondary lessons, is a matter of some educational urgency. All teachers might well contemplate the classroom implication of this."[13]

Concerned with this language situation in secondary schools, the London Association for the Teaching of English issued a document calling for teachers of all specialties to foster student classroom language through new and varied teaching approaches so as "to improve our procedures in school in such a way that language becomes a facilitating force in learning rather than a barrier bristling with formidable difficulties."[14] The document asks teachers to examine how they teach and to compare observations with their colleagues as first

12. See the research in Hyman, *Teaching: Vantage Points for Study*, and Hoetker and Ahlbrand, "The Persistence of the Recitation."

13. Douglas Barnes, "Language in the Secondary Classroom," in *Language, the Learner, and the School*, rev. ed. (Harmondsworth, England: Penguin Books, Ltd., 1971), pp. 61-62.

14. Harold Rosen, "A Language Policy Across the Curriculum," in *Language, the Learner, and the School*, p. 160.

steps toward moving to strategies that will bring about a high level of student participation, thus allowing students to develop more fully their ability to use language. The document continues:

> The more teachers work *alongside* their pupils the more likely it is that our suggestions will make sense. The more they foster the initiative of their pupils the more likely it is that their pupils will develop a confidence in their own use of language. The less they attempt to verbalize ideas for their pupils the less stereotyped will their pupils' language be.[15]

The need for pluralism also exists because of societal changes, as earlier chapters in this volume have shown. In an illuminating article, related to the points made here about strategy, the level of student participation, and pluralism, Coleman claims that our students have outgrown the schools.[16] He argues that in the past the function of the school was to serve an "information-poor society" by giving the students information about the outside world via contact with teachers and books. Through the years, however, our society has become "information-rich" due to the many sources of information now more readily available to students, such as radio, television, movies, and newspapers. At the same time, our society has moved from being "action-rich" (that is, rich in provisions for active participation in the struggle against the environment to satisfy human needs and wants) to "action-poor," with the result that our young students lack the "opportunities for responsible and productive action."

Studies by national groups concerned with secondary education support this point. According to the data, at least one quarter of our adolescents do not make the transition to adulthood well. Tyler, in commenting on this matter, noted that "few adolescents now have opportunities to try themselves out, to work with adults, to discover that they can hold up their end of a job, that they can be respected by adults. . . . They have little experience in operating in responsible ways with adults and become either alienated or plunge into the adult world unprepared for what they are going to meet."[17]

15. Ibid., p. 167.

16. James S. Coleman, "The Children Have Outgrown the Schools," *Psychology Today* 5 (February 1972): 72-75, 82.

17. Ralph W. Tyler, "Utilizing Research in Curriculum Development," *Theory Into Practice* 13 (February 1974): 10.

The conclusion from such an analysis of school and society is obvious: the schools need to offer their students a wider range of opportunities to learn. Teachers need to shift the way they teach in order "to reduce the school's dependence on its classical functions so that it can take on new ones."[18] The presenting of information to students should no longer dominate in our schools. As society changes, so must the school also change if it is to continue to be a beneficial institution to students.

Educating Teachers for Pluralistic Teaching

Teachers, supervisors, and professors will need to study teaching. Despite Dewey's call over seventy years ago for "students of teaching,"[19] few educators have engaged in such studies. Few colleges have any courses devoted to examining the research on and theories of teaching. Few school systems conduct workshops or in-service courses on research and theories of teaching. Educators do take courses concerned with the history or sociology of teaching but they spend astonishingly little time studying the activity of teaching, in terms of strategies, teacher-student relations, observation systems, or conceptual analysis. Even a mere glimpse at the mammoth *Second Handbook of Research on Teaching*[20] should convince any educator that scores of hours are needed for one to read and digest its forty-two lengthy articles concerned with these critical topics.

One example from the recent research on teaching indicates how an apparently slight change in teacher action can have significant effects on what happens in the classroom during teaching. Rowe[21] and

18. Coleman, "The Children Have Outgrown the Schools," p. 75.

19. John Dewey, "The Relation of Theory to Practice in Education," in *The Relation of Theory to Practice in the Education of Teachers,* Third Yearbook of the National Society for the Scientific Study of Education, Part I (Chicago: University of Chicago Press, 1904), p. 15.

20. Robert M. W. Travers, ed., *Second Handbook of Research on Teaching* (Chicago: Rand McNally and Company, 1973).

21. Mary Budd Rowe, "Science, Silence, and Sanctions," *Science and Children* 6 (September 1969): 11-13; idem, "Wait-Time and Rewards as Instructional Variables: Their Influence on Language, Logic, and Fate Control," abstract of a paper presented to the National Association for Research in Science Teaching, April 1972; idem, *Teaching Science as Continuous Inquiry* (New York: McGraw-Hill Book Company, 1973), pp. 243-73.

Lake[22] used observation categories developed at Columbia University[23] to investigate the amount of time teachers wait after asking a question. They found that if students do not begin a response within one second, teachers usually repeat the question or call upon other students to respond. Also, after students respond, teachers usually wait slightly less than one second before reacting to the response, or asking another question or launching a new topic. According to studies by Rowe and by Lake, when teachers increased their wait-time to three to five seconds, the following significant results occurred:

For students, the length of student responses increased; the number of unsolicited but appropriate responses increased; failure to respond decreased; confidence as reflected in fewer inflected responses increased, and fewer responses had the tone of "Is that what you want?"; the incidence of speculative thinking increased; the incidence of offering alternative explanations increased; more evidence followed by or preceded by inference statements occurred; the number of questions asked by students increased and the number of (science) experiments they proposed increased; teacher-centered show and tell decreased, and student-student comparing increased; the number of responses frôm "slow" students increased so that there was a greater variety of students participating; the incidence of students responding with congruent and more complex answers occurred (that is, ascending modal congruence increased); the incidence of conversation sequences increased (that is, sequences involving three or more related utterances increased in number).

For teachers, teachers became more flexible in their discourse, asked fewer questions, increased the variety of their questions, and improved their expectations of performance of "slow" students.

These results show that a slight change just in the pacing of the talk, done by increasing the teacher's wait-time, led to changes in pedagogical roles and cognitive performance. Students started asking more questions and participating more, as well as offering alternative explanations, increasing speculative thinking, and offering more com-

22. John H. Lake, "The Influence of Wait-Time on the Verbal Dimension of Student Inquiry Behavior" (Doctoral dissertation, Rutgers University, 1973).

23. Arno A. Bellack, Herbert M. Kliebard, Ronald T. Hyman, and Frank L. Smith, Jr., *The Language of the Classroom* (New York: Teachers College Press, 1960).

plex responses. The knowledge of such research and then the implementation of a wait-time schedule of three to five seconds will certainly aid any teacher who wishes to utilize better all three teaching strategies. The research literature abounds in other such material that educators can easily put to use so as to facilitate the advent of pluralistic teaching.

As part of studying teaching, educators will need to analyze the common metaphors applied to teaching and then to create new and fruitful ways to conceive of teaching. Educators need to stretch their imaginative minds to fashion alternative metaphors or models. Currently, several metaphors dominate our thinking: the military metaphor; the prison metaphor; the manufacturing or production metaphor; the horticulture or growth metaphor; and the sports metaphor. Negative metaphors, especially the use of the manufacturing metaphor by teachers and the use of the prison metaphor by students, are deadly and destructive.[24]

Educators will need additional and fresh metaphors in the future, positive ones that will support pluralistic teaching. Why not pursue the metaphor of "teaching as orchestrating"[25] or the teacher as blower of bubbles[26] when we think of strategies, tone, and goals? The writings by Engel[27] and Macdonald, Wolfson, and Zaret,[28] who propose a number of additional related alternative metaphors for teaching and schooling, are helpful steps in the right direction to give us fresh vision.

In order to carry through such study of teaching and the consequences flowing from it, there is a need for new courses of study in the colleges and new workshops in the school systems. A fundamental course or workshop is one where teachers will learn and then have the opportunity to practice various combinations of strategies, tone, and

24. Ronald T. Hyman, "Leadership and Metaphors in Teaching," *Notre Dame Journal of Education* 4 (Spring 1973): 80-88.

25. Ibid.

26. Philip W. Jackson, "The Way Teaching Is," in *Contemporary Thought on Teaching*, p. 12.

27. Martin Engel, "What Schooling Could Be Like: Analogies for Learning," *Elementary School Journal* 75 (October 1974): 16-27.

28. James B. Macdonald, Bernice J. Wolfson, and Esther Zaret, *Reschooling Society: A Conceptual Model* (Washington, D. C.: Association for Supervision and Curriculum Development, 1973).

goals. Through such a course or workshop, teachers will teach their classmates the characteristics of the three strategies, tones, and goals as well as data from research on teaching. They will teach their peers what they themselves are learning. The college teacher, the school supervisor, or the master teacher conducting the class will observe and give feedback to the teachers as they strive to implement what the have learned.

The advantages of in-class practice are great. First, teachers have the opportunity to practice in situations where there is little threat, where there will be helpful feedback, and where the entire group is concerned with the teacher's improvement. Second, teachers learn pluralistic teaching as they practice it and teach it. Martin makes a parallel case for having people explain something to others as a way of learning it themselves:

The point is simply that explaining can be a *way* of learning just as reading tests and figuring things out from documents can be. It is often said that to understand a subject you have to teach it. Taken literally this is false: we can all point to people who do understand a subject yet have never taught it. There is, however, something to this claim, and we should not dismiss it too hastily. For although you can understand a subject without teaching it, teaching it is one good way to improve one's understanding of it.[29]

Needed also will be courses where teachers can learn about themselves as persons and teachers. Teachers need to clarify, explicate, and justify, at least to themselves if not to others, who they are, what they hold dear, what they know, and how they act. As teachers develop and know themselves better they will become better suited to working in and understanding teaching situations. The truth of the ancient saying, "Know thyself," is as powerful today as it ever was or even more so. Furthermore, the concomitant purpose of such a course is for the teachers to learn techniques for helping others to know themselves, too. There are a number of programs and textbooks readily available for anyone wishing to initiate and teach such a course.[30]

No matter what courses are taught, however, the obligation of

29. Jane R. Martin, *Explaining, Understanding, and Teaching* (New York: McGraw-Hill Book Company, 1970), p. 217.

30. Richard L. Curwin and Barbara S. Fuhrmann, *Discovering Your Teaching Self* (Englewood Cliffs, N.J.: Prentice-Hall, Inc., 1975).

college teachers and school supervisors is the same: to practice pluralistic teaching themselves in addition to teaching about it. Professors and supervisors are exemplars. Teachers learn powerful messages from them, just as students in secondary school learn from the actions of their teachers. Professors must use strategies, positive tone, and goals in different combinations so that there is a backbone to the entire thrust of teacher preparation. Supervisors must do the same as they themselves teach in workshops, individual or group meetings, and demonstration classes. If not, the teaching of teachers will be an empty or negative gesture.

Professors of secondary education and supervisors in our high schools need to be exemplars of pluralistic teaching if the subsequent improvement of secondary teaching is to be realized. The task is great; the secondary teacher's reward greater; and the ultimate benefit to secondary students and society incalculable.

Implications for Secondary Schools

The ultimate responsibility for changing the secondary schools lies with the schools themselves. By waiting, as they have, for the colleges to change the schools through differently prepared teachers, the schools have lost the initiative for change. They also have put themselves into a highly dependent situation requiring change in another institution before change can come about. This situation is not healthy for the schools; it is not one that will lead to the needed significant and appropriate change in order to make the school a meaningful place for our youth. Hence, the secondary schools must take the initiative.

Secondary school leaders need to take steps to move the schools toward pluralistic teaching. The leaders must take the initiative and seek out those people who can help them change. They must seek out educators in their own schools who can supply expertise. They must go to all outside institutions that can help, not only to the colleges, since the latter may not be able or even willing to help.

Secondary schools should establish workshops and request specific, cooperative college courses where teachers can improve their teaching skills. Schools should involve their teachers in the planning of such workshops and courses and enable them as professionals to study during school time.

Teachers should provide the time and opportunities for students to talk over what they have learned. If the teacher invites a poet, for example, to teach by using the exemplifying strategy, then the teacher should arrange for the students to talk over among themselves and with the poet what they have learned. Although not as apparent, the same need for students to talk over what they have learned applies to the presenting and enabling strategies. It is through such talk that students clarify and solidify what they have learned.

To foster pluralism in teaching, the schools should begin to draw more heavily on community resources, as has been repeatedly suggested throughout this volume. For instance, the use of a community talent bank is not a new idea but it is one that schools have neglected. The utilization of community people is particularly important for the exemplifying strategy of teaching. A practicing poet, writer, lawyer, chef, baker, or chemist, for example, has much to teach the students by exemplifying his skills. A classroom teacher cannot exemplify all things to all students and should not even try to do so because artificiality detracts from learning. Authenticity exemplified by a community resource person should be welcomed and encouraged by teachers. If they understand the purpose and place of a talent bank, teachers need not feel threatened, insecure, or inferior.

Secondary schools should make use of available correspondence courses, programmed textbooks, and computer assisted instruction courses. When they do so, however, teachers should realize that these courses use the presenting strategy and must do so because of their very nature. Then the teachers should themselves use other strategies lest the students receive an imbalanced program.

To facilitate and support the move toward pluralistic teaching, secondary schools should initiate such supportive organizational changes as those described in chapters 7 and 9 of this volume. For instance, the schools should establish alternative schools, such as the Parkway Program in Philadelphia, which has become the prototype of the high schools that use the city as their campus. Within the regular school and also within the alternative school, there should be varying organizational plans, such as team-taught open classrooms, traditional large groups, tutorials, and independent study. Organizational change supports and fosters change in the relationships between teacher and student as well as the way the teacher teaches.[31] For example, the different arrangement of furniture and use of space in the open classroom leads the teacher to come into closer contact with the students. This closer contact can lead to the creation of a more positive tone.[32]

Secondary school leaders should consider carefully the hierarchical structure and horizontal relationships established by them for administrators, teachers, and students. Argyris has analyzed the interrelation of school structure and teacher actions, showing that unless definite changes are made in structure and groups, as well as in the theories people in fact use to guide their actions, innovations are not likely to take root.[33]

The schools should begin to employ and organize staff members according to alternative patterns. The differentiated staffing idea, for example, can be used to take advantage of differentiated skills in teaching. Schools can maximize the strengths of their teachers by recognizing what type of strategy they use best and what type of goal they value most. With employment and organizing focused on differentiated teaching talent, support for pluralism can be built into the schools.

In short, secondary schools need to move toward pluralistic teaching not only by encouraging and teaching their teachers to change their current behavior, but also by organizing their teachers, administrators, and students in alternative structures. The schools need to draw more heavily on community resources, both people and facilities. The schools need to utilize fresh materials from various sources rather than rely only on standard textbooks. The basic purpose of educational pluralism is the improvement of teaching for the ultimate benefit of the students. Pluralistic teaching aims to help the students in their present and future lives as our society continues to

31. Ronald T. Hyman, "Individualization: The Hidden Agenda," *Elementary School Journal* 73 (May 1973): 412-23.

32. David W. Cochran, An Assessment of the Process of Regular and Open Classrooms" (Doctoral dissertation, Rutgers University, 1974), p. 66.

33. Chris Argyris, "Alternative Schools: A Behavioral Analysis," *Teachers College Record* 75 (May 1974): 429-52; Chris Argyris and Donald A. Schon, *Theory in Practice: Increasing Professional Effectiveness* (San Francisco: Jossey-Bass Publishers, 1974).

change daily. It is consonant with the many recommendations made by the various committees examining the high school today.[34] It is necessary for the revitalizing of the high school curriculum as proposed by Cawelti in light of his critique[35] and by the California Commission for the Reform of Intermediate and Secondary Education.[36]

There is no one panacea. We need many avenues to bring us to an improved secondary school. Pluralistic teaching is surely one such road we need to travel on as we move into the future.

34. For a review of five major reports see Gordon Cawelti, *Vitalizing the High School: A Curriculum Critique of Major Reform Proposals* (Washington, D.C.: Association for Supervision and Curriculum Development, 1974).

35. Ibid., pp. 43-52.

36. *New York Times*, 2 March 1975, p. 33.

CHAPTER XI

How Can Learning Be Fostered?

RONALD C. DOLL

A New Setting for Educational Leadership

Suppose a "typical" American secondary school had been identified in the 1910s, the 1930s, the 1950s, and again in the 1970s. If motion pictures and written documents describing these schools in detail had been prepared at designated twenty-year intervals between the 1910s and 1970s, how would the schools have compared?

During the sixty-year period, these American secondary schools would have been housed in buildings with limited differences in basic design, buildings in which facilities and materials were increasing and improving but in which general patterns of instruction were remaining substantially the same. Curriculum offerings would have multiplied, but much of the respected learning content within the allegedly solid subjects would have been retained. Organization for learning and the learning process itself would have received too little attention. To both sophisticated and unsophisticated visitors, the schools would have continued to look decidedly institutional. Their principals and other members of the administrative hierarchy would have continued to complain that they could not get to the "important things" because so many administrative details blocked their way.

But inside and outside the secondary school of any era from the 1910s to the 1970s, there would have developed a number of ideas for reforming it. Many of the ideas would have required involvement of people who had not been involved previously in secondary education. By the 1970s the involvement would have begun to occur in unaccustomed ways.

An institution like secondary education is meant to serve people. Somewhat paradoxically, one way it can serve people is by extracting from them some substantial service to the institution. As people serve themselves in this particular way, they develop personally and also contribute to the life and the remolding of the institution. Preeminently, secondary education is bound up with the lives of people, most of them young people. If few people are directly involved in making the institution operate and thrive, its potential for doing good must be limited. If, as is the case increasingly today, more people are involved in situations in which they can perform competently, the institution's potential for doing good is enhanced.

An important thesis of this chapter is that intelligent, widespread involvement of people of varied qualifications "opens" secondary education so that it becomes more than mere secondary schooling. Fostering learning should be an important function of nearly all people who are involved in a revised version of secondary education. Fostering learning includes three major actions: planning for improved learning, supervising the learning enterprise, and administering learning programs and systems.

Thus, this chapter deals with educational leadership in a new setting. The setting is both the secondary school and its wider community. Within this wider community, educational leadership is exercised by numbers of people, some of whom have previously had leadership responsibilities in secondary education and many of whom have nǒt.

The central question to be dealt with may be worded as follows: "How can American secondary education draw fully upon the abilities of all persons who are legitimately concerned with the education of adolescents, to the end that planning, supervision, and administration of programs for improving the learning of adolescents can best occur?" The chapter will include several issues raised by question, and will indicate some of the considerations that should be kept in mind in the process of resolving the issues.

Consider, first of all, the meaning of learning to the adolescents who spend five to six hours a day, five days a week, in American secondary schools. For several years, the author interviewed public school pupils between the ages of eleven and nineteen concerning a variety of matters. The interviewees made it clear that they were learning rapidly, but that most of their learning was occurring outside the junior high schools, middle schools, and senior high schools they were attending. When pupils were asked: "What could secondary schools do to educate you in ways that no other agencies could or should?" their responses could be paraphrased as follows:

"Put what we learn in school into a framework or system which will help us understand it better." (Young people evidently think disconnected, un-associated learning content falls into the category of useless baggage.)

"Teach us 'fundamentals.' Nowhere except in school are you likely to get the tools you need for thinking and serving."

"Give us opportunities and materials in schools to help us inquire, dis-cover, and probe meaning. Getting meaning is perhaps the most important thing schools can help us do."

"Stop trying to compete with and to destroy what we learn elsewhere. Instead, seek to coordinate what we are taught in school with what we learn outside school."

In answer to a further question, "What could the secondary schools do to improve themselves?" the students replied: "The schools should not take themselves so seriously. Time given to the formal work of schools could be reduced, especially if teachers would stop unloading their pet bodies of subject matter."[1]

The words of these representative consumers of secondary school-ing are worth heeding. Though what the consumers say is far from constituting a complete answer to our central question, it does provide clues, especially in light of the ways secondary school pupils spend their out-of-school time. The pupils learn a great deal of both practical and theoretical content ouside school—in home shops and laboratories, at community centers, on street corners, in churches and temples, in business and industry, and as volunteers in hospitals and social agencies, to mention only a few uses of time over which schools usually have had little influence and even less control. A senior high school boy put a basic problem for secondary educators in this way, "Why don't the people who run the schools do something to connect what's out there with what's in the schools?"

Having already done some things in secondary schools well, educators need to emphasize these things if they are still appropriate to our roles; to discern whatever else we should be doing, and then sup-ply the ability to do it; and to coordinate the work of the secondary school with the work, formal and informal, of agencies and groups out-

1. Ronald C. Doll, "Alternative Forms of Schooling," *Educational Leadership* 29 (February 1972): 391-93.

side the school that are also engaged in teaching adolescents. If we do so, many people in American communities will then become recognized teachers and leaders. They will, however, need to be planned with, helped, supplied with additional ideas and materials, and united in achieving common purposes. The need and the possibilities for exercising leadership of this great venture linking school and community through working with varied people are sobering.

We Begin with People

An enterprise of the kind mentioned above necessarily begins with a valuing of people, and of their potential for conducting and leading important educational work. If we believe in people and trust them, we tend to involve them in doing things we ourselves value. Secondary school administrators who have worked closely with community members of all sorts have often come from their experiences with high respect for the potential of many of these persons, and also with a chilling realization that we know so little about ways of working with them to effect the best results and to avoid conflict. Among educators who have tried and do know possible ways of working, the key question about wide involvement does not contain the word "whether" but the word "how."

The kinds of persons who are likely to have enhanced roles in the secondary education of the future include parents, as individuals and in organized groups; workers and supervisors in business, industry, medical facilities, churches, museums, social agencies, and other governmental and nongovernmental organizations; special interest groups; instructors in formal and informal training programs outside the schools; adolescents and young adults, in school and out of school; legislators and bureaucrats; consultants and other special helpers; and creators and merchandisers of materials, the wherewithal of education. Persons like these should participate in decision making about secondary education, not only because it is democratic to involve people who have a stake in the decisions to be made, but also because secondary education will touch their lives more intimately as it moves out to where they are. Hidden among such people are deep wells of potential which we have seldom tapped. At the same time, the motivations and ambitions of varied individuals often run at cross purposes. Involving them appropriately and productively presents a challenge to leadership which is beyond any challenge we have previously met.

Three terms commonly used in connection with the involvement of people are leadership, management, and manipulation. Leadership has come to mean forward movement toward the acknowledged goals of the organization being led. The term management suggests nose-to-the-grindstone performance of duties that may be traditional and must, at any rate, be performed to make the organization operate with some effectiveness day by day. Manipulation means using people to attain ends that are not the people's own, but are the ends openly or subtly sought after by the manipulators. Without stirring the perennial controversy concerning these terms, one may safely say that both leadership and management of the very best sort will continue to be needed. As for manipulation, would that educators could eliminate it! Actually, however, people in the communities surrounding secondary schools are less likely to hold still to be manipulated than the teachers whom some administrators have manipulated, or the administrators whom some teachers have learned to manipulate.

If humane and efficient educational leadership and management, rather than manipulation, come into widespread use, sharing as opposed to mere delegating of responsibilities will become common. Coordination of work forces will prove to be an extremely difficult but necessary task. Lines of responsibility and authority will have to be marked out more clearly than ever before.

A List of Crucial Issues

Just how, then, can learning by adolescents be fostered in an environment that is broader and more complex than that of the traditional school? How can learning by adolescents be developed in an environment in which large numbers of people have roles to play, and in which fostering learning consists of cooperative planning to achieve cooperative decision making; careful, helpful supervision of ongoing educational activity; and skilled administration of the whole enterprise? Some of the issues raised by the central questions of the chapter are:

1. Who shall be made responsible for the varied tasks involved in fostering learning?

2. How can people's potential for performance in fostering learning be utilized to the limit?

3. How can the specific tasks involved in fostering learning be distributed and discharged best?

4. How can skills in human relations and interpersonal communication be brought to bear in fostering learning?

5. How can the work of the varied participants be balanced and coordinated?

6. How can responsibility for outcomes be increased and improved without creating a rigid system of accountability?

7. How can the effects of cooperative effort to foster learning be evaluated?

The Issue of Role Assignment

The first issue, "Who shall be made responsible for the varied tasks involved in fostering learning?" evokes two immediate observations: someone or some group needs to be generally in charge, and the tasks to be performed must be widely and carefully distributed among numbers of people.

In the past, the strongest-looking or the allegedly strongest-looking candidate, according to a mystique of strength sometimes contaminated with politics, has been appointed or elected to take charge. Public pressure on secondary schools, particularly since the 1950s, has caused school personnel to hope that their leaders would be vigorous educational statesmen and institutional managers, persons with an agenda for making progress in view of institutional goals, and with ability to keep the schools operating smoothly day by day. Concerning statesmanship, the people inside schools have wanted their leaders to be wise and foreseeing. Concerning institutional control, they have wanted them to be willing to take stands and to act decisively. Secondary school administrators have tended to perform as persons who are often called upon to make quick decisions—and are sometimes right. The cognitive facet of their competence has been assumed to be some kind of knowledge and understanding they have acquired somewhere; in addition, they were supposed to possess a kind of intuitive knowing or feeling. Such a magic combination empowered them to serve as oracles about many subjects and problems!

Laymen who like to be critical of school leaders ask why we do not have better leaders heading school systems and schools. They point to intensified programs of preparation, experience requirements, and certification standards that they often regard as sufficient to guarantee quality leadership. They do not know that there are other elements of preparation and selection which are being neglected. As the demands we make of top leaders in secondary education intensify, we must continue to stress preparation, experience requirements and certification standards as we choose potential leaders. But we must also be concerned about affective factors, awareness and self-mastery, skills in social interaction, and capacity to motivate other people.

For instance, affective difficulties are often the major handicaps crippling administrators' ability to lead. Like people in other walks of life, educational leaders may bring with them their infantilisms, their feelings of personal inadequacy, their distrust of other people, and whole catalogs of social maladjustments. Persons who are to assume top leadership roles in the future will have to be educated in those areas of affect in which we are now working with young children; for example, awareness of one's self, the meaning of mastery of self and the environment, ways to become skilled in social interaction.[2] The time will be late in their lives, but we must still make the effort.

The leaders we shall want must be aware. They must be able and willing to listen, to communicate effectively, and to discriminate among cues, evens, the magnitudes of problems, and the characteristics of people. They must be masters of themselves, possessing self-confidence and responsible competence so that, for instance, they can freely admit their mistakes as means to additional learning, and can respect the capabilities and accomplishments of other people without feeling that they themselves have lost stature by doing so.

In the area of social interaction, they must help other people understand the results of their behavior, prizing acceptance, approval, affection, and inclusion, and learning to deal with negative behaviors in themselves and others. They will need to understand that human motivation should be made to depend less on fear, competition, and charm. They will need to recognize that people are better motivated through learning that there is something in an experience for one's self, through having success experiences, and through receiving realistic, constructive feedback concerning one's own successes.

2. See, for instance, Harold Bessell and Uvaldo Palomares, *Methods in Human Development*, Theory Manual, 1973 Revision (San Diego: Human Development Training Institute, 1973), *passim*.

In brief, top-level leadership for fostering learning properly depends on the quality of human beings and on the continuing, functional education of these human beings. In response to those who believe that adulthood is too late a time in life to increase people's sensitivity and concern, there are already available records of success in re-educating school administrators in areas of affective education. For example, Combs and Fisk found, when they examined the effects of training programs in human relations conducted in three universities, that the attitudes and behaviors of school administrators who were students in the programs had changed.[3] We need to educate and re-educate administrators to become cultured persons, knowledgeable in useful arts and sciences, and also skilled in making use of their own potential and in interacting with other people. We want people in the highest positions of leadership to be genuine, personally secure, open, and willing to share with others whatever responsibility they can legitimately share.

One of the significant functions of leaders who are in first-line positions in secondary schools is to work with other people as though they were indeed worthy people, as indeed they almost always are. When leaders do this, they recognize the intrinsic worth, the present contributions, and the potential of the people around them. They realize that every teacher, pupil, parent, and other community member is unique. As Argyris says, three norms should exist in a desirable climate for human beings. The first is the norm of individuality; the second, the norm of concern; the third, the norm of trust.[4]

Where individuality, concern, and trust are emphasized, emergent leadership can thrive. Fostering learning in secondary education should depend in part on applying the theory of emergent leadership, which has been tested often, if carelessly, in practice. A major responsibility of a first-line leader is to cause new leaders to emerge by giving previously uninitiated people real opportunities to lead. The first-line leader thus becomes a leader of leaders.

Some superintendents of public school systems in the nation were striving hard to provide leadership opportunities to both teachers and

3. Arthur W. Combs and Robert S. Fisk, eds., "Human Relations Training for School Administrators," *The Journal of Social Issues* 10 (no. 2 (1954): entire issue.

4. Chris Argyris, *Organization and Innovation* (Homewood, Ill.: Richard D. Irwin, Inc., 1965).

laymen long before teachers' unions and other organizations of professionals were rightly insisting that the making of decisions be shared more widely. The consequence was usually a strengthening of the persons with whom decision making was shared. Many a distinguished professional had his or her start in a school system where sharing was the norm.[5] If planning, supervising, and administering programs in secondary education are to become the responsibilities of numbers of persons of varied ages, backgrounds, capacities, and competencies, leadership opportunities must be distributed among all these persons. Levels of leadership will vary and specific tasks will differ, but all will be involved in leading.

Leadership in the secondary education of the future will need to be based increasingly in competence as opposed to position. As professional personnel become even more professional than they are now, they will accept leadership only from persons who are truly competent in the arena of service in which the leadership is being provided.

As promising, exciting, and democratic as distribution of leadership responsibility is, it can hardly function unless certain considerations guide the making of role assignments. The need for these considerations has been noted by many secondary educators during the era of school-community ferment in the late 1960s and the early 1970s, when persons who were previously deprived of the right to participate and even of the right to be regarded with respect have made their presence strongly felt, especially in the inner cities. With special reference to the right to participate and to be respected, matters of competence, authority, motivation, and philosophy are important considerations.

Competence. People who are competent to perform particular tasks should perform them. It is easily possible, in times of bursting enthusiasm for increased involvement, to put incompetent people in charge of assignments. Then all involved live to regret it. For instance, teachers should not be put in charge of curriculum planning and budget-making until they are prepared for these assignments. Some parents are obviously abler in leading discussion groups than other

5. Ronald C. Doll, *Leadership to Improve Schools* (Worthington, Ohio: Charles A. Jones Publishing Co., 1972), p. 49.

parents. Though pupils are often competent to participate in planning their learning experiences and to tutor younger children, they usually lack background about how to apply curriculum theory and how to effect curriculum change.

The ranges of competence of the new participants in leadership will broaden as secondary education moves further into the community. Laymen who know their own specialties can be helped to teach adolescents in the settings in which the laymen feel most at home, and in which they have the necessary equipment and materials. When the curriculum is opened to include more and more experiences in the community, much work will be available to all persons who should be teaching and leading. The challenge to leaders of leaders is obvious: it is possible to keep people doing, for a time, the things they are competent to do, but helping them to expand their competence and to feel comfortable with their new responsibilities is much more difficult.

Authority. People tend to feel contented and satisfied if they feel right about authority—their own and other people's. Giving and receiving authority will remain a difficult matter in reorganized systems of secondary education. Hard experience teaches that authority, sufficient and functional, must accompany responsibility. Trouble arises, however, when some people feel an insatiable lust for power, so that the energies of numbers of participants are redirected into undesirable power struggles.

Secondary education, in any changed format, will continue to face the questions, "Who is now *really* in charge?" and "Who *should* be in charge?" In many school systems, administrators have lost part of their former power, while teachers and paraprofessionals have gained power. Parent groups and other community groups of varying motivations have become rivals of boards of education. The expression "the schools belong to the people" has rightly been taken literally, but particular literal interpretations have sometimes become so skewed that power distribution has been without order or reason. Extending adolescents' learning experiences to new sites and circumstances might so spread whole secondary education programs that consequent uncontrolled power-grabbing could result and become detrimental to the sprawling programs themselves.

However, if we increase opportunities for people to participate, we should provide many more opportunities for them to lead; thus we would reduce the frustration that comes from an individual's never having his or her desire to lead satisfied. Planners in secondary education had better have a healthy view of the enhancing worth of power in the lives of people. The numbers of people who feel the urge to possess power should be identified; the many opportunities to exercise power should be distributed judiciously; and the few persons who need special help in controlling their hunger for power should be helped. For instance, in one school system a start toward a studied attempt to deal more effectively with people's desire for power was made by keeping a "power opportunity card file" for each full-time school employee, professional and nonprofessional.

Motivation. Most persons who participate in planning, supervising, and administering educational programs have generally affirmative feelings about their own work and about the people with whom they serve. Teachers, administrators, school board members, and members of parent groups have characteristically undertaken burdensome tasks primarily to be helpful to children. Education has seemed so important a field of endeavor that it has attracted a great deal of volunteer assistance as well as low-paid help in the development of professional programs. Apparently it will continue to do so. In broadened, open programs of secondary education, the vast domain within which service is needed should be shown and described to potential participants. Participants and those who recruit them had best recognize that conditions of work may be less than ideal. Recruiters of personnel may wish to ask, for example, "If things were just right, what do you think you would most like to do?" Continual inquiring, observing, guiding, and readjusting will be necessary in the attempt to get feelings to fit assignments.

In rare instances, people are motivated to destroy ongoing programs and the workers who serve in them. When psychopathology takes this form, it must be dealt with directly. Destructiveness by the few will not routinely disappear, and must not be allowed to interfere with the constructive efforts of their participants.

Philosophy. People who believe most strongly in a program of secondary education will make it an object of their deep concern and effort. The philosophy underlying a program should be discussed frequently because philosophy can be clarified and "purified" through discussion and a clearly stated philosophy leads to realistic goal setting.

People who are philosophically opposed to an educational idea can scarcely be expected to help put the idea into effect, not because they are benighted or perverse but because they have other preferences.

Utilizing Human Potential

The second issue, "How can people's potential for performance in fostering learning be utilized to the limit?" may be confronted in several major ways. The first way would seem to be helping people know themselves. Self-concept has been defined as all the things a person feels to be true about him- or herself. These feelings, however, are necessarily unclear, for they are distorted by what the person would like to feel about himself, what he believes others feel about him, and how his situation at the moment affects his self-vision.[6] Inasmuch as one's self-concept is formed from the outside in, what leaders do or fail to do becomes very significant in the formation of self-concepts by those who follow the leadership.

The individual must do everything he can to clarify his perception of himself. What Lewis and Miel say about methods by which supervisors can come to understand themselves may apply to the many people who will assume leadership in the new secondary education. Lewis and Miel suggest that supervisors keep records of their uses of time, watching for possible areas of neglect. Supervisors should notice whether they spend more time with people or with things; more time with individuals than with groups, or vice versa; more time working in classrooms than working alone, recording, reflecting, studying, and preparing; more time with professionals than with community members; more time on management than on leadership. How one voluntarily spends one's time is an index to one's preferences and attitudes.[7]

One may gather additional data about oneself in an educational situation by analyzing the questions, suggestions, and comments of other persons who are in a similar situation. Through analyzing

---

6. See, for example, Florida Educational Research and Development Council, *Enhancement of the Self-Concept: A Case Study* (Gainesville, Fla.: The Council, 1971).

7. Arthur J. Lewis and Alice Miel, *Supervision for Improved Instruction: New Challenges, New Responses* (Belmont, Cal.: Wadsworth Publishing Company, 1972), pp. 243-44.

related situations one may also detect one's own vanities, satisfactions, irritations, insistence on winning, and tendency to succumb to "power poison." Sometimes it is possible to recognize and verbalize one's strengths, weaknesses, desires, and interests. The varying individuals who now participate and who will participate in secondary education need to feel that it is natural and respectable to have weaknesses as well as strengths; they may learn that people in comparable situations also have strengths and weaknesses—even offbeat desires and aberrant interests. One may expect to see in others, and thus in oneself, immaturities which seem strange and unacceptable to other people. Analysis of others in similar situations contributes to self-analysis. Self-analysis leads to self-awareness, which in turn can strengthen a striving toward attainable goals.

Accurate understanding of what an individual can do may also be aided by other people's favorable assessment. The individual is freed to do better than his or her imagined best by feeling the empathy or depth understanding displayed by other people; by feeling others' respect as revealed in their message that he or she is uniquely capable; and by feeling the warmth of those who care enough to increase their investment in his or her life. Perhaps after a while we shall learn about adults what we have known, at least in the abstract, about children and youth—that accentuating the positive in our dealings with them pays rich dividends. What we currently know about developing potential in other people is conveyed in these messages that people would like to communicate to us:

"Act on your affirmative judgments about me. Hold back discreetly before acting on your negative ones."

"Show both verbally and nonverbally that you think I am worthy of associating and working with you."

"Show me gently how well I am doing things that help youngsters learn. Then show me just as gently what I can do to improve."

When one knows oneself well and has had adequate feedback concerning what other people think, one may be ready to help oneself change. The object of change which increases human potential is, in Maslow's term, self-actualization. Maslow believes that what the person can be, the person must be. Certain preconditions provided by leadership need to exist before an individual can approach the state of self-actualization. One of these preconditions is having success in some basic but worthwhile experiences. A second related one is receiving honest approval for what one has done. A third is being given freedom to act responsibly in a work assignment to which one is suited. After these preconditions have been fulfilled, change becomes, in part, a consequence of one's own will and initiative.

A person's will to change is assisted materially by appropriate kinds of in-service education and experience. Continuing education for individuals and small groups cannot be provided entirely by colleges and universities. In the years to come, continuing education of secondary educators must be tailored more often to the needs of people in school systems and education complexes. Constant cataloging and analysis of the in-service requirements of individuals will be necessary if in-service education is to be effective at the local level.

The case of a secondary school paraprofessional in an eastern city is illustrative of what can be done to develop the potential of a person charged with helping adolescents learn. The paraprofessional had been regarded by teachers in the school as a run-of-the-mine assistant to an industrial arts teacher who himself was considered to be one of the least able professionals in the school. Two department chairmen discovered almost simultaneously that the paraprofessional was a potentially competent and imaginative mathematician with an interest in computer programming. They tried to increase the paraprofessional's self-confidence by talking with him. They took him to the principal for a conversation about possible uses for his hidden talents, helped him find in-service opportunities which enhanced his understanding and creativity in applying mathematics to solving school problems, and sponsored him in a new assignment in programming, scheduling, and budgeting. Such cases are not rare; they can be multiplied in number.

Distributing and Discharging Specific Tasks

The third stated issue is, "How can the specific tasks involved in fostering learning be distributed and discharged best?" The specific tasks are of several types, including leading innovation, learning more about the adolescents being served, managing the arrangements that already exist, searching for and inquiring about new opportunities for learning, marshaling and distributing resources, coordinating people's work, serving intimately with peer groups and individuals, and engaging in down-to-earth activity in classrooms and at other learning sites. These tasks are comprehended within the three responsibilities referred to at the beginning of this chapter: planning, supervising, and administering. Each responsibility involves job assignments and sets of duties. For example, curriculum planning may involve the following job classifications and related sets of duties:

1. *Curriculum Coordinator*

Sample Duties: Directing the development of an organizational plan and the selection of planning procedures; guiding the assignment of planners' roles; stimulating planners to avoid superficiality, duplication, and other planning difficulties; arranging for time for curriculum development and for places and materials to be used in planning; guiding the process of change and innovation.

2. *Professional Team Leader*

Sample Duties: Guiding selection and involvement in planning of team leaders; conducting planning meetings of the team; directing inquiry and experimentation by team members; advising about the planning of curriculum sequences, the preparation of curriculum guides, and the development of instructional units.

3. *Lay Participant in Planning*

Sample Duties: Discussing with professional and lay persons the aims and procedures of programs and projects; suggesting ways of using resource persons who have competence in specialized areas of human knowledge; working as a member of a team creating instructional materials; exploring and investigating out-of-school instructional sites and arrangements.

4. *Classroom Aide*

Sample Duties: Soliciting from instructional team members ideas for the agenda of a forthcoming meeting; planning with pupils the itinerary of a field trip; making preliminary lists of instructional materials to be ordered; collecting materials and arranging facilities for a planning meeting; keeping records of uses of pupil time in education centers.

5. *Pupil Representative*

Sample Duties: Planning with adults toward introduction of an innovation; responding to a curriculum committee's request for pupil reaction to an instructional experiment; leading other pupils in planning to utilize a newly-opened section of a building; making contacts with youth groups that should be involved in a comprehensive program of secondary education.

The current differentiated staffing in some secondary schools is sufficiently experimental to permit some tasks to be moved about freely among, for instance, master teachers, instructional researchers, specialist teachers, curriculum team leaders, helping teachers, interns, aides, instructional materials assistants, and student teachers. When secondary education becomes genuinely more than secondary schooling, the distribution of tasks will become an even more complicated problem. Both quality of performance and development of the potential of the new facilitators will need to be considered in assigning and reassigning specific tasks.

Some tasks will necessarily be broader than the specific ones in the preceding paragraph. Those tasks will be of the spirit of the new open and broadened secondary education. As Margaret Mead has pointed out, future attempts to provide quality secondary education will require administrators and teachers, both professional and amateur, to learn where pupils are in their development, what different or out of the ordinary experiences individual pupils have had, what can be done to increase the flexibility of individuals' learning programs, and what can be done to make learning continually more relevant.[8] In answer to the question, "Do you think that there's a way of providing excitement in high schools and simultaneously keeping fifteen to eighteen year olds within a single building, removed from the rest of the community, for five to seven hours a day?" Dr. Mead pointed to the importance of "letting the students out." She mentioned that "the ecology problem" provided many appropriate activities for students in American communities.[9]

Planning closely for thorough and efficient education of adolescent learners requires much coordinated effort. If decision making in the planning process is to be shared, control over administration and

8. Margaret Mead, "Are Any School Administrators Listening?" *Nation's Schools* 87 (June 1971): 41-42.

9. Ibid., p. 42.

supervision should be shared similarly. Typically, a planning group sets directions and then frees administrators and supervisors to make specific decisions about how a given project is to be carried out. Both the makers of basic decisions who are members of the planning group and the controllers of the activity who administer and supervise the project should provide people with stability and stimulate them to productive activity.

Utilizing Skills in Human Relations and Human Communication

The fourth stated issue is, "How can skills in human relations and human communication be brought to bear in fostering learning?" At a broad and general level, commendable human relations consists of enunciating the Golden Rule, using enlightened ethics and applied common sense, and practicing humanely appropriate behavior. At the educational practitioner's level, the "Index of Perception" developed by Gazda and others shows how a person who truly helps others responds in interview or conference with the person to be helped. The helper who responds appropriately goes beyond merely reflecting the "helpee's" communication; the helper identifies underlying feelings and meanings. The helper is clearly committed to the helpee's welfare. He or she tries to be attentive, specific, and genuine; volunteers his or her personal feelings, thoughts, and experiences; points out gently the discrepancies in the helpee's behavior; and discusses the relationship between helper and helpee.[10] Even clinical psychologists, who know the practical worth of behaviors like these, have difficulty in achieving and maintaining them. When leadership in secondary education is dispersed, large numbers of people will need education and training in just such skills of human relations and interpersonal communication.

The education and training of the new helpers might well begin with an identification of the psychological needs which people manifest on the job. Some of these needs have been identified by groups of teachers as follows:

1. The need to be dealt with fairly, according to participants' perceptions of the meaning of fairness

---

10. George M. Gazda et al., *Instructor's Manual to Accompany Human Relations Development: A Manual for Educators* (Boston: Allyn and Bacon, Inc., 1973) p. 3.

2. The need to be treated in a friendly manner. Friendliness encourages the many people who feel ill at ease and even lost in their social and occupational relationships

3. The need to be dealt with consistently, so that one knows what to expect in similar circumstances day by day

4. The need to find one's immediate superior dependable, so that trust in the leader and his or her authority begin to grow

5. The need to be listened to, a need which waxes as life in an organization continues.[11]

Teachers and administrators who have had long experience in schools report that the helpers whose behavior they most respect do three things particularly well: they show that they are conscious of the impact of what they themselves do and say; they obviously recognize the worth of people around them; and they are unusually willing to help others. The first of these actions, taking cognizance of what one does and says, may begin with trying to sense the image one projects. It may involve trying to make one's words fit one's deeds, and vice versa. It reaches its acme in a developed system of personal monitoring of what one does and personal editing of what one says.

The leader who shows willingness to recognize the worth of other people believes that everyone is in the process of becoming. The person who believes in this kind of human evolution has exceptional patience with stumbling, bumbling human beings. Since many of the future helpers in secondary education will bring to their tasks very limited background and experience, today's administrators must themselves practice helpfulness if they are to aid the newcomers.

Before one begins to help, one must show in every way possible that there is nothing intrinsically wrong with being helped. Furthermore, one needs to engage in a great deal of interpersonal inquiry to learn what one's associates think helpfulness really is. When the helper knows, he or she should help unstintingly.

Although elaborate communication arrangements may have to be developed in a large organization, the all-round best communication system still is closely interpersonal. Opening secondary education to widespread interaction will occasion many more interpersonal contacts than have ever existed in and around secondary schools. Without continuing education in the art of communicating, these interpersonal con-

11. Doll, *Leadership to Improve Schools*, pp. 40-44.

tacts will be poorly made and maintained. A goal of administrators must be to open channels and create networks of communication that involve people who have most in common and most to share. The channels and networks will function satisfactorily only if the messages within them move freely in as many directions as possible within networks, thereby giving ample opportunity for feedback and reexamination of ideas. People who send and receive messages will need in-service education in skilled communication and reeducation in managing the feelings that miscommunication creates.

Sometimes a new leader learns more about desirable human relations and human communication from negative examples than from affirmative preachment. The administrators around us who get into trouble because they are too dictatorial or too laissez faire, unwise in involving people, inclined to create escapes from involvement, neglectful of the right of other people to know, and unreasonable in their expectations can serve as negative examples to new leaders seeking constructive ways of working.

Achieving Balance and Coordination in Participation

The fifth issue is, "How can the work of the varied participants be balanced and coordinated?"

Balancing and coordinating the work of in-school and out-of-school participants in a broadened program of secondary education is a mammoth assignment. It calls for carefully specifying goals, determining necessary functions which relate to the goals, realigning and reassigning tasks, supervising performance of the tasks with concern for combining resources, and encouraging cooperation to achieve a masterful pulling together of all the forces instrumental in attaining the goals.

The goals of the new secondary education must be made clearer than the goals of secondary schooling have been made in the past. The recommendations of the National Commission on the Reform of Secondary Education properly began with a call for definition of secondary school expectations. The Commission asked every secondary school and its departments to formulate a statement of goals in consultation with people of the community.[12] The community itself,

12. National Commission on the Reform of Secondary Education, *The Reform of Secondary Education* (New York: McGraw-Hill Book Company, 1973).

and not merely that subsection of the community that is the secondary school, can then be made responsible for the eventual achievement of the goals.

Respect for established goals and careful interpretation of the meanings of goals should lead to determining what educational functions the goals mandate. Where the functions should be discharged—in the secondary school, outside it, or both inside and outside it— becomes an important subsequent question. At present, some secondary schools are catch-alls for all sorts of functions, educational and noneducational. This state of affairs is often a direct consequence of absence or insufficiency of planning within the schools and their constituent communities.

Cataloging valid functions and assigning them to locations in educational settings lead naturally to according status and position to specified tasks within an appropriate, modifiable hierarchy. Some of the tasks that have been allocated earlier will have to be reallocated. The supervision of staff performance will surely result in further alignments and assignments. What would easily become a mechanistic distribution of tasks must instead be undertaken with a spirit of cooperation, to the end that persons assigned as program coordinators achieve a meshing of large numbers of activities.

Supervising staff performance in the secondary education that is emerging will become the responsibility of many more people than those presently serving in paid supervisory positions. Lewis and Miel say that "not only may official leaders like general and special supervisors (consultants) and principals share with others the responsibility for the quality of the instructional process, but teachers also may assume responsibility for the quality of their work."[13] One might add that, as more lay persons become involved in teaching, some lay persons will necessarily help with supervising the work of the lay teachers. Supervisory leaders, as these authors say, might serve best as visionaries, catalysts, coordinators, and stimulators as they work with teachers, laymen, and new helpers.

Coordination is a masterful pulling together of all the forces contributing to progress toward desired goals. Persons charged with coordinating people and programs contend with two special difficulties.

13. Lewis and Miel, *Supervision for Improved Instruction*, p. 342.

The first is the variety of perceptions of people's roles and tasks. Discussions, case studies, and sociodramas are useful in causing perceptions to converge. The second difficulty is duplication in roletaking, resulting in conflict among roletakers who are attempting to do the same work. People tend to "step on each other's toes" especially when new job assignments are made and new lines of responsibility are left unclear. The solution may be frank discussion and a subsequent written recording of agreements. Responsibilities may be noted in writing as being primary, that is, particular to one person only, or cooperative, that is, shared by several participants. Subsequently, adjustments can be made in role assignments as personnel and circumstances change.

Coordinators should prize diversity in people's thinking, but their central task is to help achieve a workable unity. They can do this by keeping people talking about things and people to be coordinated; by helping people commit themselves to common themes-for-the-year; and by involving people in cooperative projects in which they find excitement and stimulation.

A centralized work area such as the central offices of a school system must accept a high degree of responsibility for coordination. Though the units "out there" should remain functionally diffuse, a considerable degree of pulling together through the center is needed if unity of action in pursuing common purposes is to be achieved.

Balance and coordination are so difficult to achieve that they are sometimes said to provide the sternest test of the viability of an organization. But reasonable achievement of both balance and coordination is not an impossibility.

Fixing Responsibility or Accountability without Causing Threat

The sixth issue is definitely a current concern: "How can responsibility for outcomes be increased and improved without creating a rigid system of accountability?" We live in a day in which accountability, desirable as it is for roletakers in any productive organization, threatens further to harden institutional arteries. Accountability threatens to damage the initiative and creativity of participants in planning, supervising, and administering systems of secondary education. Yet, people in all walks of life should be held accountable for the direct results of their efforts when it can be clearly proved that they are responsible for the results. They should not be held accountable for results which are only obliquely, casually, or partially the results of their own efforts.

In professional education today, conflicts rage about both the content for which people are accountable and the means of determining their accountability. Consider the propriety of holding supervisors and administrators who work with numbers of people of differing backgrounds and qualifications accountable for the total personal and professional development of these people. Obviously, both the favorable and adverse influences that play upon the lives of persons who are developing in their personal responses and through their work experiences are partially beyond anything supervisors and administrators can help or hinder. Provide then, some critics urge, a requirement that leaders in secondary education be held accountable only for measurable results of their efforts to influence and help, conceived strictly in behavioral terms and gauged by means of narrowly defined evaluation instruments. But can small pieces of an associate's behavior, no matter how carefully measured, represent what the associate can do as a direct consequence of his or her mentor's intervention? If the goal of the supervisor is intelligent behavior manifested by the supervised person, can the behavior of the supervised be examined and measured in small pieces, or can it only be viewed and evaluated holistically?

A fair question to ask of leaders in secondary education concerning their own accountability is, "What do you leaders do to 'turn people on' or otherwise alter their perceptions constructively so that the people show additional evidences of intelligent behavior?" This question recognizes that people's behavior is less fruitful to work with than the underlying causes of their behavior—what people perceive and what meanings they attach to their perceptions. It implies further that supervisors and administrators can be held accountable for helping alter people's perceptions within prescribed frames of reference, and for helping them arrive at meanings which will affect their actions. That is, they can be expected to learn how people *feel* and to help influence their thoughts and feelings. But they cannot, except in a very limited and limiting sense, be held accountable for what other people *do*.

Leaders can and should be held responsible for helping to influence the thoughts and feelings of the people with whom they work through programs of in-service education. Both cognitive and affective in-service education are necessary for people who are altering their perceptions and arriving at new meanings. For secondary education in the future, this fact suggests the importance of massive new in-service developments. Modifying and intensifying feelings and helping people identify with others in desirable professional interaction will call for a kind of affective education to which school personnel are unaccustomed. New in-service procedures, including interaction workshops and exercises in interpersonal and small-group facilitation, will be required.

In the new secondary education, teachers of differing backgrounds and abilities are likely to be everywhere in a given system. A look at some of their probable tasks offers an example of a responsibility-accountability base. Teachers will probably work with pupils increasingly on a one-to-one basis. With communication of information being taken over to some extent by electronic equipment and related materials, teachers will interact more closely and affectively with pupils, engage in educational diagnosis, lead discussions, plan with pupils, help answer specific questions, keep growth charts and other ongoing records, supervise experiencing by pupils, provide instructional prescriptions, and give advice about the availability and location of additional help. The accountability of these teachers will be based in what they are required or expected to do, as indicated above. But the question that will be pertinent in gauging their competence and achievement remains, "What do these teachers do to 'turn pupils on' or otherwise alter their perceptions constructively so that the pupils show additional evidences of intelligent behavior?" The teachers will be expected to help alter their pupils' perceptions and to help influence their thoughts and feelings so that the pupils' actions become more constructive.

Teachers currently complain, through their associations and unions, that boards of education, administrators, and communities attempt to hold them accountable for what pupils know and fail to know, and for what they do and fail to do. They rightly consider this version of accountability to be unfair because teachers should not be made responsible for either the advantages or the decrements in students' total learning environments. Teachers of adolescents should be responsible and accountable only for whatever they can influence directly and solely by their own efforts. They must remain responsible and accountable without threat.

Evaluating the Effects of Planning, Supervising, and Administering

The seventh and final issue to be discussed briefly in this chapter is, "How can the effects of cooperative effort to foster learning be evaluated?" Like the behavior of other people, the behavior of supervisors and administrators of secondary education should be viewed holistically rather than in pieces and bits. It should then be *evaluated* rather than *measured*. Nonatomistic evaluation requires setting broad criteria. These criteria would center on the impact that supervisors and administrators make in releasing people's feelings, changing their attitudes, and stimulating development and clarification of their meanings.

Most evaluation devices in this domain are, of course, yet to be created. The new devices, which may be regarded by some researchers and evaluators as being too "loose," will emphasize close observation and subsequent exercise of judgment. Both observational systems and procedures for establishing judgments in secondary education can be made exact and exacting. Yet the judgments that will be made as a consequence of observation will necessarily be largely subjective. To try for high levels of objectivity may, in fact, be foolhardy. At the University of Florida, investigators found that objectivity in gauging teaching correlated negatively with effectiveness in teaching. What is being learned in teacher education may be applied in large measure to the in-service teaching done by supervisors and administrators.[14] The work of supervisors and administrators, like the work of preservice teacher educators, involves teaching adults.

With Combs and his group, we may say that a person's behavior is symptom, and that the meaning the person affixes to what he or she perceives is cause. Accordingly, by intensive observation and judgment-making, supervisors and administrators should "read their clients" to infer the nature of these clients' or associates' perceptions and the meanings they attach to their perceptions. This is, of course, a difficult thing to do, but by coming to know one's associates better

---

14. Arthur W. Combs et al., *Florida Studies in the Helping Professions*, University of Florida Social Science Monograph No. 37 (Gainesville, Fla.: University of Florida Press, 1969).

and better, one finds it increasingly easy. By drawing inferences from associates' behavior, by asking them the probable sources of selected meanings they have acquired, and by noting meanings which they could have gained only from their mentors, the effectiveness of supervisors and administrators in building power in their associates, in teaching them cognitively and affectively, and in helping them identify with and relate to other people, can be gauged by supervisors and administrators themselves or by evaluators.

Furthermore, the competence of supervisors and administrators may be assessed in part without reference to their associates by finding out how much they know about the processes of planning, supervising, and administering; how skilled they are in dealing constructively with people outside groups of their own associates; how clear they are as to their own purposes; and how broad a repertory of procedures they have available for use. Both observational and pencil-and-paper devices can be used in conducting such evaluation of their work. The fact that many people, working at different levels of responsibility, will be needed in the future to direct planning, to supervise instruction, and to administer portions of programs suggests that certain ready-made instruments should be at hand for immediate use in meeting evaluation needs.

New instruments for evaluating attitude change may show that the impact of a leader, wherever he or she is placed in a system of secondary education, is not as great as might have been hoped. If so, the suspicion will grow stronger that the brief contacts that leaders have customarily had with their associates may help to explain why leaders' impact has often been slight. "Resocialization" of personnel by extending working relationships with them may in the future prove to be a significant factor in increasing leader impact. Evaluation data may reveal the importance of this factor.[15]

Summary

If learning is fostered in the new secondary education in the terms discussed above, the effects will be similar to those desired by Harold Howe II in his article predicting the nature of education in the year

15. See Joseph B. Giacquinta, "The Process of Organizational Change in Schools," *Review of Research in Education I*, ed. Fred N. Kerlinger, a publication of the American Educational Research Association (Itasca, Ill.: F. E. Peacock Publishers, Inc., 1973), pp. 192-94.

2024.[16] According to Howe, cooperation, as opposed to competition, will be cherished, and the contributions of individuals to the achievement of other people will be rewarded. As a consequence, education will become a more pleasant experience, learning will increase, "problems" will decrease, and educational institutions will improve their relationships with other institutions in society.

To attain such conditions in the new secondary education, we shall need enlightened leaders who know how to fix responsibility among available personnel, how to develop people's potential, how to assign tasks, how to encourage desirable human relationships and communication, how to assist in balancing and coordinating people's efforts, how to make themselves and others reasonably responsible for outcomes, and how to evaluate the actual effects of fostering learning.

16. Harold Howe II, "Report to the President of the United States from the Chairman of the White House Conference on Education, August 1, 2024," *Saturday Review-World* 1 (August 24, 1974): 73-76, 131.

CHAPTER XII

The Future, Social Decisions, and Educational Change in Secondary Schools

VIRGIL CLIFT AND HAROLD G. SHANE

Introduction

The methodical study of the future has become a new discipline, particularly during the past decade. The interest in reasoned speculations about tomorrow is reflected in a number of books and articles published during this ten-year interval.[1] Furthermore, widespread public awareness as to the importance of the future is reflected in the popularity of such books as Toffler's *Future Shock* and his *Learning for Tomorrow*.[2]

In this concluding chapter the writers look at certain premises for approaching the future; at probable developments of the next decade that are relevant to secondary education; and at portentous social decisions that need to be made if an American secondary education program, designed for the 1980s as well as anticipating the next century, is to be moved from our ideological drawing boards to the oftentimes harsh world of reality. The writers also have chosen to explore some of the possible implications for tomorrow's education to be derived from cultural pluralism. The challenge of meeting the needs of

1. For example, see Herman Kahn and Anthony J. Wiener, *The Year 2000* (New York: Macmillan Co., 1967); Paul Dickson, *Think Tanks* (New York: Atheneum, 1971); Kenneth Boulding, *The Meaning of the Twentieth Century* (New York: Harper Colophon Books, 1964); "Toward the Year 2000," *Daedalus* 96 (Summer 1967): whole issue; Herman Kahn and B. Bruce-Briggs, *Things to Come* (New York: Macmillan Co., 1972); Harold G. Shane, *The Educational Significance of the Future* (Bloomington, Ind.: Phi Delta Kappa, 1973); Richard W. Hostrop, ed., *Foundations of Futurology in Education* (Homewood, Ill.: ETC Publications, 1973); Louis Rubin, ed., *The Future of Education: Perspectives on Tomorrow's Schooling* (Boston: Allyn & Bacon, Inc., 1975).

2. Alvin Toffler, *Future Shock* (New York: Random House, 1970); and Alvin Toffler et al., *Learning for Tomorrow: The Role of the Future in Education* (New York: Random House, 1974).

our human subsets, we believe, is so important as to merit selection as an exemplar of the many decisions that are long overdue for attention and follow-up action in society and in secondary education.

It is our conviction that secondary education (as well as elementary and postsecondary education) tends for the most part to reflect rather than to create significant social change. Evidence for this observation is abundant. For instance, the schools offered little leadership in pointing the United States toward greater awareness of the special needs of minority groups, and various liberation movements owe a very small debt for any boosts they have received either from the average teacher or from most professional associations. We believe that schools should both reflect and create significant social change.

This viewpoint emphasizes the need for persons in secondary education (1) to examine and accept sound premises for approaching the future, (2) to study and learn from data and from selected trends that suggest what the future may be like, and (3) to recognize that there are portentous decisions pertaining to the governance of society that must be made wisely and soon. Each of these three points will be discussed briefly.

Some Premises for Approaching the
Future of Secondary Education

As Toffler correctly reminded us in 1974, "All education springs from some image of the future. If the image . . . held by a society is grossly inaccurate, its education system will betray its youth."[3] What, then, are some examples of broad premises that should govern the thinking of educators as they contemplate tomorrow?

First, we need to be prepared to be surprised. Will Rogers once said that "the schools ain't what they used to be—and they probably never wuz." As far as the future is concerned, it is not what it used to be either—and doubtless never really was. That is, the futures we once anticipated have only rarely turned out to be the way we conceived them at a given time in the past. Our images of abundance, of unlimited energy, and of technological futures swarming with servomechanisms to cater to our whims have become rather badly frayed

---

3. Toffler et al., *Learning for Tomorrow*, p. 3.

during the past five years. Two billion or more poorly fed people and perhaps ten million threatened with actual starvation[4] remind us in the mid-1970s that population is outstripping food production, a development to which most Americans were blind in the 1960s. A decade ago, only a few gloom-and-doom prophets—seers who were ignored in their own land—foresaw the inevitability of energy pro problems stemming from growing demand and the depletion of reserves.

Second, in confronting the future, one needs to recognize that it is unwise to apply the supposedly "infallible" guidelines of today and yesterday to emerging tomorrows. If we try to colonize the future with the many flawed ideas that are still reflected in contemporary culture, we shall partially paralyze the progress we might otherwise make. For example, it once was desirable to have large families. Now population threatens to assume a role analogous to that of a cancer on the planet. Old ideas regarding population, extravagant use of resources, and the threat of war as an instrument of national policy must be discarded rather than carried over into tomorrow.

Third, on the positive side, our posture for coming decades must anticipate that human capacities, both intellectual and technological, will continue to extend. This is an especially important concept to accept. We need all of our talent for survival and all of our technological skills, prudently employed, to increase food production until population growth tops off and to find long-range nuclear and solar substitutes for fossil fuels.

Fourth, we can anticipate that the "dizzying disorientation" of future shock will abate. Patently, we are learning to accept and to live with phenomenal changes. It is well that we are, since the rate of change is unlikely to diminish in the next several decades. We thus have no choice other than to begin more successfully to adjust to the presence of new developments and to cope with the problems that some of these developments create.

Fifth, we should be skeptical of any specific predictions made about the future. The future is not a topic neatly organized for study and futurists are not infallible. Indeed, their research data sometimes can be the enemy of truth when based on incomplete information or

4. See the report of an interview with Lester R. Brown, international expert on food problems, in "The Coming Global Famine," *Phi Delta Kappan* 56 (September 1974): 34-38.

when based on linear projections that suffer from the problem of tunnel vision.

The educational implications of our five premises for secondary schools are at least three in number. In the first place, confronted as we are by alternative futures that can be anticipated and controlled only in limited ways, we need to keep an open mind with regard to what "good" and "appropriate" schooling will be in the future. As authors of earlier chapters have implied, we almost certainly are on the threshold of a major discontinuity in human history. Certain old practices in secondary schools will be less relevant or irrelevant on the far side of this threshold, and new instructional policies will be highly important in a world recreating its values and its life-styles. It seems wise at this juncture, during a convulsive "ecospasm," as Toffler labeled it in 1975, to clean our educational house and to seek deliberately to conceive genuinely new programs. There is no longer any security to be found, per se, in Carnegie Units, in diplomas, and in scores on tests of scholastic aptitude. Indeed, in the 1980s, they may be remembered more for their limiting influence than for their virtues.

Not only do we need to re-examine past assumptions about secondary education. We also need to accept Lasswell's view that policy makers have an obligation to attain the security that resides in factual knowledge, including an awareness of lacunae, if they are to function with conviction and with merited security.[5] Secondary education, particularly in the realm of new content, needs to reflect meticulous study of what is really worth knowing and what supports the conclusions that are reached in this regard.

We round off our three suggestions with the point that secondary educators need to be less tense in the future than they have been in the past with regard to newer emergent life-styles. The passing years and future perspectives combine to suggest that we have been too "up tight" about male youth's ulotrichous haircuts (or the lack of any haircuts at all), about the "proper" skirt length for female youth, or about armbands worn to school in support of controversial causes and movements. After all, we were alarmed by the "quiet generation" of the 1950s, then more alarmed than ever when youth turned turbulent

---

5. Harold D. Lasswell, "The Future of Government and Politics in the United States," in *The Future of Education: Perspectives on Tomorrow's Schooling*, pp. 6-8.

in the 1960s. Can we not learn to reconcile ourselves to a tomorrow that seems so antic while it is being born and so nostalgic in retrospect a decade later?

Let us try to free ourselves from unexamined loyalty to irrational rules and conventions, and from an inability to sense, to grasp, and to act in terms of the changing fabric of society—both nationally and transnationally. As Walter Lippmann advised in *The Public Philosophy*, let us not be more willing to be *wrong*, than to be *right* at the *wrong time*.[6]

What Can We Anticipate Tomorrow?

As practitioners endeavor to improve practices and to allay some of the problems of secondary education, such as those identified by Coleman,[7] what kind of a world can they contemplate? While forecasts can be misleading, as noted above, events that already are taking place suggest at least a few of the developments likely to characterize the quarter century that lies ahead. Let us consider, then, what we are likely to encounter in the next decade or two and what this suggests for secondary education.

As Harman pointed out in chapter 5 of this yearbook, it seems more than likely that in the United States our lives will continue to be complicated by the paradox of too much success. Science and technology have created dissatisfaction with routine, production-line tasks and have bred the problems and responsibilities associated with nuclear weaponry. Material comforts that were unknown in 1900 or even 1920—air conditioning and a plethora of automobiles, for example—have contributed to a continuing energy crisis and severe pollution. Better transportation has made us more vulnerable to sky-jacking. Even our success in meeting some basic human needs has led to the frustrations of a world-wide "revolution of expectation" with which a planet with limited resources cannot cope.

The problems of success have led us toward an era that history may record as the post-affluent society in which we become careful users rather than open-handed consumers of industrial products. This

6. Walter Lippmann, *The Public Philosophy* (New York: New American Library, 1956).

7. "An Interview with James S. Coleman on Youth," *Today's Education* 64 (March-April 1975): 2.

needs a word of explanation. Beginning around 1950, the United States entered what was to be a brief interval of incredible resource depletion, a period that was characterized by a blend of applied technology and greed hitherto unattained in the developed world.[8] In a twenty-year interval, for instance, consumption of oil in the United States increased fourfold, and by 1974 domestic per capita energy consumption was double that of West Germany, and triple that of Switzerland. The authors of *Mankind at the Turning Point* estimate that if the entire world used oil at the rate it was used in the United States in 1973-74 all known reserves would be used up by 1982. Patently, such rates of use can not be continued insofar as oil and other nonrenewable earth resources are concerned. "Waste not and want less" may well be a geopolitical slogan of the 1980s.

We inevitably are approaching what Margaret Mead once labeled a return to "a string-saving society"—a recycling economy in which extravagance and conspicuous consumption are ruled out by cultural pressures. This suggests that tomorrow's society is very likely to be a more disciplined one. One can only hope that it will also be more equitable and that the discipline will be self-imposed rather than imposed by an authoritarian state.

Although not yet entirely clear, the implications of the future for secondary education are almost certain to be momentous ones. This is especially true when one contemplates the opportunites for schooling to reach new levels of significance during an epidemic of crises. But, certain social decisions must be reached if the schools are to develop programs that are designed more adequately to meet the demands that a changing social and economic structure are likely to make.

Social Decisions: Their Relations to
Schooling at the Secondary Level

Social decisions that are prerequisite to meaningful educational changes transcend discussions regarding methods or content in the secondary school. They focus on goals for humankind rather than

8. Our comments in this paragraph are based on Mihajlo Mesarovic and Eduard Pestel, *Mankind at the Turning Point* (New York: E. P. Dutton & Co., Inc./Reader's Digest Press, 1974); Lester Brown, *In the Human Interest* (New York: W. W. Norton, 1974); idem, *World Without Borders* (New York: W. W. Norton, 1972); and Andre van Dam, "The Limits to Waste," *The Futurist* 9 (February 1975): 18-21.

solely on education in the United States, as, for instance, was done in *The Purposes of Education in American Democracy*, an influential book at the time it was prepared by the Educational Policies Commission.[9]

A SPECIFIC ROSTER OF PRESSING DECISIONS

Among the social decisions that United States citizens must reach in order to give new directions to themselves (and thus to their secondary schools) we would list the following, phrased as questions for purposes of clarity. Explicit reference is made to instruction and curriculum when feasible, for new content and new directions in classroom discussions are suggested by all of these questions.

1. *What policies shall govern our future use of technology?* We need the power that our technological skills give us in mediating the environment but find that we have great difficulty in living with the consequences. This dilemma is one of particular portent for high school age youth, most of whom know only a world permeated by technology. They sometimes seem tremendously enamored of its products as represented by the hi-fi system, the transistorized radio, the auto, snowmobile, and the like. When inevitable cutbacks occur in the products of technology, what concomitant changes will occur in a youth culture so heavily impacted by its power? What policies will youth support as to the future use of technology?

2. *At a global level, what shall our goals be, and how can we reach them?* The growing interdependence of the world's national states and numerous related transnational problems require enlightened decisions in the next several years. At the classroom level it makes a great deal of sense, in the writers' opinion, to introduce methodically the world's realities, the alternatives that humankind may have as it faces global problems such as hunger, the probable consequences of alternatives, and the choices that seem most appropriate when data have been gathered.

3. *What shall we identify as the "good life"?* Opinions continue to vary sharply and, as a consequence, society and its schools lack a suitable image of the educated individual to hold up to youth. Social

9. Educational Policies Commission, *The Purposes of Education in American Democracy* (Washington, D. C.: National Education Association, 1938).

decisions made in this realm are of particular significance to the teacher of young adolescents who are deeply involved in the quest for a satisfying future-focused role-image. By precept and in the "hidden curriculum"—the things that are really being learned—what will the school of 1980 or 1985 really stand for?

4. *How shall we deploy our limited resources in meeting the needs of our human subsets?* The United States is made up of very many subsets: young children, the very poor, the old, youth, various ethnic and religious minorities, women, occupational groups, and so on. With a finite amount of tax monies available, how shall our treasure be invested in the well-being of each subgroup? Each youth in our schools is a part of one or more of our subsets, hence intimately affected by the policies and practices that will reflect social thinking in the coming decade. Also each young man and woman will be involved in paying the cost of human welfare programs, which as of 1976 are costing in excess of $100 billion annually. Again, as present and prospective policies are supported or assailed there is much opportunity to begin motivating youth to think of what it means to anticipate living in the twenty-first century.   •

5. *Shall we seek to modify the wide range in income that characterizes the so-called "haves" and "have-nots," and, if so, how?* In the United States there are enormous discrepancies in the standard of living. Shall we contemplate such innovations as a ceiling on earnings, as was seriously proposed for the Swedes by Professor Gunnar Adler-Karlsson?[10] Here we do, indeed, have a difficult problem. Those below the median—the "have-nots"—possess little to trade off with those "haves" above the median, except perhaps freedom from harassment. Major tensions build up quickly, too, since for every person who moves across the median to become a "have," someone must slip below it to preserve the fifty-fifty balance. Our discussion on subsequent pages casts some light on the complexities here. We cannot let it become a matter that is "out of sight, out of mind."

6. *How can we, without censorship or other imposed controls, maximize the value of the mass media—particularly television—and minimize their shortcomings?* In an era of incipient panic, great responsibility and maturity are essential in the distribution and selection of news and

10. Reported in the *Washington Post*, August 8, 1974.

other programs. In the secondary schools the task of alerting youth to the media's merits as well as to their occasionally minacious products is of high importance. Both programs involving extreme violence, overemphasizing sex, and featuring giveaways and the illusion that the media present accurate and comprehensive images of what is happening are representative of problems that require social decisions and social education. Already there is ample information available on how the impact of the mass media facilitates decision-making, but up to the present time (particularly where television is concerned) the American public has been willing to see changes made just so long as its televiewing and reading foibles remain unimpeded. That is, we are delighted to see gore, sex, and giveaway programs repudiated—just so long as our favorite bloodbath, sexy movie, or puerile guessing game remains to delight us. The enemy is "us," as Pogo, the comic strip character, reminded us back in the 1960s.

7. *What use shall be made of psychological, chemical, and electronic approaches to the modification of behavior?* In certain respects humans have developed Jovian powers before they matured to a point at which such powers could be wisely used. To what extent, if any, should behavior be the target of what Krech has called "psychoneurobiochemeducational" developments?[11] At least for the current decade, we advise caution. There is the danger that in our present state of knowledge we might make a faulty diagnosis or be influenced by what physicians call a "false positive" and apply the wrong approach, be it chemical, psychological, or electronic.

8. *What steps shall we take to insure the future integrity of our political-military-economic-industrial systems?* The systems that operate in a democracy reflect, at least to a substantial degree, implicit public resignation to the existence of dubious practices. The present parlous period in history suggests that the abuses typified by the Watergate scandals (but by no means limited to government) demand public decisions to reduce past abuses for which the public eventually pays. We probably should not expect too much gentleness in our political-military and economic-industrial systems; when all is said and done, *Adler bruten keine Tauben.*[12] Nonetheless, abuses by the systems can be

11. David Krech, "Psychoneurobiochemeducation," *Phi Delta Kappan* 50 (March 1969): 50.

12. "Eagles do not give birth to doves."

countered. For instance, Willard Wirtz has suggested the importance of eliminating huge contributions to political parties, more carefully policing politics so that persons do not abuse the power of their office for personal gain, and the need to reduce pressures for "deals" urged upon persons running for office by individuals or groups proposing to provide support only in return for promised concessions.[13] Again, it is important for society to weigh ways in which it can become more responsible for its general welfare.

9. *What, if anything, are we willing to relinquish—and in what order?* As a people, United States citizens are a privileged group, ranking among the world's best fed and sheltered, despite some notable exceptions in inner cities and on Appalachian mountain slopes. Are we to do with less during years ahead to help insure what the poor of the nation and the world would acclaim as greater equity? Any decision made here is vastly complicated by the rapidly mounting costs of government in its many forms. Consider our education bill as an example. According to Terrel H. Bell, U.S. Commissioner of Education, the cost of education in our nation for the fiscal year 1975-1976 will total $108 billion.[14] In this same fiscal year, subsidies such as Medicaid, Medicare, and veterans' education benefits will jump to $111 billion. The extent of increasing costs perhaps can better be expressed in terms of percent, since the billions involved stagger the imagination. Without counting Social Security cash benefits, the cost of federal welfare measures increased by 738 percent from 1964 to June, 1975.[15] Any viable decisions regarding the future are closely related to the long-range ability of the economy to support tax-based programs. And the more people become dependent on them, the more politically unpopular it will be to turn off the flow of funds.

10. *Since perfection presumably is unattainable, what honorable compromises shall we make as we contemplate the nine previous questions?* This concluding social decision differs from the first nine in that it per-

13. Mr. Wirtz, Secretary of Labor in the Kennedy and Johnson administrations, made this comment to one of the writers during a conversation on October 10, 1974.

14. This breaks down as follows: elementary and secondary schools, $68 billion (including $6 billion for nonpublic institutions); $40 billion for higher education (including $13 billion for private schools). Cited in *Medianews* (Winter 1975): 1.

15. Federal fiscal data are abstracted from *U. S. News and World Report* 78 (March 24, 1975): 70, 76.

meates all of them. Since we cannot attain all of our goals and our aspirations, and since we cannot quickly solve all of our problems, where do we begin to move toward greater justice and equity?

TOWARD IMPROVED SECONDARY EDUCATION

Before we ever reach a consensus on such comprehensive problems as the ten exemplars above, it is essential to act now on some of these problems at the secondary school level. This can be done, since society in the United States already has begun to reach, or has at least come in sight of, certain basic policy decisions regarding improved human opportunity through schooling. As an illustration of an area in which social decisions and applications are in sight, *and where we are ready to implement them*, consider cultural pluralism, listed as Point 4 above, "How shall we deploy our limited resources in meeting the needs of our human subsets?" Here we contemplate what is perhaps the most important investment we can make with finite tax monies.

Cultural Pluralism as an Exemplar of Social
Decisions Confronting Secondary Education

There are a number of problems peculiar to the cultural subgroups in America and education can and should play a special role in their solution. As we look to the future, it is important that these problems be identified and understood by the cultural subgroups themselves, as well as by the other spectra of society if solutions are to be found. Education for the future—education that is to serve adequately the various minority and disadvantaged groups—should take into account the special problems of these groups, the appropriate purposes and objectives of their education, and also the special features of educational programs that give greatest promise of helping to move the groups served into the mainstream of human development.

PROBLEMS IN IMPLEMENTING
THE CONCEPTS OF CULTURAL PLURALISM

The protests of the 1960s for civil rights brought blacks, Chicanos, women, students, native Americans, and others a sense of pride and personal dignity. It brought a sense of political power and enabled them to attract the attention of major establishment institutions. As American participation in the war in Vietnam dragged on and as attendant domestic problems increased, more and more of the sub-groups sensed that there was something fundamentally wrong with society.

Leading educators today are focusing attention on the proper relationship between education and society. For example, Lawrence A. Cremin seeks a new understanding of "the relationship between education and social ideals to which we aspire. Any narrow definition of education that ignores the large issues of society is just not sufficient."[16]

During the decade of the 1960s increased attention was given to the education of the disadvantaged, a large number of whom were members of the minorities. As a result secondary educators (along with those at the elementary and postsecondary level) developed a better understanding of the problems minorities group students faced, some of the most important of which are discussed in the following paragraphs.

First of all, the stigma of minority status creates many problems for students and adversely affects aspirations, motivation, and learning. All individuals need a sense of belonging, a feeling of acceptance, and a sense of personal worth. It is demeaning when they are relegated to inferior status on the basis of race, religion, sex, national origin, or social class. The consequences of stripping an individual of his dignity because of accident of birth are inhumane and undemocratic. It is impossible for persons to grow to their full stature when such conditions exist.

Further, most cultural minorities in America have a double problem to overcome. In addition to the stigma attached to individuals by their minority status, their institutions are regarded as inferior whether or not they are in reality. Their schools, churches, neighborhoods, and organizations are considered as inferior, regardless of the contribution they may make. Thus the individual of a minority group or lower social class who attends a school for minorities or for people of low economic status is almost invariably assumed to be receiving an inferior education. The end result is that the minority individual is nearly always regarded as inferior regardless of his strength of character, his achievement against odds, or the skills

16. Fred M. Hechinger, "Lawrence Cremin: Looking Toward the Heights," *Saturday Review-World* 2 (October 19, 1974): 56.

and competencies he has developed. The negative influence of this appraisal on individuals and groups has never been adequately assessed. It breaks the human spirit, the will, and produces helplessness and despair. The physical pain individuals suffer as a result of illness, accidents, and the like is soon forgotten. On the other hand, scars and pain—the psychological scar tissues—resulting from discrimination are never erased from one's memory and have a negative influence on the individual throughout life. Consequently large numbers of individuals in the various cultural minorities in America have negative images of themselves, negative self-concepts or low self-esteem, and frustrating future-focused role-images.

As an adult, Joyce A. Lander wrote, "I can vividly recall at a very early age (in Mississippi), when I cried in sorrow and anguish because I could not attend the newly built brick school for white children. Nothing my mother said in the way of explanation could erase my sorrow and bitterness. This was the first lesson of racial oppression I experienced, and for which I am still bitter."[17] This explains, at least in part, why some go to great lengths to achieve integrated education.

Let us also bear in mind that society is organized in a way that assigns roles to individuals. This is the second major problem on our list. The social class or caste system determines to a large extent the neighborhoods in which individuals reside, the schools they attend, and the vocational groups or classifications in which they earn a living. Persons from low socioeconomic backgrounds or from racial, national, and religious minorities are often viewed by the larger society as being of less worth, and in some cases as being something less than human. The broader society expects these individuals to achieve very little academically; to accept hard, dirty, demeaning work as their lot; and to live in slums. Whatever the lot of the unfortunates, it long has been erroneously assumed to be due to some fault of their own: lack of ambition, lack of talent or ability, limited intelligence.

The truth of the matter is that socioeconomic status and racial or ethnic origin largely determine what the individual is and what he may become. These factors determine the role society assigns to the individual, the quality and quantity of his education, and the levels of his

17. Joyce A. Lander, "Tomorrow's Tomorrow," in *The Black Woman*, ed. Tony Cade (New York: New American Library, 1974), p. 24.

aspirations and the extent of his motivation. Formal and informal agents of socialization cause the individual, often grudgingly or dispiritedly, to accept the role society assigns. In short, the individual tends to operate in terms of the "self-fulfilling prophecy" that is thrust upon him. When society makes known to the individual again and again in subtle ways that it views the individual to be of less worth or inferior, the individual comes to accept this verdict and to perform in a manner that is consistent with it. This helps to explain much of the apathy, the lack of concern, and the lack of achievement on the part of a large proportion of students from the various subgroups. They tend to achieve what society expects them to.

To continue our roster of problems, most minorities are at a disadvantage in acquiring the skills and competencies that are needed for higher levels of employment. Because they are locked into low-paying, dead-end jobs, parents simply cannot provide an environment for their children that helps them to acquire the skills and competencies prerequisite to the better educational and employment opportunities. How can we expect students who are hampered by this sort of limited background to aspire to more contributive jobs and better life-styles about which they do not even know? How can we expect them to strive for educational and vocational goals that society implicitly or explicitly tells them they cannot attain?

It has long been recognized that schools seldom offer programs that help minority students to achieve upward mobility. Quite the reverse! Studies show that schools attended typically by these students are not only supposed by the majority to be inferior in quality and quantity but often in actuality *are* inferior. Schools reflect the attitudes of society, some of which are not even remotely consistent with democracy. For example, because society does not expect women to be presidents of universities, they generally are not. Society does not expect blacks, American Indians, Chicanos, or women to serve as directors on boards of the major corporations, and generally they do not.[18]

18. It must be noted in all fairness that women and blacks *have* made some progress in solving these problems and in advancing themselves since 1970. There were 125 blacks on the boards of directors of the 100 major corporations in 1974, whereas there were only three in 1970. There were over 3,000 black elected officials in 1974, as compared with 1,184 in 1970. These included 125 city mayors, 17 United State Congressmen (four of whom were women), one United States Senator, and two lieutenant governors. For at least a decade the number of women in the professions has increased sharply and many more are employed in the labor force in jobs of their choosing.

This is largely because education heretofore has not helped to develop more positive attitudes in society, nor has education helped minority students to deal adequately with the three problems discussed so far.

A fourth difficulty is that our subgroups are confronted with the problems of maintaining cultural identity yet at the same time are expected to acquire social competencies and a life-style acceptable to the broader society. The decade of the 1960s, of course, witnessed an upsurge among minorities toward maintaining their cultural identity. At present this trend shows no sign of diminishing.

In the past, the broader society has generally looked with disdain on the unique cultural features and mores of minorities. The minorities recognized, at least tacitly, that their self-esteem and ego structure were damaged because of this disdain. In fact, the practice of being denied one's heritage and culture tended to cause severe identity problems. It frequently forced the minority person to reject the "real" self and to strive for values and life-styles that were probably no better or no more desirable than his own and which might be even less desirable. Yet no group should be made to feel ashamed of, or apologetic for, its art, music, and other general cultural attributes. Nor should individuals ever be forced to feel at a disadvantage because of their race or sex.

The attempts of minorities and of women to deal with the identity problem have led to considerable confusion and many contradictions. The struggle for identity also has resulted in a wide variety of demands. Among them were black studies, women's studies, and Indian studies. To some people in the larger society it seemed that the groups seeking to find themselves rejected everything characteristic of the majority society, including styles in dress, values, and established life-styles. Because of their visibility, clamor, and attention from the mass media, persons "rejecting" society and seeking to create counter cultures seemed more numerous than they were.

In a democracy individuals should have a wide range of options and choices by means of which they can satisfy their cultural tastes and engage in their chosen social practices. Nonetheless, many people reject what they deem to be bizarre behavior and conduct. Those in society who deviate too far from the norm are therefore likely to be penalized, rejected, or discriminated against. It follows that while the secondary school should respect students' rights, these students also should be helped to understand the risks involved in striving for identity through engaging in practices that are in conflict with those acceptable to the broader culture.

Let us elaborate on this point. Some educators feel that nonstandard English is acceptable as long as it conveys meanings adequately. Hence, to demand standard English of students whose culture has taught them nonstandard usage is regarded by some educators as demeaning. Certainly there are situations where nonstandard English is acceptable and adequate. There are, however, other situations that demand standard usage; in some situations one's position, status, and personal improvement patently cannot be achieved without it.

Thus, as students strive to resolve the identity crisis and to preserve their culture, the secondary school should help them take careful note of the distinction between substance and symbols. This is to say that some of the things associated with a counter culture to which students cling may be of no substantive significance. Indeed, they may be harmful if they enrich neither life nor the purse, and extremely harmful if they impair one's health. Some practices in an attempt to maintain identity may, on the other side of the coin, be of therapeutic value to the student. Even so, they may lead to discrimination and rejection, a point which youth should be helped to understand.

We now turn to our fifth and final problem. It is generally agreed that students should receive an education that is oriented toward the future. One of the most serious problems confronting students and parents from low income subgroups is that they are so obsessed with daily survival problems that no time or effort is left for thinking and planning for more than a day or two ahead. When the problems of securing adequate food, shelter, clothing, and other daily necessities are pressing, to speak of the future becomes irrelevant. As one result, it becomes the responsibility of society to give needed assistance and compensatory aid so that disadvantaged students are able to begin to think and plan for the future: to develop a positive future-focused role-image. Providing basically the same "equal" educational opportunity for students of vastly different socio-economic subsets is to provide education that ignores the concept of *equity*. It simply does not give students an *equitable* chance for successful self-realization in life. The special needs and problems of subgroups must receive more special attention if a future-oriented education is to have any meaning.

PURPOSES OF EDUCATION
IN A MULTIETHNIC PLURALISTIC SOCIETY

The problems and priorities of education at all levels, as of 1976, are more complex than they have ever been before. Much disagreement on policy and uncertainty of action resides in the lack of an adequate philosophical base for a culturally pluralistic education. This may be ascribed to the fact that American society is suffering from the same inadequacy. Norman Cousins has argued convincingly that "We live in a time of philosophical poverty. The vast increase of new knowledge and therefore of problems has not produced new philosophies that speak uniquely to the new conditions in human affairs."[19] When one considers the various goals and programs of the various subgroups in America, it quickly becomes apparent that Cousins' point is well made and that an adequate philosophical base is needed.

In general, the overall purposes and objectives for secondary education should be much the same for all American young people. If the goals of Americans of the various racial, cultural, or national groups are to gain respect for the dignity and worth of each individual and group; to gain equality of opportunity in education, employment, and housing; and to achieve equal justice before the law, then there ought to be some relationship between these goals and the education that will make them a reality. Yet too frequently no such positive relationship exists. Education, therefore, should help both minority and majority group students become aware of the value conflicts expressed as social and political contradictions in society and should aim to help them learn effective ways to take action against those oppressive elements which threaten the welfare and the relationships existing between minority and majority groups in the United States.

Philip Werdell provides a source of direction and a guide to purposes of education to which educators should give thoughtful and critical attention:

The greatest public service education can perform is to develop people who can help solve society's emerging problems—who can articulate their own needs, who can understand the needs of others, and who can thus go on to create new goals and develop new forms of learning and doing. Only people so

19. Norman Cousins, "Life Without Helplessness," *Saturday Review-World* 1 (December 4, 1973): 4.

trained will be able to assume new roles as old ones become obsolete. Only those who have gained confidence in their own identity and direction can create healthy future goals for society. The challenge is to develop future-oriented self-directed learners.[20]

If a more perfect society is to be achieved—one that truly reflects democratic ideals—education must be permeated with these ideals. Students will also need to learn nonviolent strategies for improving society, including tactics for removing those elements in it who behave in ways that are inconsistent with freedom, justice, and equality. Learning by itself is not enough. Political, economic, and social action skills also are needed to overcome inequities and to extend a larger measure of democracy to all. These are things the secondary school must communicate as it seeks to prepare students for the future. They are ingredients of prime importance in the education of members of subsets in a culturally pluralistic society.

DESIRABLE CHARACTERISTICS
OF SECONDARY EDUCATION FOR SUBGROUPS
IN A MULTIETHNIC SOCIETY

Let us examine even more closely the implications of cultural pluralism, always keeping in mind that this is but one exemplar of our challenging social decisions.

The task of providing effective secondary education for subgroups will be made much easier when the inequities in the financial support of education are removed and when the general public accepts more widely the view that society and schools have an obligation to help our youth overcome handicaps growing out of the social situations into which they were thrust by the accident of birth.

Two recent U.S. Supreme Court landmark decisions bear directly on the more equitable funding of educational opportunity. In the case *Rodriguez* v. *San Antonio Independent School District*, March 1973, the plaintiff held that the low tax base of the district did not support education equal to that of the more affluent districts. But the court held by a five to four vote that the State of Texas could continue the unequal system for financing public education. Many educators and legal au-

20. Philip Werdell, "Futurism and the Reform of Higher Education," in *Learning for Tomorrow*, p. 286.

thorities have become persuaded that an educational amendment to the Constitution has become essential to remove a broad range of financial inequities. In another case, *Lau* v. *Nichols*, the high court ruled unanimously that San Francisco had violated the 1964 Civil Rights Act by failing to provide 1,800 non-English-speaking Chinese students with special language instruction.

These two decisions have far-reaching implications for the future education of minorities, namely: (1) further agitation for equality in financial support can be expected, and (2) the principle laid down in *Lau* v. *Nichols* probably can be applied to other kinds of inadequacies and cultural disadvantages that characterize many students in our schools. Almost certainly, this decision paves the way to the development of a variety of programs in compensatory education. In time, we hope, *compensatory* experiences will be replaced by *preclusive* education. "Preclusive education" refers to schooling begun soon enough, in early childhood, to make needless any subsequent compensatory measures.

To summarize, the secondary school must help racial, cultural, and religious groups achieve both a better education and a better way of life by aiding them in their struggle to overcome ridicule, hostility, guilt, lack of confidence, insecurity, and a feeling of shame. As we pointed out earlier, the inhospitable environment in which many of these students live often has caused severe and sometimes irreparable personality problems. These are frequently so severe that students cannot muster their resources to achieve success in school. The school should not only provide a happy environment; it must also help students feel the warm glow of personal worth, and make it possible for them to experience success that they have at last achieved on their own merits. There are literally hundreds of ways of attacking these tasks. The role of educational leadership is one of supporting thoughtful and resourceful teachers who can operate programs that help disadvantaged individuals to overcome deeply ingrained negative self-images, the feeling of failure, and the feeling of being of no worth.

Toward A Better Society

The industrial revolution and early forms of capitalism are giving way to new electronic, nuclear, biological, and solar technologies and to a new form of economy unlike pre-1970 capitalism, yet not like any form of conventional socialism. Our industrial society certainly is still with us, yet at the same time the emergent future will witness the formation of a new society.

One of the tasks of secondary education, then, is to help students establish confidence in the nation's institutions, not as they are, but as they should and could be. Educators likewise will need to understand their new role in making the emerging institutions responsive to the needs and problems of individuals. For instance, secondary school staffs also must help students understand the nature of work and careers in the emerging society. Minority group members are among those who most need to understand what is necessary to prepare for careers related to their own personal and social values and their continued personal worth.

As the writers have noted, society will be deeply plagued for the foreseeable future by the old and by new problems we have directly or indirectly mentioned: food shortages, threats of war, inflation, recession, resource depletion, energy shortage, unemployment, and a general weakening or deterioration of many onetime powerful institutions. Some of these problems are worldwide. But whatever their nature may be, haphazard and improvised "solutions" are not appropriate. Furthermore, we believe that new and creative solutions will demand the involvement of all the people, not a selected few. Leadership, we believe, will begin to reside not in "status positions" but in ideas. One of our great opportunities is to help youth learn how to generate, to express, and to apply creative thinking to group interaction and in a human welfare context.

Education, unfortunately, has not adequately prepared large masses of our youth to discharge their responsibilities in solving the problems that have confronted society. Surely the strength and welfare of the nation will depend to a considerable degree on our subsequent ability to provide education which helps all of the people to function effectively in the future. Developing the secondary school "learning segment" in a lifelong educational continuum will be an outstanding challenge to our professional maturity. Our maturity as a species will be tested as we seek further to develop the heightened consciousness which, hopefully, will lead immediately to at least a number of the insightful social decisions which are prerequisite to a world in which youth can develop a motivating, satisfying, future-focused image of their role ten, twenty, and thirty years hence.

We should bear in mind that as of 1976 time is short and increasingly precious. Decisions in society and in education should be undergoing critical study between 1976 and 1980. Also, *there should be substantial and prompt implementation of our planning, since many scholars in futures research see no more than twenty years and perhaps only ten before irreversible harm is done to the biosphere and to our long-range prospects for a viable life for humankind.* Let us not use the enormity of our problems as a pretext for expressing fatalism and the deadly dangerous inactivity that it encourages.

As for secondary school reform in the next fifteen years, fifteen years while we reach quintessentially important decisions as a species, let us remember that:

1. We must bring education and life together so that they are a unity.

2. We must make this life-and-education partnership one that is associated with clear goals for every youth's socioeconomic literacy and vocational success.

3. We must wipe out the gap between what we *say* and what we *do* as educators. High school youth must literally experience the achievement of values and of the human goals these values select for us.

4. We must design our curricula to help our young people to anticipate change and inculcate them with a sense of the future that will enable them not only to cope with newness but to use the changing scene so skillfully, as they work side by side with older generations, that the best of alternative worlds can become a reality in the span of the single lifetime that stretches ahead of youth in secondary schools today.

Index

CONSTITUTION AND BY-LAWS
OF
THE NATIONAL SOCIETY FOR THE
STUDY OF EDUCATION

(As adopted May, 1944, and amended June, 1945, February, 1949, September, 1962, February, 1968 and September, 1973)

Article I

NAME

The name of this corporation shall be "The National Society for the Study of Education," an Illinois corporation not for profit.

Article II

PURPOSES

Its purposes are to carry on the investigation of educational problems, to publish the results of same, and to promote their discussion.

The corporation also has such powers as are now, or may hereafter be, granted by the General Not For Profit Corporation Act of the State of Illinois.

Article III

OFFICES

The corporation shall have and continuously maintain in this state a registered office and a registered agent whose office is identical with such registered office, and may have other offices within or without the State of Illinois as the Board of Directors may from time to time determine.

Article IV

MEMBERSHIP

Section 1. *Classes.* There shall be two classes of members—active and honorary. The qualifications and rights of the members of such classes shall be as follows:

(*a*) Any person who is desirous of promoting the purposes of this corporation is eligible to active membership and shall become such on payment of dues as prescribed.

(*b*) Active members shall be entitled to vote, to participate in discussion, and, subject to the conditions set forth in Article V, to hold office.

(*c*) Honorary members shall be entitled to all the privileges of active members, with the exception of voting and holding office, and shall be exempt from the payment of dues. A person may be elected to honorary membership by vote of the active members of the corporation on nomination by the Board of Directors.

(*d*) Any active member of the Society may, at any time after reaching the age of sixty, become a life member on payment of the aggregate amount of the regular annual dues for the period of life expectancy, as determined by standard actuarial tables, such membership to entitle the member to receive all yearbooks and to enjoy all other privileges of active membership in the Society for the lifetime of the member.

Section 2. *Termination of Membership.*

(*a*) The Board of Directors by affirmative vote of two-thirds of the members of the Board may suspend or expel a member for cause after appropriate hearing.

(*b*) Termination of membership for nonpayment of dues shall become effective as provided in Article XIV.

Section 3. *Reinstatement.* The Board of Directors may by the affirmation vote of two-thirds of the members of the Board reinstate a former member whose membership was previously terminated for cause other than nonpayment of dues.

Section 4. *Transfer of Membership.* Membership in this corporation is not transferable or assignable.

Article V

BOARD OF DIRECTORS

Section 1. *General Powers.* The business and affairs of the corporation shall be managed by its Board of Directors. It shall appoint the Chairman and Vice-Chairman of the Board of Directors, the Secretary-Treasurer, and Members of the Council. It may appoint a member to fill any vacancy on the Board until such vacancy shall have been filled by election as provided in Section 3 of this Article.

Section 2. *Number, Tenure, and Qualifications.* The Board of Directors shall consist of seven members, namely, six to be elected by the members of the corporation, and the Secretary-Treasurer to be the seventh member. Only active members who have contributed to the yearbook shall be eligible for election to serve as directors. A member who has been elected for a full term of three years as director and has not attended at least two-thirds of the meetings duly called and held during that term shall not be eligible for election again before the fifth annual election after the expiration of the term for which he was first elected. No member who has been elected for two full terms as director in immediate succession shall be elected a director for a term next succeeding. This provision shall not apply to the Secretary-Treasurer who is appointed by the Board of Directors. Each director shall hold office for the term for which he is elected or appointed and until his successor shall have been selected and qualified. Directors need not be residents of Illinois.

Section 3. *Election.*

(*a*) The directors named in the Articles of Incorporation shall hold office until their successors shall have been duly selected and shall have qualified. Thereafter, two directors shall be elected annually to serve three years, beginning March first after their election. If, at the time of any annual election, a vacancy exists in the Board of Directors, a director shall be elected at such election to fill such vacancy.

(*b*) Elections of directors shall be held by ballots sent by United States mail as follows: A nominating ballot together with a list of members eligible to be directors shall be mailed by the Secretary-Treasurer to all active members of the corporation in October. From such list, the active members shall nominate on such ballot one eligible member for each of the two regular terms and for any vacancy to be filled and return such ballots to the office of the Secretary-Treasurer within twenty-one days after said date of mailing by the Secretary-Treasurer. The Secretary-Treasurer shall prepare an election ballot and place thereon in alphabetical order the names of persons equal to three times the number of offices to be filled, these persons to be those who received the highest number of votes on the nominating ballot, provided, however, that not more than one person connected with a given institution or agency shall be named on such final ballot, the person so named to be the one receiving the highest vote on the nominating ballot. Such election ballot shall be mailed by the Secretary-Treasurer to all active members in November next succeeding. The active members shall vote thereon for one member for each such office. Election ballots must be in the office of the Secretary-Treasurer within twenty-one days after the said date of mailing by the Secretary-Treasurer. The ballots shall be counted by the Secretary-Treasurer, or by an election committee, if any, appointed by the Board. The two members receiving the highest number of votes shall be declared elected for the regular term and the member or members receiving the next highest number of votes shall be declared elected for any vacancy or vacancies to be filled.

Section 4. *Regular Meetings.* A regular annual meeting of the Board of Directors shall be held, without other notice than this by-law, at the same place and as nearly as possible on the same date as the annual meeting of the corporation. The Board of Directors may provide the time and place, either within or without the State of Illinois, for the holding of additional regular meetings of the Board.

Section 5. *Special Meetings.* Special meetings of the Board of Directors may be called by or at the request of the Chairman or a majority of the directors. Such special meetings shall be held at the office of the corporation unless a majority of the directors agree upon a different place for such meetings.

Section 6. *Notice.* Notice of any special meeting of the Board of Directors shall be given at least fifteen days previously thereto by written notice delivered personally or mailed to each director at his business address, or by telegram. If mailed, such notice shall be deemed to be delivered when deposited in the United States mail in a sealed envelope so addressed, with postage thereon prepaid. If notice be given by telegram, such notice shall be deemed to be delivered when the telegram is delivered to the telegraph company. Any director may waive notice of any meeting. The attendance of a director at any meeting shall constitute a waiver of notice of such meeting, except where a director attends a meeting for the express purpose of objecting to the transaction of any business because the meeting is not lawfully called or convened. Neither the business to be transacted at, nor the purpose of, any regular or special meeting of the Board need be specified in the notice or waiver of notice of such meeting.

Section 7. *Quorum.* A majority of the Board of Directors shall constitute a quorum for the transaction of business at any meeting of the Board, provided, that if less than a majority of the directors are present at said meeting, a majority of the directors present may adjourn the meeting from time to time without further notice.

Section 8. *Manner of Acting.* The act of the majority of the directors present at a meeting at which a quorum is present shall be the act of the Board of Directors, except where otherwise provided by law or by these by-laws.

Article VI

THE COUNCIL

Section 1. *Appointment.* The Council shall consist of the Board of Directors, the Chairmen of the corporation's Yearbook and Research Committees, and such other active members of the corporation as the Board of Directors may appoint.

Section 2. *Duties.* The duties of the Council shall be to further the objects of the corporation by assisting the Board of Directors in planning and carrying forward the educational undertakings of the corporation.

Article VII

OFFICERS

Section 1. *Officers.* The officers of the corporation shall be a Chairman of the Board of Directors, a Vice-Chairman of the Board of Directors, and a Secretary-Treasurer. The Board of Directors, by resolution, may create additional offices. Any two or more offices may be held by the same person, except the offices of Chairman and Secretary-Treasurer.

Section 2. *Election and Term of Office.* The officers of the corporation shall be elected annually by the Board of Directors at the annual regular meeting of the Board of Directors, provided, however, that the Secretary-Treasurer may be elected for a term longer than one year. If the election of officers shall not be held at such meeting, such election shall be held as soon thereafter as conveniently may be. Vacancies may be filled or new offices created and filled at any meeting of the Board of Directors. Each officer shall hold office until his successor shall have been duly elected and shall have qualified or until his death or until he shall resign or shall have been removed in the manner hereinafter provided.

Section 3. *Removal.* Any officer or agent elected or appointed by the Board of Directors may be removed by the Board of Directors whenever in its judgment the best interests of the corporation would be served thereby, but such removal shall be without prejudice to the contract rights, if any, of the person so removed.

Section 4. *Chairman of the Board of Directors.* The Chairman of the Board of Directors shall be the principal officer of the corporation. He shall preside at all meetings of the members of the Board of Directors, shall perform all duties incident to the office of chairman of the Board of Directors and such other duties as may be prescribed by the Board of Directors from time to time.

Section 5. *Vice-Chairman of the Board of Directors.* In the absence of the Chairman of the Board of Directors or in the event of his inability or refusal to act, the Vice-Chairman of the Board of Directors shall perform the duties of the Chairman of the Board of Directors, and when so acting, shall have all the powers of and be subject to all the restrictions upon the Chairman of the Board of Directors. Any Vice-Chairman of the Board of Directors shall perform such other duties as from time to time may be assigned to him by the Board of Directors.

Section 6. *Secretary-Treasurer.* The Secretary-Treasurer shall be the managing executive officer of the corporation. He shall: (a) keep the minutes of the meetings of the members and of the Board of Directors in one or more books provided for that purpose; (b) see that all notices are duly given in accordance with the provisions of these by-laws or as required by law; (c) be custodian of the corporate records and of the seal of the corporation and see that the seal of the corporation is affixed to all documents, the execution of which on behalf of the corporation under its seal is duly authorized in accordance with the provisions of these by-laws; (d) keep a register of the postoffice address of each member as furnished to the Secretary-Treasurer by such member; (e) in general perform all duties incident to the office of secretary and such other duties as from time to time may be assigned to him by the Chairman of the Board of Directors or by the Board of Directors. He shall also: (1) have charge and custody of and be responsible for all funds and securities of the corporation; receive and give receipts for moneys due and payable to the corporation from any source whatsoever, and deposit all such moneys in the name of the corporation in such banks, trust companies or other depositories as shall be selected in accordance with the provisions of Article XI of these by-laws; (2) in general perform all the duties incident to the office of Treasurer and such other duties as from time to time may be assigned to him by the Chairman of the Board of Directors or by the Board of Directors. The Secretary-Treasurer shall give a bond for the faithful discharge of his duties in such sum and with such surety or sureties as the Board of Directors shall determine, said bond to be placed in the custody of the Chairman of the Board of Directors.

Article VIII

COMMITTEES

The Board of Directors, by appropriate resolution duly passed, may create and appoint such committees for such purposes and periods of time as it may deem advisable.

Article IX

PUBLICATIONS

Section 1. The corporation shall publish *The Yearbook of the National Society for the Study of Education*, such supplements thereto, and such other materials as the Board of Directors may provide for.

Section 2. *Names of Members*. The names of the active and honorary members shall be printed in the Yearbook in alternate years or, at the direction of the Board of Directors, may be published in a special list.

Article X

ANNUAL MEETINGS

The corporation shall hold its annual meetings at the time and place of the Annual Meeting of the American Association of School Administrators of the National Education Association. Other meetings may be held when authorized by the corporation or by the Board of Directors.

Article XI

CONTRACTS, CHECKS, DEPOSITS, AND GIFTS

Section 1. *Contracts*. The Board of Directors may authorize any officer or officers, agent or agents of the corporation, in addition to the officers so authorized by these by-laws to enter into any contract or execute and deliver any instrument in the name of and on behalf of the corporation and such authority may be general or confined to specific instances.

Section 2. *Checks, drafts, etc.* All checks, drafts, or other orders for the payment of money, notes, or other evidences of indebtedness issued in the name of the corporation, shall be signed by such officer or officers, agent or agents of the corporation and in such manner as shall from time to time be determined by resolution of the Board of Directors. In the absence of such determination of the Board of Directors, such instruments shall be signed by the Secretary-Treasurer.

Section 3. *Deposits.* All funds of the corporation shall be deposited from time to time to the credit of the corporation in such banks, trust companies, or other depositories as the Board of Directors may select.

Section 4. *Gifts.* The Board of Directors may accept on behalf of the corporation any contribution, gift, bequest, or device for the general purposes or for any special purpose of the corporation.

Section 5. *Dissolution.* In case of dissolution of the National Society for the Study of Education (incorporated under the GENERAL NOT FOR PROFIT CORPORATION ACT of the State of Illinois), the Board of Directors shall, after paying or making provision for the payment of all liabilities of the Corporation, dispose of all assets of the Corporation to such organization or organizations organized and operated exclusively for charitable, educational, or scientific purposes as shall at the time qualify as an exempt organization or organizations under Section 561 (C) (3) of the Internal Revenue Code of 1954 (or the corresponding provision of any future United States Internal Revenue Law), as the Board of Directors shall determine.

Article XII

BOOKS AND RECORDS

The corporation shall keep correct and complete books and records of account and shall also keep minutes of the proceedings of its members, Board of Directors, and committees having any of the authority of the Board of Directors, and shall keep at the registered or principal office a record giving the names and addresses of the members entitled to vote. All books and records of the corporation may be inspected by any member or his agent or attorney for any proper purpose at any reasonable time.

Article XIII

FISCAL YEAR

The fiscal year of the corporation shall begin on the first day of July in each year and end on the last day of June of the following year.

Article XIV

DUES

Section 1. *Annual Dues.* The annual dues for active members of the Society shall be determined by vote of the Board of Directors at a regular meeting duly called and held.

Section 2. *Election Fee.* An election fee of $1.00 shall be paid in advance by each applicant for active membership.

Section 3. *Payment of Dues.* Dues for each calendar year shall be payable in advance on or before the first day of January of that year. Notice of dues for the ensuing year shall be mailed to members at the time set for mailing the primary ballots.

Section 4. *Default and Termination of Membership.* Annual membership shall terminate automatically for those members whose dues remain unpaid after the first day of January of each year. Members so in default will be reinstated on payment of the annual dues plus a reinstatement fee of fifty cents.

Article XV

SEAL

The Board of Directors shall provide a corporate seal which shall be in the form of a circle and shall have inscribed thereon the name of the corporation and the words "Corporate Seal, Illinois."

Article XVI

WAIVER OF NOTICE

Whenever any notice whatever is required to be given under the provision of the General Not For Profit Corporation Act of Illinois or under the provisions of the Articles of Incorporation or the by-laws of the corporation, a waiver thereof in writing signed by the person or persons entitled to such notice, whether before or after the time stated therein, shall be deemed equivalent to the giving of such notice.

Article XVII

AMENDMENTS

Section 1. *Amendments by Directors.* The constitution and by-laws may be altered or amended at any meeting of the Board of Directors duly called and held, provided that affirmative vote of at least five directors shall be required for such action.

Section 2. *Amendments by Members.* By petition of twenty-five or more active members duly filed with the Secretary-Treasurer, a proposal to amend the constitution and by-laws shall be submitted to all active members by United States mail together with ballots on which the members shall vote for or against the proposal. Such ballots shall be returned by United States mail to the office of the Secretary-Treasurer within twenty-one days after date of mailing of the proposal and ballots by the Secretary-Treasurer. The Secretary-Treasurer or a committee appointed by the Board of Directors for that purpose shall count the ballots and advise the members of the result. A vote in favor of such proposal by two-thirds of the members voting thereon shall be required for adoption of such amendment.

ANNUAL MEETINGS OF THE SOCIETY

In 1975, meetings of the Society were held in Dallas, Washington, D.C., and New Orleans. At each of these meetings one part of the seventy-fourth yearbook was presented.

Part I

Part I (*Youth*) was presented in Dallas on February 23 at a meeting cosponsored by the American Association of School Administrators with the following persons participating:

Presiding and presenting the yearbook: Robert J. Havighurst, Cochairman (with Philip H. Dreyer) of the Yearbook Committee and Professor of Education and Human Development, University of Chicago.

Commenting on the yearbook: John B. Davis, Jr., Superintendent of Schools, Minneapolis, Minnesota.

Participating in a panel discussion on the "Youth Crisis and the Schools": Mr. William Cotton and Mrs. Ruby Morris, Dallas Public Schools, and Mrs. Joanne H. Pratt, educational consultant, Dallas.

Another presentation of the volume on *Youth* was made at a meeting cosponsored by the American Education Research Association in Washington, D.C. on April 4 with the following persons participating:

Presiding and presenting the yearbook: Philip H. Dreyer, Cochairman (with Robert J. Havighurst) of the Yearbook Committee and Professor of Psychology, Emory University.

Reactors to the yearbook: Elizabeth Douvan, Professor of Psychology, University of Michigan; Robert E. Grinder, Associate Dean, College of Education, Arizona State University; and Lawrence Kohlberg, Professor of Education and Social Psychology, Harvard University.

Part II

Part II (*Teacher Education*) was presented in New Orleans on April 4 at a meeting cosponsored by the Association for Supervision and Curriculum Development, with the following persons participating:

Presiding and presenting the yearbook: Kevin Ryan, Chairman of the Yearbook Committee and Associate Professor of Education, University of Chicago.

Reacting to the yearbook: M. Karl Openshaw, Dean, School of Education, University of Colorado; A. Harry Passow, Professor of Education, Teachers College, Columbia University and member of the Board of Directors of the Society; Harold G. Shane, University Professor of Education, Indiana University; and Morris L. Cogan, Professor of Education, University of Pittsburgh.

The volume on Teacher Education was also presented by Mr. Ryan, together with Mr. Joel Burdin, Associate Director of the American Association of Colleges for Teacher Education, and Martin Haberman, Professor of Education, University of Wisconsin (Milwaukee) at the annual banquet of the AACTE in Chicago in March, 1975.

SYNOPSIS OF THE PROCEEDINGS OF THE BOARD
OF DIRECTORS OF THE SOCIETY FOR 1975

I. MEETING OF APRIL 1, 1975

The Board of Directors of the National Society for the Study of Education met at the Sheraton Park Hotel (Washington) at 9 A.M. on Wednesday, April 1, 1975 with the following members present: Jeanne Chall, Luvern L. Cunningham (Chairman), Jacob W. Getzels, John I. Goodlad, A. Harry Passow, Ralph W. Tyler, and Kenneth J. Rehage (Secretary).

1. The Secretary presented reports on membership, income, and expenditures for the first eight months of the fiscal year, together with projects of income and expenditures for the balance of the fiscal year.

2. Because of increasing costs of reprinting past yearbooks for which there is still some demand it was agreed that expenditures for this purpose should hereafter not exceed $5,000 in any one year.

3. The Board approved a proposal to appoint a committee to review existing categories of membership in the Society and to make such recommendations as it felt appropriate with regard to the establishment of other membership categories.

4. The Secretary reported on the status of the Expanded Publication Program, and on plans for paperbacks to be published in 1976.

5. The Board considered a proposal from the McCutchan Publishing Corporation for an arrangement under which that firm would become distributor for the Society's yearbooks. Action was deferred pending an inquiry by a special committee of the Board regarding the details of the present arrangements with the University of Chicago Press, which has served as distributor for the yearbooks since 1945. The Secretary reported that he had received a request from the Press to increase the Commission it receives for its services in distributing the yearbooks.

6. The Board heard reports on previously authorized yearbooks—*Issues in Secondary Education* and *The Psychology of Teaching Methods* (1976); *The Politics of Education* and *The Teaching of English* (1977); *Education and the Brain* and *The Law and Education* (1978).

7. Several topics for future yearbooks were discussed but no action was taken pending the receipt of formal proposals.

8. It was agreed that action on a proposal to index NSSE yearbooks should be deferred.

9. The Board approved a proposal to retain the present Secretary-Treasurer for the fiscal year 1975-76 on a half-time basis. It was further agreed that the post of full-time editorial assistant should be discontinued and that an editorial assistant should be employed on a half-time basis.

10. The Secretary reported that the autumn election had resulted in the election of Messrs. Getzels and Passow to three-year terms on the Board.

11. The next meeting of the Board was set for October 24 and 25 at the O'Hare Hilton Hotel in Chicago.

II. MEETING OF OCTOBER 24 AND 25, 1975

The Board of Directors of the National Society for the Study of Education met at 8 P.M. on Friday, October 24 and again at 8:30 A.M. on Saturday, October 25, 1975 at the O'Hare Hilton Hotel (Chicago) with the following members present: Jeanne Chall, LUvern L. Cunningham (Chairman), Jacob W. Getzels, John I. Goodlad, A. Harry Passow, Ralph W. Tyler, and Kenneth J. Rehage (Secretary).

1. The Secretary presented a report on membership and a report of the financial position of the Society at the close of the fiscal year 1974-75.

2. Note was taken of the recurring deficits in operating expenditures during the past few years. It was agreed that the following measures should be taken to reduce expenditures: (a) reduce the number of copies of the yearbooks printed on the initial order; (b) discontinue the practice of printing the list of members in the yearbooks, but prepare an annual list of members for distribution to members on request. An earlier agreement to restrict reprinting orders to $5,000 per year was reaffirmed. The Secretary was instructed to develop plans for interesting new members in the Society, concentrating especially on the audiences most likely to be interested in the forthcoming yearbooks. The Secretary was also requested to prepare a report that could serve as the basis for Board discussion of the present dues structure for the Society.

3. The Secretary reported that, in general, the Expanded Publication Program appears to be accomplishing the purposes for which it was originally intended. The interest in the paperback series has grown each year and the Society is beginning to realize some income from from royalties on the sale of these volumes to nonmembers.

4. The Secretary was instructed to devise a suitable means of gathering information that would permit an analysis of the Society's membership with respect to such matters as age distribution, geographical location, professional positions, and the like. In addition, the Board wished to get suggestions of members for future topics to be considered in its publication programs.

5. After hearing a report of the special committee on relationships with the University of Chicago Press, the Board unanimously approved the request of the Press to have its commission on yearbook sales to nonmembers increased from 35 percent to 45 percent. The Board agreed that the nature of the Society's relationship with the Press precluded the possibility of entering into arrangements with other firms for the distribution of the yearbooks.

6. The Board heard reports on yearbooks in progress. Dr. Alan Mersky will serve as cochairman for the volume on *Education and the Brain*. Dr. Clifford Hooker of the University of Minnesota will chair the committee that is to work on the volume on *The Law and Education*.

7. After hearing a proposal from Mr. Passow for a yearbook on the Gifted,

the Board authorized him to organize a committee and also allocated $2,000 for the support of the committee's work.

8. Mr. Goodlad was requested to convene a meeting of individuals who would explore the prospects for a yearbook on classroom management. Mr. Goodlad was also asked to inquire into the possibilities of a yearbook that would review recent experience with alternative arrangements for education. Action on Mr. Passow's proposal for a yearbook on the middle school was deferred until the next meeting. It was agreed that proposals for a publication on bilingual education and another on the current status of the accountability movement should be referred to the Commission on the Expanded Publication Program. Mr. Cunningham agreed to give thought to the possibility of a publication in the general area of the governance of education. A proposal to do a yearbook on "Education for the 21st Century" was not approved by the Board.

9. The next meeting of the Board will be held April 18 and 19, 1976 in San Francisco.

REPORT OF THE TREASURER OF THE SOCIETY
1974-75

Receipts:

Membership dues and fees	$ 63,907.50
Sales, royalties, and permissions	46,635.43
Interest and dividends	5,743.56
Refunds and transfers	23.50
Bequest from Ruth Strang	17,655.96
Miscellaneous	1,472.91
Total	$135,438.86

Disbursements:

Yearbooks:	
Manufacturing	$ 54,396.66
Reprinting and binding	9,258.80
Preparation	1,785.90
Meetings of the Board and Society	2,934.63
Secretary's Office:	
Editorial, secretarial, clerical	28,450.26
Supplies, equipment, telephone	4,240.57
New Publication Program expenses:	
Purchase of 1975 paperbacks	20,075.36
Preparation	428.45
Refunds and transfers	84.00
Bank charges	132.10
Miscellaneous	27.00
Transfer to Investment Fund	20,000.00
Total	$141,813.73
Excess disbursements over receipts	$ 6,374.87
Cash account, July 1, 1974	17,009.02
Cash account, June 30, 1975	10,634.15

STATEMENT OF CASH AND SECURITIES

As of June 30, 1975

Cash:

New University Bank, Chicago, Checking Account ......$ 10,646.15

Savings Account:

New University Bank, Chicago 8,159.80

Savings and Loan Certificates:

Chicago Federal Savings and Loan Association........... 10,000.00
Home Federal Savings and Loan Association 10,000.00

Certificate of Deposit:

New University Bank, Chicago 12,000.00

Bonds:

American Telephone & Telegraph ($21,000, 1985)....... 14,679.42
ML Corporate Income Fund (25 units) 25,925.25
U. S. Government Bonds (H) due March, 1977 .... 15,000.00

Stock:

First National Bank of Boston, 57 shares capital stock 1,300.00

Total Cash and Securities on Hand $107,710.62

Charges Against Current Assets

Annual dues paid for 1976 .... 250.00
Paid up Life Memberships 4,534.00
Total..$ 4,784.00
Unencumbered assets...........................$102,926.62

A Note to Members of the Society

The practice of including a list of the members of the Society in the yearbooks has added substantially to the cost of manufacturing the volumes. The Board of Directors, at its meeting in October, 1975, directed the Secretary-Treasurer to discontinue this practice. Instead, a list of members will be prepared each year and will include all individuals whose dues are paid as of the close of the calendar year. This list will be sent to any member of the Society whose written request for it is received by February 1.

KENNETH J. REHAGE
Secretary-Treasurer

INFORMATION CONCERNING
THE NATIONAL SOCIETY FOR THE STUDY OF EDUCATION

1. *Purpose.* The purpose of the National Society is to promote the investigation and discussion of educational questions. To this end it holds an annual meeting and publishes a series of yearbooks and a series of paperbacks on Contemporary Educational Issues.

2. *Membership.* Any person interested in the purpose of the Society and in receiving its publications may become a member by sending in name, title, address, and a check covering dues and the entrance fee (see items 4 and 5). Graduate students may become members, upon recommendation of a faculty member, at a reduced rate for the first year of membership. Dues for all subsequent years are the same as for other members.

Membership is not transferable. It is limited to individuals and may not be held by libraries, schools, or other institutions, either directly or indirectly.

3. *Period of Membership.* Membership is for the calendar year and terminates automatically on December 31, unless dues for the ensuing year are paid as indicated in item 6. Applicants for membership may not date their entrance back of the current calendar year.

4. *Categories of Membership.* The following categories of membership have been established:

Regular. Annual dues are $10.00. The member receives a clothbound copy of each part of the yearbook.

Comprehensive. Annual dues are $20.00. The member receives a clothbound copy of the yearbook and all volumes in the current year's series on Contemporary Educational Issues.

Life Membership. Persons sixty years of age or above may become life members on payment of a fee based on the average life expectancy of their age group. Regular life members may take out a Comprehensive membership for any year by payment of an additional fee of 10.00. For information apply to the Secretary-Treasurer.

Graduate Students. First year dues for the Regular and Comprehensive membership are $8.00 and $18.00 respectively, plus the $1.00 entrance fee in either case.

5. *Privileges of Membership.* Members receive the publications of the Society as described above. All members are entitled to vote, to participate in meetings of the Society, and (under certain conditions) to hold office. The names of members are printed in the yearbook in alternate years.

6. *Entrance Fee.* New members are required to pay an entrance fee of one dollar, in addition to the dues, for the first year of membership.

7. *Payment of Dues.* Statements of dues are rendered in October for the following calendar year. Any member so notified whose dues remain unpaid on January 1 thereby loses membership and can be reinstated only by paying the dues plus a reinstatement fee of fifty cents ($.50).

School warrants and vouchers from institutions must be accompanied by definite information concerning the name and address of the person for whom the membership fee is being paid. Statements of dues are rendered on our own form only. The Secretary's office cannot undertake to fill out special invoice forms of any kind or to a affix a notary's affidavit to statements or receipts.

Cancelled checks serve as receipts. Members desiring an additional receipt must enclose a stamped and addressed envelope therefor.

8. *Distribution of Yearbooks to Members.* The yearbooks, normally ready prior to the February meeting of the Society, will be mailed from the office of the distributor only to members whose dues for that year have been paid.

9. *Commercial Sales.* The distribution of all yearbooks prior to the

current year, and also of those of the current year not regularly mailed to members in exchange for their dues, is in the hands of the distributor, not of the Secretary. Orders may be placed with the University of Chicago Press, Chicago, Illinois 60637, which distributes the yearbooks of the Society. Orders for paperbacks in the series on Contemporary Educational Issues should be placed with the designated publisher of that series. The list of the Society's publications is printed in each yearbook.

10. *Yearbooks.* The yearbooks are issued about one month before the February meeting. Published in two volumess, each of which contains 300 to 400 pages, the yearbooks are planned to be of immediate practical value as well as representative of sound scholarship and scientific investigation.

11. *Series on Contemporary Educational Issues.* This series, in paperback format, is designed to supplement the yearbooks by timely publications on topics of current interest. There will usually be three of these volumes each year.

12. *Meetings.* The annual meeting, at which the yearbooks are presented and critiqued, is held as a rule in February at the same time and place as the meeting of the American Association of School Administrators. Members will be notified of other meetings.

Applications for membership will be handled promptly at any time. New members will receive the yearbook scheduled for publication during the calendar year in which application for Regular Membership is made. New members who elect to take out the Comprehensive membership will receive both the yearbook and the paperbacks scheduled for publication during the year in which application is made.

KENNETH J. REHAGE, Secretary-Treasurer

5835 Kimbark Avenue
Chicago, Illinois 60637

PUBLICATIONS OF THE NATIONAL SOCIETY FOR THE STUDY OF EDUCATION

1. The Yearbooks

NOTICE: Many of the early yearbooks of this series are now out of print. In the following list, those titles to which an asterisk is prefixed are not available for purchase.

*First Yearbook, 1902, Part I—*Some Principles in the Teaching of History.* Lucy M. Salmon.

*First Yearbook, 1902, Part II—*The Progress of Geography in the Schools.* W. M. Davis and H. M. Wilson.

*Second Yearbook, 1903, Part I—*The Course of Study in History in the Common School.* Isabel Lawrence, C. A. McMurry, Frank McMurry, E. C. Page, and E. J. Rice.

*Second Yearbook, 1903, Part II—*The Relation of Theory to Pratice in Education.* M. J. Holmes, J. A. Keith, and Levi Seeley.

*Third Yearbook, 1904, Part I—*The Relation of Theory to Practice in the Education of Teachers.* John Dewey, Sarah C. Brooks, F. M. McMurry, et al.

*Third Yearbook, 1904, Part II—*Nature Study.* W. S. Jackman.

*Fourth Yearbook, 1905, Part I—*The Education and Training of Secondary Teachers.* E. C. Elliott, E. G. Dexter, M. J. Holmes, et al.

*Fourth Yearbook, 1905, Part II—*The Place of Vocational Subjects in the High-School Curriculum.* J. S. Brown, G. B. Morrison, and Ellen Richards.

*Fifth Yearbook, 1906, Part I—*On the Teaching of English in Elementary and High Schools.* G. P. Brown and Emerson Davis.

*Fifth Yearbook, 1906, Part II—*The Certification of Teachers.* E. P. Cubberley.

*Sixth Yearbook, 1907, Part I—*Vocational Studies for College Entrance.* C. A. Herrick, H. W. Holmes, T. deLaguna, V. Prettyman, and W. J. S. Bryan.

*Sixth Yearbook, 1907, Part II—*The Kindergarten and Its Relation to Elementary Education.* Ada Van Stone Harris, E. A. Kirkpatrick, Marie Kraus-Boelté, Patty S. Hill, Harriette M. Mills, and Nina Vandewalker.

*Seventh Yearbook, 1908, Part I—*The Relation of Superintendents and Principals to the Training and Professional Improvement of Their Teachers.* Charles D. Lowry.

*Seventh Yearbook, 1908, Part II—*The Co-ordination of the Kindergarten and the Elementary School.* B. J. Gregory, Jennie B. Merrill, Bertha Payne, and Margaret Giddings.

*Eighth Yearbook, 1909, Part I—*Education with Reference to Sex: Pathological, Economic, and Social Aspects.* C. R. Henderson.

*Eighth Yearbook, 1909, Part II—*Education with Reference to Sex: Agencies and Methods.* C. R. Henderson and Helen C. Putnam.

*Ninth Yearbook, 1910, Part I—*Health and Education.* T. D. Wood.

*Ninth Yearbook, 1910, Part II—*The Nurses in Education.* T. D. Wood, et al.

*Tenth Yearbook, 1911, Part I—*The City School as a Community Center.* H. C. Leipziger, Sarah E. Hyre, R. D. Warden, C. Ward Crampton, E. W. Stitt, E. J. Ward, Mrs. T. C. Grice, and C. A. Perry.

*Tenth Yearbook, 1911, Part II—*The Rural School as a Community Center.* B. H. Crocheron, Jessie Field, F. W. Howe, E. C. Bishop, A. B. Graham, O. J. Kern, M. T. Scudder, and B. M. Davis.

*Eleventh Yearbook, 1912, Part I—*Industrial Education: Typical Experiments Described and Interpreted.* J. F. Barker, M. Bloomfield, B. W. Johnson, P. Johnson, L. M. Leavitt, G. A. Mirick, M. W. Murray, C. F. Perry, A. L. Stafford, and H. B. Wilson.

*Eleventh Yearbook, 1912, Part II—*Agricultural Education in Secondary Schools.* A. C. Monahan, R. W. Stimson, D. J. Crosby, W. H. French, H. F. Button, F. R. Crane, W. R. Hart, and G. F. Warren.

*Twelfth Yearbook, 1913, Part I—*The Supervision of City Schools.* Franklin Bobbitt, J. W. Hall, and J. D. Wolcott.

*Twelfth Yearbook, 1913, Part II—*The Supervision of Rural Schools.* A. C. Monahan, L. J. Hanifan, J. E. Warren, Wallace Lund, U. J. Hoffman, A. S. Cook, E. M. Rapp, Jackson Davis, J. D. Wolcott.

*Thirteenth Yearbook, 1914, Part I—*Some Aspects of High-School Instruc'ion and Administration.* H. C. Morrison, E. R. Breslich, W. A. Jessup, and L. D. Coffman.

*Thirteenth Yearbook, 1914, Part II—*Plans for Organizing School Surveys, with a Summary of Typical School Surveys.* Charles H. Judd and Henry L. Smith.

*Fourteenth Yearbook, 1915. Part I—*Minimum Essentials in Elementary School Subjects—Standards and Current Practices.* H. B. Wilson, H. W. Holmes, F. E. Thompson, R. G. Jones, S. A. Courtis, W. S. Gray, F. N. Freeman, H. C. Pryor, J. F. Hosic, W. A. Jessup, and W. C. Bagley.

*Fourteenth Yearbook, 1915, Part II—*Methods for Measuring Teachers' Efficiency.* Arthur C. Boyce.

*Fifteenth Yearbook, 1916, Part I—*Standards and Tests for the Measurement of the Efficiency of Schools and School Systems.* G. D. Strayer, Bird T. Baldwin, B. R. Buckingham, F. W. Ballou, D. C. Bliss. H. G. Childs, S. A. Courtis, E. P. Cubberley, C. H. Judd, George Melcher, E. E. Oberholtzer, J. B. Sears, Daniel Starch, M. R. Trabue, and G. M. Whipple.

*Fifteenth Yearbook, 1916, Part II—*The Relationship between Persistence in School and Home Conditions.* Charles E. Holley.
*Fifteenth Yearbook, 1916, Part III—*The Junior High School.* Aubrey A. Douglas.
*Sixteenth Yearbook, 1917, Part I—*Second Report of the Committee on Minimum Essentials in Elementary-School Subjects.* W. C. Bagley, W. W. Charters, F. N. Freeman, W. S. Gray, Ernest Horn, J. H. Hoskinson, W. S. Monroe, C. F. Munson, H. C. Pryor, L. W. Rapeer, G. M. Wilson, and H. B. Wilson.
*Sixteenth Yearbook, 1917, Part II—*The Efficiency of College Students as Conditioned by Age at Entrance and Size of High School.* B. F. Pittenger.
*Seventeenth Yearbook, 1918, Part I—*Third Report of the Committee on Economy of Time in Education.* W. C. Bagley, B. B. Bassett, M. E. Branom, Alice Camerer, J. E. Dealey, C. A. Ellwood, E. B. Greene, A. B. Hart, J. F. Hosic, E. T. Housh, W. H. Mace, L. R. Marston, H. C. McKown, H. E. Mitchell, W. V. Reavis, D. Snedden, and H. B. Wilson.
*Seventeenth Yearbook, 1918, Part II—*The Measurement of Educational Products.* E. J. Ashbaugh, W. A. Averill, L. P. Ayers, F. W. Ballou, Edna Bryner, B. R. Buckingham, S. A. Courtis, M. E. Haggerty, C. H. Judd, George Melcher, W. S. Monroe, E. A. Nifenecker, and E. L. Thorndike.
*Eighteenth Yearbook, 1919, Part I—*The Professional Preparation of High-School Teachers.* G. N. Cade, S. S. Colvin, Charles Fordyce, H. H. Foster, T. S. Gosling, W. S. Gray, L. V. Koos, A. R. Mead, H. L. Miller, F. C. Whitcomb, and Clifford Woody.
*Eighteenth Yearbook, 1919, Part II—*Fourth Report of Committee on Economy of Time in Education.* F. C. Ayer, F. N. Freeman, W. S. Gray, Ernest Horn, W. S. Monroe, and C. E. Seashore.
*Nineteenth Yearbook, 1920, Part I—*New Materials of Instruction.* Prepared by the Society's Committee on Materials of Instruction.
*Nineteenth Yearbook, 1920, Part II—*Classroom Problems in the Education of Gifted Children.* T. S. Henry.
*Twentieth Yearbook, 1921, Part I—*New Materials of Instruction.* Second Report by Society's Committee.
*Twentieth Yearbook, 1921, Part II—*Report of the Society's Committee on Silent Reading.* M. A. Burgess, S. A. Courtis, C. E. Germane, W. S. Gray, H. A. Greene, Regina R. Heller, J. H. Hoover, J. A. O'Brien, J. L. Packer, Daniel Starch, W. W. Theisen, G. A. Yoakam, and representatives of other school systems.
*Twenty-first Yearbook, 1922, Parts I and II—*Intelligence Tests and Their Use.* Part I—*The Nature, History, and General Principles of Intelligence Testing.* E. L. Thorndike, S. S. Colvin, Harold Rugg, G. M. Whipple, Part II—*The Administrative Use of Intelligence Tests.* H. W. Holmes, W. K. Layton, Helen Davis, Agnes L. Rogers, Rudolf Pintner, M. R. Trabue, W. S. Miller, Bessie L. Gambrill, and others. The two parts are bound together.
*Twenty-second Yearbook, 1923, Part I—*English Composition: Its Aims, Methods and Measurements.* Earl Hudelson.
*Twenty-second Yearbook, 1923, Part II—*The Social Studies in the Elementary and Secondary School.* A. S. Barr, J. J. Coss, Henry Harap, R. W. Hatch, H. C. Hill, Ernest Horn, C. H. Judd, L. C. Marshall, F. M. McMurry, Earle Rugg, H. O. Rugg, Emma Schweppe, Mabel Snedaker, and C. W. Washburne.
*Twenty-third Yearbook, 1924, Part I—*The Education of Gifted Children.* Report of the Society's Committee. Guy M. Whipple, Chairman.
*Twenty-third Yearbook, 1924, Part II—*Vocational Guidance and Vocational Education for Industries.* A. H. Edgerton and others.
*Twenty-fourth Yearbook, 1925, Part I—*Report of the National Committee on Reading.* W. S. Gray, Chairman, F. W. Ballou, Rose L. Hardy, Ernest Horn, Francis Jenkins, S. A. Leonard, Estaline Wilson, and Laura Zirbes.
*Twenty-fourth Yearbook, 1925, Part II—*Adapting the Schools to Individual Differences.* Report of the Society's Committee. Carleton W. Washburne, Chairman.
*Twenty-fifth Yearbook, 1926, Part I—*The Present Status of Safety Education.* Report of the Society's Committee. Guy M. Whipple, Chairman.
*Twenty-fifth Yearbook, 1926, Part II—*Extra-Curricular Activities.* Report of the Society's Committee. Leonard V. Koos, Chairman.
*Twenty-sixth Yearbook, 1927, Part I—*Curriculum-making: Past and Present.* Report of the Society's Committee. Harold O. Rugg, Chairman.
*Twenty-sixth Yearbook, 1927, Part II—*The Foundations of Curriculum-making.* Prepared by individual members of the Society's Committee. Harold O. Rugg, Chairman.
*Twenty-seventh Yearbook, 1928, Part I—*Nature and Nurture: Their Influence upon Intelligence.* Prepared by the Society's Committee. Lewis M. Terman, Chairman.
*Twenty-seventh Yearbook, 1928, Part II—*Nature and Nurture: Their Influence upon Achievement.* Prepared by the Society's Committee. Lewis M. Terman, Chairman.
Twenty-eighth Yearbook, 1929, Parts I and II—*Preschool and Parental Education.* Part I—*Organization and Development.* Part II—*Research and Method.* Prepared by the Society's Committee. Lois H. Meek, Chairman. Bound in one volume. Cloth.
*Twenty-ninth Yearbook, 1930, Parts I and II—*Report of the Society's Committee on Arithmetic.* Part I—*Some Aspects of Modern Thought on Arithmetic.* Part II—*Research in Arithmetic.* Prepared by the Society's Committee. F. B. Knight, Chairman. Bound in one volume.
*Thirtieth Yearbook, 1931— Part I—*The Status of Rural Education.* First Report of the Society's Committee on Rural Education. Orville G. Brim, Chairman.
Thirtieth Yearbook, 1931, Part II—*The Textbook in American Education.* Report of the Society's Committee on the Textbook, J. B. Edmonson, Chairman. Cloth, Paper.

*Thirty-first Yearbook, 1932, Part I—*A Program for Teaching Science*. Prepared by the Society's Committee on the Teaching of Science. S. Ralph Powers, Chairman.
*Thirty-first Yearbook, 1932, Part II—*Changes and Experiments in Liberal-Arts Education*. Prepared by Kathryn McHale, with numerous collaborators.
*Thirty-second Yearbook, 1933—*The Teaching of Geography*. Prepared by the Society's Committee on the Teaching of Geography. A. E. Parkins, Chairman.
*Thirty-third Yearbook, 1934, Part I—*The Planning and Construction of School Buildings*. Prepared by the Society's Committee on School Buildings. N. L. Engelhardt, Chairman.
*Thirty-third Yearbook, 1934, Part II—*The Activity Movement*. Prepared by the Society's Committee on the Activity Movement. Lois Coffey Mossman, Chairman.
Thirty-fourth Yearbook, 1935—*Educational Diagnosis*. Prepared by the Society's Committee on Educational Diagnosis. L. J. Brueckner, Chairman. Paper.
*Thirty-fifth Yearbook, 1936, Part I—*The Grouping of Pupils*. Prepared by the Society's Committee. W. W. Coxe, Chairman.
*Thirty-fifth Yearbook, 1936, Part II—*Music Education*. Prepared by the Society's Committee. W. L. Uhl, Chairman.
*Thirty-sixth Yearbook, 1937, Part I—*The Teaching of Reading*. Prepared by the Society's Committee. W. S. Gray, Chairman.
*Thirty-sixth Yearbook, 1937, Part II—*International Understanding through the Public-School Curriculum*. Prepared by the Society's Committee. I. L. Kandel, Chairman.
*Thirty-seventh Yearbook, 1938, Part I—*Guidance in Educational Institutions*. Prepared by the Society's Committee. G. N. Kefauver, Chairman.
*Thirty-seventh Yearbook, 1938, Part II—*The Scientific Movement in Education*. Prepared by the Society's Committee. F. N. Freeman, Chairman.
*Thirty-eighth Yearbook, 1939, Part I—*Child Development and the Curriculum*. Prepared by the Society's Committee. Carleton Washburne, Chairman.
Thirty-eighth Yearbook, 1939, Part II—*General Education in the American College*. Prepared by the Society's Committee. Alvin Eurich, Chairman. Cloth.
*Thirty-ninth Yearbook, 1940, Part I—*Intelligence: Its Nature and Nurture. Comparative and Critical Exposition*. Prepared by the Society's Committee. G. D. Stoddard, Chairman.
*Thirty-ninth Yearbook, 1940, Part II—*Intelligence: Its Nature and Nurture. Original Studies and Experiments*. Prepared by the Society's Committee. G. D. Stoddard, Chairman.
*Fortieth Yearbook, 1941—*Art in American Life and Education*. Prepared by the Society's Committee. Thomas Munro, Chairman.
Forty-first Yearbook, 1942, Part I—*Philosophies of Education*. Prepared by the Society's Committee. John S. Brubacher, Chairman. Cloth, Paper.
Forty-first Yearbook, 1942, Part II—*The Psychology of Learning*. Prepared by the Society's Committee. T. R. McConnell, Chairman. Cloth.
*Forty-second Yearbook, 1943, Part I—*Vocational Education*. Prepared by the Society's Committee. F. J. Keller, Chairman.
*Forty-second Yearbook, 1943, Part II—*The Library in General Education*. Prepared by the Society's Committee. L. R. Wilson, Chairman.
Forty-third Yearbook, 1944, Part I—*Adolescence*. Prepared by the Society's Committee. Harold E. Jones, Chairman. Paper.
*Forty-third Yearbook, 1944, Part II—*Teaching Language in the Elementary School*. Prepared by the Society's Committee. M. R. Trabue, Chairman.
*Forty-fourth Yearbook, 1945, Part I—*American Education in the Postwar Period: Curriculum Reconstruction*. Prepared by the Society's Committee. Ralph W. Tyler, Chairman.
Forty-fourth Yearbook, 1945, Part II—*American Education in the Postwar Period: Structural Reorganization*. Prepared by the Society's Committee. Bess Goodykoontz, Chairman. Paper.
*Forty-fifth Yearbook, 1946, Part I—*The Measurement of Understanding*. Prepared by the Society's Committee. William A. Brownell, Chairman.
*Forty-fifth Yearbook, 1946, Part II—*Changing Conceptions in Educational Administration*. Prepared by the Society's Committee. Alonzo G. Grace, Chairman.
*Forty-sixth Yearbook, 1947, Part I—*Science Education in American Schools*. Prepared by the Society's Committee. Victor H. Noll, Chairman.
Forty-sixth Yearbook, 1947, Part II—*Early Childhood Education*. Prepared by the Society's Committee. N. Searle Light, Chairman. Paper.
Forty-seventh Yearbook, 1948, Part I—*Juvenile Delinquency and the Schools*. Prepared by the Society's Committee. Ruth Strang, Chairman. Cloth.
Forty-seventh Yearbook, 1948, Part II—*Reading in the High School and College*. Prepared by the Society's Committee. William S. Gray, Chairman. Cloth, Paper.
Forty-eighth Yearbook, 1949, Part I—*Audio-visual Materials of Instruction*. Prepared by the Society's Committee. Stephen M. Corey, Chairman. Cloth.
*Forty-eighth Yearbook, 1949, Part II—*Reading in the Elementary School*. Prepared by the Society's Committee. Arthur I. Gates, Chairman.
*Forty-ninth Yearbook, 1950, Part I—*Learning and Instruction*. Prepared by the Society's Committee. G. Lester Anderson, Chairman.
Forty-ninth Yearbook, 1950, Part II—*The Education of Exceptional Children*. Prepared by the Society's Committee. Samuel A. Kirk, Chairman. Paper.
Fiftieth Yearbook, 1951, Part I—*Graduate Study in Education*. Prepared by the Society's Board of Directors. Ralph W. Tyler, Chairman. Paper.
Fiftieth Yearbook, 1951, Part II—*The Teaching of Arithmetic*. Prepared by the Society's Committee. G. T. Buswell, Chairman. Cloth, Paper.

Fifty-first Yearbook, 1952, Part I—*General Education.* Prepared by the Society's Committee. T. R. McConnell, Chairman. Cloth, Paper.

Fifty-first Yearbook, 1952, Part II—*Education in Rural Communities.* Prepared by the Society's Committee. Ruth Strang, Chairman. Cloth, Paper.

*Fifty-second Yearbook, 1953, Part I—*Adapting the Secondary-School Program to the Needs of Youth.* Prepared by the Society's Committee: William G. Brink, Chairman.

Fifty-second Yearbook, 1953, Part II—*The Community School.* Prepared by the Society's Committee. Maurice F. Seay, Chairman. Cloth.

Fifty-third Yearbook, 1954, Part I—*Citizen Co-operation for Better Public Schools.* Prepared by the Society's Committee. Edgar L. Morphet, Chairman. Cloth, Paper.

Fifty-third Yearbook, 1954, Part II—*Mass Media and Education.* Prepared by the Society's Committee. Edgar Dale, Chairman. Paper.

*Fifty-fourth Yearbook, 1955, Part I—*Modern Philosophies and Education.* Prepared by the Society's Committee. John S. Brubacher, Chairman.

Fifty-fourth Yearbook, 1955, Part II—*Mental Health in Modern Education.* Prepared by the Society's Committee. Paul A. Witty, Chairman. Paper.

*Fifty-fifth Yearbook, 1956, Part I—*The Public Junior College.* Prepared by the Society's Committee. B. Lamar Johnson, Chairman.

Fifty-fifth Yearbook, 1956, Part II—*Adult Reading.* Prepared by the Society's Committee. David H. Clift, Chairman. Paper.

Fifty-sixth Yearbook, 1957, Part I—*In-service Education of Teachers, Supervisors, and Administrators.* Prepared by the Society's Committee. Stephen M. Corey, Chairman. Cloth, Paper.

Fifty-sixth Yearbook, 1957, Part II—*Social Studies in the Elementary School.* Prepared by the Society's Committee. Ralph C. Preston, Chairman. Cloth, Paper.

Fifty-seventh Yearbook, 1958, Part I—*Basic Concepts in Music Education.* Prepared by the Society's Committee. Thurber H. Madison, Chairman. Cloth.

Fifty-seventh Yearbook, 1958, Part II—*Education for the Gifted.* Prepared by the Society's Committee. Robert J. Havighurst, Chairman. Cloth, Paper.

Fifty-seventh Yearbook, 1958, Part III—*The Integration of Educational Experiences.* Prepared by the Society's Committee. Paul L. Dressel, Chairman. Cloth.

Fifty-eighth Yearbook, 1959, Part I—*Community Education: Principles and Practices from World-wide Experience.* Prepared by the Society's Committee. C. O. Arndt, Chairman. Cloth, Paper.

Fifty-eighth Yearbook, 1959, Part II—*Personnel Services in Education.* Prepared by the Society's Committee. Melvene D. Hardee, Chairman. Paper.

*Fifty-ninth Yearbook, 1960, Part I—*Rethinking Science Education.* Prepared by the Society's Committee. J. Darrell Barnard, Chairman.

Fifty-ninth Yearbook, 1960, Part II—*The Dynamics of Instructional Groups.* Prepared by the Society's Committee. Gale E. Jensen, Chairman. Cloth, Paper.

Sixtieth Yearbook, 1961, Part I—*Development in and through Reading.* Prepared by the Society's Committee. Paul A. Witty, Chairman. Cloth, Paper.

Sixtieth Yearbook, 1961, Part II—*Social Forces Influencing American Education.* Prepared by the Society's Committee. Ralph W. Tyler, Chairman. Cloth.

Sixty-first Yearbook, 1962, Part I—*Individualizing Instruction.* Prepared by the Society's Committee. Fred T. Tyler, Chairman. Cloth.

Sixty-first Yearbook, 1962, Part II—*Education for the Professions.* Prepared by the Society's Committee. G. Lester Anderson, Chairman. Cloth.

Sixty-second Yearbook, 1963, Part I—*Child Psychology.* Prepared by the Society's Committee. Harold W. Stevenson, Editor. Cloth, Paper.

Sixty-second Yearbook, 1963, Part II—*The Impact and Improvement of School Testing Programs.* Prepared by the Society's Committee. Warren G. Findley, Editor. Cloth.

Sixty-third Yearbook, 1964, Part I—*Theories of Learning and Instruction.* Prepared by the Society's Committee. Ernest R. Hilgard, Editor. Paper.

Sixty-third Yearbook, 1964, Part II—*Behavioral Science and Educational Administration.* Prepared by the Society' Committee. Daniel E. Griffiths, Editor. Paper.

Sixty-fourth Yearbook, 1965, Part I—*Vocational Education.* Prepared by the Society's Committee. Melvin L. Barlow, Editor. Cloth.

Sixty-fourth Yearbook, 1965, Part II—*Art Education.* Prepared by the Society's Committee. W. Reid Hastie, Editor. Cloth.

Sixty-fifth Yearbook, 1966, Part I—*Social Deviancy among Youth.* Prepared by the Society's Committee. William W. Wattenberg, Editor. Cloth.

Sixty-fifth Yearbook, 1966, Part II—*The Changing American School.* Prepared by the Society's Committee. John I. Goodlad, Editor. Cloth.

Sixty-sixth Yearbook, 1967, Part I—*The Educationally Retarded and Disadvantaged.* Prepared by the Society's Committee. Paul A. Witty, Editor. Cloth.

Sixty-sixth Yearbook, 1967, Part II—*Programed Instruction.* Prepared by the Society's Committee. Phil C. Lange, Editor. Cloth.

Sixty-seventh Yearbook, 1968, Part I—*Metropolitanism: Its Challenge to Education.* Prepared by the Society's Committee. Robert J. Havighurst, Editor. Cloth.

Sixty-seventh Yearbook, 1968, Part II—*Innovation and Change in Reading Instruction.* Prepared by the Society's Committee. Helen M. Robinson, Editor. Cloth.

Sixty-eighth Yearbook, 1969, Part I—*The United States and International Education.* Prepared by the Society's Committee. Harold G. Shane, Editor. Cloth.

Sixty-eighth Yearbook, 1969, Part II—*Educational Evaluation: New Roles, New Means.* Prepared by the Society's Committee. Ralph W. Tyler, Editor. Cloth.

Sixty-ninth Yearbook, 1970, Part I—*Mathematics Education.* Prepared by the Society's Committee. Edward G. Begle, Editor. Cloth.

Sixty-ninth Yearbook, 1970, Part II—*Linguistics in School Programs.* Prepared by the Society's Committee. Albert H. Marckwardt, Editor. Cloth.

Seventieth Yearbook, 1971, Part I—*The Curriculum: Retrospect and Prospect.* Prepared by the Society's Committee. Robert M. McClure, Editor. Paper.

Seventieth Yearbook, 1971, Part II—*Leaders in American Education.* Prepared by the Society's Committee. Robert J. Havighurst, Editor. Cloth.

Seventy-first Yearbook, 1972, Part I—*Philosophical Redirection of Educational Research.* Prepared by the Society's Committee. Lawrence G. Thomas, Editor. Cloth.

Seventy-first Yearbook, 1972, Part II—*Early Childhood Education.* Prepared by the Society's Committee. Ira J. Gordon, Editor. Cloth, Paper.

Seventy-second Yearbook, 1973, Part I—*Behavior Modification in Education.* Prepared by the Society's Committee. Carl E. Thoresen, Editor. Cloth.

Seventy-second Yearbook, 1973, Part II—*The Elementary School in the United States.* Prepared by the Society's Committee. John I. Goodlad and Harold G. Shane, Editors. Cloth.

Seventy-third Yearbook, 1974, Part I—*Media and Symbols: The Forms of Expression, Communication, and Education.* Prepared by the Society's Committee. David R. Olson, Editor. Cloth.

Seventy-third Yearbook, 1974, Part II—*Uses of the Sociology of Education.* Prepared by the Society's Committee. C. Wayne Gordon, Editor. Cloth.

Seventy-fourth Yearbook, 1975, Part I—*Youth.* Prepared by the Society's Committee. Robert J. Havighurst and Philip H. Dreyer, Editors. Cloth.

Seventy-fourth Yearbook, 1975, Part II—*Teacher Education.* Prepared by the Society's Committee. Kevin Ryan, Editor. Cloth.

Seventy-fifth Yearbook, 1976, Part I—*Psychology of Teaching Methods.* Prepared by the Society's Committee. N. L. Gage, Editor. Cloth.

Seventy-fifth Yearbook, 1976, Part II—*Issues in Secondary Education.* Prepared by the Society's Committee. William Van Til, Editor. Cloth.

Yearbooks of the National Society are distributed by

THE UNIVERSITY OF CHICAGO PRESS, CHICAGO, ILLINOIS 60637

Please direct inquiries regarding prices of volumes still available to the University of Chicago Press. Orders for these volumes should be sent to the University of Chicago Press, not to the offices of the National Society.

2. The Series on Contemporary Educational Issues

In addition to its Yearbooks the Society now publishes volumes in a series on Contemporary Educational Issues. These volumes are prepared under the supervision of the Society's Commission on an Expanded Publication Program.

The 1976 Titles

> *Prospects for Research and Development in Education* (Ralph W. Tyler, ed.)
> *Public Testimony on Public Schools* (Commission on Educational Governance)
> *Counseling Children and Adolescents* (William M. Walsh, ed.)

The 1975 Titles

> *Schooling and the Rights of Children* (Vernon Haubrich and Michael Apple, eds.)
> *Systems of Individualized Education* (Harriet Talmage, ed.)
> *Educational Policy and International Assessment: Implications of the IEA Assessment of Achievement* (Alan Purves and Daniel U. Levine, eds.)

The 1974 Titles

> *Crucial Issues in Testing* (Ralph W. Tyler and Richard M. Wolf, eds.)
> *Conflicting Conceptions of Curriculum* (Elliott Eisner and Elizabeth Vallance, eds.)
> *Cultural Pluralism* (Edgar G. Epps, ed.)
> *Rethinking Educational Equality* (Andrew T. Kopan and Herbert J. Walberg, eds.)

All of the above volumes may be ordered from

McCutchan Publishing Corporation
2526 Grove Street
Berkeley, California 94704

The 1972 Titles

> *Black Students in White Schools* (Edgar G. Epps, ed.)
> *Flexibility in School Programs* (W. J. Congreve and G. L. Rinehart, eds.)
> *Performance Contracting—1969–1971* (J. A. Mecklenburger)
> *The Potential of Educational Futures* (Michael Marien and W. L. Ziegler, eds.)
> *Sex Differences and Discrimination in Education* (Scarvia Anderson, ed.)

The 1971 Titles

> *Accountability in Education* (Leon M. Lessinger and Ralph W. Tyler, eds.)
> *Farewell to Schools???* (D. U. Levine and R. J. Havighurst, eds.)
> *Models for Integrated Education* (D. U. Levine, ed.)
> PYGMALION *Reconsidered* (J. D. Elashoff and R. E. Snow)
> *Reactions to Silberman's* CRISIS IN THE CLASSROOM (A. Harry Passow, ed.)

Titles in the 1971 and 1972 series may be ordered from
Charles A. Jones Publishing Company
Worthington, Ohio 43085